SCHOLASTIC

ALPHA Mathematics

Develops mathematical thinking and problem-solving skills

Coursebook

4

Scholastic ALPHA™ Mathematics is adapted from the Primary Mathematics Project series (3rd Edition), originally developed by the Ministry of Education, Singapore. This edition contains new content developed by Scholastic Education International (Singapore) Private Limited, which is not attributable to the Ministry of Education, Singapore.

First edition: 2014
Reprinted: 2014 (twice), 2015 (twice), 2016, 2017 (twice), 2018, 2019, 2021, 2022 (twice), 2023, 2024, 2025 (twice), 2026

ISBN 978-93-5103-031-7

SCHOLASTIC

About ALPHA™ Mathematics

Welcome to **Scholastic ALPHA™ Mathematics**.

The programme covers four strands of mathematics across five grades: **Numbers and Operations**, **Measurement**, **Geometry** and **Data Analysis**.

Numbers and Operations

Data Analysis

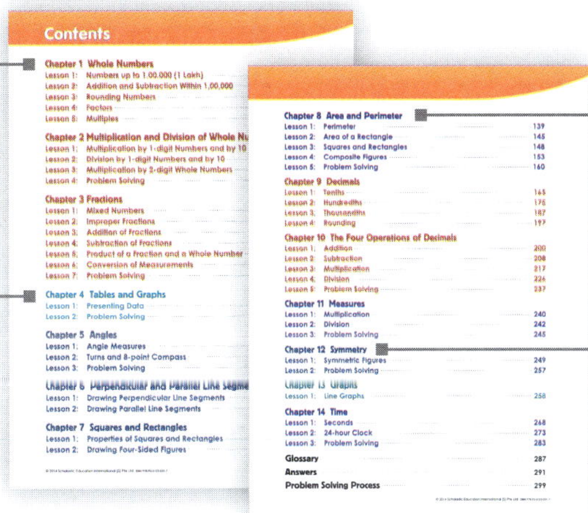

Measurement

Geometry

Each chapter of the Coursebook comprises two parts, **Lessons** and **Practice**.

1 Each chapter contains **lessons**, each focusing on a concept or an aspect of it. Concepts and skills are introduced in **Let's Learn**, and **Let's Do** provides opportunities for immediate formative assessment.

In **Let's Learn**, concepts and skills are introduced and developed to mastery using the *concrete-pictorial-abstract* approach. This proven, research-based approach develops deep conceptual understanding.

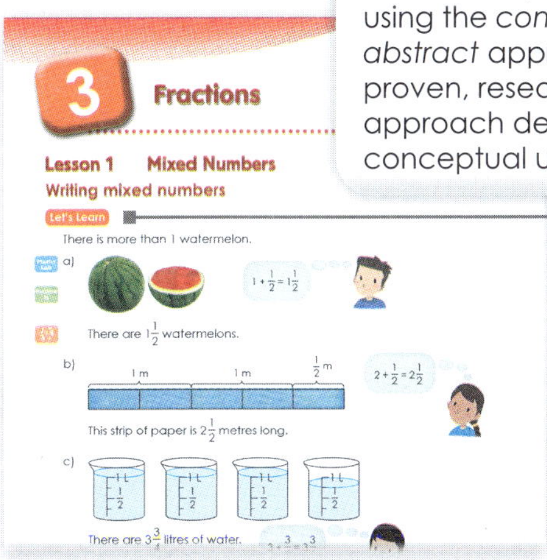

Let's Do provides opportunities for formative assessment. Systematic variation of tasks reinforces students' understanding and enables teachers to check learning and identify remediation needs.

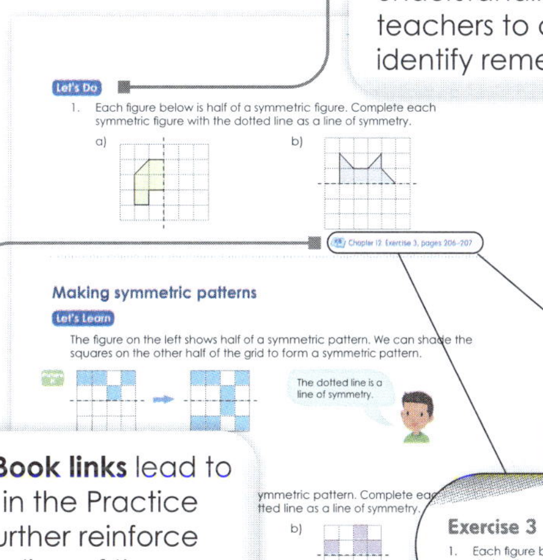

Practice Book links lead to exercises in the Practice Book to further reinforce understanding of the concepts and skills learnt.

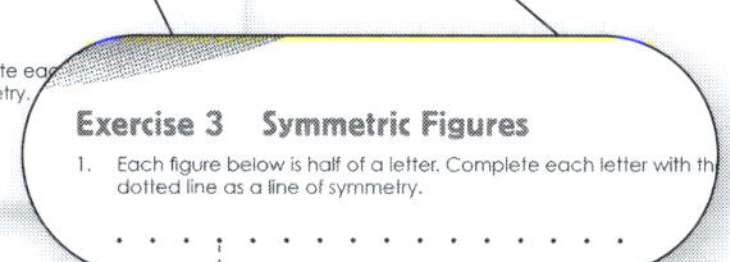

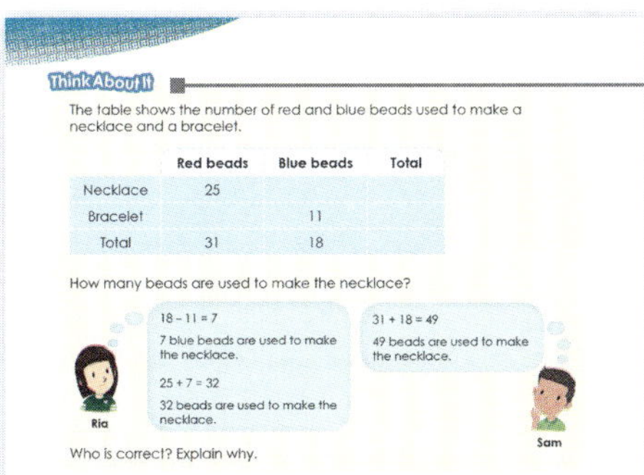

Think About It develops metacognitive skills by providing opportunities for mathematical communication, reasoning and justification.

 ISBN 978-93-5103-031-7

2 **Practice** provides opportunities for summative assessment and independent practice.

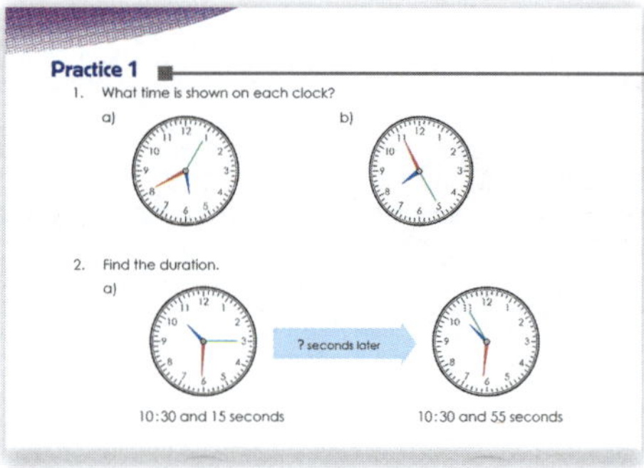

The questions are graded and allow for consolidation of concepts and skills learnt within the lesson.

Chapters end with a **Problem Solving** lesson.
Word problems provide a meaningful context for students to apply mathematical knowledge.
The focus is on both the strategies and the process of problem solving.

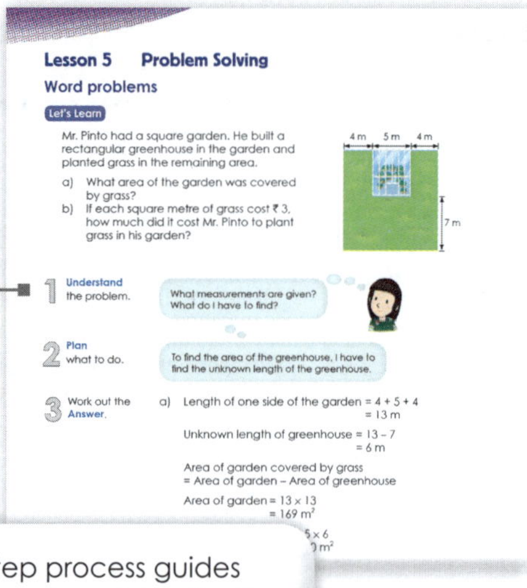

A 4-step process guides students to systematically solve problems and to apply appropriate problem-solving strategies.

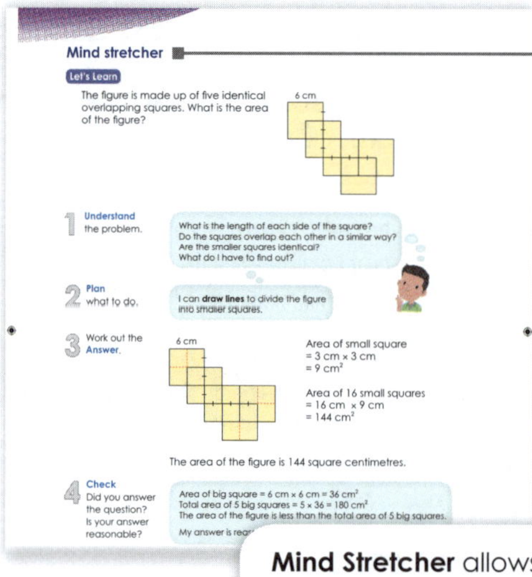

Mind Stretcher allows students to apply knowledge gained to non-routine problem situations to develop higher-order thinking skills.

The **Glossary** combines pictorial representation and simple explanations for easy reference by students.

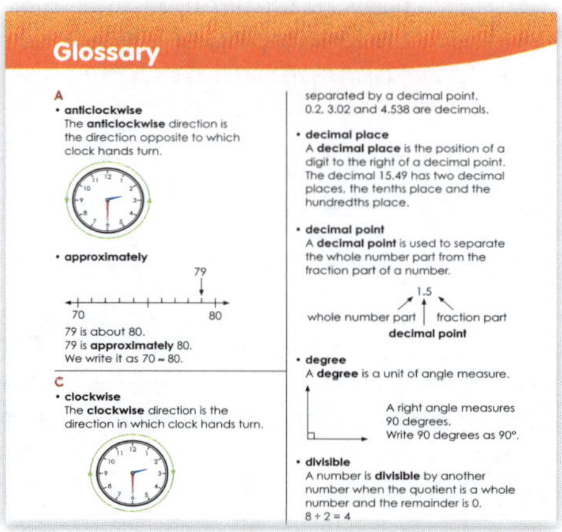

 ISBN 978-93-5103-031-7

Contents

 ISBN 978-93-5103-031-7

 ISBN 978-93-5103-031-7

1 Whole Numbers

Lesson 1 Numbers up to 1,00,000 (1 Lakh)

Reading and writing numbers

Let's Learn

a) This block is made up of unit cubes. How many unit cubes are there?

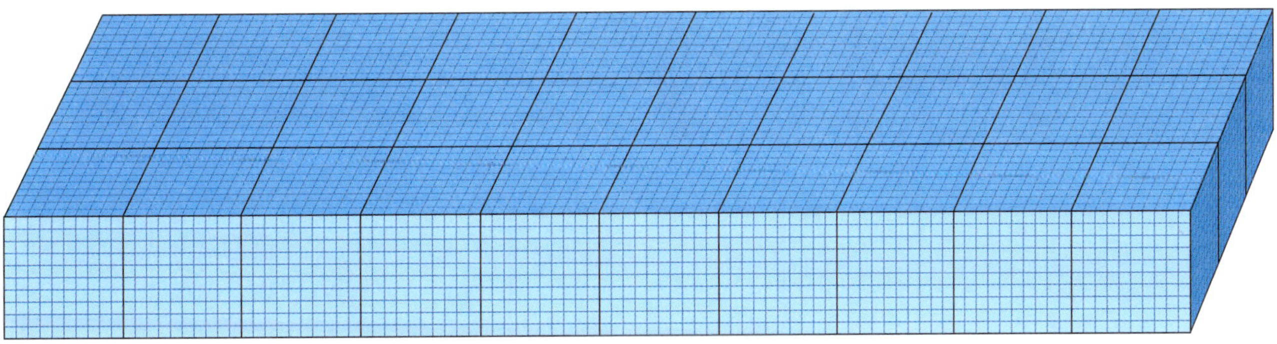

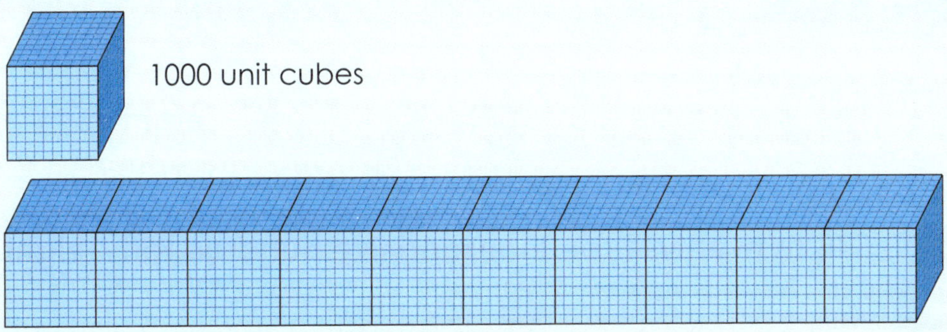

There are 30,000 unit cubes.
Read 30,000 as **thirty thousand**.

 ISBN 978-93-5103-031-7

b) How many unit cubes are there altogether?

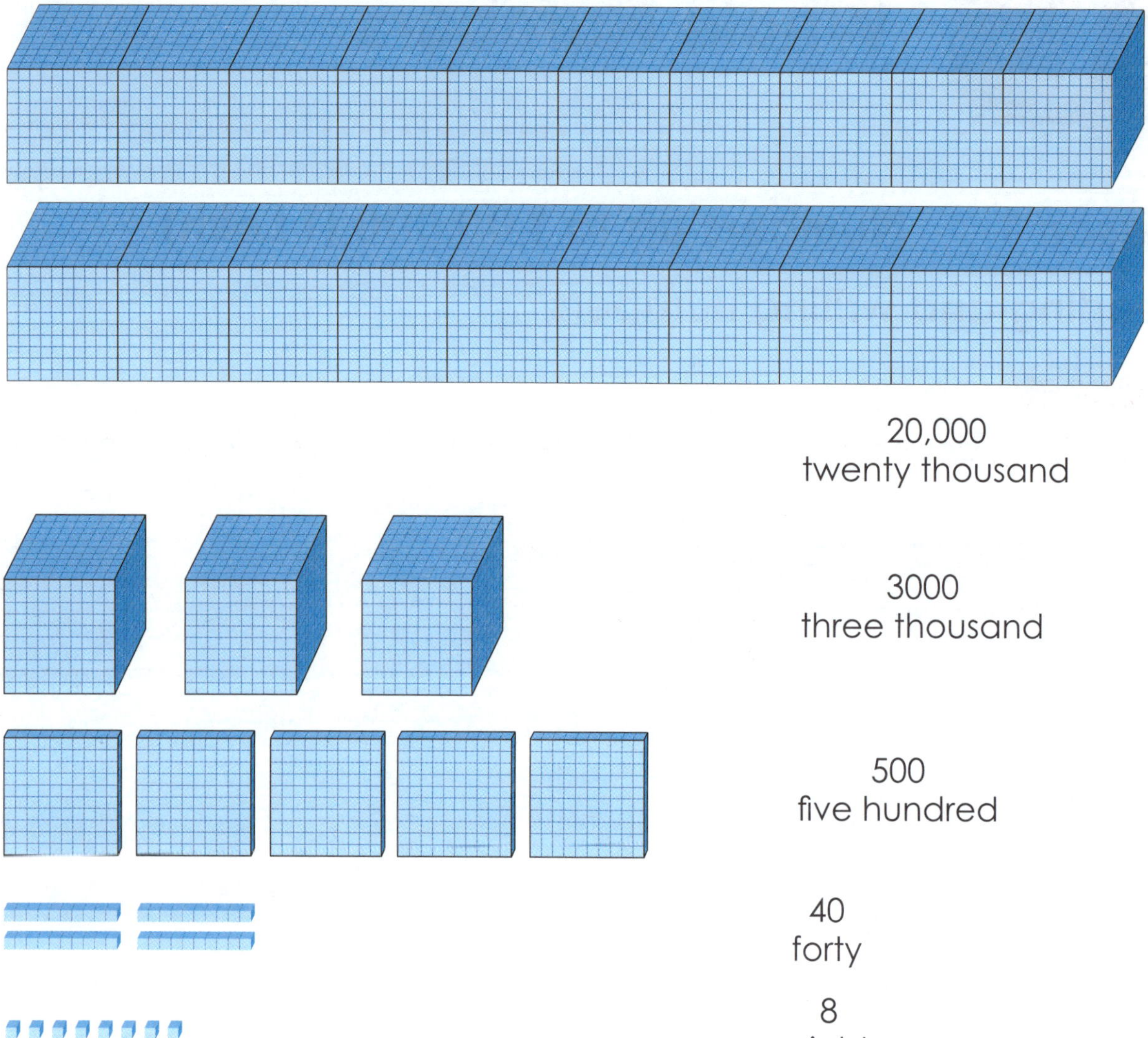

20,000
twenty thousand

3000
three thousand

500
five hundred

40
forty

8
eight

The total number of unit cubes is 23,548.

Read 23,548 as **twenty-three thousand five hundred forty-eight**.

Ten Thousands	Thousands	Hundreds	Tens	Ones
● ●	● ● ●	● ● ● ● ●	● ● ● ●	● ● ● ● ● ● ● ●
2	3	5	4	8

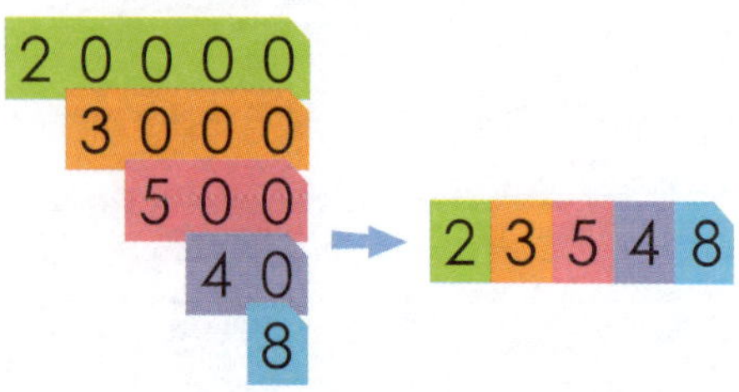

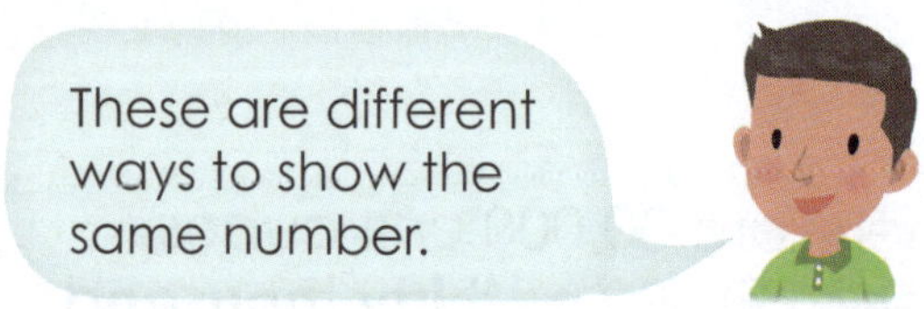

 ISBN 978-93-5103-031-7

20,000 + 3000 + 500 + 40 + 8 = 23,548
23,000 + 548 = 23,548

Read 23,548 as **twenty-three thousand five hundred forty-eight**.

Let's Do

1. Write the numbers.
   a) eight thousand twelve ______
   b) forty-nine thousand five hundred one ______
   c) ninety thousand ninety ______

2. Write the numbers in words.
   a) 4908 ______________________________
   b) 27,165 ______________________________
   c) 81,900 ______________________________

Chapter 1: Exercise 1, pages 7–8

Identifying values of digits

Let's Learn

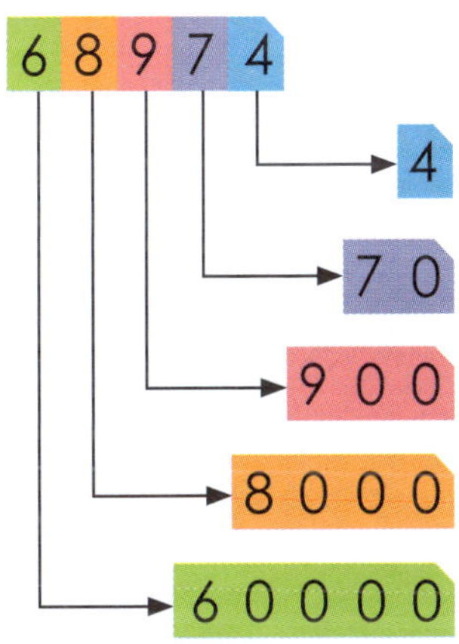

68,974 is a 5-digit number.

The digit 9 stands for 900.
The digit 8 stands for ____.
The digit 6 stands for ____.

68,974 = ____ + 8000 + 900 + 70 + 4

Let's Do

1. Fill in the missing numbers.
   a) 25,168 = 20,000 + ______ + 100 + 60 + 8
   b) 42,065 = 40,000 + ______ + 60 + 5
   c) 60,140 = 60,000 + ______ + 40

 ISBN 978-93-5103-031-7

2. What does the digit **8** stand for in each of the following numbers?

a) 16,**8**14 ______ b) **8**2,114 ______ c) 4**8**,050 ______

Identifying values of digits and place values

Let's Learn

Count the ten thousands, thousands, hundreds, tens and ones.

Picture It

T Th	Th	H	T	O
●●●	●●●●●	●●	●●●●●●	
3	5	2	6	0

In 35,260, the digit 3 is in the ten thousands place.
Its value is 30,000.

The digit 5 is in the thousands place.
Its value is ☐.

The digit ☐ is in the ones place.
Its value is 0.

Let's Do

1. Read the table. Then, fill in the blanks.

T Th	Th	H	T	O
7	6	3	4	8

In 76,348,

a) the digit 7 is in the ______________ place and its value is ______.

b) the digit ______ is in the thousands place and its value is 6000.

P/B Chapter 1: Exercise 2, pages 9–10

 ISBN 978-93-5103-031-7

Finding 'more than' and 'less than'

Let's Learn

a) What number is 100 more than 73,125?

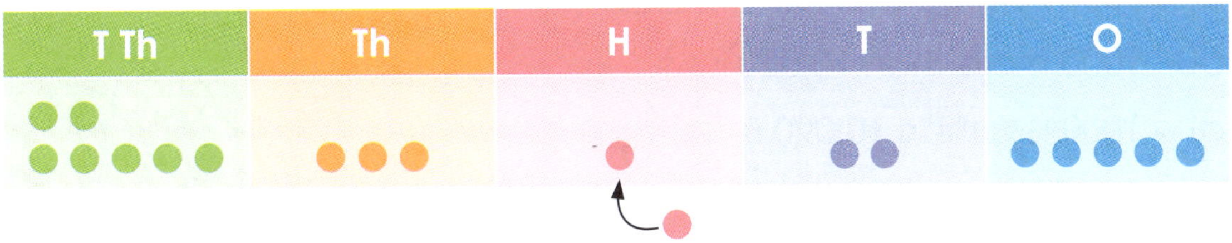

$73{,}\mathbf{1}25 \xrightarrow{+\,100} 73{,}\mathbf{2}25$

100 more than 73,**1**25 is 73,**2**25.

b) What number is 10,000 more than 73,125?

$\mathbf{73}{,}125 \xrightarrow{+\,10{,}000}$ □

10,000 more than **73**,125 is □.

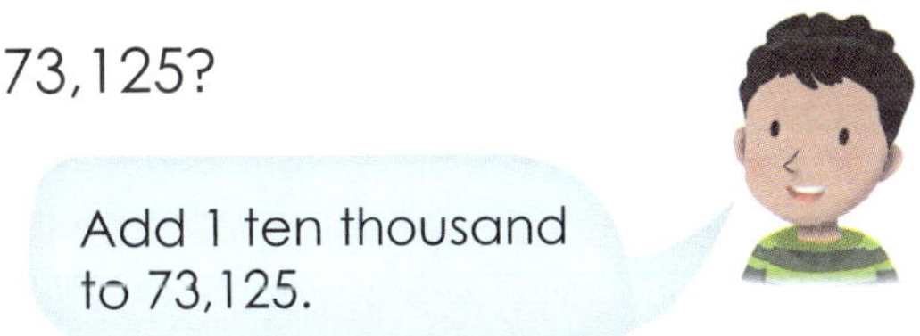

c) What number is 1000 less than 64,352?

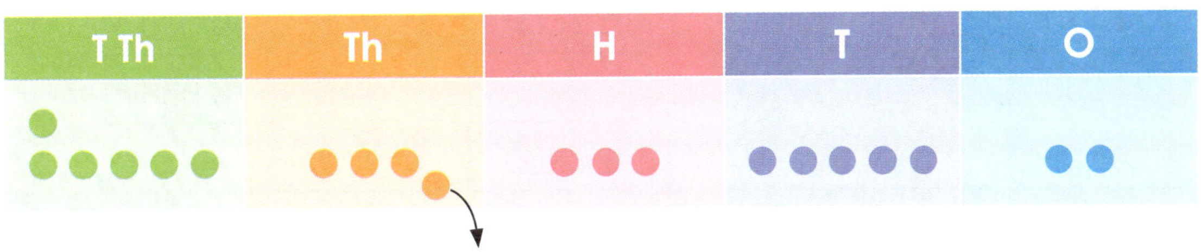

$6\mathbf{4}{,}352 \xrightarrow{-\,1000} 6\mathbf{3}{,}352$

1000 less than 6**4**,352 is 6**3**,352.

d) What number is 10 less than 64,352?

$64{,}3\mathbf{5}2 \xrightarrow{-\,10}$ □

10 less than 64,3**5**2 is □.

 ISBN 978-93-5103-031-7

Let's Do

1. Fill in the blanks.

 a) 10 more than 50,640 is ______.

 b) 100 less than 81,406 is ______.

 c) 1000 more than 10,020 is ______.

 d) 1000 less than 10,020 is ______.

 e) 10,000 more than 90,000 is ______.

2. Complete the number patterns.

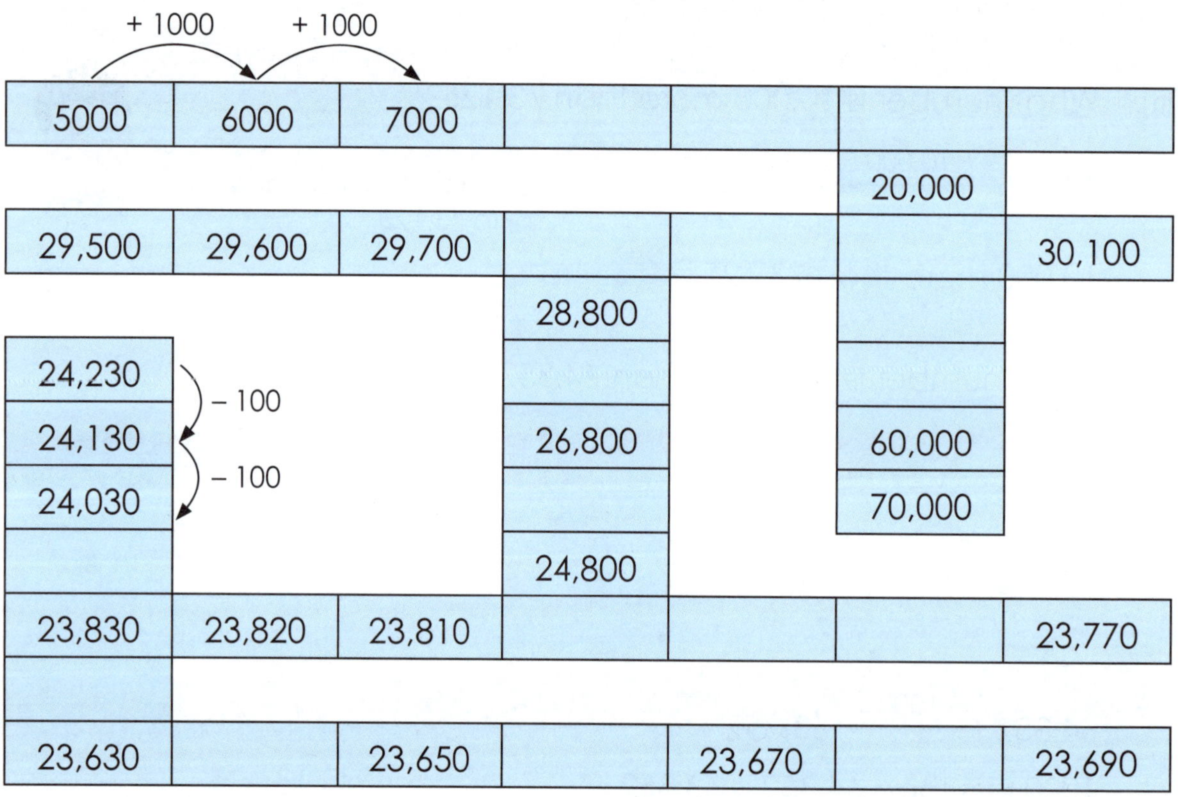

P/B Chapter 1: Exercise 3, page 11

  ISBN 978-93-5103-031-7

Reading number lines

Let's Learn

a) Numbers are arranged in **increasing order** from left to right on a number line.

There are 10 equal intervals between 0 and 1000 on this number line. Each interval stands for 100.

Picture It

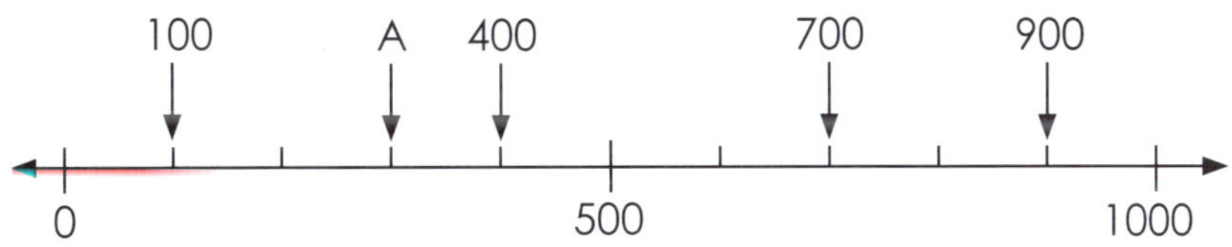

A represents 300.

b)

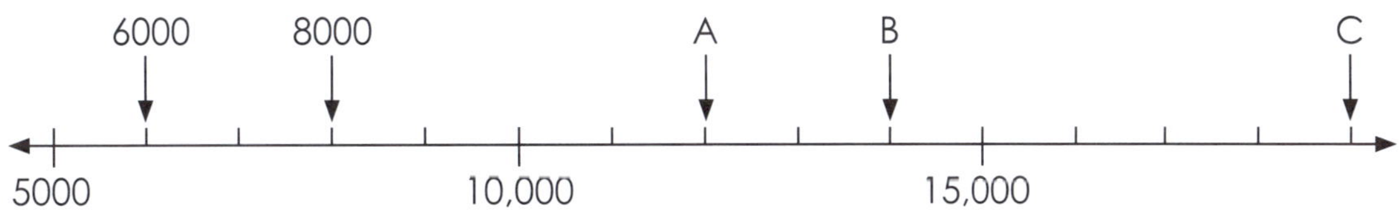

There are 10 equal intervals between 5000 and 15,000 on this number line. Each interval stands for 1000.

A represents 12,000.

B represents ____.

C represents ____.

Let's Do

1. Write the number represented by each letter.

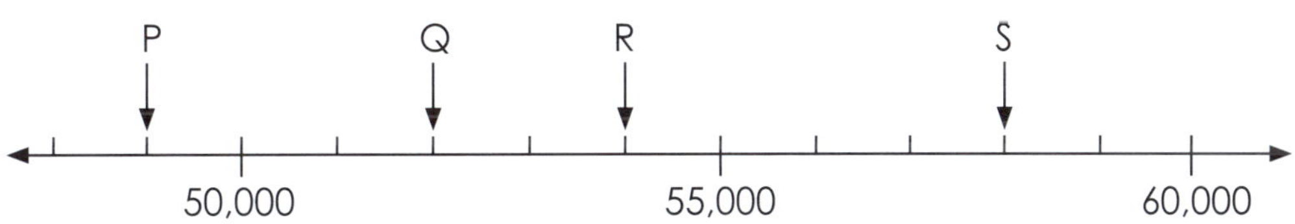

a) P: ______ b) Q: ______

c) R: ______ d) S: ______

P/B Chapter 1: Exercise 4, page 12

 ISBN 978-93-5103-031-7

Comparing and ordering numbers

Let's Learn

Compare 39,625, 39,562 and 40,025.

	T Th	Th	H	T	O
39,625	3	9	6	2	5
39,562	3	9	5	6	2
40,025	4	0	0	2	5

First, compare the ten thousands. 4 ten thousands is greater than 3 ten thousands. 40,025 is the greatest number.

Next, compare the thousands of 39,625 and 39,562. They are the same.

Then, compare the hundreds of 39,625 and 39,562. 6 hundreds is greater than 5 hundreds.

39,625 is greater than 39,562.
39,562 is the smallest number.

Arranging the numbers in order from the smallest, we have:

39,562, 39,625, 40,025
(smallest)

Let's Do

1. Fill in the circles with **>** or **<**.

   a) 46,729 ◯ 46,732 b) 70,060 ◯ 70,006

2. Arrange the numbers in order. Begin with the greatest.

78,430	78,409	79,021

   ______, ______, ______
   (greatest)

 ISBN 978-93-5103-031-7

3. | 6 | 0 | 5 | 9 |

Do not start with 0.

Use each digit once to form the

a) greatest 4-digit number. ______

b) smallest 4-digit number. ______

Chapter 1: Exercise 5, page 13

Think About It

| 9876 | 76,543 | 87,654 |

9876 is the greatest number because its first digit is the greatest.

Ria

Is Ria correct? Explain why.

Practice 1

1. Write the numbers.
   - a) twelve thousand eight hundred three
   - b) twenty thousand fifty
   - c) seventy thousand

2. Write the numbers in words.
   - a) 1758 b) 5306 c) 72,903 d) 91,120

3. What are the missing numbers?
   - a) 38,276 = 30,000 + ______ + 200 + 70 + 6
   - b) 29,168 = ______ + 9000 + 100 + 60 + 8
   - c) 50,000 + 4000 + 600 + 7 = ______
   - d) 40,000 + 800 + 30 = ______

4. What is the value of the digit **6** in each of the following numbers?
   - a) 54,0**6**0 b) 34,**6**20 c) **6**0,143 d) 27,00**6**

 ISBN 978-93-5103-031-7

5. In the number 80,647,
   a) which digit is in the ten thousands place?
   b) what place is the digit 0 in?

6. Complete the number patterns.
   a) 5780, 5880, ______, ______, 6180
   b) 32,465, 33,465, ______, ______, 36,465
   c) 93,700, 83,700, 73,700, ______, ______

7. What number does each letter represent?

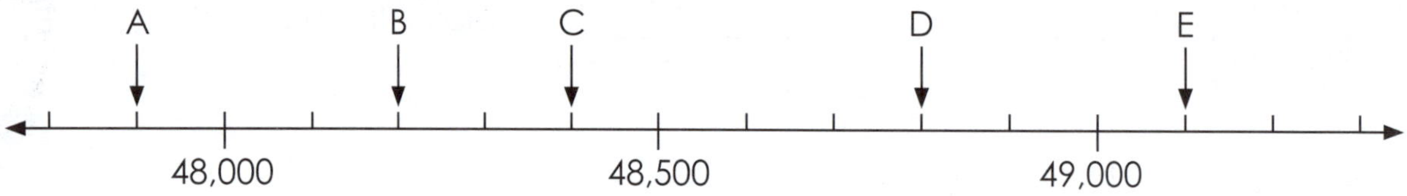

8. a) Which number is greater, 35,618 or 35,620?
   b) Which number is smaller, 40,006 or 4600?

9. Circle the greatest number. Cross out the smallest number.

   90,530   90,350   90,305

10. Arrange the numbers in order. Begin with the smallest.
   a) 30,601, 30,061, 30,160, 30,016
   b) 29,999, 90,000, 20,990, 29,909

11. | 5 | 8 | 9 | 0 | 7 |

   Use each digit once to form the
   a) greatest 5-digit number.
   b) smallest 5-digit number.

12. Rearrange the digits in the number 40,793, so that the new number is the greatest possible number that can be formed using these digits.

 ISBN 978-93-5103-031-7

Lesson 2 Addition and Subtraction Within 1,00,000

Adding within 1,00,000

Let's Learn

Find the sum of 37,340 and 35,067.

37,340 + 35,067 = ☐

	T Th	Th	H	T	O
	1		1		
	3	7	3	4	0
+	3	5	0	6	7
	7	2	4	0	7

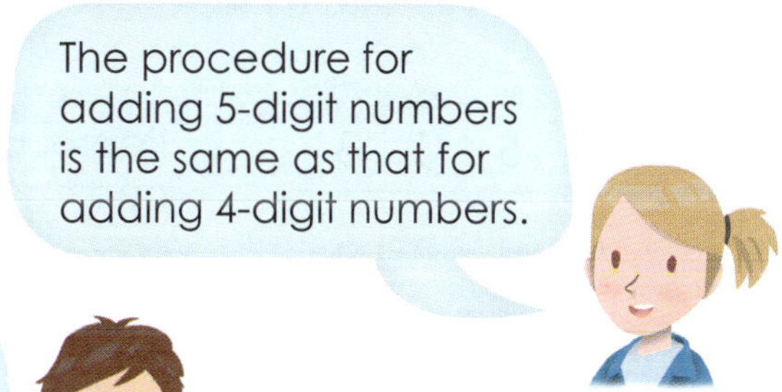

37,340 + 35,067 = 72,407

Let's Do

1. Add.

a)
$$\begin{array}{r} 4680 \\ +\ 6231 \\ \hline \\ \hline \end{array}$$

b)
$$\begin{array}{r} 65310 \\ +\ 25407 \\ \hline \\ \hline \end{array}$$

c)
$$\begin{array}{r} 58635 \\ +\ 40518 \\ \hline \\ \hline \end{array}$$

2. 36,811 + 7901 = ________

Chapter 1: Exercise 6, page 14

 ISBN 978-93-5103-031-7

Subtracting within 1,00,000

Let's Learn

Find the difference between 98,764 and 80,608.

98,764 – 80,608 = ▢

	T Th	Th	H	T	O
				5	1
	9	8	7	~~6~~	4
–	8	0	6	0	8
	1	8	1	5	6

98,764 – 80,608 = 18,156

Let's Do

1. Subtract.

a)
```
   9 9 7 6 0
 – 1 8 4 5 3
 ___________
```

b)
```
   7 5 8 4 2
 – 2 3 9 1 7
 ___________
```

c)
```
   6 8 5 3 1
 – 4 8 7 4 0
 ___________
```

2. 65,928 – 9909 = ________

Chapter 1: Exercise 7, page 15

 ISBN 978-93-5103-031-7

Solving word problems

Let's Learn

a) Factory A has 66,295 workers. After the shutdown of Factory B, 29,148 workers from Factory B join Factory A. How many workers will Factory A have now?

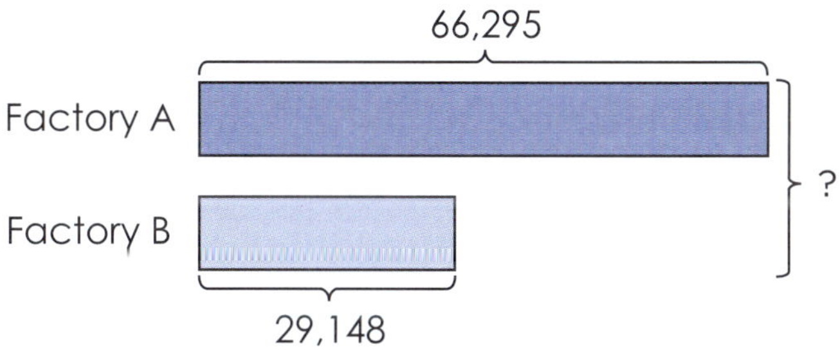

$$\begin{array}{r} \;\;^{1}6\;6\;^{1}2\;^{1}9\;5 \\ +\;\;2\;9\;1\;4\;8 \\ \hline \;\;9\;5\;4\;4\;3 \\ \hline \end{array}$$

Factory A will now have 95,443 workers.

b) A plane is flying at a height of 12,530 metres above sea-level. After flying for half an hour, its height drops by 1900 metres. At what height is the plane flying now?

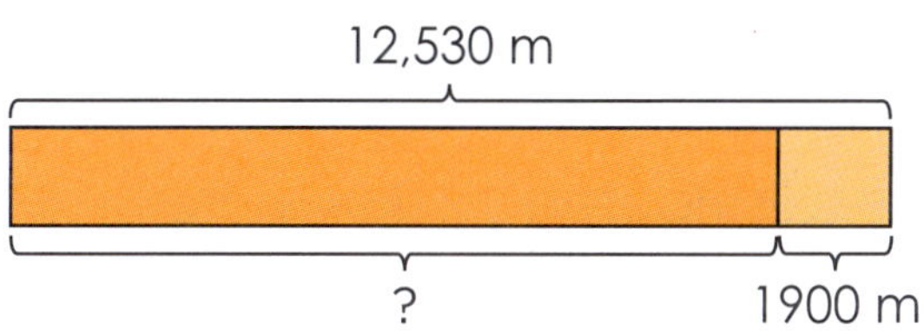

$$\begin{array}{r} 1\;\not{2}^{1}\;{}^{1}5\;3\;0 \\ -\;\;\;1\;9\;0\;0 \\ \hline 1\;0\;6\;3\;0 \\ \hline \end{array}$$

If 12,530 – 1900 = 10,630,
then, 10,630 + 1900 = 12,530.

$$\begin{array}{r} 1\;\overset{1}{0}\;6\;3\;0 \\ +\;\;\;1\;9\;0\;0 \\ \hline 1\;2\;5\;3\;0 \\ \hline \end{array}$$

My answer is correct.

The plane is flying at a height of 10,630 metres now.

Let's Do

1. After paying ₹ 32,240 for a laptop, Mr. Kapoor still had an instalment of ₹ 4160 left to pay. How much did the laptop cost altogether?

2. A property developer needs 27,386 bricks to build a house. The developer has 17,897 bricks in their warehouse now. How many more bricks must the developer buy?

P/B Chapter 1: Exercise 8, page 16

Practice 2

1. Add.

   a) 67,482 + 2509 b) 34,810 + 29,146 c) 48,395 + 30,613

2. Subtract.

   a) 82,653 – 1822 b) 96,254 – 87,512 c) 46,231 – 16,729

Solve the word problems. You may draw bar models to help you. Show your work clearly.

3. University A has 25,416 students. University B has 2273 more students than University A. How many students does University B have?

4. May distributed 35,860 pamphlets. She distributed 12,264 more pamphlets than Sheila. How many pamphlets did Sheila distribute?

5. There were 32,345 people at a parade. 14,000 of them were men and 9800 were women. How many children were at the parade?

 ISBN 978-93-5103-031-7

Lesson 3 Rounding Numbers

Rounding 2-digit numbers to the nearest ten

Let's Learn

Carol

Kamal

Siti

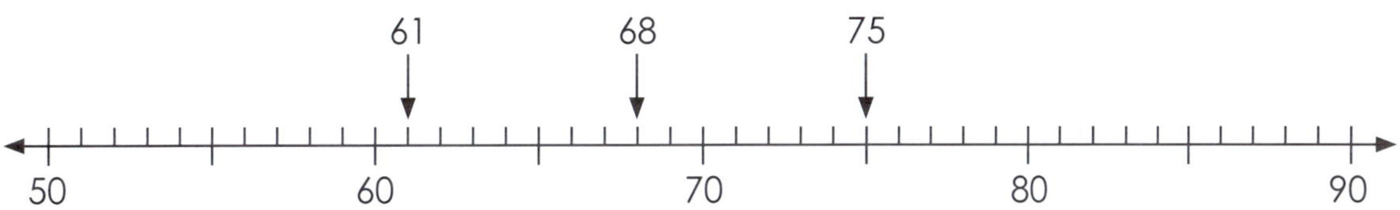

The children **round** each of the numbers 61, 68 and 75 to the nearest ten.

a)

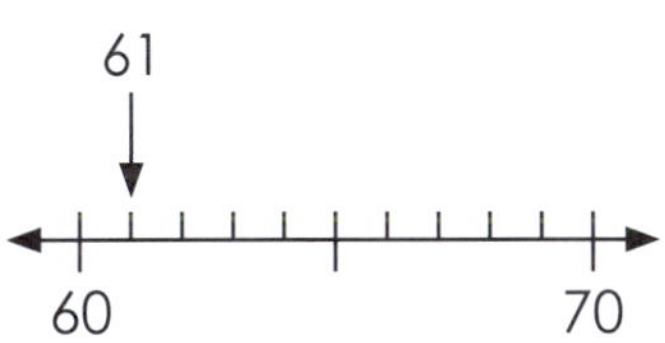

61 is between 60 and 70.
It is nearer to 60 than to 70.
So, the nearest ten is 60.

61 is 60 when rounded to the nearest ten.
$61 \approx 60$
61 is **approximately** 60.

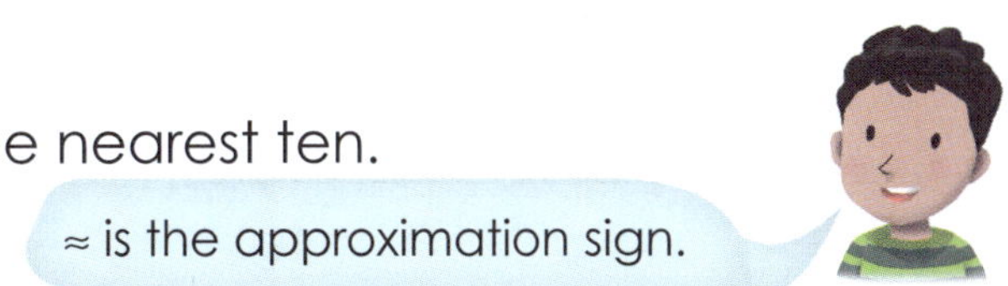

 ISBN 978-93-5103-031-7

b) 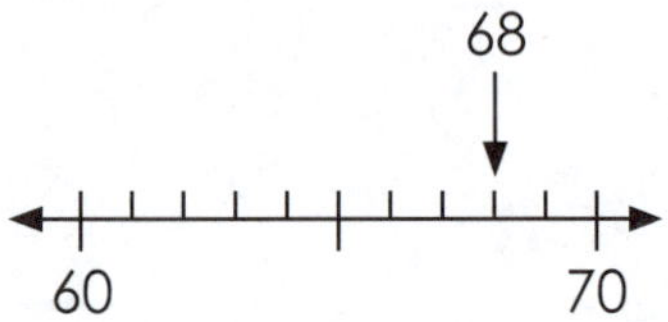

68 is between 60 and 70.
It is nearer to 70 than to 60.
So, the nearest ten is 70.

68 is 70 when rounded to the nearest ten.
$68 \approx 70$
68 is approximately 70.

c) 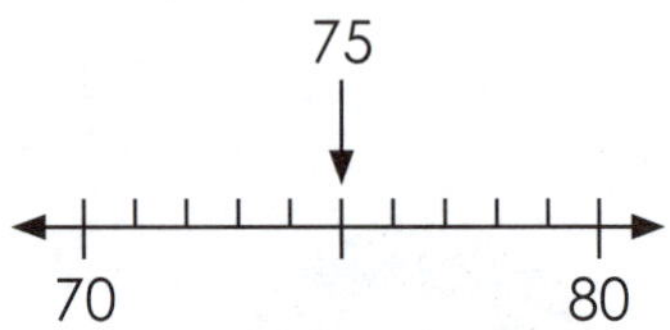

75 is halfway between 70 and 80.
Take 80 to be the nearest ten.

75 is 80 when rounded to the nearest ten.
$75 \approx 80$
75 is approximately 80.

Let's Do

1. Round each number to the nearest ten.

a) $29 \approx$ ______

b) $82 \approx$ ______

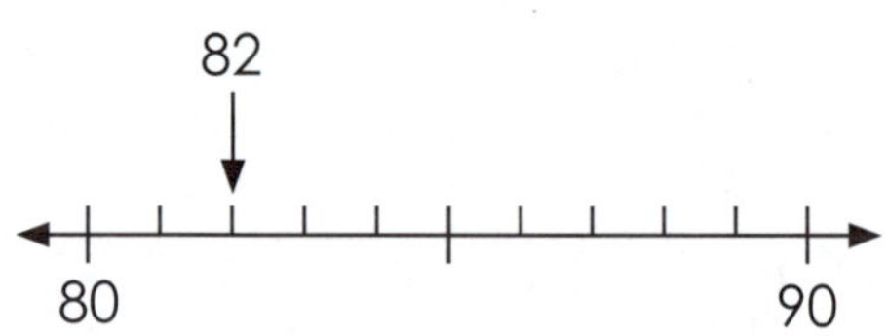

c) $95 \approx$ ______

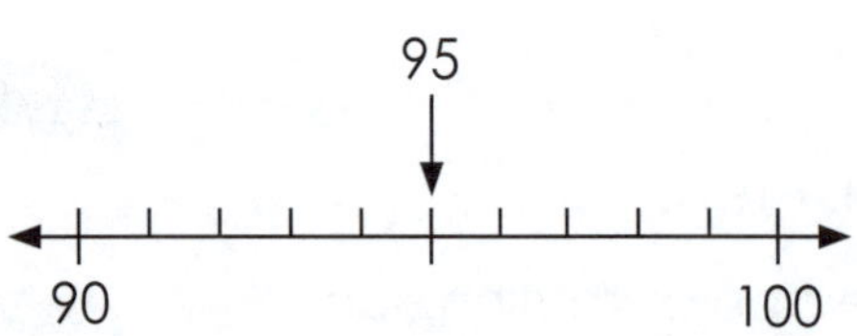

 ISBN 978-93-5103-031-7

Rounding 3-digit and 4-digit numbers to the nearest ten

Let's Learn

a) Round 234 to the nearest ten.

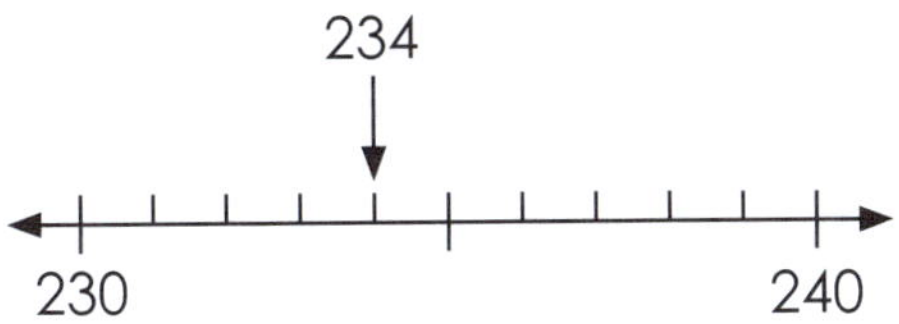

234 is between 230 and 240.
It is nearer to 230 than to 240.
234 is ____ when rounded to the nearest ten.
234 ≈ ____

b) Round 1458 to the nearest ten.

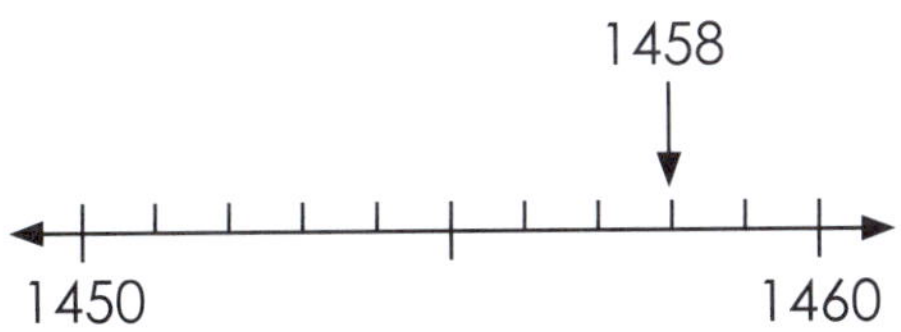

1458 is between 1450 and 1460.
It is nearer to 1460 than to 1450.
1458 is ____ when rounded to the nearest ten.
1458 ≈ ____

c) Round 2735 to the nearest ten.

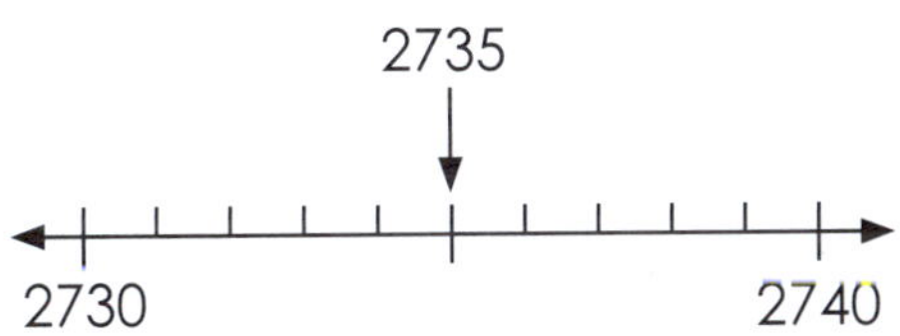

2735 is halfway between 2730 and 2740.
2735 is ____ when rounded to the nearest ten.
2735 ≈ ____

 ISBN 978-93-5103-031-7

Let's Do

1. Round each number to the nearest ten.

a) 128 ≈ ______

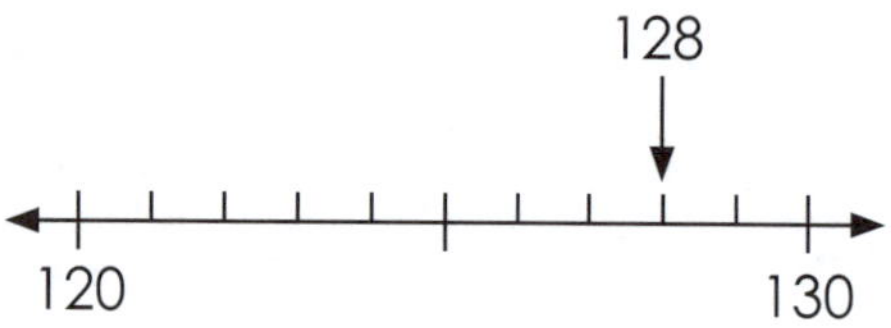

b) 452 ≈ ______

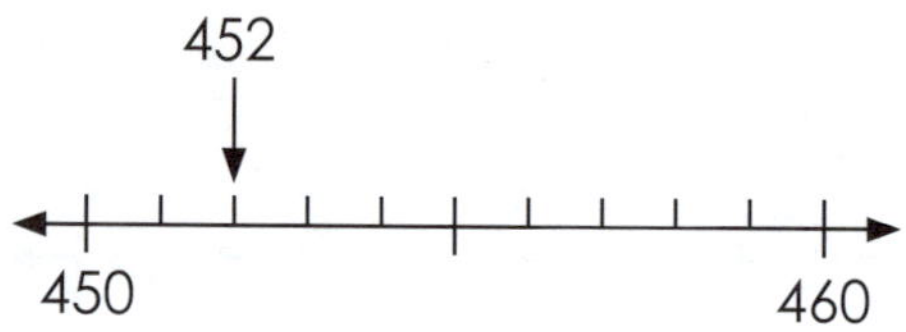

c) 4805 ≈ ______

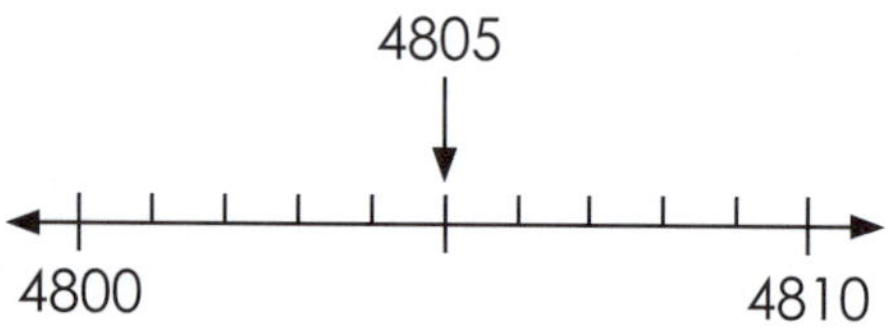

Chapter 1: Exercise 9, pages 17–18

Rounding numbers to the nearest hundred

Let's Learn

a) There are 2478 students in Lakeview School.

i) Round the number of students to the nearest ten.

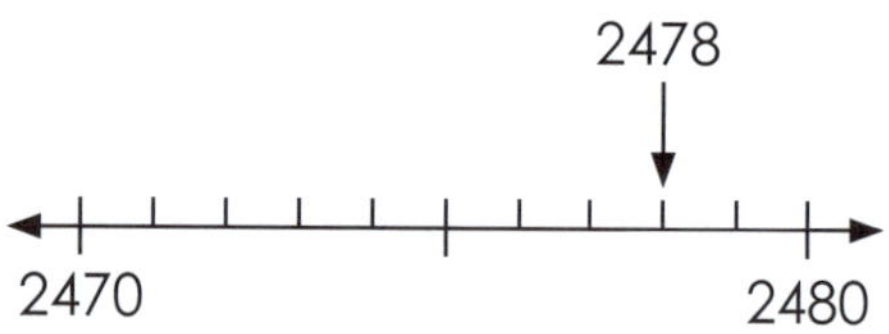

2478 is more than halfway between 2470 and 2480.
It is nearer to 2480 than to 2470.
2478 is 2480 when rounded to the nearest ten.
2478 ≈ 2480

ii) Round the number of students to the nearest hundred.

2478 is more than halfway between 2400 and 2500.
It is nearer to 2500 than to 2400.
2478 is 2500 when rounded to the nearest hundred.
2478 ≈ 2500

 ISBN 978-93-5103-031-7

b) Mr. Kumar sold his car for ₹ 34,125. Round this amount to the nearest ₹ 100.

34,125 is less than halfway between 34,100 and 34,200.
It is nearer to 34,100 than to 34,200.
34,125 is 34,100 when rounded to the nearest hundred.

₹ 34,125 ≈ ₹ ☐

c) Round 27,050 to the nearest hundred.

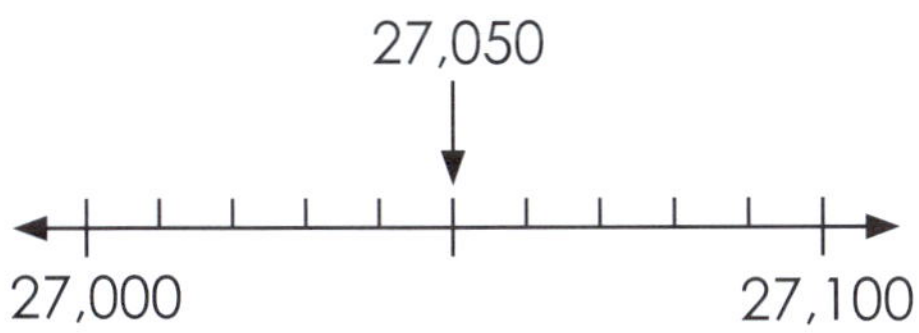

27,050 is halfway between 27,000 and 27,100.
27,050 is 27,100 when rounded to the nearest hundred.

27,050 ≈ ☐

Think About It

Round 3462 to the nearest hundred.

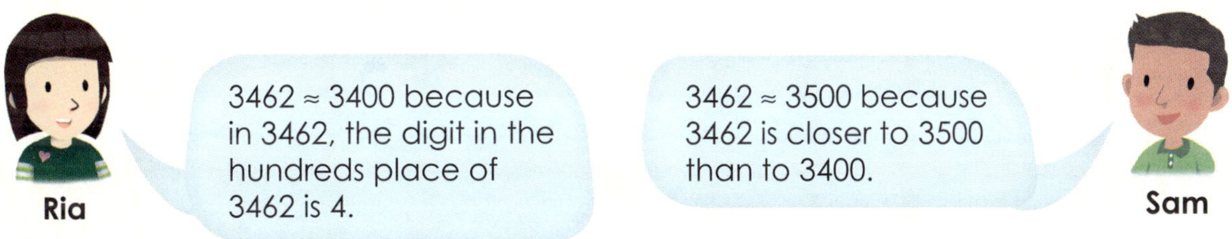

Who is correct? Explain why.

Let's Do

1. Round each number to the nearest hundred.

a) 345 ≈ ______

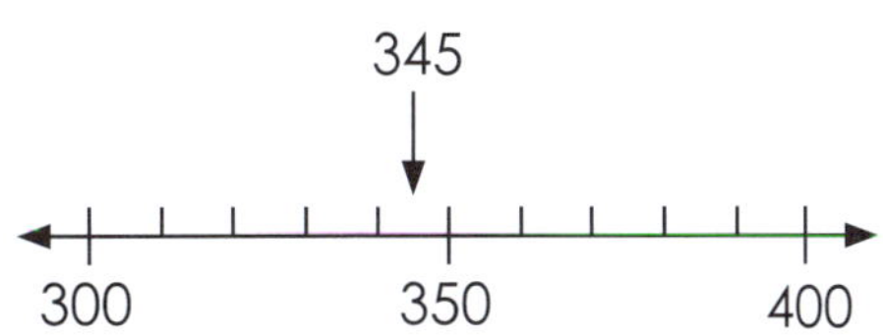

 ISBN 978-93-5103-031-7

b) 3670 ≈ ______

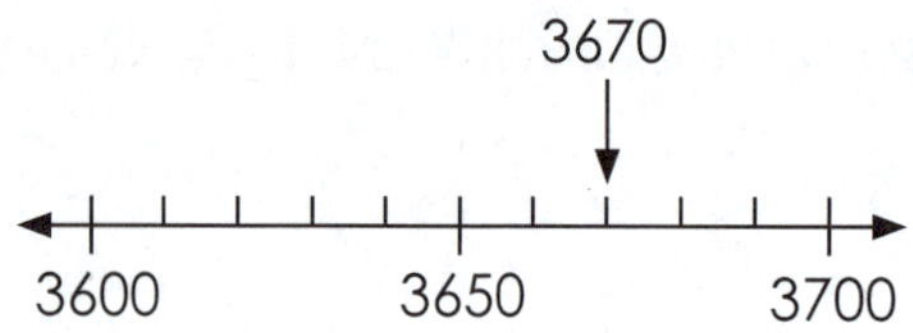

c) 4850 ≈ ______

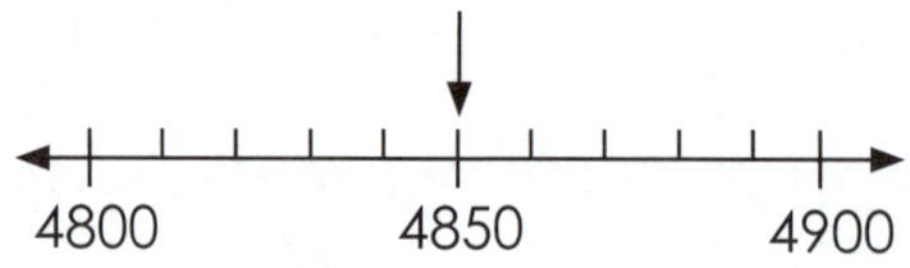

d) 42,629 ≈ ______

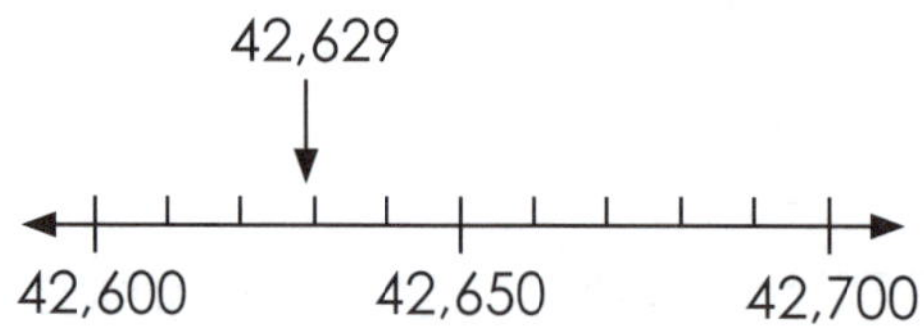

PB Chapter 1: Exercise 10, pages 19–20

Estimating sums and differences

Let's Learn

a) **Estimate** the value of 712 + 492.
Round each number to the nearest hundred.

712 + 492 ≈ 700 + 500
= ▭

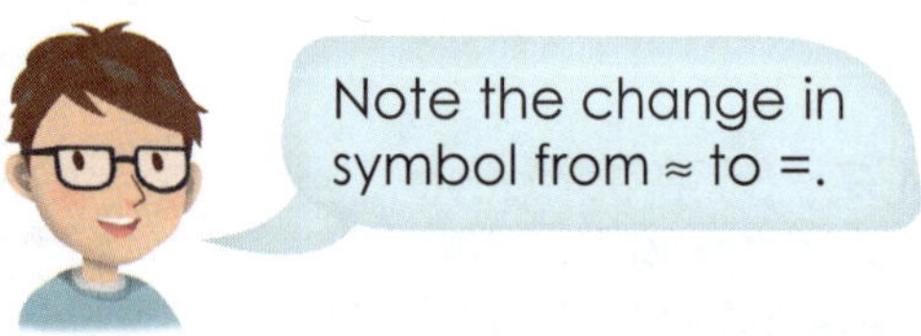

b) Estimate the value of 14,480 – 390.
Round each number to the nearest hundred.

14,480 – 390 ≈ 14,500 – 400
= ▭

Let's Do

1. Round each number to the nearest hundred to estimate the value of each of the following.

a) 384 + 296 ≈ ______ + ______
= ______

b) 1095 + 211 ≈ ______ + ______
= ______

 ISBN 978-93-5103-031-7

c) 716 – 382 ≈ _______ – _______

= _______

d) 85,402 – 419 ≈ _______ – _______

= _______

Chapter 1: Exercise 11, page 21

Think About It

Estimate the value of 341 + 2138.

Ria

341 + 2138 ≈ 300 + 2100
= 2400

341 + 2138 ≈ 340 + 2140
= 2480

Sam

Who is correct? Explain why.

Using estimation to check sums and differences

Let's Learn

Find the value of 914 + 707. Then, use estimation to check your answer.

914 + 707 = 1621

914 + 707 ≈ 900 + 700
= 1600

1621 is about 1600.
My answer is **reasonable**.

Let's Do

1. Find the value of 1208 – 587. Then, use estimation to check your answer.

   1208 – 587 = _______

   Check: 1208 – 587 ≈ _______ – _______

   = _______

Chapter 1: Exercise 12, page 22

 ISBN 978-93-5103-031-7

Practice 3

1. Round each number to the nearest ten.

   a) 89 b) 725 c) 4621 d) 9099

2. Round each number to the nearest hundred.

   a) 837 b) 15,468 c) 39,963 d) 46,050

3. Find the sum or difference. Then, use estimation to check your answer.

   a) 576 + 329 b) 2154 + 887 c) 39,480 + 208

   d) 682 – 207 e) 7078 – 238 f) 71,408 – 382

Lesson 4 Factors

Finding factors of a whole number

Let's Learn

a)

$3 \times 4 = 12$

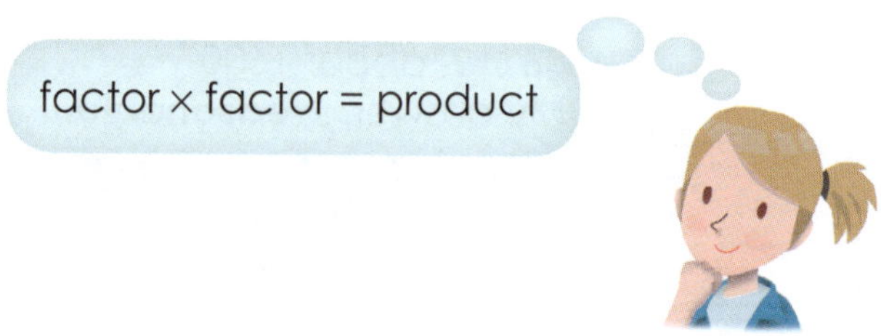

12 is the **product** of 3 and 4.
3 and 4 are **factors** of 12.

$2 \times 3 \times 4 = 24$

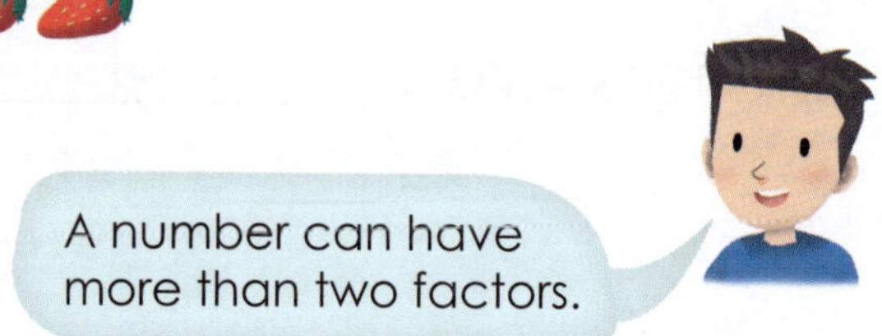

24 is the product of 2, 3 and 4.
2, 3 and 4 are factors of 24.

 ISBN 978-93-5103-031-7

Maths Lab

b) 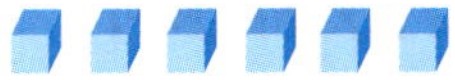

$1 \times 6 = 6$
1 and 6 are factors of 6.

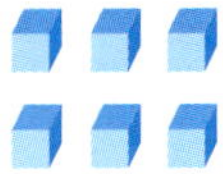

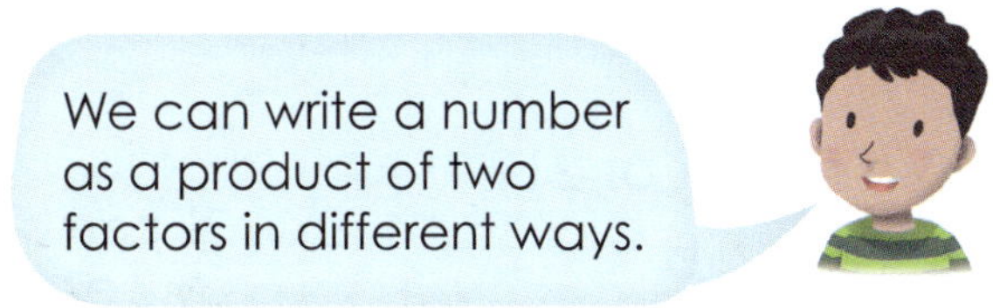

$2 \times 3 = 6$

2 and 3 are also factors of 6.

1, 2, 3 and 6 are factors of 6.

Is 4 a factor of 6?

Is 5 a factor of 6?

Let's Do

1. Find the factors of 16.

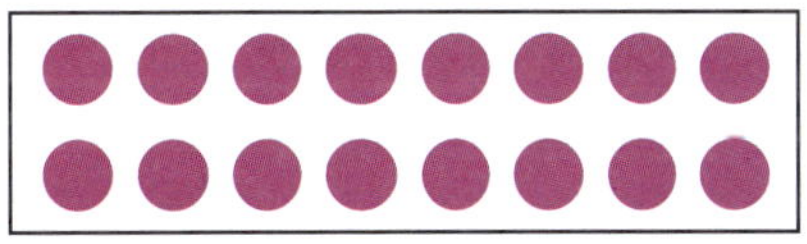

$2 \times 8 = 16$

_______ and _______ are factors of 16.

_______ × _______ = 16

_______ × _______ = 16

The factors of 16 are _______, _______, _______, _______ and _______.

2. Find the factors of 12.

$1 \times$ _______ = 12

$2 \times$ _______ = 12

$3 \times$ _______ = 12

The factors of 12 are _______, _______, _______, _______, _______ and _______.

3. Which of the following numbers have 2 as a factor?

8, 10, 15, 24

____

P/B Chapter 1: Exercise 13, pages 23–24

Finding out if a number is a factor of another number

Let's Learn

a) Is 3 a factor of 21?

$$\begin{array}{r} 7 \\ 3\overline{)21} \\ 21 \\ \hline 0 \end{array}$$

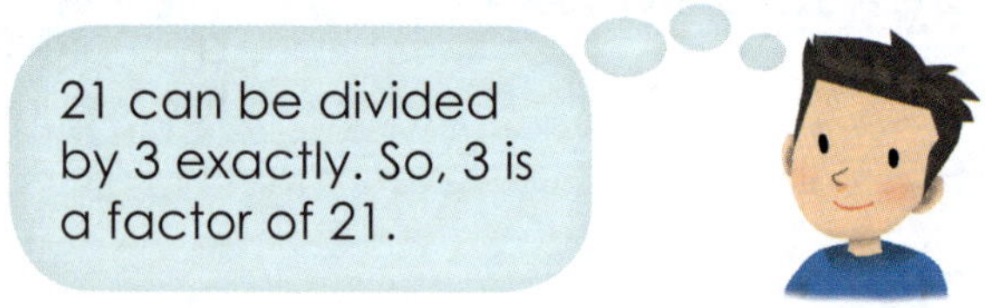

b) Is 3 a factor of 26?

$$\begin{array}{r} 8 \\ 3\overline{)26} \\ 24 \\ \hline 2 \end{array}$$

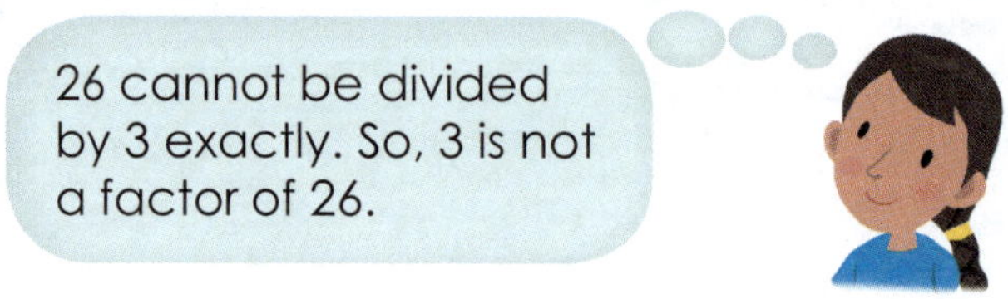

Let's Do

1. a) Is 2 a factor of 98? ______

   $2\overline{)98}$

   b) Is 4 a factor of 98? ______

   $4\overline{)98}$

Chapter 1: Exercise 14, page 25

ISBN 978-93-5103-031-7

Prime and composite numbers

Let's Learn

a) 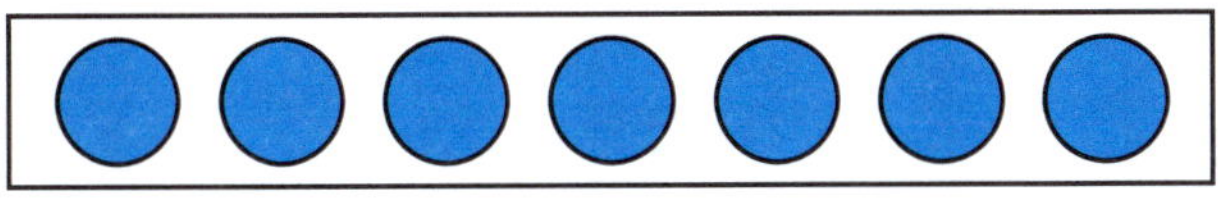

$1 \times 7 = 7$

The factors of 7 are 1 and 7.

Numbers that have only two factors, 1 and the number itself, are called **prime numbers**.
So, 7 is a prime number.

b) 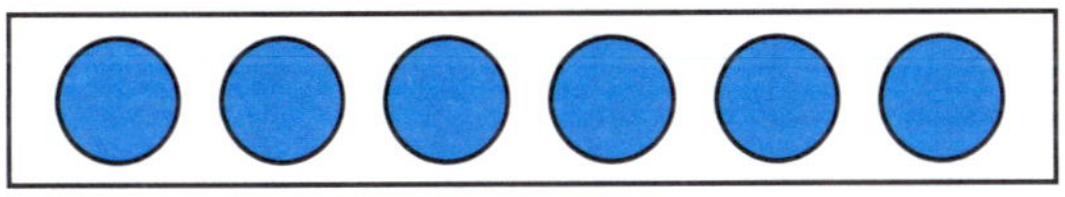

$1 \times 6 = 6$

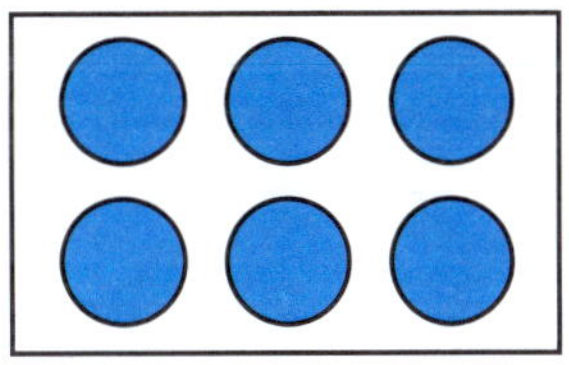

$2 \times 3 = 6$

The factors of 6 are 1, 2, 3 and 6.

Numbers that have more than two factors are called **composite numbers**.
So, 6 is a composite number.

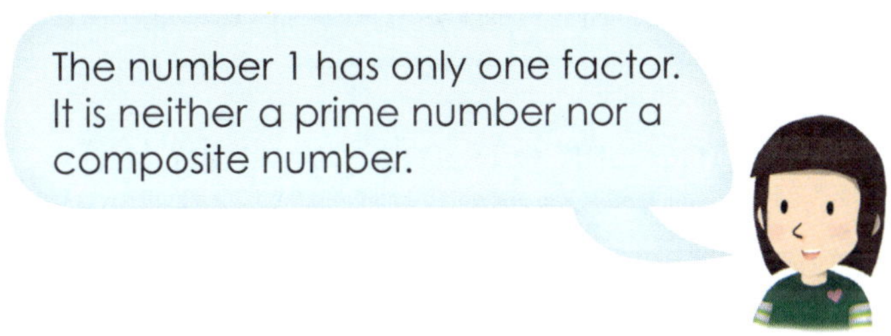

Let's Do

1. Circle the prime numbers. Cross out the composite numbers.

   8 23 17 12

2. List the first six prime numbers.

 ISBN 978-93-5103-031-7

Finding prime numbers within 100

Let's Learn

1	2	3	4	5	6	7	8	9	10
11	12	13	14	15	16	17	18	19	20
21	22	23	24	25	26	27	28	29	30
31	32	33	34	35	36	37	38	39	40
41	42	43	44	45	46	47	48	49	50
51	52	53	54	55	56	57	58	59	60
61	62	63	64	65	66	67	68	69	70
71	72	73	74	75	76	77	78	79	80
81	82	83	84	85	86	87	88	89	90
91	92	93	94	95	96	97	98	99	100

Follow these steps to find all the prime numbers within 100.

Step 1: Cross out 1 in the grid as it is neither a prime nor a composite number.

Step 2: 2 is the first prime number. Circle it and cross out all multiples of 2 that are greater than 2.

Step 3: 3 is the next prime number. Circle it and cross out all multiples of 3 that are greater than 3.

Step 4: 5 is the next prime number. Circle it and cross out all multiples of 5 that are greater than 5.

Step 5: Continue this process until all the numbers are circled or crossed out.

All the numbers that are circled are the prime numbers between 1 and 100.

 ISBN 978-93-5103-031-7

Let's Do

Use the grid on the previous page to help you answer these questions.

1. What are the prime numbers from 1 to 10?

   ____

2. What are the composite numbers from 11 to 20?

3. What is the smallest prime number? _______

4. What is the first odd composite number? _______

P/B Chapter 1: Exercise 15, page 26

Practice 4

1. What arc the factors of 18?

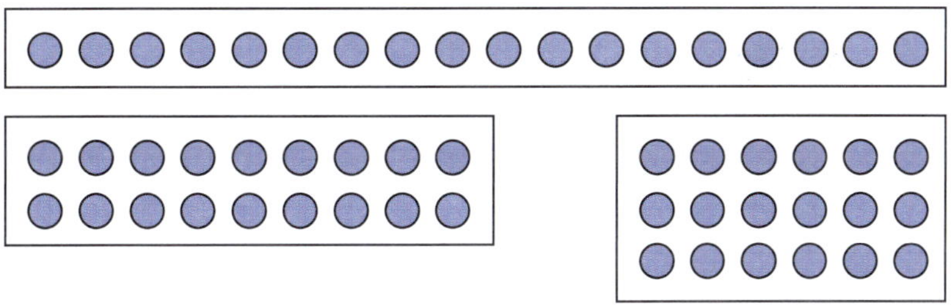

2. Find the missing factors.

   a) 28 = 7 × _____ b) 40 = 5 × _____ c) 72 = 8 × _____

3. Find the factors of 32.

4. Find the factors of each number.

   a) 8 b) 15 c) 20 d) 50 e) 75 f) 98

5. Which of the following numbers have 5 as a factor?

   15, 20, 25, 32, 67, 80

6. List all the prime numbers from 1 to 100.

7. List all the composite numbers from 71 to 90.

 ISBN 978-93-5103-031-7

Lesson 5 Multiples

Finding multiples of a whole number

Let's Learn

Picture It

$1 \times 3 = 3$ $2 \times 3 = 6$

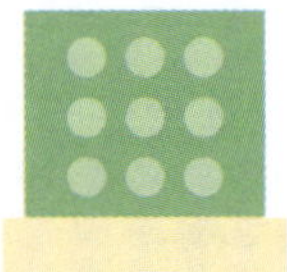

$3 \times 3 = 9$ $4 \times 3 = 12$

3, 6, 9 and 12 are **multiples** of 3.

List other multiples of 3.

Let's Do

1. List the next four multiples of 5.

   5, 10, ______, ______, ______, ______

2. List the next four multiples of 9.

   9, 18, ______, ______, ______, ______

PB Chapter 1: Exercise 16, page 27

ISBN 978-93-5103-031-7

Relating factors and multiples

Let's Learn

a) 12 can be divided by 3 exactly.
12 is a multiple of 3.
3 is a factor of 12.

$$\begin{array}{r} 4 \\ 3\overline{)12} \\ 12 \\ \hline 0 \end{array}$$

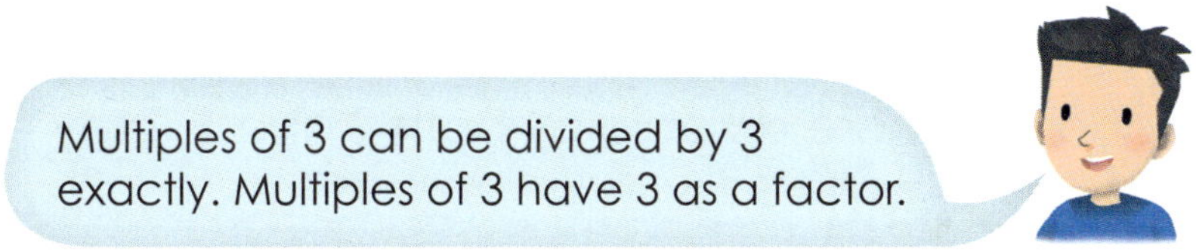

b) 23 cannot be divided by 3 exactly.
23 is not a multiple of 3.
3 is not a factor of 23.

$$\begin{array}{r} 7 \\ 3\overline{)23} \\ 21 \\ \hline 2 \end{array}$$

Let's Do

1. Fill in the blanks with **factor** or **multiple**.

$$3 \times 5 = 15$$

a) 5 is a ______ of 15.

b) 15 is a ______ of 3.

c) 3 is a ______ of 15.

2. a) Is 12 a multiple of 2? ______
Is 2 a factor of 12? ______ $2\overline{)12}$

b) Is 12 a multiple of 6? ______
Is 6 a factor of 12? ______ $6\overline{)12}$

c) Is 12 a multiple of 4? ______

d) Is 12 a multiple of 5? ______

 ISBN 978-93-5103-031-7

Divisibility rules of 2, 5 and 10

Let's Learn

Multiples of 2 can be divided by 2 exactly. We say that these numbers are **divisible** by 2. In this chart, these numbers are circled.

Multiples of 5 or numbers that are divisible by 5 are shown in red.

Numbers that are circled and in red are divisible by both 2 and 5. They are divisible by 10.

Picture It

1	2	3	4	5	6	7	8	9	10
11	12	13	14	15	16	17	18	19	20
21	22	23	24	25	26	27	28	29	30
31	32	33	34	35	36	37	38	39	40
41	42	43	44	45	46	47	48	49	50
51	52	53	54	55	56	57	58	59	60
61	62	63	64	65	66	67	68	69	70
71	72	73	74	75	76	77	78	79	80
81	82	83	84	85	86	87	88	89	90
91	92	93	94	95	96	97	98	99	100

2, 4, 6, ... are multiples of 2. They are divisible by 2.

5, 10, 15, ... are multiples of 5. They are divisible by ___.

10, 20, 30, ... are multiples of 2, 5 and 10. They are divisible by 2, ___ and ___.

a) When a number is divisible by 2, its ones digit is 0, 2, ___, ___ or ___.

b) When a number is divisible by 5, its ones digit is ___ or ___.

c) When a number is divisible by 10, its ones digit is ___.

 ISBN 978-93-5103-031-7

Let's Do

1. Is 75 divisible by the following numbers?

   a) 2 ______ b) 5 ______ c) 10 ______

Chapter 1: Exercise 17, page 28

Practice 5

1. a) What are the next two multiples of 3?

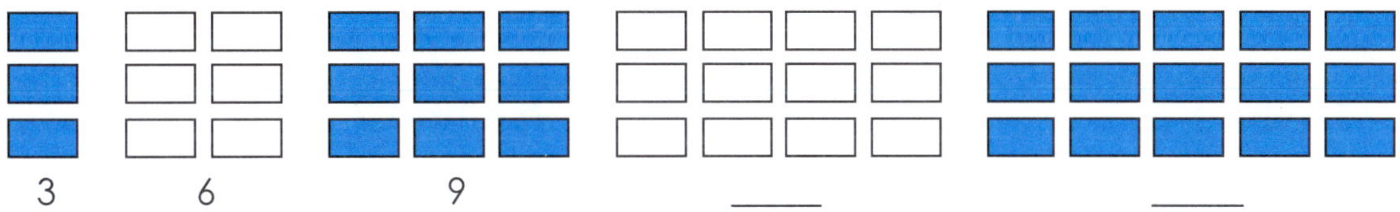

   b) What are the next four multiples of 5?

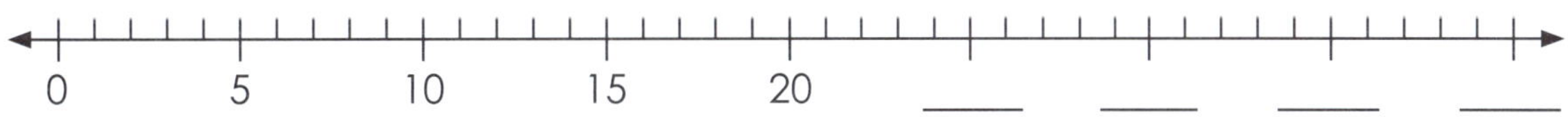

2. Circle the numbers that are divisible by 2.

   98 45 50 88 54 67 32

3. Complete the number patterns.

   a) 4, 8, 12, 16, _____, _____, _____

   b) 6, 12, 18, 24, _____, _____, _____

4. Fill in the blanks with **factor** or **multiple**.

   a) 4 is a ______ of 16. b) 20 is a ______ of 5.

5. a) Is 84 a multiple of 6?

   b) Is 96 a multiple of 8?

6. Is 85 divisible by the following numbers?

   a) 2 ______ b) 5 ______ c) 10 ______

7. Write any number that is a multiple of 3. Find the sum of the digits of the number. Is the sum a multiple of 3?

 ISBN 978-93-5103-031-7

2 Multiplication and Division of Whole Numbers

Lesson 1 Multiplication by 1-digit Numbers and by 10

Multiplying three 1-digit numbers

Let's Learn

Find the value of $2 \times 3 \times 4$.

Method 1

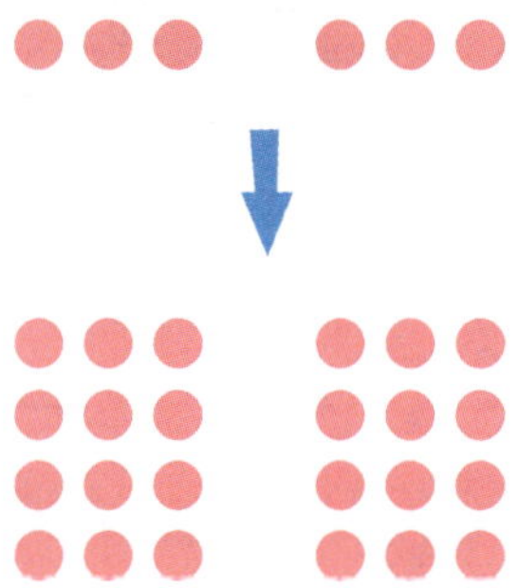

$2 \times 3 = 6$

$2 \times 3 \times 4 = 6 \times 4$
$= 24$

Method 2

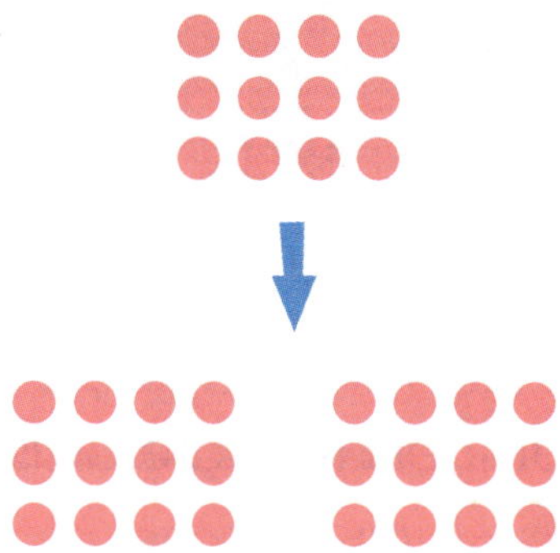

$3 \times 4 = 12$

$2 \times 3 \times 4 = 2 \times 12$
$= 24$

$2 \times 3 \times 4 = 6 \times 4 = 2 \times 12 = 24$

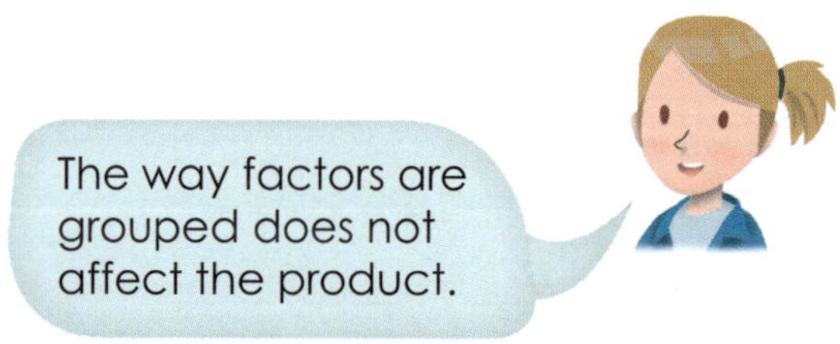

Let's Do

1. Find the value of $3 \times 5 \times 6$.

Method 1

$3 \times 5 \times 6 =$ ______ $\times 6$
$=$ ______

Method 2

$3 \times 5 \times 6 = 3 \times$ ______
$=$ ______

Which method is easier? ________________

 ISBN 978-93-5103-031-7

Let's Learn

Find the value of $8 \times 9 \times 5$.

Method 1 $8 \times 9 \times 5 = 72 \times 5$
$= 360$

Method 2 $8 \times 9 \times 5 = 8 \times 45$
$= 360$

Method 3 $8 \times 9 \times 5 = 9 \times 8 \times 5$
$= 9 \times 40$
$= 360$

Which method is the easiest? ▢

Let's Do

1. Multiply.

a) $5 \times 7 \times 4 = 5 \times 4 \times 7$
$= \_\_\_\_ \times 7$
$= \_\_\_\_$

b) $4 \times 3 \times 5 = \_\_\_\_ \times \_\_\_\_ \times \_\_\_\_$
$= \_\_\_\_ \times \_\_\_\_$
$= \_\_\_\_$

PB Chapter 2: Exercise 1, page 29

Multiplying 4-digit whole numbers by 1-digit numbers

Let's Learn

a) Multiply 1135 by 4.

$1135 \times 4 =$ ▢

1 Multiply the ones by 4.
5 ones × 4 = 20 ones

Regroup the ones.
20 ones = 2 tens

$$\begin{array}{r} {}^{2} \\ 1\,1\,3\,5 \\ \times \quad\ 4 \\ \hline 0 \\ \hline \end{array}$$

2 Multiply the tens by 4.
3 tens × 4 = 12 tens

Add the tens.
12 tens + 2 tens = 14 tens

Regroup the tens.
14 tens = 1 hundred 4 tens

$$\begin{array}{r} {}^{1\ 2} \\ 1\,1\,3\,5 \\ \times \quad\ 4 \\ \hline 4\,0 \\ \hline \end{array}$$

③ Multiply the hundreds by 4.
1 hundred × 4 = 4 hundreds

Add the hundreds.
4 hundreds + 1 hundred = 5 hundreds

$$\begin{array}{r} {}^{1}\ {}^{2}\ \ \\ 1\ 1\ 3\ 5 \\ \times\ \ \ \ \ \ \ 4 \\ \hline 5\ 4\ 0 \\ \hline \end{array}$$

④ Multiply the thousands by 4.
1 thousand × 4 = 4 thousands

$$\begin{array}{r} {}^{1}\ {}^{2}\ \ \\ 1\ 1\ 3\ 5 \\ \times\ \ \ \ \ \ \ 4 \\ \hline 4\ 5\ 4\ 0 \\ \hline \end{array}$$

1135 × 4 = 4540
When 1135 is multiplied by 4, the product is 4540.

b) Multiply 3726 by 5.

3726 × 5 = ▭

① Multiply 6 ones by 5.

$$\begin{array}{r} {}^{3}\ \ \\ 3\ 7\ 2\ 6 \\ \times\ \ \ \ \ \ \ 5 \\ \hline 0 \\ \hline \end{array}$$

② Multiply 2 tens by 5. Add 3 tens.

$$\begin{array}{r} {}^{1}\ {}^{3}\ \ \\ 3\ 7\ 2\ 6 \\ \times\ \ \ \ \ \ \ 5 \\ \hline 3\ 0 \\ \hline \end{array}$$

③ Multiply 7 hundreds by 5. Add 1 hundred.

$$\begin{array}{r} {}^{3}\ {}^{1}\ {}^{3}\ \ \\ 3\ 7\ 2\ 6 \\ \times\ \ \ \ \ \ \ 5 \\ \hline 6\ 3\ 0 \\ \hline \end{array}$$

④ Multiply 3 thousands by 5. Add 3 thousands.

$$\begin{array}{r} {}^{3}\ {}^{1}\ {}^{3}\ \ \\ 3\ 7\ 2\ 6 \\ \times\ \ \ \ \ \ \ 5 \\ \hline 1\ 8\ 6\ 3\ 0 \\ \hline \end{array}$$

3726 × 5 = 18,630

Let's Do

1. Multiply.

a) 2950 × 6 = ______

$$\begin{array}{r} 2\ 9\ 5\ 0 \\ \times\ \ \ \ \ \ \ 6 \\ \hline \\ \hline \end{array}$$

b) 8 × 3245 = ______

$$\begin{array}{r} 3\ 2\ 4\ 5 \\ \times\ \ \ \ \ \ \ 8 \\ \hline \\ \hline \end{array}$$

P/B Chapter 2: Exercise 2, page 30

 ISBN 978-93-5103-031-7

Multiplying whole numbers by 10

Let's Learn

a) Multiply 4 by 10.

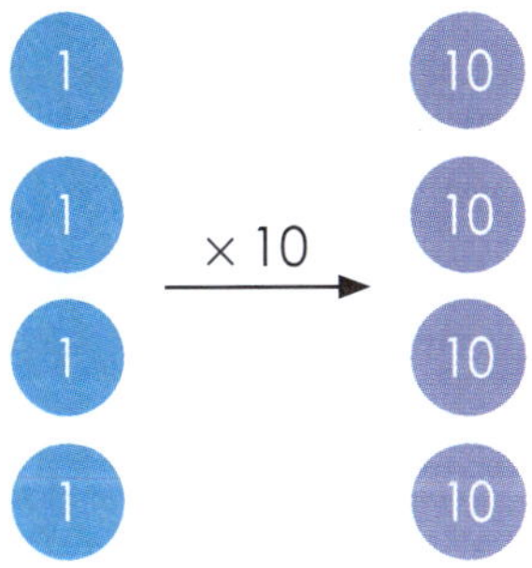

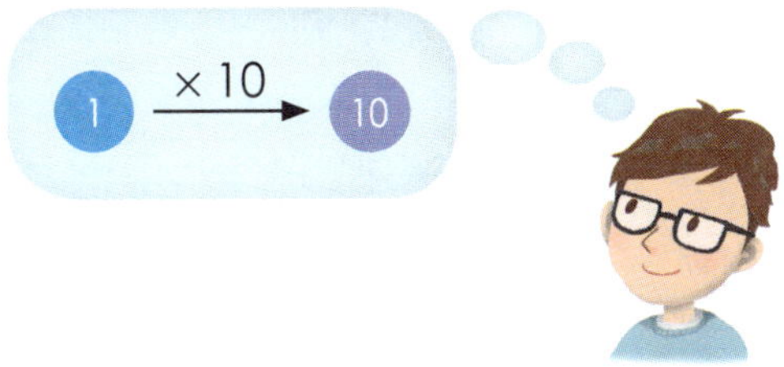

$4 \times 10 = 40$

b) Multiply 40 by 10.

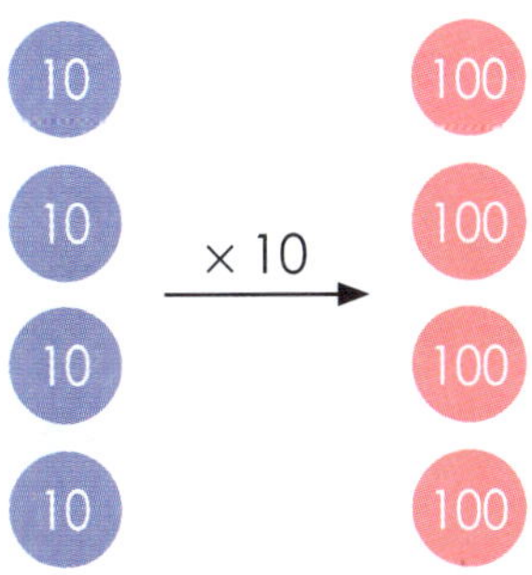

$40 \times 10 = 400$

c) Multiply 400 by 10.

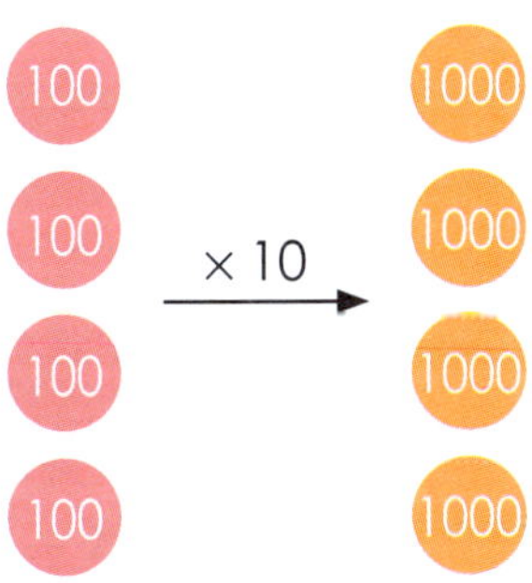

$400 \times 10 = 4000$

 ISBN 978-93-5103-031-7

Let's Do

1. Multiply.

   a) $440 \times 10 =$ ______

   b) $4440 \times 10 =$ ______

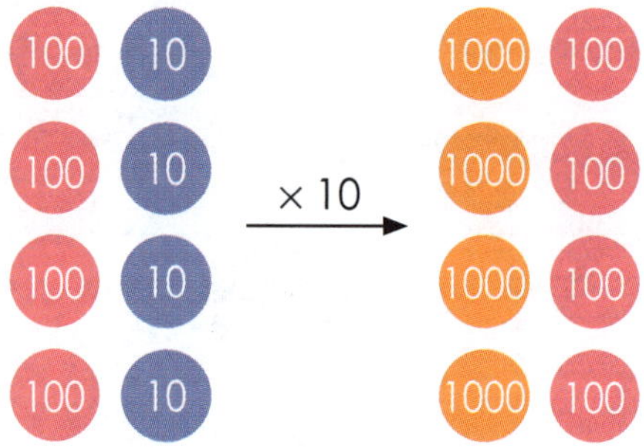

Estimating products

Let's Learn

Estimate the value of 6018×4.

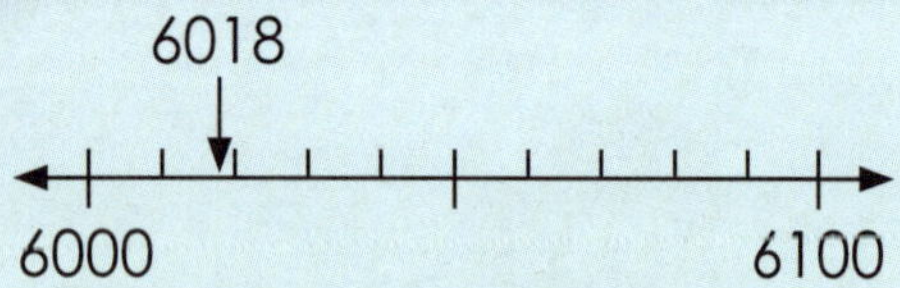

6018 is nearer to 6000 than to 6100.
$6018 \approx 6000$

$$6018 \times 4 \approx 6000 \times 4$$
$$= 24{,}000$$

6 thousands × 4 = 24 thousands

Let's Do

1. Estimate and then multiply.

   a) 4976×5

   Estimate: $4976 \times 5 \approx$ ______ $\times 5$

   $=$ ______

   $$\begin{array}{r} 4\ 9\ 7\ 6 \\ \times \quad\quad 5 \\ \hline \\ \hline \end{array}$$

   b) 6×3040

   Estimate: $6 \times 3040 \approx 6 \times$ ______

   $=$ ______

   $$\begin{array}{r} 3\ 0\ 4\ 0 \\ \times \quad\quad 6 \\ \hline \\ \hline \end{array}$$

PB Chapter 2: Exercise 3, page 31

 ISBN 978-93-5103-031-7

Solving word problems

Let's Learn

There are 2975 children at a stadium watching a football match. There are 3 times as many adults as children at the stadium. How many adults are there?

Picture It

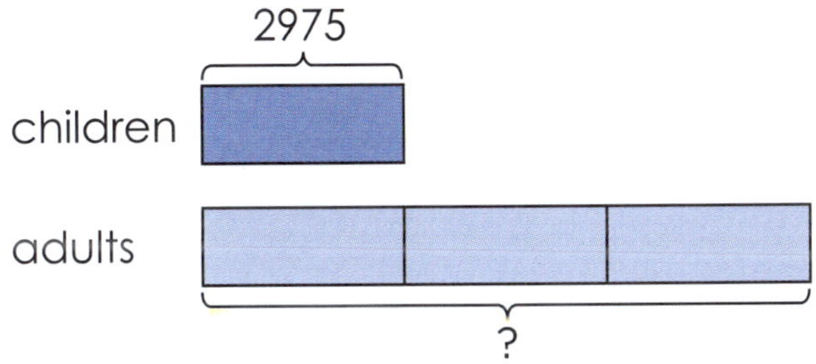

1 unit → 2975
3 units → $3 \times 2975 = 8925$

There are ____ adults.

$2975 \times 3 \approx 3000 \times 3$
$= 9000$
8925 is about 9000.
My answer is reasonable.

Let's Do

1. A printer costs ₹ 1978. Find the total cost of 5 such printers.

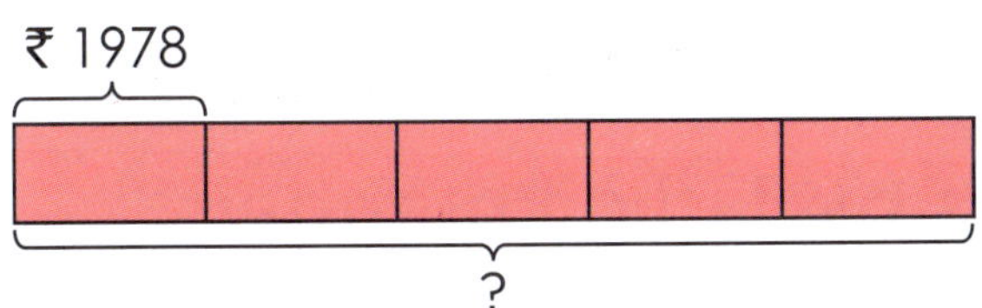

1 unit → ₹ 1978
5 units → 5 × ₹ 1978 = ₹ ______

The total cost of 5 printers is ₹ ______.

P/B Chapter 2: Exercise 4, page 32

 ISBN 978-93-5103-031-7

Practice 1

1. Multiply.

   a) $2 \times 5 \times 6$ b) $4 \times 7 \times 3$ c) $8 \times 6 \times 5$

2. Multiply.

   a) 2011×3 b) 2107×4 c) 3450×5

   d) 6×4215 e) 7×3917 f) 9×6258

3. Estimate and then multiply.

   a) 4076×5 b) 3987×6 c) 2050×9

   d) 7×6971 e) 5×6032 f) 8×5980

Solve the word problems. Show your work clearly.

4. A baker sold 1980 loaves of bread last month. He sold 3 times as many loaves this month as last month. How many loaves of bread did he sell this month?

5. Mr. Rao earns ₹ 2048 a week. How much does he earn in 4 weeks?

Lesson 2 Division by 1-digit Numbers and by 10

Dividing 4-digit whole numbers by 1-digit numbers

Let's Learn

a) Divide 4206 by 3.

$4206 \div 3 = \square$

❶ Divide the thousands by 3.

$$\begin{array}{r l} & \underline{\;1} \\ 3\,)\!\! & 4206 \\ & \underline{3} \leftarrow 3 \times 1 \text{ thousand} = 3 \text{ thousands} \\ & 1 \leftarrow \text{remainder 1 thousand} \end{array}$$

 ISBN 978-93-5103-031-7

2 Divide the hundreds by 3.

```
    1 4
  ------
3 ) 4 2 0 6
    3
    ---
    1 2    ← 1 thousand 2 hundreds = 12 hundreds
    1 2    ← 3 × 4 hundreds = 12 hundreds
    ----
```

3 Divide the tens by 3.

```
    1 4 0
  --------
3 ) 4 2 0 6
    3
    ---
    1 2
    1 2
    -----
        0    ← 0 tens
        0    ← 3 × 0 tens = 0 tens
        -
```

4 Divide the ones by 3.

```
    1 4 0 2
  ---------
3 ) 4 2 0 6
    3
    ---
    1 2
    1 2
    -----
        0
        0
        ---
          6   ← 6 ones
          6   ← 3 × 2 ones = 6 ones
          -
          0
```

4206 ÷ 3 = 1402

When 4206 is divided by 3, the quotient is 1402.

b) Divide 5630 by 6.

5630 ÷ 6 = ▢

1 Divide the thousands by 6.

```
  ---------
6 ) 5 6 3 0
```

I do not have enough 1000 to put a 1000 each into 6 groups. So, I regroup the thousands and hundreds.

5 thousands 6 hundreds = 56 hundreds

 ISBN 978-93-5103-031-7

❷ Divide the hundreds by 6.

```
     9
6 ) 5 6 3 0
    5 4      ← 6 × 9 hundreds = 54 hundreds
    ---
      2      ← remainder 2 hundreds
```

❸ Divide the tens by 6.

```
      9 3
6 ) 5 6 3 0
    5 4
    ---
      2 3    ← 2 hundreds 3 tens = 23 tens
      1 8    ← 6 × 3 tens = 18 tens
      ---
        5    ← remainder 5 tens
```

❹ Divide the ones by 6.

```
      9 3 8
6 ) 5 6 3 0
    5 4
    ---
      2 3
      1 8
      ---
        5 0  ← 5 tens = 50 ones
        4 8  ← 6 × 8 ones = 48 ones
        ---
          2  ← remainder 2 ones
```

5630 ÷ 6 = 938 R2

Let's Do

1. Divide.

a) 5) 7 1 9 5

b) 5) 3 2 5 4

c) 7) 4 2 3 5

P/B Chapter 2: Exercise 5, page 33

 ISBN 978-93-5103-031-7

Dividing whole numbers by 10

Let's Learn

a) Divide 40 by 10.

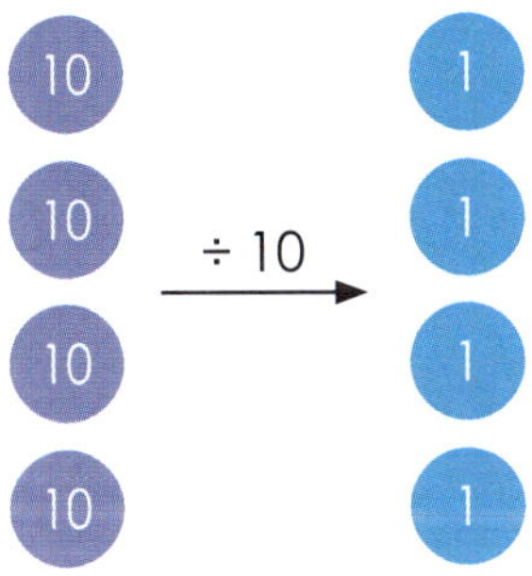

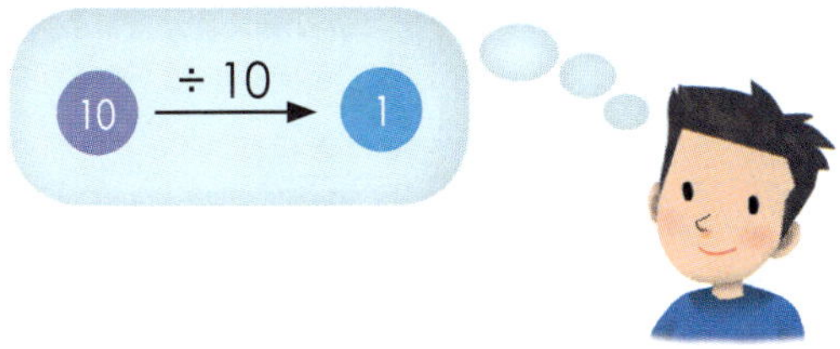

40 ÷ 10 = 4

b) Divide 400 by 10.

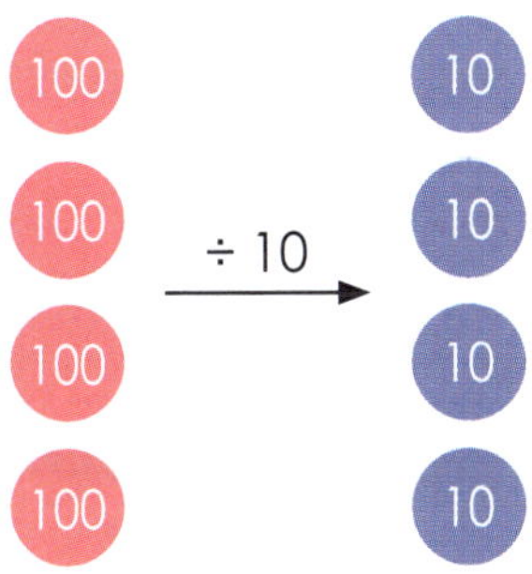

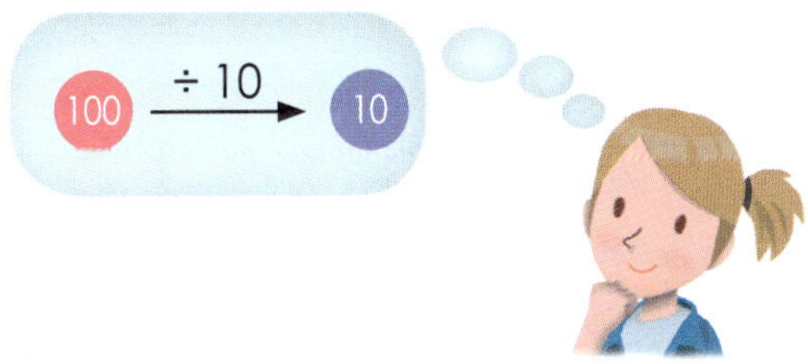

400 ÷ 10 = 40

c) Divide 4000 by 10.

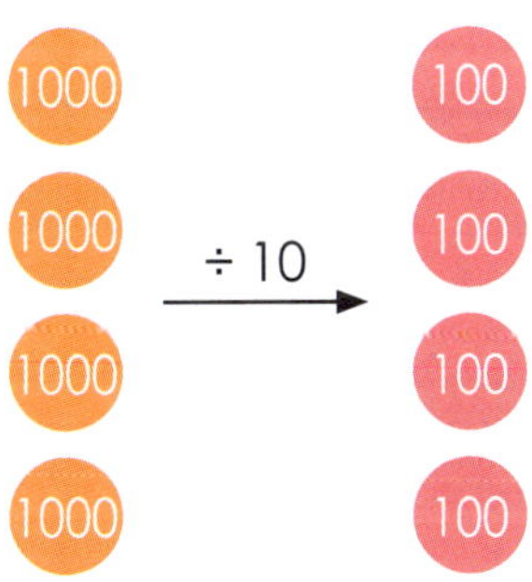

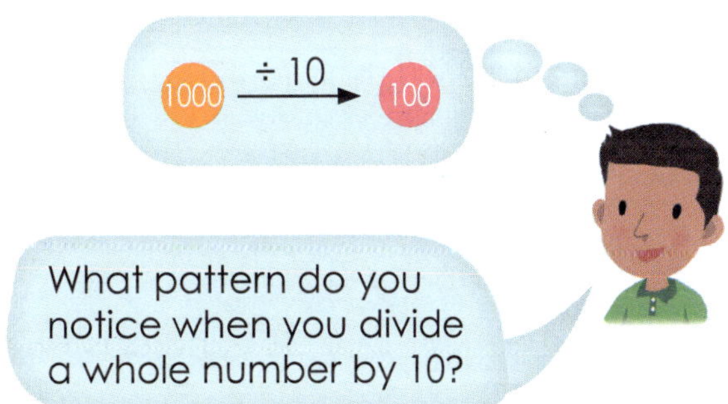

4000 ÷ 10 = 400

 ISBN 978-93-5103-031-7

Let's Do

1. Divide.

   a) 440 ÷ 10 = ______ b) 4400 ÷ 10 = ______

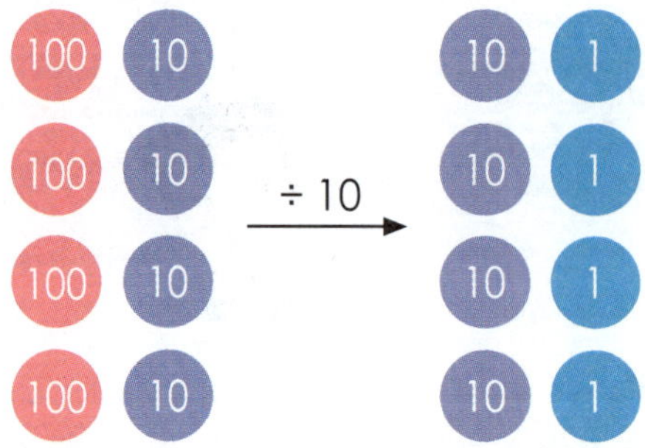

Estimating quotients

Let's Learn

Estimate the value of 3840 ÷ 6.

Multiples of 6:
... 30, 36, 42 ...
... **30**00, **36**00, **42**00 ...

3840 is between 3600 and 4200.

Picture It

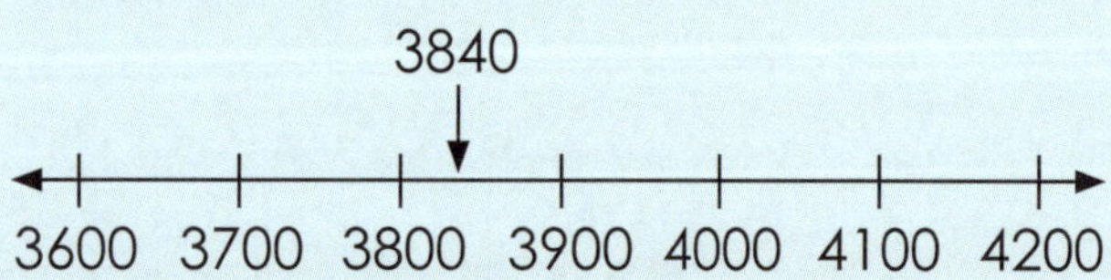

3840 is nearer to 3600 than to 4200.
3840 ≈ 3600

$3840 \div 6 \approx 3600 \div 6$
$= 600$

36 hundreds ÷ 6 = 6 hundreds

 ISBN 978-93-5103-031-7

Let's Do

1. Estimate and then divide.

a) $3604 \div 9$

Estimate:

What numbers are multiples of 9?

$3604 \div 9 \rightarrow 3600 \div 9$

$3604 \div 9 \rightarrow 4500 \div 9$

3604 is nearer to ______ than to ______.

$3604 \div 9 \approx$ ______ $\div 9$

$=$ ______

$9\overline{)3604}$

b) $3120 \div 8$

Estimate:

What numbers are multiples of 8?

$3120 \div 8 \approx$ ______ $\div 8$

$=$ ______

$8\overline{)3120}$

PB Chapter 2: Exercise 6, page 34

Solving word problems

Let's Learn

Mr. Roy had 1455 buttons. He packed all the buttons equally into 3 bags. How many buttons were there in each bag?

Picture It

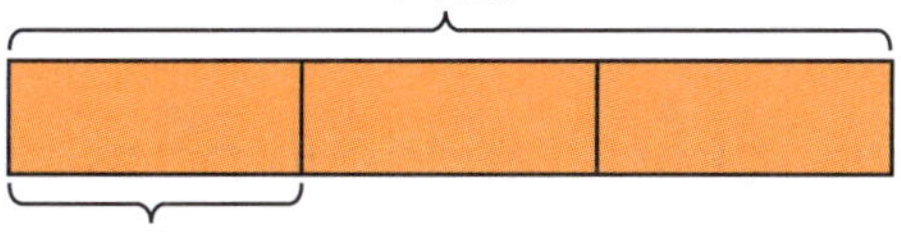

3 units → 1455
1 unit → $1455 \div 3 = 485$

$1455 \div 3 \approx 1500 \div 3$
$= 500$

485 is about 500.
My answer is reasonable.

There were 485 buttons in each bag.

 ISBN 978-93-5103-031-7

Let's Do

1. There are 2630 adults at a carnival. There are 5 times as many adults as children at the carnival. How many children are there?

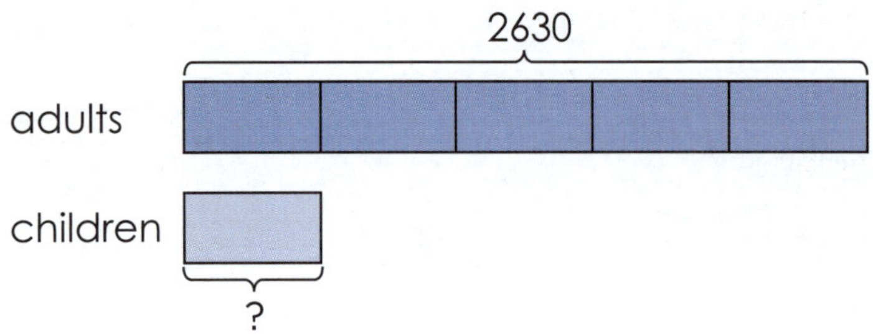

There are more adults than children.

5 units → 2630
1 unit → 2630 ÷ 5 = ______

There are ______ children.

2630 ÷ 5 ≈ ______ ÷ 5
= ______

Is my answer reasonable?

PB Chapter 2: Exercise 7, page 35

Practice 2

1. Divide.

a)	2109 ÷ 3	b)	4036 ÷ 4	c)	2510 ÷ 5	d)	7212 ÷ 6
e)	3968 ÷ 8	f)	8181 ÷ 9	g)	6431 ÷ 7	h)	4750 ÷ 10

2. Estimate and then divide.

a)	2115 ÷ 9	b)	3580 ÷ 7	c)	3104 ÷ 8
d)	8128 ÷ 10	e)	7528 ÷ 3	f)	7180 ÷ 6

Solve the word problems. Show your work clearly.

3. The cost of a microwave oven is 4 times the cost of a blender. If the microwave oven costs ₹ 7200, find the cost of the blender.

4. Ali had 1536 rubber bands. He put them equally into 6 boxes. How many rubber bands were there in each box?

5. Mr. Sharma bought 3750 kilograms of rice. He packed the rice in bags of 10 kilograms each. How many bags of rice did Mr. Sharma have?

6. Trisha bought 6 similar pairs of earrings for ₹ 8040. How much did she pay for each pair of earrings?

 ISBN 978-93-5103-031-7

Lesson 3 Multiplication by 2-digit Whole Numbers

Multiplying 2-digit whole numbers by tens

Let's Learn

Multiply 32 by 20.

Maths Lab

Picture It

Method 1

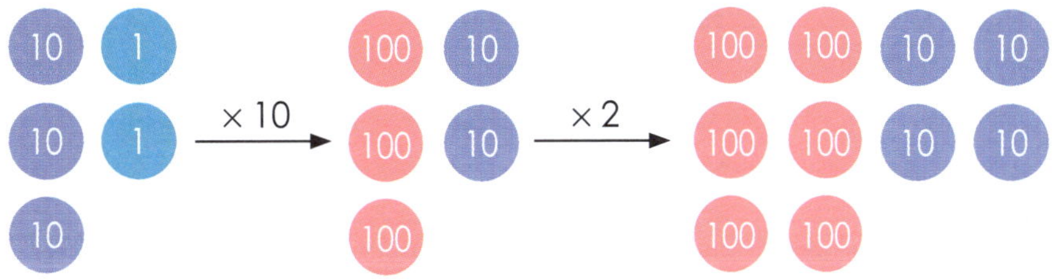

$32 \times 10 = 320$ $320 \times 2 = 640$

$$\begin{aligned} 32 \times 20 &= 32 \times 10 \times 2 \\ &= 320 \times 2 \\ &= 640 \end{aligned}$$

Method 2

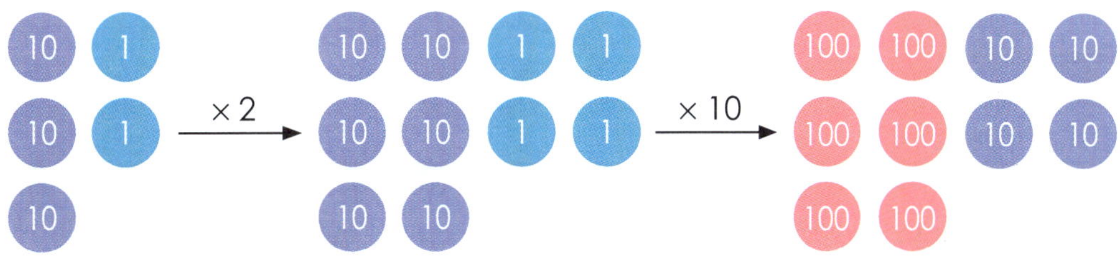

$32 \times 2 = 64$ $64 \times 10 = 640$

$$\begin{aligned} 32 \times 20 &= 32 \times 2 \times 10 \\ &= 64 \times 10 \\ &= 640 \end{aligned}$$

Method 3

❶ Multiply 32 by 0 ones.

$$\begin{array}{r} 3\ 2 \\ \times\ 2\ 0 \\ \hline 0 \\ \hline \end{array}$$

❷ Multiply 2 ones by 2 tens.

$$\begin{array}{r} 3\ 2 \\ \times\ 2\ 0 \\ \hline 4\ 0 \\ \hline \end{array}$$

❸ Multiply 3 tens by 2 tens.

$$\begin{array}{r} 3\ 2 \\ \times\ \ 2\ 0 \\ \hline 6\ 4\ 0 \\ \hline \end{array}$$

Let's Do

1. Find the product of 14 and 30.

Method 1

$14 \times 30 = 14 \times 10 \times$ ______

$= $ ______ $\times$ ______

$= $ ______

Method 2

$14 \times 30 = 14 \times 3 \times$ ______

$= $ ______ $\times$ ______

$= $ ______

Method 3

$$\begin{array}{r} 1\ 4 \\ \times\ 3\ 0 \\ \hline \\ \hline \end{array}$$

Multiplying 3-digit whole numbers by tens

Let's Learn

Multiply 284 by 20.

Method 1

$284 \times 20 = 284 \times 10 \times 2$
$= 2840 \times 2$
$= 5680$

Method 2

$284 \times 20 = 284 \times 2 \times 10$
$= 568 \times 10$
$= 5680$

Method 3

1. Multiply 284 by 0 ones.

$$\begin{array}{r} 2\ 8\ 4 \\ \times\quad 2\ 0 \\ \hline 0 \\ \hline \end{array}$$

2. Multiply 4 ones by 2 tens.

$$\begin{array}{r} 2\ 8\ 4 \\ \times\quad 2\ 0 \\ \hline 8\ 0 \\ \hline \end{array}$$

3. Multiply 8 tens by 2 tens.

$$\begin{array}{r} {}^{1}\quad \\ 2\ 8\ 4 \\ \times\quad 2\ 0 \\ \hline 6\ 8\ 0 \\ \hline \end{array}$$

4. Multiply 2 hundreds by 2 tens.

$$\begin{array}{r} {}^{1}\quad \\ 2\ 8\ 4 \\ \times\quad 2\ 0 \\ \hline 5\ 6\ 8\ 0 \\ \hline \end{array}$$

 ISBN 978-93-5103-031-7

Let's Do

1. Multiply.

a) **Method 1 or 2**

$392 \times 80 = 392 \times$ ______ $\times$ ______

$=$ ______ $\times$ ______

$=$ ______

Method 3

$$\begin{array}{r} 3\ 9\ 2 \\ \times \quad 8\ 0 \\ \hline \\ \hline \end{array}$$

b) **Method 1 or 2**

$40 \times 309 = 309 \times 40$

$= 309 \times$ ______ $\times$ ______

$=$ ______ $\times$ ______

$=$ ______

Method 3

$$\begin{array}{r} 3\ 0\ 9 \\ \times \quad 4\ 0 \\ \hline \\ \hline \end{array}$$

Chapter 2: Exercise 8, page 36

Multiplying 2-digit whole numbers by 2-digit whole numbers

Let's Learn

Multiply 34 by 15.

❶ Multiply 34 by 5.

$$\begin{array}{r} ^{2} \\ 3\ 4 \\ \times \quad 1\ 5 \\ \hline 1\ 7\ 0 \end{array}$$

❷ Multiply 34 by 10.

$$\begin{array}{r} ^{2} \\ 3\ 4 \\ \times \quad 1\ 5 \\ \hline 1\ 7\ 0 \\ 3\ 4\ 0 \end{array}$$

❸ Add.

$$\begin{array}{rl} ^{2} & \\ 3\ 4 & \\ \times \quad 1\ 5 & \\ \hline 1\ 7\ 0 & \leftarrow 34 \times 5 \\ 3\ 4\ 0 & \leftarrow 34 \times 10 \\ \hline 5\ 1\ 0 & \leftarrow 34 \times 15 \\ \hline \end{array}$$

 ISBN 978-93-5103-031-7

Let's Do

1. Multiply.

a)
```
      6 4
×     2 7
---------
            ← 64 × 7
            ← 64 × 20
---------
            ← 64 × 27
---------
```

b)
```
      5 4
×     3 1
---------
            ← 54 × 1
            ← 54 × 30
---------
            ← 54 × 31
---------
```

c)
```
      9 3
×     2 4
---------
            ← 93 × 4
            ← 93 × 20
---------
            ← 93 × 24
---------
```

d)
```
      8 7
×     1 9
---------
            ← 87 × 9
            ← 87 × 10
---------
            ← 87 × 19
---------
```

Chapter 2: Exercise 9, page 37

Multiplying 3-digit whole numbers by 2-digit whole numbers

Let's Learn

Multiply 19 by 278.

1 Multiply 278 by 9.

```
   7 7
   2 7 8
×    1 9
--------
 2 5 0 2
```

2 Multiply 278 by 10.

```
   7 7
   2 7 8
×    1 9
--------
 2 5 0 2
 2 7 8 0
```

3 Add.

```
   7 7
   2 7 8
×    1 9
--------
 2 5 0 2  ← 278 × 9
 2 7 8 0  ← 278 × 10
--------
 5 2 8 2  ← 278 × 19
--------
```


 ISBN 978-93-5103-031-7

Let's Do

1. Multiply.

a) $\begin{array}{r} 4\ 9\ 0 \\ \times \quad 5\ 1 \\ \hline \end{array}$

b) $\begin{array}{r} 6\ 1\ 2 \\ \times \quad 2\ 5 \\ \hline \end{array}$

c) $\begin{array}{r} 3\ 8\ 3 \\ \times \quad 5\ 8 \\ \hline \end{array}$

d) $\begin{array}{r} 7\ 8\ 6 \\ \times \quad 6\ 9 \\ \hline \end{array}$

P/B Chapter 2: Exercise 10, page 38

Think About It

Multiply 538 by 31.

Ria **Sam**

Who is correct? Explain why.

Estimating products

Let's Learn

a) Estimate the value of 32 × 68. Round 32 and 68 to the nearest tens.

Picture It

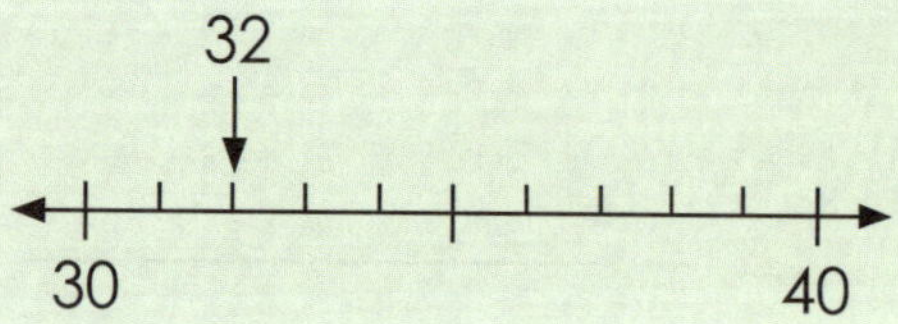

32 is nearer to 30 than to 40.
32 ≈ 30

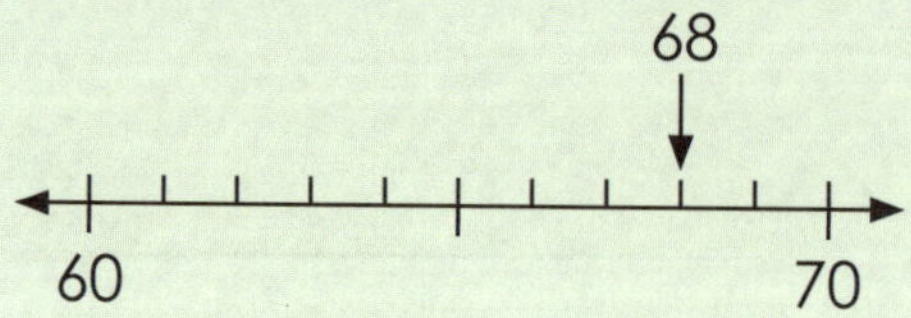

68 is nearer to 70 than to 60.
68 ≈ 70

$32 \times 68 \approx 30 \times 70$
$= 2100$

$3 \times 7 = 21$
$30 \times 70 = 2100$

b) Estimate the value of 48 × 315. Round 48 to the nearest ten.
Round 315 to the nearest hundred.

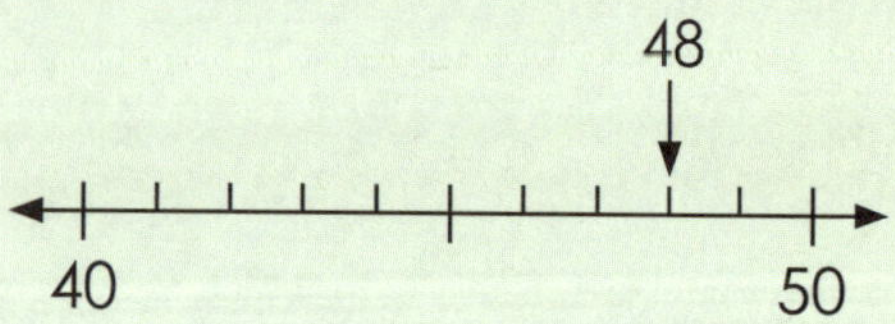

48 is nearer to 50 than to 40.
48 ≈ 50

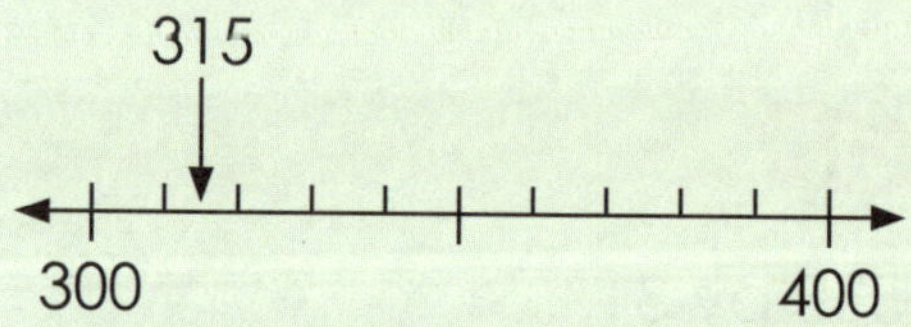

315 is nearer to 300 than to 400.
315 ≈ 300

$48 \times 315 \approx 50 \times 300$
$= 15{,}000$

$5 \times 3 = 15$
$50 \times 300 = 15{,}000$

Let's Do

1. Estimate and then multiply.

a) 49 × 18

Estimate: 49 × 18 ≈ ______ × ______
= ______

$$\begin{array}{r} 4\ 9 \\ \times\ 1\ 8 \\ \hline \end{array}$$

 ISBN 978-93-5103-031-7

b) 412×23

Estimate: $412 \times 23 \approx$ ______ $\times$ ______

$=$ ______

$$\begin{array}{r} 4\ 1\ 2 \\ \times \quad 2\ 3 \\ \hline \end{array}$$

c) 32×685

Estimate: $32 \times 685 \approx$ ______ $\times$ ______

$=$ ______

$$\begin{array}{r} 6\ 8\ 5 \\ \times \quad 3\ 2 \\ \hline \end{array}$$

P/B Chapter 2: Exercise 11, pages 39–40

Solving word problems

Let's Learn

There are 48 classes in a school. There are 32 students in each class. How many students are there altogether?

$32 \times 48 = 1536$

There are 1536 students altogether.

$32 \times 48 \approx 30 \times 50$
$= 1500$

1536 is about 1500.
My answer is reasonable.

Let's Do

1. Chef Gopal has 29 bags of flour. Each bag of flour weighs 505 grams. Find the total weight of the bags of flour.

   ______ $\times$ ______ $=$ ______

   The total weight of the bags of flour is ______ grams.

Check your answer.
Is it reasonable?

P/B Chapter 2: Exercise 12, page 41

 ISBN 978-93-5103-031-7

Practice 3

1. Multiply.

a) 23×30	b) 68×70	c) 36×50
d) 90×45	e) 281×50	f) 560×60

2. Estimate and then multiply.

a) 48×11	b) 61×29	c) 88×67
d) 101×13	e) 289×53	f) 786×78

Solve the word problems. Show your work clearly.

3. John delivers 165 copies of newspaper every day. How many copies of newspaper will he deliver in 30 days?

4. Gaurav bought 15 sheets of stamps. If there were 25 stamps on each sheet, how many stamps did he buy?

5. Mr. Johnson bought 27 shelves for the school library. Each shelf cost ₹ 125. How much did the shelves cost altogether?

6. Mrs. Singh ordered 35 cheese sandwiches and 3 times as many chicken sandwiches for a party. How many chicken sandwiches did she order?

7. There are 576 green balls in a box. There are 23 times as many red balls as green balls in the box. How many red balls are there?

Lesson 4 Problem Solving

Word problems

Let's Learn

Kabir trained for a marathon by running 36 kilometres every week except for the first week when he ran 15 kilometres less.

a) How far did he run in the first week?
b) How far did he run in the first 13 weeks?

 ISBN 978-93-5103-031-7

1 Understand the problem.

How far did Kabir run each week?
Did he run the same distance every week?
What do I have to find?

2 Plan what to do.

First, find the distance he ran in the first week.
Then, find the distance he ran in the next 12 weeks.

3 Work out the **Answer**.

a) $36 - 15 = 21$
He ran 21 kilometres in the first week.

b) $36 \text{ km} \times 12 = 432$
He ran 432 kilometres in the next 12 weeks.

$21 + 432 = 453$
He ran 453 kilometres in the first 13 weeks.

4 Check
Did you answer the question?
Is your answer reasonable?

$36 \times 13 \approx 40 \times 10$
$= 400$
453 is about 400.
My answer is reasonable.

- ☑ 1. Understand
- ☑ 2. Plan
- ☑ 3. Answer
- ☑ 4. Check

Let's Do

1. The admission fee to a zoo was ₹ 21 for each person. In a day, the zoo had 124 visitors in the afternoon and 78 fewer visitors in the evening. How much admission fee did the zoo collect that day?

How many people visited the zoo in the afternoon?
How many people visited the zoo in the evening?
What was the total number of visitors that day?

- ☐ 1. Understand
- ☐ 2. Plan
- ☐ 3. Answer
- ☐ 4. Check

PB Chapter 2: Exercise 13, pages 42–43

 ISBN 978-93-5103-031-7

Practice 4

Solve the word problems. Show your work clearly.

1. Sara bakes 11 pies each day. If she bakes for 20 days each month, how many pies will she bake in a year?

2. There are 3140 children at a camp. 11 of the children are put into one group. The remaining children are put into groups of 7. How many groups are there altogether?

3. The cost of a bicycle is 3 times the cost of a skateboard.
   A guitar is 10 times as expensive as the skateboard.
   If the bicycle costs ₹ 1437,
   a) what is the cost of the guitar?
   b) what is the total cost of the bicycle and the guitar?

4. Mr. Harding gave 3390 grams of clay to 15 boys and 9 girls. Each boy was given 130 grams of clay. If the remaining clay was divided equally among the girls, how many grams of clay did each girl receive?

Mind stretcher

Let's Learn

Noor had 3 times as many stickers as Ben at first. She put her stickers into packets of 16 and gave away 16 such packets. In the end, Ben had 3 times as many stickers as Noor. How many stickers did Noor have at first?

1 Understand the problem.

Who had more stickers at first?
Who had more stickers in the end?
How many stickers were given away?
Did Ben's number of stickers change?

2 Plan what to do.

I can **draw bar models** to help me solve the problem.

 ISBN 978-93-5103-031-7

3 Work out the **Answer**.

At first

In the end

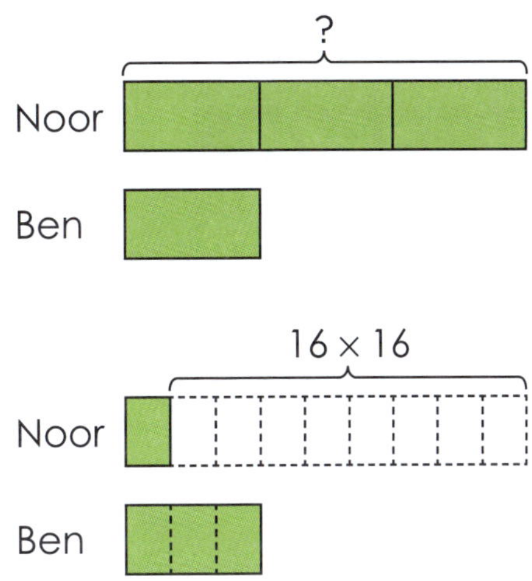

$16 \times 16 = 256$
Noor gave away 256 stickers.

8 units $\rightarrow$ 256
1 unit $\rightarrow 256 \div 8 = 32$
9 units $\rightarrow 9 \times 32 = 288$

Noor had 288 stickers at first.

4 Check

Did you answer the question?
Is your answer correct?

3 units $\rightarrow 3 \times 32 = 96$
Ben had 96 stickers.

Noor had 3 times as many stickers as Ben at first.
$3 \times 96 = 288$
She had 288 stickers at first.

My answer is correct.

- ☑ 1. Understand
- ☑ 2. Plan
- ☑ 3. Answer
- ☑ 4. Check

 ISBN 978-93-5103-031-7

3 Fractions

Lesson 1 Mixed Numbers

Writing mixed numbers

Let's Learn

There is more than 1 watermelon.

a)

$1 + \frac{1}{2} = 1\frac{1}{2}$

There are $1\frac{1}{2}$ watermelons.

b)

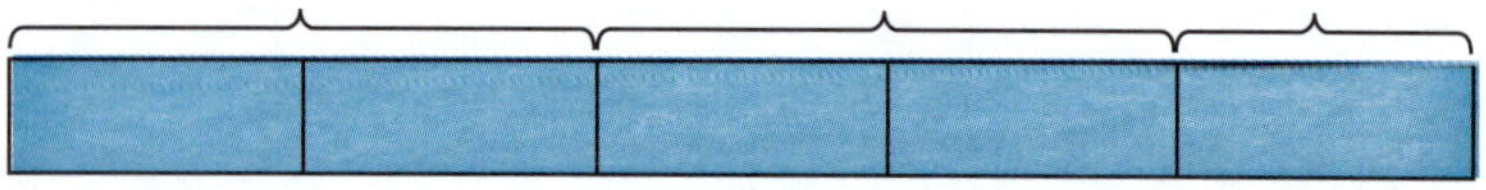

$2 + \frac{1}{2} = 2\frac{1}{2}$

This strip of paper is $2\frac{1}{2}$ metres long.

c)

There are $3\frac{3}{4}$ litres of water.

$3 + \frac{3}{4} = 3\frac{3}{4}$

$1\frac{1}{2}$, $2\frac{1}{2}$ and $3\frac{3}{4}$ are **mixed numbers**.

When we add a whole number and a fraction, the result is a mixed number.

d)

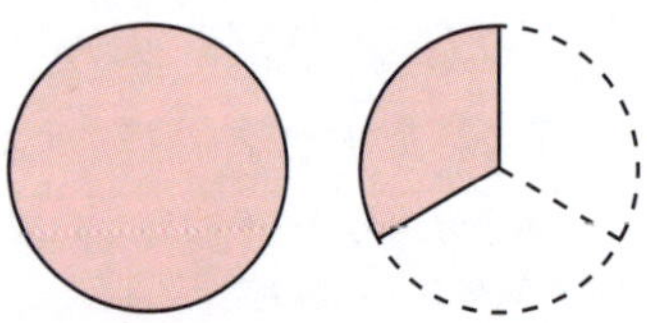

$1 + \frac{1}{3} = 1\frac{1}{3}$

1 whole and 1 third = $1\frac{1}{3}$

 ISBN 978-93-5103-031-7

e) 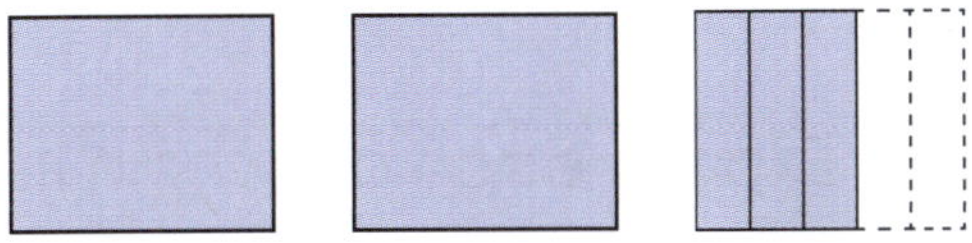

2 wholes and 3 fifths = ____

Let's Do

1. Fill in the blanks.

a) 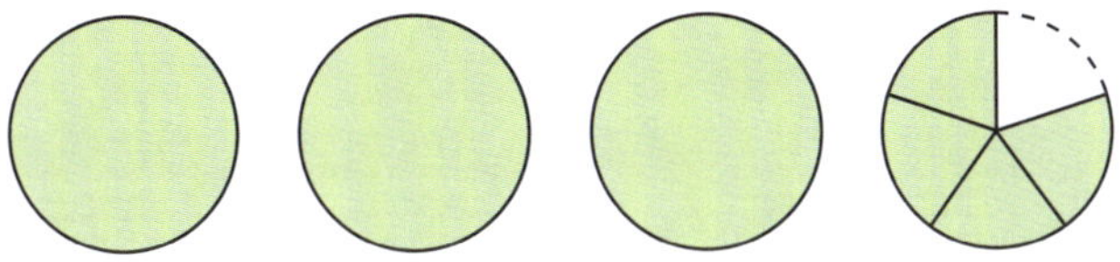

3 wholes and 4 fifths = ______

b) 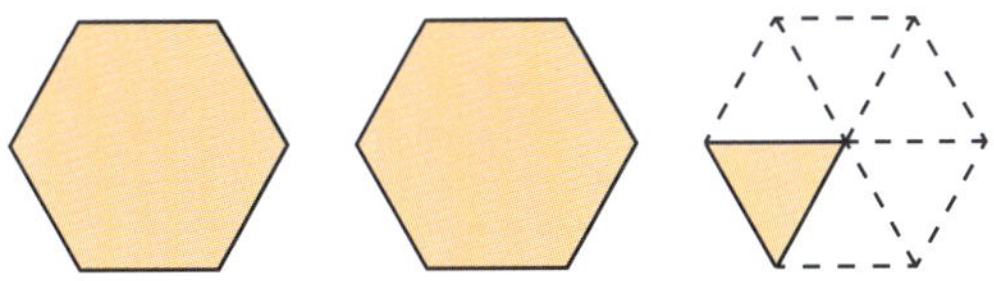

______ wholes and ______ sixth = ______

Reading mixed numbers on a number line

Let's Learn

Picture It

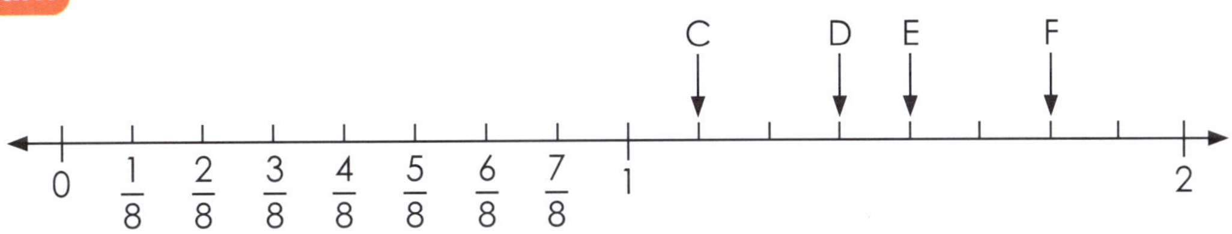

C represents $1\frac{1}{8}$.

D represents $1\frac{\square}{\square}$.

E represents $1\frac{4}{8}$.

$E = 1\frac{4}{8}$

$= 1\frac{1}{2}$

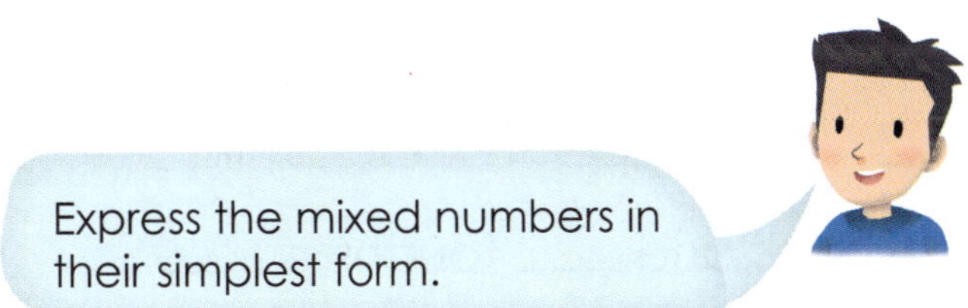

F represents $1\frac{6}{8}$.

$F = 1\frac{6}{8}$

= ____

Let's Do

1. What number does each letter represent? Express each answer in its simplest form.

a)

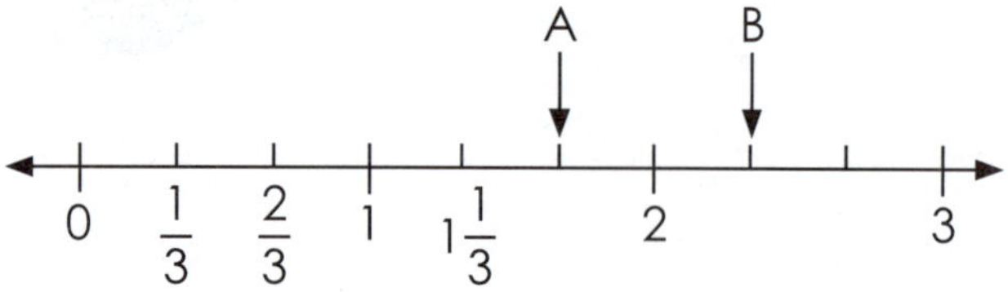

A: ______

B: ______

b)

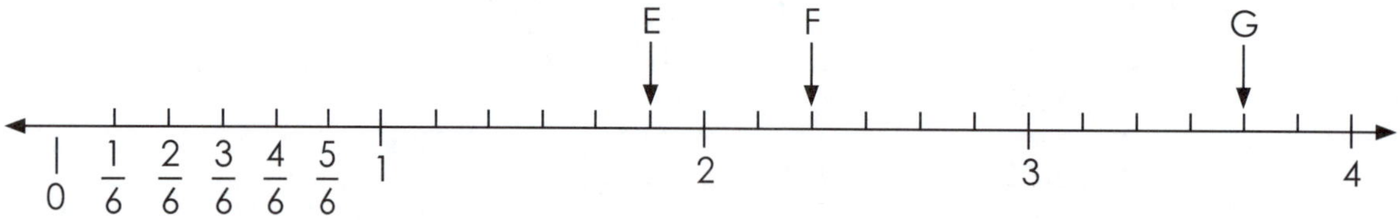

E: ______ F: ______ G: ______

2. Express each mixed number in its simplest form.

a) $1\frac{4}{8}$ = ______ b) $2\frac{2}{6}$ = ______ c) $4\frac{10}{15}$ = ______

PB Chapter 3: Exercise 1, pages 44–45

Practice 1

1. What are the missing numbers?

a)

____ wholes and ____ half = ____

b)

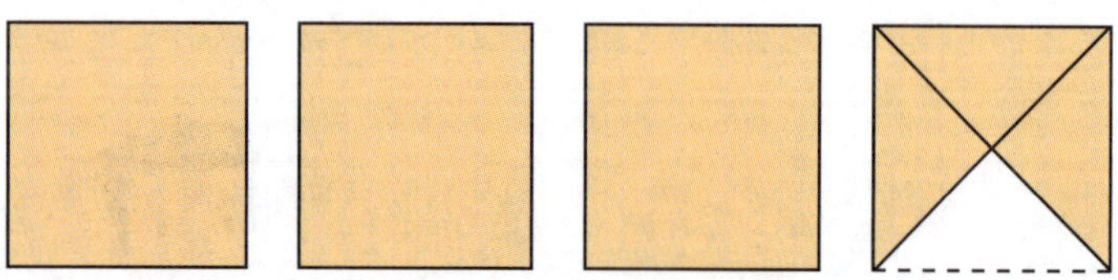

____ wholes and ____ fourths = ____

2. Express each answer as a mixed number.

a) $3 + \frac{2}{3}$ b) $\frac{4}{5} + 2$ c) $\frac{7}{10} + 4$

 ISBN 978-93-5103-031-7

3. What number does each letter represent? Express each answer in its simplest form.

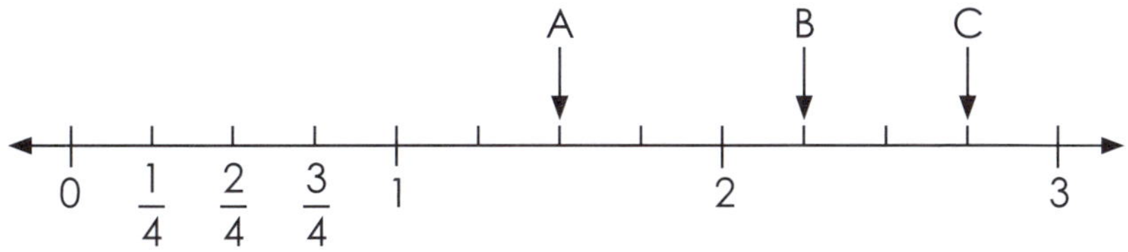

4. Express each mixed number in its simplest form.

a) $1\frac{3}{6}$ b) $2\frac{5}{10}$ c) $3\frac{10}{12}$ d) $7\frac{6}{9}$

Lesson 2 Improper Fractions

Writing improper fractions

Let's Learn

a) Each slice of cheese is cut into thirds.

Maths Lab

Picture It

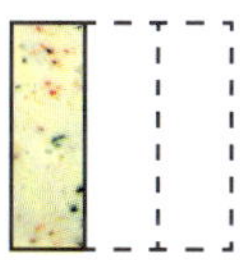

1 third = $\frac{1}{3}$

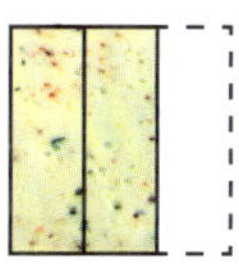

2 thirds = $\frac{2}{3}$

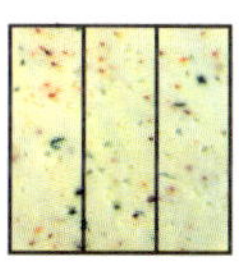

3 thirds = $\frac{3}{3}$

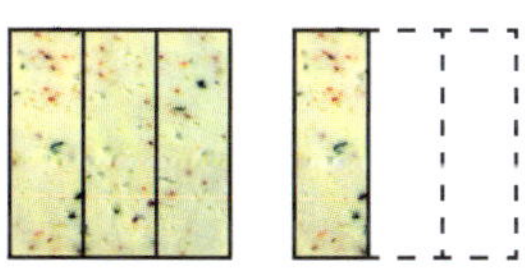

4 thirds = $\frac{4}{3}$

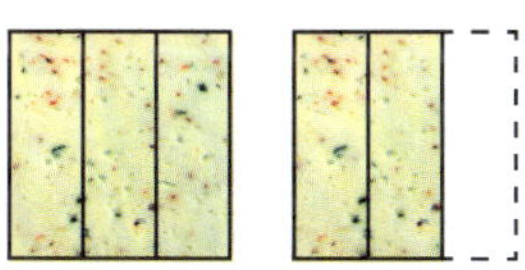

5 thirds = $\frac{5}{3}$

$\frac{3}{3}$, $\frac{4}{3}$ and $\frac{5}{3}$ are **improper fractions**.

An improper fraction is equal to or greater than 1.
Its numerator is equal to or greater than its denominator.

 ISBN 978-93-5103-031-7

b)

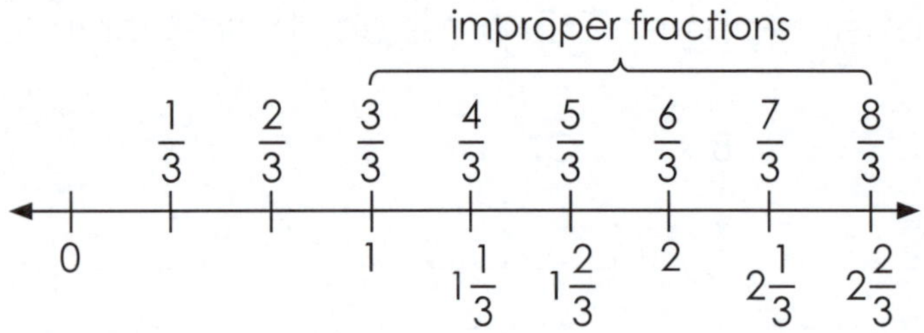

An improper fraction can be expressed as a whole number or a mixed number.

c) How many halves are there in $3\frac{1}{2}$?

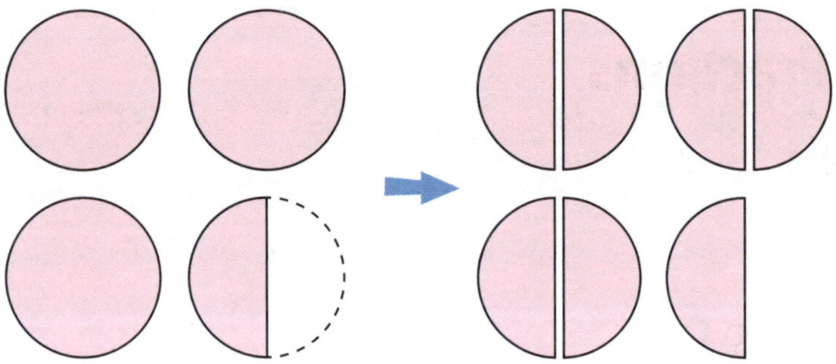

$3\frac{1}{2} = \frac{7}{2}$

There are 7 halves in $3\frac{1}{2}$.

Let's Do

1. Write an improper fraction for each of the following.

a)

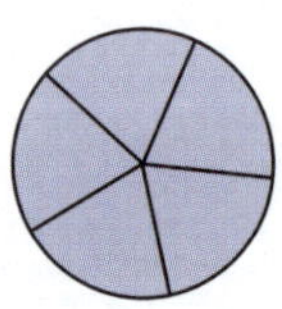

5 fifths = ______

$\frac{1}{5} + \frac{1}{5} + \frac{1}{5} + \frac{1}{5} + \frac{1}{5} =$ ______

b)

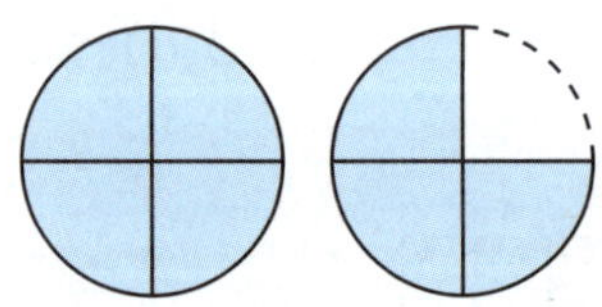

7 quarters = ______

$\frac{1}{4} + \frac{1}{4} + \frac{1}{4} + \frac{1}{4} + \frac{1}{4} + \frac{1}{4} + \frac{1}{4} =$ ______

 ISBN 978-93-5103-031-7

2. How many quarters are there in $2\frac{1}{4}$?

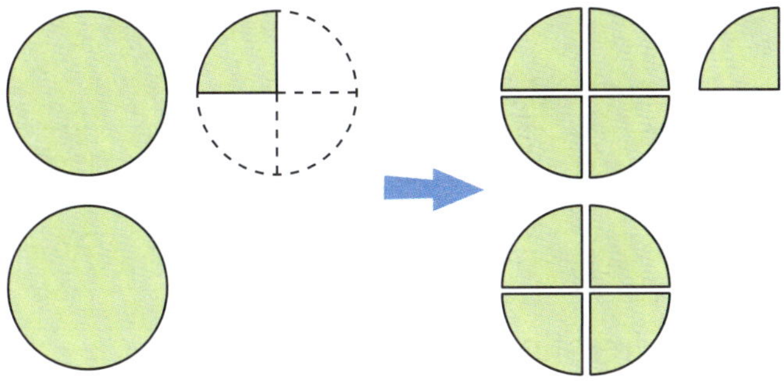

$2\frac{1}{4}$ = _______

There are _______ quarters in $2\frac{1}{4}$

P/B Chapter 3: Exercise 2, pages 46–47

Expressing improper fractions as mixed numbers

Let's Learn

Picture It

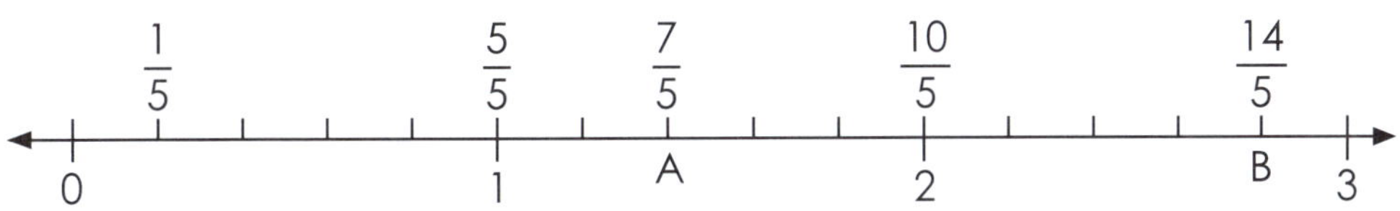

A and B can be expressed as mixed numbers.

$\frac{7}{5} = \frac{5}{5} + \frac{2}{5}$

$= 1 + \frac{2}{5}$

$= 1\frac{2}{5}$

So, A is $1\frac{2}{5}$.

$\frac{14}{5} = \frac{10}{5} + \frac{4}{5}$

$=$ ▢ $+ \frac{4}{5}$

$=$ ▢

So, B is ▢.

Let's Do

1. Express each improper fraction as a mixed number or a whole number.

a) $\frac{12}{4}$ = _______

b) $\frac{13}{6}$ = _______ $+ \frac{1}{6}$

= _______ $+ \frac{1}{6}$

= _______

P/B Chapter 3: Exercise 3, pages 48–49

 ISBN 978-93-5103-031-7

Expressing mixed numbers as improper fractions

Let's Learn

Picture It

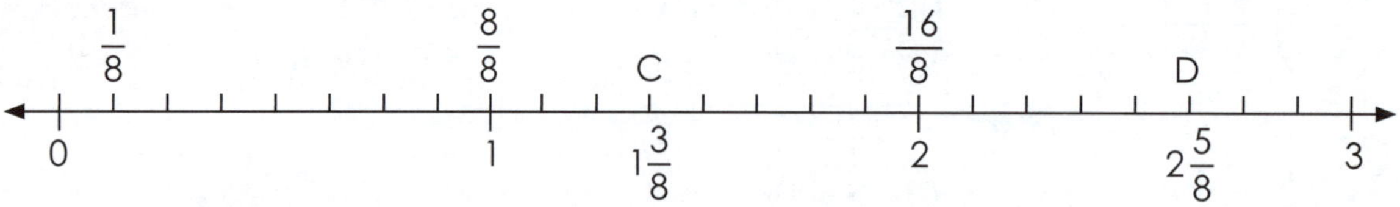

C and D can be expressed as improper fractions.

$$1\frac{3}{8} = 1 + \frac{3}{8}$$
$$= \frac{8}{8} + \frac{3}{8}$$
$$= \frac{11}{8}$$

So, C is $\frac{11}{8}$.

$1 = \frac{8}{8}$

$$2\frac{5}{8} = 2 + \frac{5}{8}$$
$$= \square + \frac{5}{8}$$
$$= \square$$

So, D is $\square$.

$2 = \frac{\square}{8}$

Let's Do

1. Express each mixed number as an improper fraction.

a) $3\frac{1}{6}$ = ______ + $\frac{1}{6}$

= ______ + $\frac{1}{6}$

= ______

$1 = \frac{6}{6}$
$2 = \frac{12}{6}$
$3 = \frac{18}{6}$

b) $2\frac{3}{5}$ = ______ + $\frac{3}{5}$

= ______ + $\frac{3}{5}$

= ______

$1 = \frac{5}{5}$
$2 = \frac{10}{5}$

P/B Chapter 3: Exercise 4, pages 50–51

 ISBN 978-93-5103-031-7

Expressing a mixed number as another mixed number with an improper fraction

Let's Learn

What is the missing numerator?

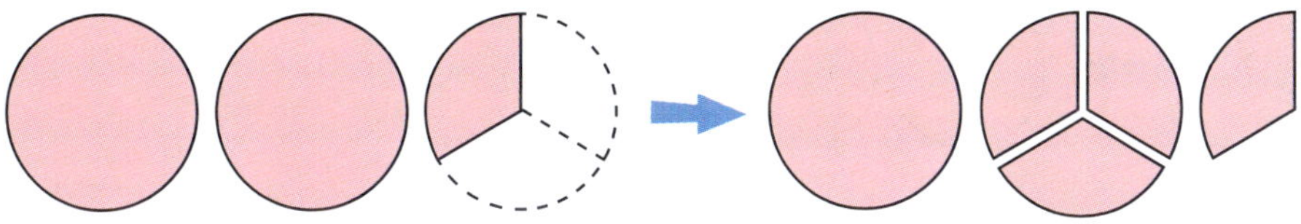

$$2\frac{1}{3} = 1\frac{\square}{3}$$

$$2\frac{1}{3} = 1 + 1 + \frac{1}{3}$$
$$= 1 + \frac{3}{3} + \frac{1}{3}$$
$$= 1\frac{\square}{3}$$

Let's Do

1. Find the missing numerators or fractions.

a) $2\frac{2}{5} = 1\frac{\square}{5}$

$2\frac{2}{5} = 1 + 1 + \frac{2}{5}$

$= 1 + \_\_\_\_\_\_ + \frac{2}{5}$

$= 1\frac{\square}{5}$

b) $3\frac{1}{4} = 2\frac{\square}{4}$

$3\frac{1}{4} = 2 + 1 + \frac{1}{4}$

$= 2 + \_\_\_\_\_\_ + \frac{1}{4}$

$= 2\frac{\square}{4}$

 ISBN 978-93-5103-031-7

Simplifying mixed numbers

Let's Learn

Express $2\frac{5}{3}$ in its simplest form.

Maths Lab

Picture It

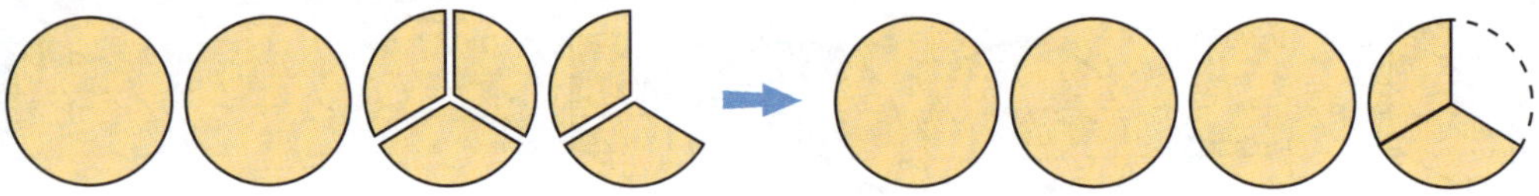

$2\frac{5}{3}$ = ▢

$2\frac{5}{3} = 2 + \frac{5}{3}$

$= 2 + \frac{3}{3} + \frac{2}{3}$

$= 2 + 1 + \frac{2}{3}$

= ▢

Let's Do

1. Express each mixed number in its simplest form.

a) $2\frac{8}{5} = 2 + \frac{8}{5}$

$= 2 +$ ______ $+ \frac{3}{5}$

$= 2 +$ ______ $+ \frac{3}{5}$

= ______

b) $3\frac{7}{4} = 3 + \frac{7}{4}$

$= 3 +$ ______ $+$ ______

$= 3 +$ ______ $+$ ______

= ______

P/B Chapter 3: Exercise 5, page 52

Practice 2

1. Express each of the following as an improper fraction.

a)

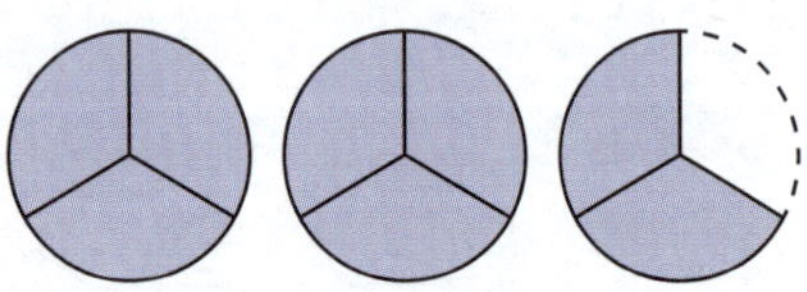

8 thirds

b)

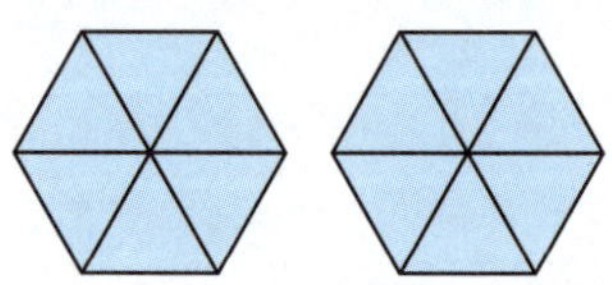

12 sixths

 ISBN 978-93-5103-031-7

2. How many halves are there in $4\frac{1}{2}$?

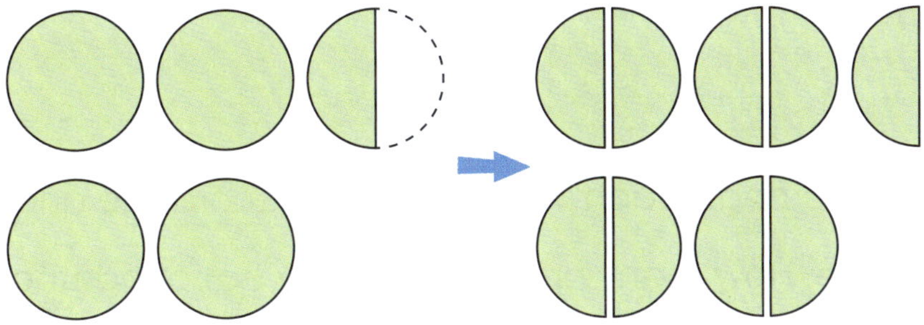

3. How many fifths are there in $3\frac{2}{5}$?

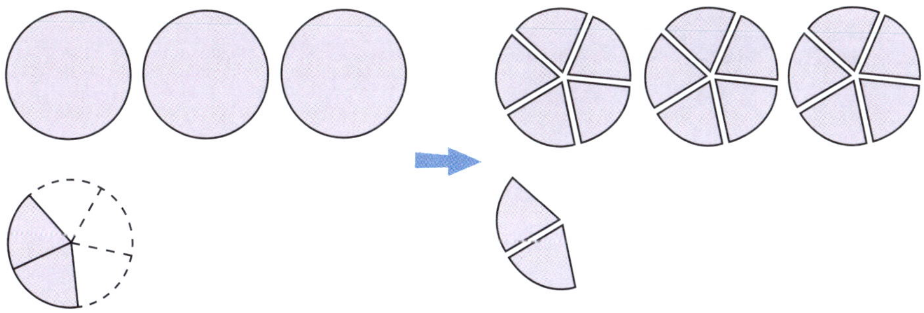

4. Express each improper fraction as a mixed number or a whole number.

a) $\frac{17}{4}$ b) $\frac{10}{3}$ c) $\frac{8}{2}$

d) $\frac{12}{5}$ e) $\frac{10}{4}$ f) $\frac{12}{8}$

5. Express each mixed number as an improper fraction.

a) $1\frac{4}{5}$ b) $2\frac{2}{3}$ c) $2\frac{1}{4}$ d) $3\frac{5}{6}$

6. Find the missing numerators.

a) $3\frac{2}{7} = 2\frac{\square}{7}$ b) $3\frac{1}{2} = 2\frac{\square}{2}$

c) $4\frac{1}{6} = 3\frac{\square}{6}$ d) $4\frac{3}{4} = 3\frac{\square}{4}$

7. Express each mixed number in its simplest form.

a) $1\frac{5}{4}$ b) $2\frac{6}{3}$ c) $3\frac{11}{8}$ d) $4\frac{17}{9}$

 ISBN 978-93-5103-031-7

Lesson 3 Addition of Fractions

Adding two fractions

Let's Learn

a) Mala and Ken had an orange each. Mala ate $\frac{5}{6}$ of her orange and Ken ate $\frac{5}{6}$ of his orange. How many oranges did they eat altogether?

Maths Lab

Picture It

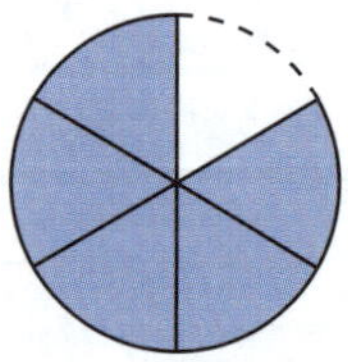

$\frac{5}{6}$

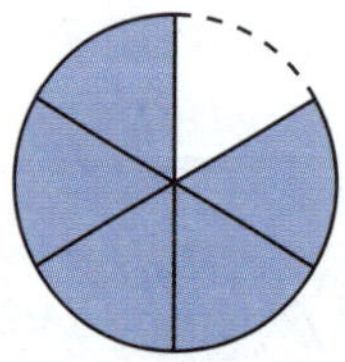

$\frac{5}{6}$

$$\frac{5}{6} + \frac{5}{6} = \frac{10}{6}$$
$$= 1\frac{4}{6}$$
$$= 1\frac{2}{3}$$

$$\frac{10}{6} = \frac{6}{6} + \frac{4}{6}$$
$$= 1 + \frac{4}{6}$$
$$= 1\frac{4}{6}$$

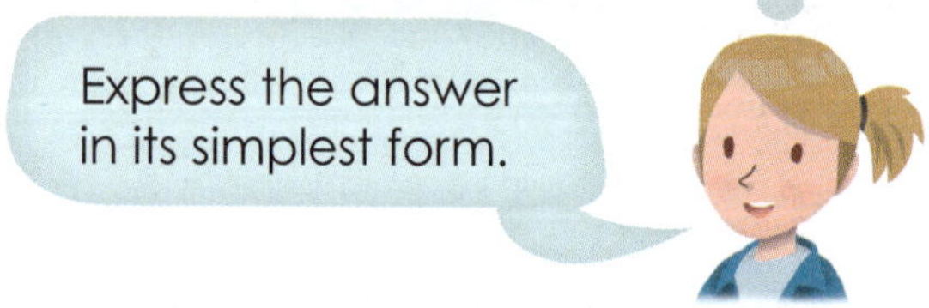

They ate $1\frac{2}{3}$ oranges altogether.

 ISBN 978-93-5103-031-7

b) Add $\frac{7}{10}$ and $\frac{4}{5}$.

$\frac{7}{10}$

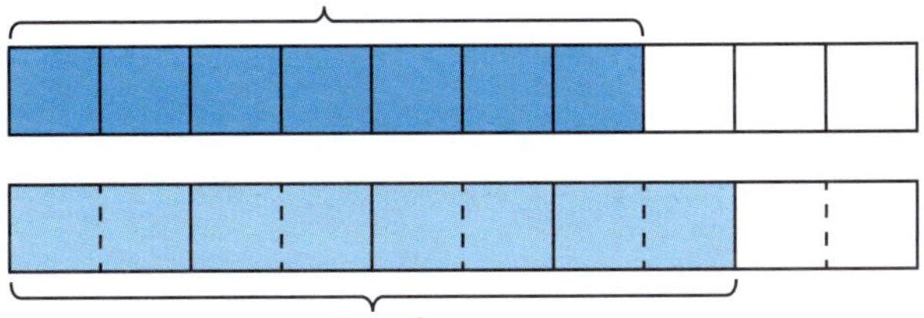

$\frac{4}{5} = \frac{8}{10}$

$$\frac{7}{10} + \frac{4}{5} = \frac{7}{10} + \frac{8}{10}$$
$$= \frac{15}{10}$$
$$= 1\frac{5}{10}$$
$$= \square$$

$$\frac{15}{10} = \frac{10}{10} + \frac{5}{10}$$
$$= 1 + \frac{5}{10}$$
$$= 1\frac{5}{10}$$

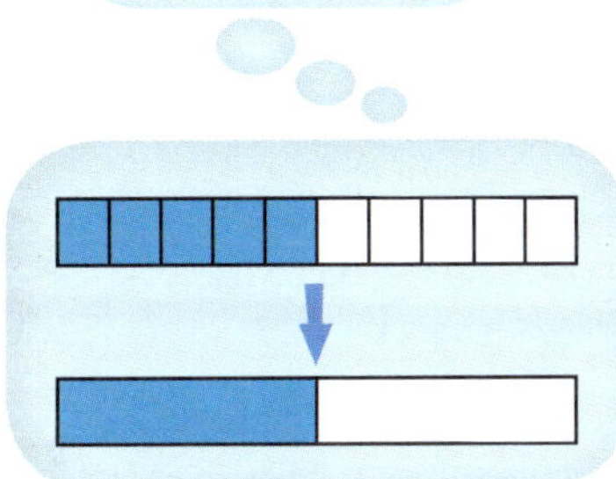

Let's Do

1. Add. Express each answer in its simplest form.

a) $\frac{8}{9} + \frac{7}{9} = \frac{\square}{9}$

$= \_\_\_\_ \frac{\square}{9}$

$= \_\_\_\_$

b) $\frac{7}{10} + \frac{1}{2} = \frac{7}{10} + \frac{\square}{10}$

$= \frac{\square}{10}$

$= \_\_\_\_ \frac{\square}{10}$

$= \_\_\_\_$

P/B Chapter 3: Exercise 6, page 53

 ISBN 978-93-5103-031-7

Adding three fractions

Let's Learn

Add $\frac{7}{10}$, $\frac{3}{5}$ and $\frac{4}{5}$.

Maths Lab

Picture It

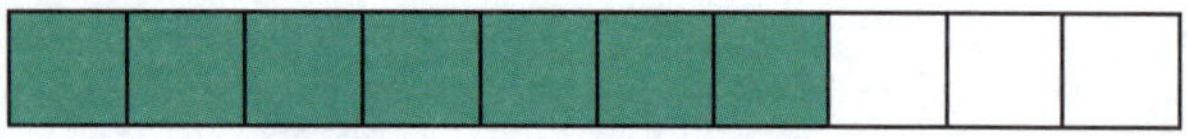

$\frac{7}{10}$

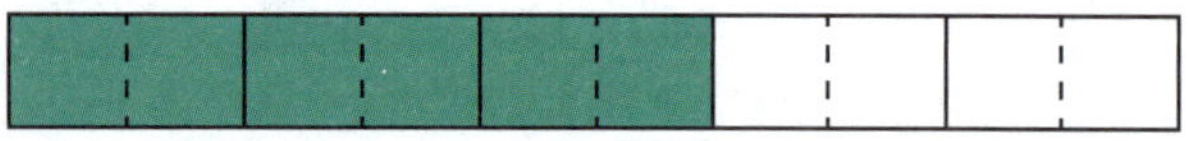

$\frac{3}{5}$

$$\frac{3}{5} \overset{\times 2}{=} \frac{6}{10}$$

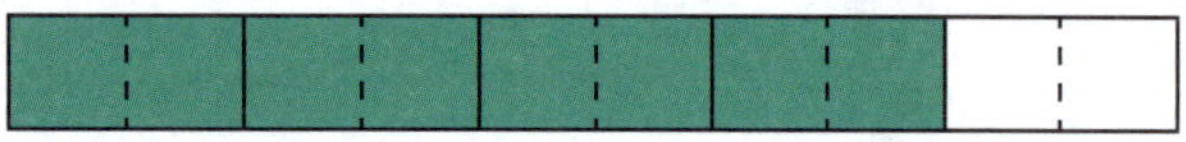

$\frac{4}{5}$

$$\frac{4}{5} \overset{\times 2}{=} \frac{8}{10}$$

$$\frac{7}{10} + \frac{3}{5} + \frac{4}{5} = \frac{7}{10} + \frac{6}{10} + \frac{8}{10}$$
$$= \frac{21}{10}$$
$$= 2\frac{1}{10}$$

$$\frac{21}{10} = \frac{20}{10} + \frac{1}{10}$$
$$= 2 + \frac{1}{10}$$
$$= 2\frac{1}{10}$$

Let's Do

1. Add. Express each answer in its simplest form.

a) $\frac{4}{9} + \frac{1}{9} + \frac{7}{9} = \frac{\square}{9}$

$= \_\_\_\_\_ \frac{\square}{9}$

$= \_\_\_\_\_$

b) $\frac{11}{12} + \frac{7}{12} + \frac{1}{4} = \frac{11}{12} + \frac{7}{12} + \frac{\square}{12}$

$= \frac{\square}{12}$

$= \_\_\_\_\_ \frac{\square}{12}$

$= \_\_\_\_\_$

$$\frac{1}{4} \overset{\times 3}{=} \frac{\square}{12}$$

PB Chapter 3: Exercise 7, page 54

 ISBN 978-93-5103-031-7

Solving word problems

Let's Learn

Abdul had two slices of cheese. He used $\frac{1}{2}$ of a slice to make a sandwich. He used $\frac{3}{4}$ of another slice in a salad. How many slices of cheese did Abdul use altogether?

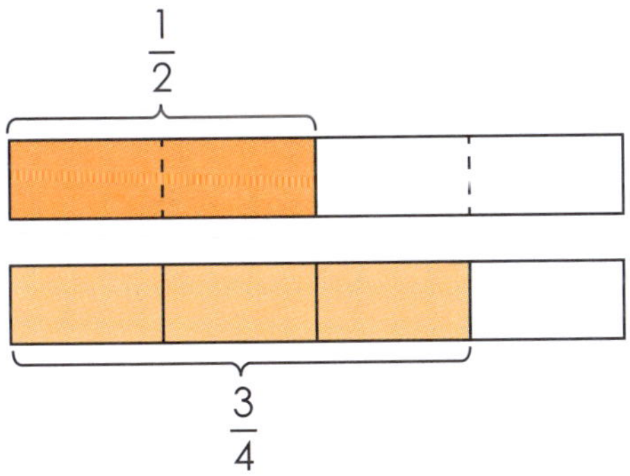

$$\frac{1}{2} + \frac{3}{4} = \frac{2}{4} + \frac{3}{4}$$
$$= \frac{5}{4}$$
$$= 1\frac{1}{4}$$

Abdul used $1\frac{1}{4}$ slices of cheese altogether.

Let's Do

1. Karmen and Rehan had an apple each. Karmen ate $\frac{5}{8}$ of an apple and Rehan ate $\frac{1}{2}$ of another apple. How many apples did they eat altogether?

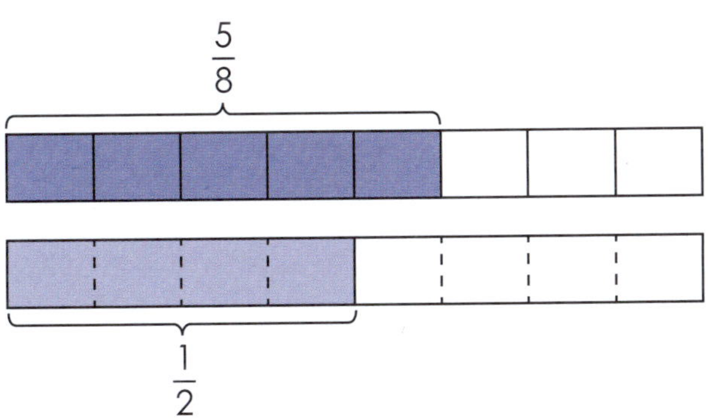

$$\frac{5}{8} + \frac{1}{2} = \frac{5}{8} + \_\_\_\_$$
$$= \frac{\square}{8}$$
$$= \_\_\_\_$$

They ate ______ apples altogether.

Chapter 3: Exercise 8, page 55

 ISBN 978-93-5103-031-7

Practice 3

1. Add. Express each answer in its simplest form.

   a) $\frac{3}{5} + \frac{4}{5}$ b) $\frac{6}{7} + \frac{5}{7}$ c) $\frac{7}{8} + \frac{3}{4}$ d) $\frac{7}{9} + \frac{2}{3}$

2. Add. Express each answer in its simplest form.

   a) $\frac{1}{8} + \frac{1}{4} + \frac{3}{4}$ b) $\frac{2}{3} + \frac{1}{6} + \frac{5}{6}$ c) $\frac{2}{3} + \frac{5}{9} + \frac{7}{9}$ d) $\frac{1}{5} + \frac{3}{5} + \frac{7}{10}$

Solve the word problems. Show your work clearly.

3. Mr. Jackson measures the length of two wooden planks. Plank A is $\frac{5}{6}$ metre long and Plank B is $\frac{2}{3}$ metre long. What is the total length of the two planks?

4. Sita mixed $\frac{7}{12}$ kilogram of flour, $\frac{3}{4}$ kilogram of sugar and $\frac{1}{4}$ kilogram of nuts. What was the weight of the mixture?

Lesson 4 Subtraction of Fractions

Subtracting a fraction from a whole number

Let's Learn

Ruth had a plank 3 metres long. She used $\frac{3}{4}$ metre of the plank to mend a bookshelf. How many metres of the plank were left?

Maths Lab

Picture It

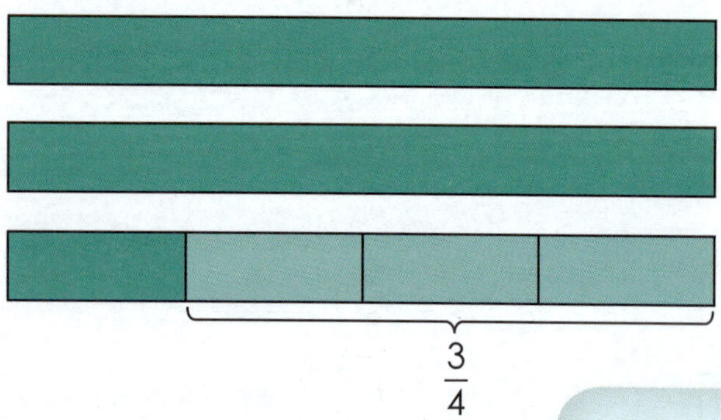

$$3 - \frac{3}{4} = 2\frac{4}{4} - \frac{3}{4}$$
$$= 2\frac{1}{4}$$

$2\frac{1}{4}$ metres of the plank were left.

 ISBN 978-93-5103-031-7

Let's Do

1. Subtract. Express each answer in its simplest form.

a) $2 - \frac{4}{5} = 1\frac{\square}{5} - \frac{4}{5}$

$= \_\_\_\_\_\_$

b) $5 - \frac{2}{3} = 4\frac{\square}{3} - \frac{2}{3}$

$= \_\_\_\_\_\_$

P/B Chapter 3: Exercise 9, page 56

Subtracting two fractions from a whole number

Let's Learn

Subtract $\frac{1}{12}$ and $\frac{7}{12}$ from 2.

Maths Lab

Picture It

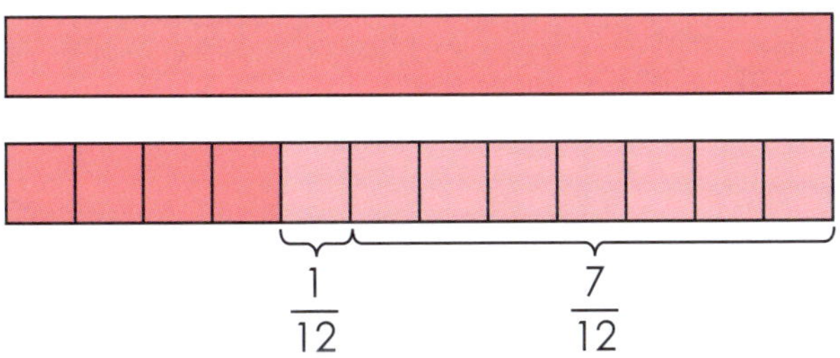

$$2 - \frac{1}{12} - \frac{7}{12} = 1\frac{12}{12} - \frac{1}{12} - \frac{7}{12}$$
$$= 1\frac{11}{12} - \frac{7}{12}$$
$$= 1\frac{\square}{12}$$
$$= \square$$

$2 = 1 + 1$
$= 1 + \frac{12}{12}$
$= 1\frac{12}{12}$

Express the answer in its simplest form.

Let's Do

1. Subtract. Express each answer in its simplest form.

a) $3 - \frac{1}{9} - \frac{5}{9} = 2\frac{9}{9} - \frac{1}{9} - \frac{5}{9}$

$= 2\frac{\square}{9} - \frac{5}{9}$

$= 2\frac{\square}{9}$

$= \_\_\_\_\_\_$

$3 = 2 + 1$
$= 2 + \frac{9}{9}$
$= 2\frac{9}{9}$

 ISBN 978-93-5103-031-7

b) $4 - \frac{1}{4} - \frac{5}{12} = 3\frac{12}{12} - \frac{\square}{12} - \frac{5}{12}$

$= 3\frac{\square}{12} - \frac{5}{12}$

$= 3\frac{\square}{12}$

= ______

$4 = 3 + 1$

$= 3 + \frac{\square}{12}$

$= 3\frac{\square}{12}$

Chapter 3: Exercise 10, page 57

Solving word problems

Let's Learn

A shop has 2 pumpkin pies. A customer buys $\frac{3}{8}$ of a pumpkin pie. How many pumpkin pies are left?

Picture It

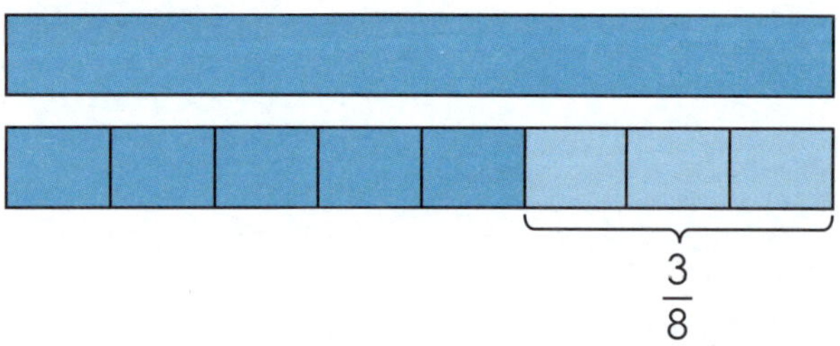

$2 - \frac{3}{8} = 1\frac{8}{8} - \frac{3}{8}$

$= 1\frac{5}{8}$

$1\frac{5}{8}$ pumpkin pies are left.

$2 = 1 + 1$

$= 1 + \frac{8}{8}$

$= 1\frac{8}{8}$

Let's Do

1. Trisha has 3 kilograms of flour. She uses $\frac{5}{6}$ kilogram to make some bread. How many kilograms of flour does Trisha have left?

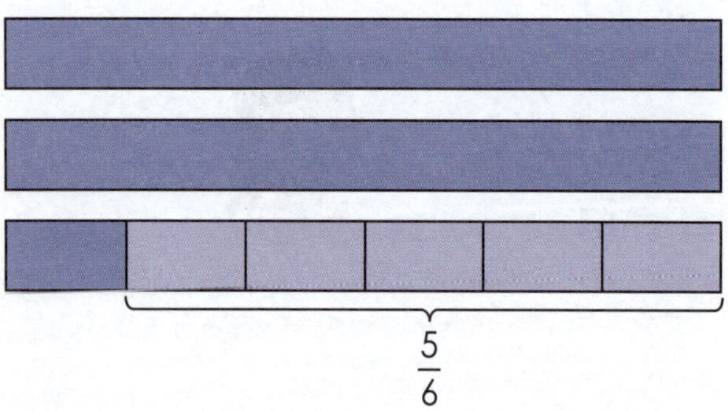

$3 - \frac{5}{6} = 2\frac{\square}{6} - \frac{5}{6}$

= ______

Trisha has ______ kilograms of flour left.

Chapter 3: Exercise 11, page 58

 ISBN 978-93-5103-031-7

Practice 4

1. Subtract. Express each answer in its simplest form.

a) $4 - \frac{3}{4}$　　b) $2 - \frac{1}{6}$　　c) $4 - \frac{1}{2}$

d) $2 - \frac{3}{10}$　　e) $3 - \frac{3}{5}$　　f) $3 - \frac{5}{7}$

2. Subtract. Express each answer in its simplest form.

a) $2 - \frac{1}{8} - \frac{3}{8}$　　b) $3 - \frac{1}{5} - \frac{2}{5}$

c) $1 - \frac{1}{6} - \frac{5}{12}$　　d) $6 - \frac{1}{10} - \frac{2}{5}$

Solve the word problems. Show your work clearly.

3. Mr. Rao made 2 mushroom pizzas. His children ate $\frac{2}{3}$ of a pizza. How many pizzas were left?

4. A grocery store has 10 kilograms of peanuts. One customer buys $\frac{1}{4}$ kilogram of peanuts and another customer buys $\frac{3}{8}$ kilogram. How many kilograms of peanuts are left?

5. There were 2 litres of orange juice in a jug. Leela poured $\frac{1}{5}$ litre of juice into a glass and $\frac{3}{10}$ litre of juice into a mug. How much orange juice was left in the jug?

Lesson 5 Product of a Fraction and a Whole Number

Understanding fraction of a group

Let's Learn

Maths Lab

Picture It

a) 

2 out of the 5 toys are cars.

$\frac{2}{5}$ of the toys are cars.

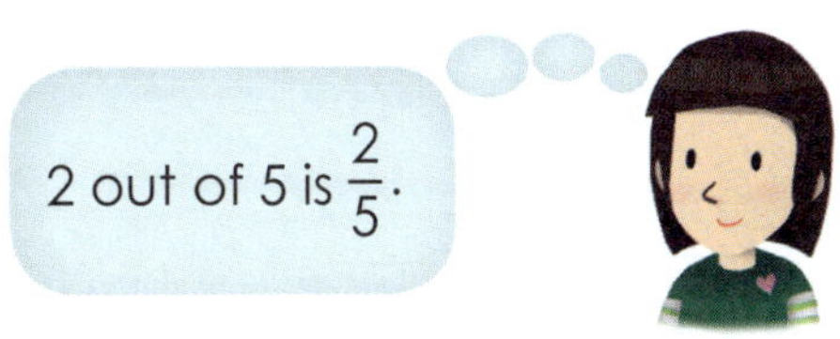

 ISBN 978-93-5103-031-7

b) There are 5 equal groups of toys.

2 out of the 5 groups are cars.

$\frac{2}{5}$ of the toys are cars.

Let's Do

1. What fraction of each group is shaded?

a) 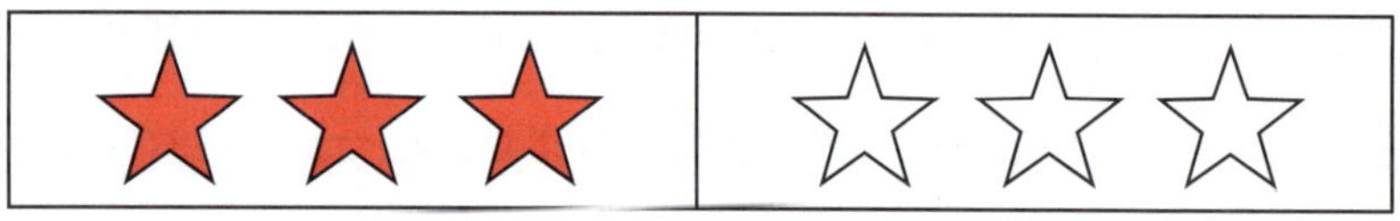 ______

b) 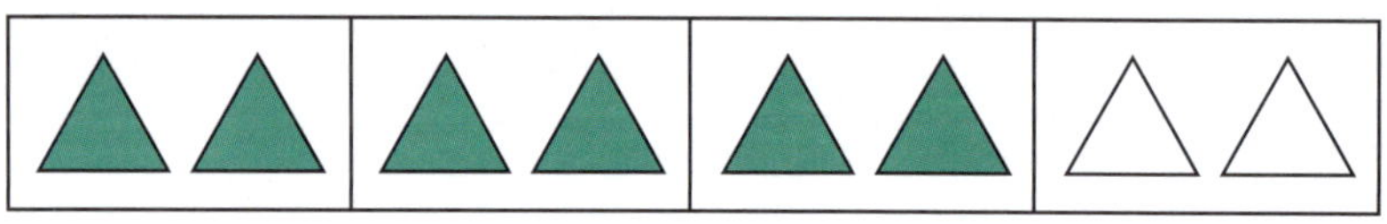 ______

Chapter 3: Exercise 12, pages 59–60

Finding a fractional part of a quantity

Let's Learn

a) Find the value of $\frac{1}{3}$ of 12.

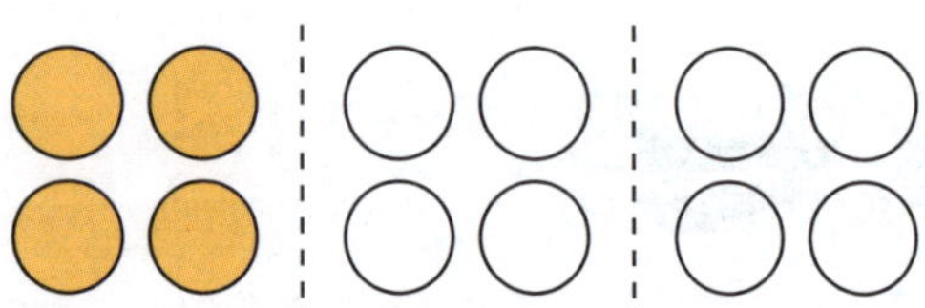

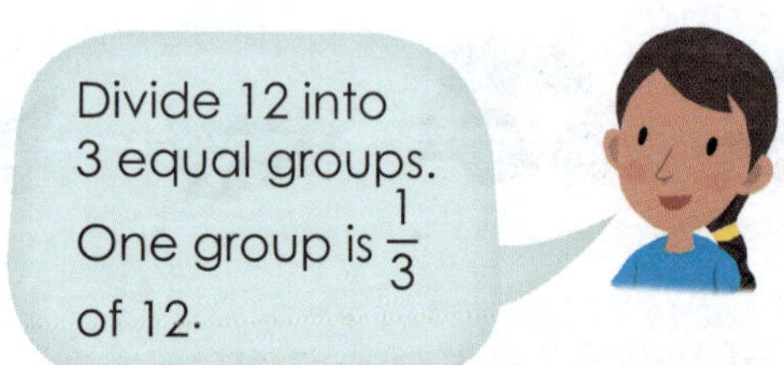

$\frac{1}{3}$ of 12 = ▢

 ISBN 978-93-5103-031-7

b) Find the value of $\frac{3}{4}$ of 20.

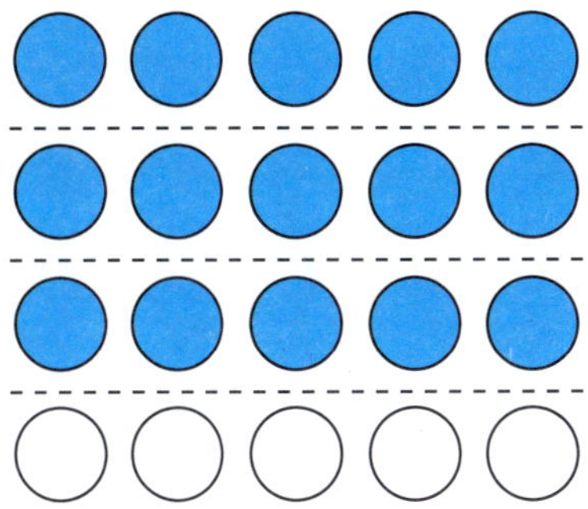

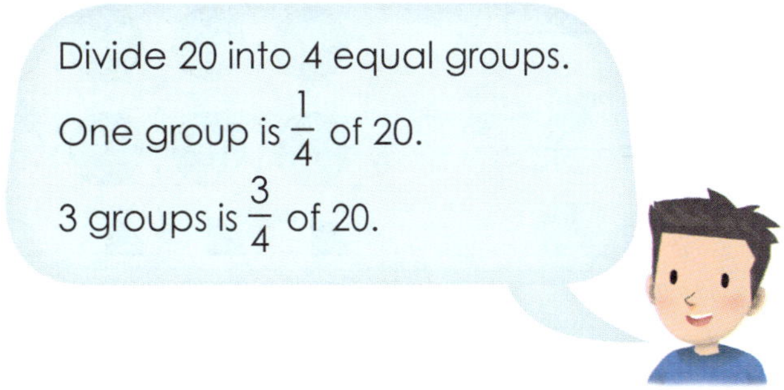

$\frac{1}{4}$ of 20 = $\square$ $\qquad$ $\frac{3}{4}$ of 20 = $\square$

Let's Do

1. What is the value of $\frac{4}{5}$ of 15?

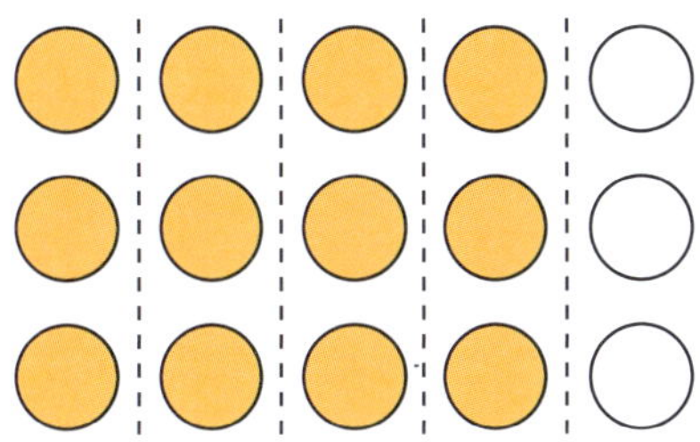

$\frac{1}{5}$ of 15 = ______

$\frac{4}{5}$ of 15 = ______

P/B Chapter 3: Exercise 13, page 61

Multiplying a fraction and a whole number

Let's Learn

a) Find the value of $\frac{1}{5}$ of 15.

Picture It

$$\frac{1}{5} \text{ of } 15 = \frac{1}{5} \times 15 = \frac{1 \times 15}{5} = \frac{\square}{5} = \square$$

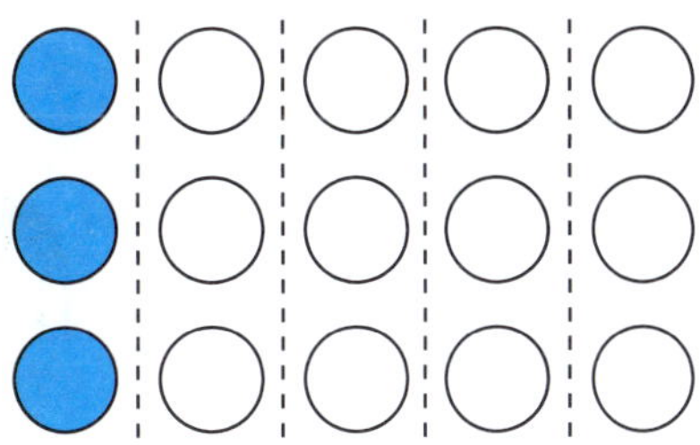

 ISBN 978-93-5103-031-7

b) Find the value of $\frac{3}{4} \times 9$.

$$\frac{3}{4} \times 9 = \frac{3 \times 9}{4} = \frac{\square}{4} = \square$$

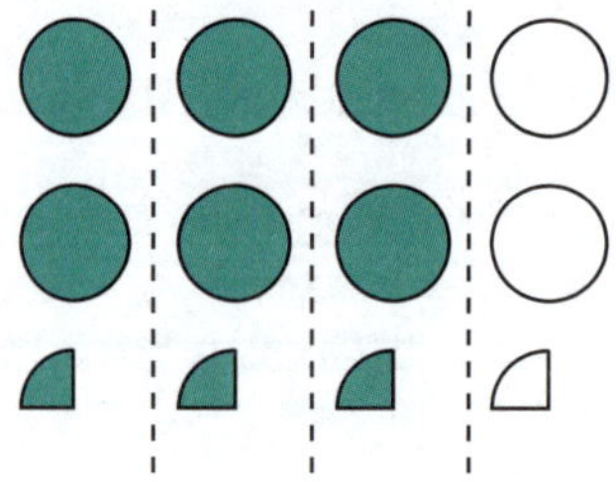

Let's Do

1. Find the value of $\frac{5}{6}$ of 18.

$$\frac{5}{6} \text{ of } 18 = \frac{5}{6} \times 18 = \frac{\square \times 18}{6} = \frac{\square}{6} = \_\_\_\_\_$$

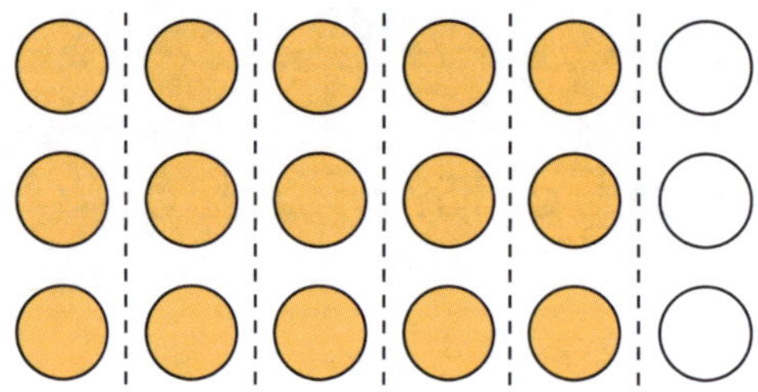

2. Find the value of $\frac{2}{3} \times 10$.

$$\frac{2}{3} \times 10 = \frac{\square \times 10}{3} = \frac{\square}{3} = \_\_\_\_\_$$

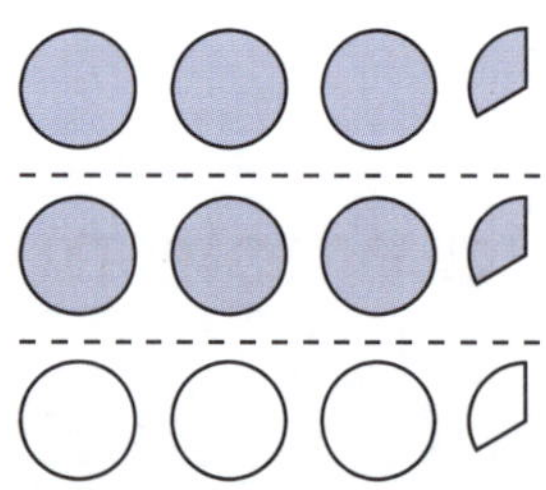

3. Find the value of $5 \times \frac{7}{3}$.

$$5 \times \frac{7}{3} = \frac{5 \times \square}{\square} = \_\_\_\_\_ = \_\_\_\_\_$$

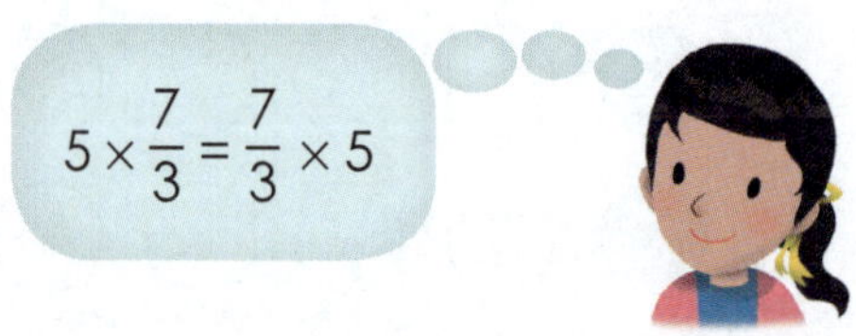

P/B Chapter 3: Exercise 14, pages 62–64

 ISBN 978-93-5103-031-7

Solving word problems

Let's Learn

a) Mary had 24 eggs. She cooked $\frac{2}{3}$ of them. How many eggs did she cook?

Method 1

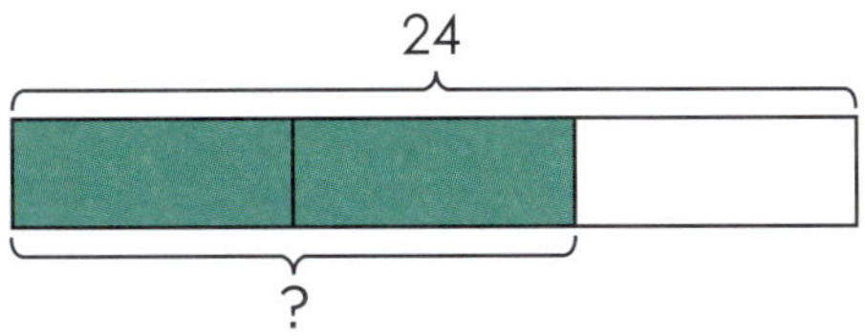

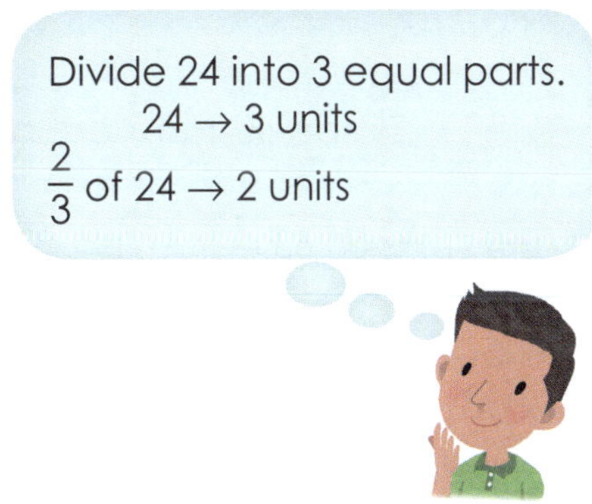

3 units → 24
1 unit → 24 ÷ 3 = 8
2 units → 2 × 8 = 16

Method 2

$$\frac{2}{3} \times 24 = \frac{2 \times \cancel{24}^{8}}{\cancel{3}_{1}}$$
$$= \frac{2 \times 8}{1}$$
$$= 16$$

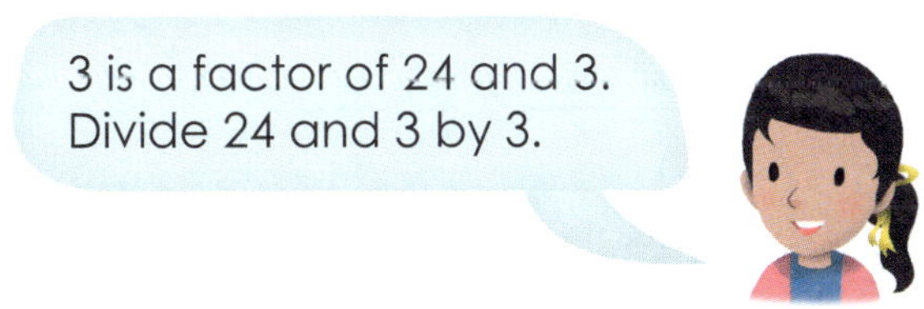

She cooked 16 eggs.

b) Ram practises playing the violin for $\frac{3}{4}$ hour a day. How many hours does he practise playing the violin in 5 days?

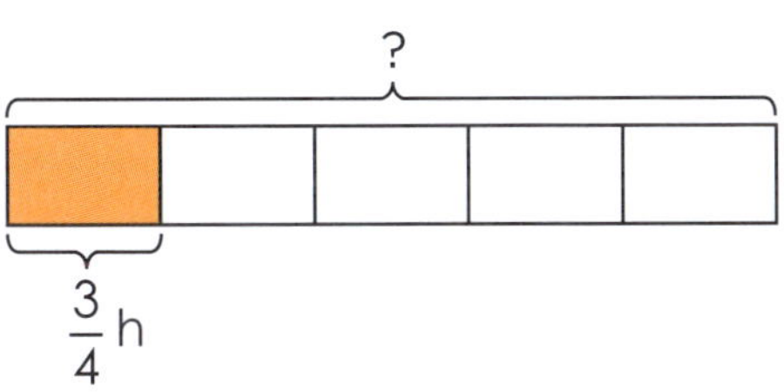

1 unit → $\frac{3}{4}$ h

5 units → $5 \times \frac{3}{4} = \frac{5 \times 3}{4}$

$= \frac{\square}{4}$

$= \square$ h

He practises playing the violin for $\square$ hours.

 ISBN 978-93-5103-031-7

Let's Do

1. There are 63 children in a choir. $\frac{4}{7}$ of the children are boys. How many boys are there in the choir?

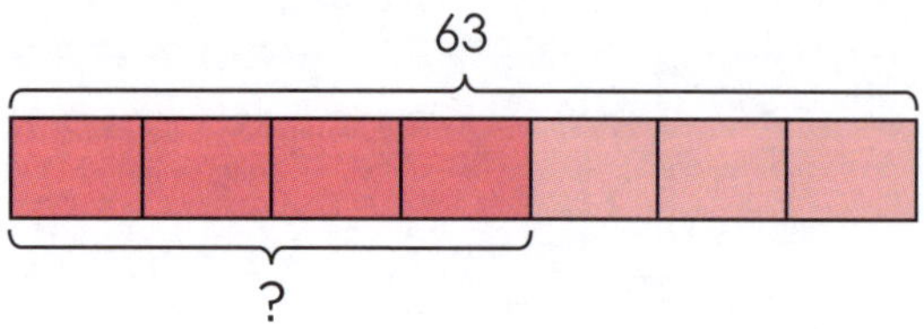

Divide 63 into 7 equal parts.
$63 \rightarrow 7$ units
$\frac{4}{7}$ of $63 \rightarrow 4$ units

7 units $\rightarrow$ 63

1 unit $\rightarrow$ ______

4 units $\rightarrow$ ______ $\times$ ______ = ______

There are ______ boys in the choir.

2. Ram has 6 packets of raisins. Each packet weighs $\frac{3}{8}$ kilogram. What is the total weight of the 6 packets?

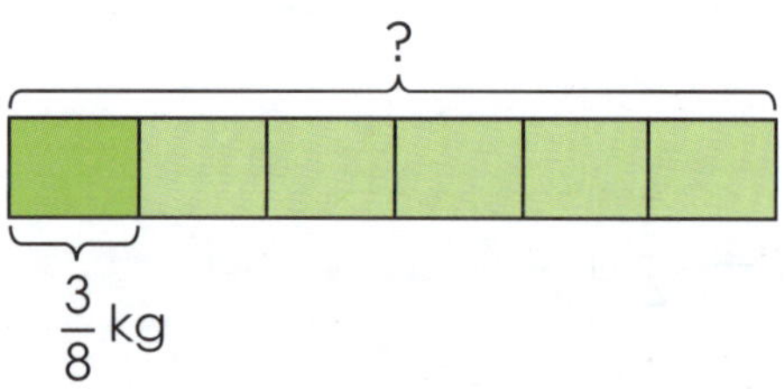

Express the answer in its simplest form.

1 unit $\rightarrow$ ______ kg

______ units $\rightarrow$ ______ $\times$ ______

= ______

= ______ kg

The total weight of the 6 packets is ______ kilograms.

P/B Chapter 3: Exercise 15, page 65

 ISBN 978-93-5103-031-7

Let's Learn

Maria has 8 coins. 6 of them are five-rupee coins. What fraction of the coins are five-rupee coins?

Picture It

6 out of 8 is $\frac{6}{8}$.

$$\frac{6}{8} \overset{\div 2}{=} \frac{3}{4} \quad (\div 2)$$

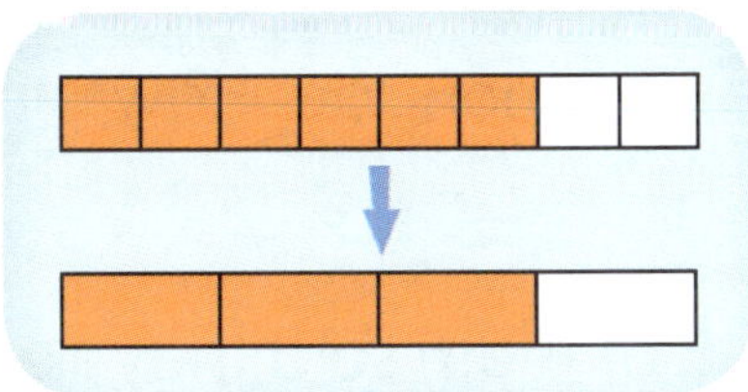

☐ of the coins are five-rupee coins.

Let's Do

1. Harry had 42 stickers. He lost 6 of them. What fraction of the stickers did he lose?

He lost ______ of the stickers.

P/B Chapter 3: Exercise 16, page 66

Practice 5

1. What fraction of each group is shaded?

a)

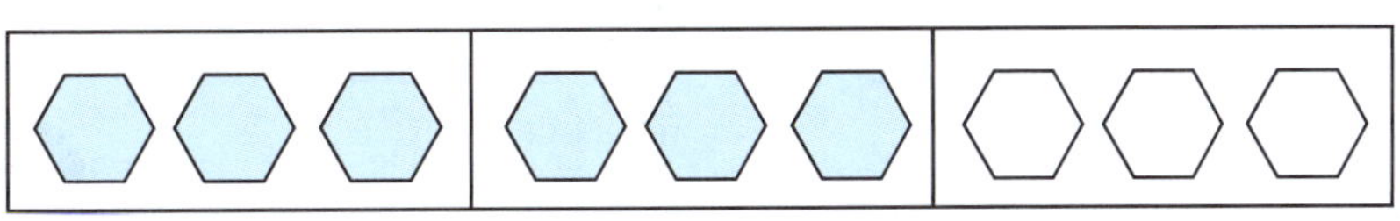

b)

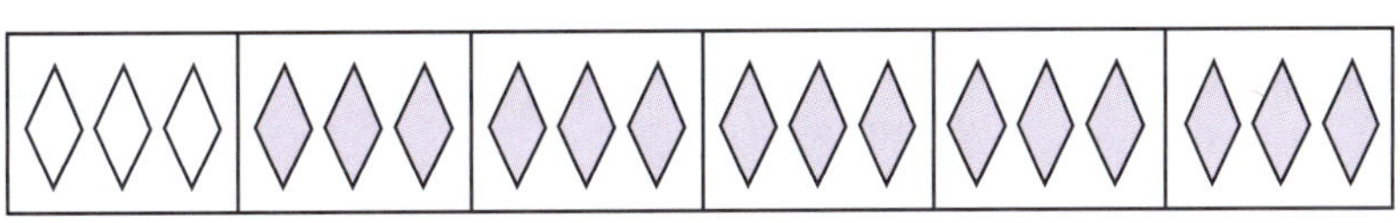

 ISBN 978-93-5103-031-7

2. Find the value of:

a) $\frac{1}{5}$ of 20 b) $\frac{3}{4}$ of 32 c) $4 \times \frac{1}{6}$

d) $15 \times \frac{3}{8}$ e) $\frac{7}{3} \times 21$ f) $40 \times \frac{9}{8}$

Solve the word problems. Show your work clearly.

3. Divya had a roll of tape 5 metres long. She used $\frac{3}{4}$ of its length for her art project. How much tape did she use?

4. At a lemonade stand, there were 6 pitchers of lemonade. Each pitcher contained $\frac{2}{3}$ litre of lemonade. How much lemonade was there altogether?

5. In a class of 40 children, 8 of them said they liked the colour purple. What fraction of the children liked the colour purple?

6. Gavin bought 81 game cards. He gave $\frac{2}{9}$ of them to Mohan. How many cards did Gavin give Mohan?

Lesson 6 Conversion of Measurements

Units of measurements

Let's Learn

Length

1 centimetre = 10 millimetres
1 metre = 100 centimetres
1 kilometre = 1000 metres

Mass

1 kilogram = 1000 grams

Volume of liquid

1 litre = 1000 millilitres

Time

1 year = 12 months
1 week = 7 days
1 day = 24 hours
1 hour = 60 minutes
1 minute = 60 seconds

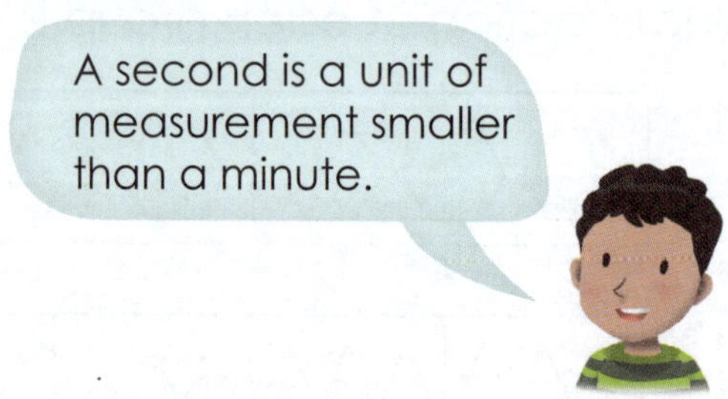

 ISBN 978-93-5103-031-7

Converting a measurement from a larger unit involving fractions to a smaller unit

Let's Learn

Express $\frac{1}{2}$ minute in seconds.

$$\frac{1}{2}\text{ min} = \frac{1}{2} \times 60$$
$$= \frac{1 \times \cancel{60}^{30}}{\cancel{2}_{1}}$$
$$= 30\text{ s}$$

$\frac{1}{2}$ min $= \frac{1}{2}$ of a minute
$= \frac{1}{2} \times 60$ seconds

2 is a factor of 60 and 2.
Divide 60 and 2 by 2.

Let's Do

1. Find the equivalent measures.

a) $\frac{3}{10}$ L = ______ ml

$\frac{3}{10}$ L $= \frac{3}{10} \times$ ______

$= \frac{3 \times \square}{10}$

= ______ ml

b) $\frac{3}{4}$ year = ______ months

$\frac{3}{4}$ year $= \frac{3}{4} \times$ ______

$= \frac{3 \times \square}{4}$

= ______ months

P/B Chapter 3: Exercise 17, page 67

Converting a measurement from a larger unit to compound units

Let's Learn

Express $2\frac{3}{4}$ hours in hours and minutes.

$$\frac{3}{4}\text{ h} = \frac{3}{4} \times 60$$
$$= \frac{3 \times \cancel{60}^{15}}{\cancel{4}_{1}}$$
$$= 45\text{ min}$$

4 is a factor of 60 and 4.
Divide 60 and 4 by 4.

$$2\frac{3}{4}\text{ h} = 2\text{ h } 45\text{ min}$$

 ISBN 978-93-5103-031-7

Let's Do

1. Find the equivalent measures.

a) $4\frac{2}{3}$ min = ____ min ____ s

$\frac{2}{3}$ min $= \frac{2}{3} \times$ ____

$= \frac{2 \times \square}{3}$

= ____ s

b) $14\frac{9}{10}$ L = ____ L ____ ml

$\frac{9}{10}$ L $= \frac{9}{10} \times$ ____

$= \frac{9 \times \square}{10}$

= ____ ml

Chapter 3: Exercise 18, page 68

Converting a measurement from a larger unit involving a mixed number to a smaller unit

Let's Learn

Express $3\frac{2}{5}$ kilometres in metres.

$3 \text{ km} = 3 \times 1000$
$= 3000 \text{ m}$

$\frac{2}{5} \text{ km} = \frac{2}{5} \times 1000$
$= \frac{2 \times \cancel{1000}^{200}}{\cancel{5}_1}$
$= 400 \text{ m}$

$3\frac{2}{5} \text{ km} = 3000 + 400$
$= 3400 \text{ m}$

$3\frac{2}{5}$ km = 3 km + $\frac{2}{5}$ km

5 is a factor of 1000 and 5.
Divide 1000 and 5 by 5.

Let's Do

1. Express $2\frac{1}{4}$ days in hours.

2 days = 2×24

= ____ h

$\frac{1}{4}$ day $= \frac{1}{4} \times 24$

= ____ h

$2\frac{1}{4}$ days = ____ + ____

= ____ h

1 day = 24 h

Chapter 3: Exercise 19, pages 69–70

 ISBN 978-93-5103-031-7

Expressing a measurement in a smaller unit as a fraction of a larger unit

Let's Learn

a) We can write 600 millilitres as a fraction of 1 litre.

$$\frac{\cancel{600}^{\,6}}{\cancel{1000}_{\,10}} = \frac{\cancel{6}^{\,3}}{\cancel{10}_{\,5}} = \frac{3}{5}$$

1 L = 1000 ml

First, divide 600 and 1000 by 100. Then, divide 6 and 10 by 2.

600 millilitres is $\frac{3}{5}$ of 1 litre.

b) Bob's handspan is 16 centimetres. What fraction of 1 metre is 16 centimetres?

$$\frac{\cancel{16}^{\,8}}{\cancel{100}_{\,50}} = \frac{\cancel{8}^{\,4}}{\cancel{50}_{\,25}} = \frac{\square}{\square}$$

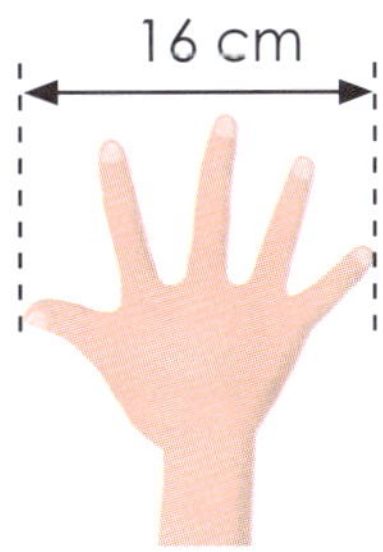

1 m = 100 cm

16 centimetres is $\square$ of 1 metre.

Let's Do

1. Express 80 paise as a fraction of ₹ 2.

$$\frac{80}{200} = \frac{8}{20} = \frac{\square}{\square}$$

₹ 1 = 100 paise
₹ 2 = 200 paise

Chapter 3: Exercise 20, page 71

Practice 6

1. Find the equivalent measures.

a) $\frac{1}{4}$ kg = ____ g

b) $\frac{2}{5}$ cm = ____ mm

c) $\frac{1}{6}$ h = ____ min

d) $\frac{3}{4}$ day = ____ h

 ISBN 978-93-5103-031-7

2. Find the equivalent measures.

a) $2\frac{1}{3}$ h = ____ h ____ min b) $7\frac{1}{2}$ km = ____ km ____ m

c) $5\frac{3}{10}$ L = ____ L ____ ml d) $6\frac{1}{4}$ years = ____ years ____ months

3. Find the equivalent measures.

a) $2\frac{1}{2}$ m = ____ cm b) $1\frac{9}{10}$ kg = ____ g

c) $3\frac{1}{2}$ days = ____ h d) $2\frac{3}{4}$ years = ____ months

e) $1\frac{3}{10}$ L = ____ ml f) $2\frac{1}{10}$ km = ____ m

4. Express 45 seconds as a fraction of 1 minute.

5. Express 60 paise as a fraction of ₹ 1.

6. Express 90 centimetres as a fraction of 3 metres.

7. Express 50 minutes as a fraction of 2 hours.

Lesson 7 Problem Solving

Word problems

Let's Learn

Jimmy spent $\frac{2}{5}$ of his money on a shirt. The shirt cost ₹ 200. How much money did Jimmy have at first?

1 Understand the problem.

How much did the shirt cost?
What fraction of Jimmy's money was spent on the shirt?
What do I have to find?

2 Plan what to do.

I can **draw a bar model** to help me solve the problem.

 ISBN 978-93-5103-031-7

3 Work out the **Answer**.

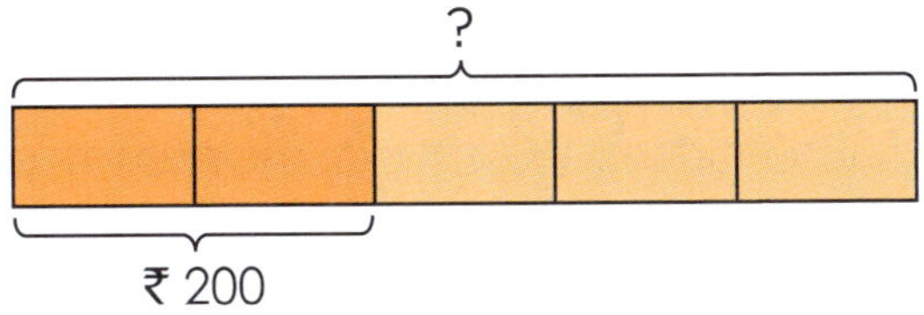

2 units → ₹ 200
1 unit → ₹ 200 ÷ 2 = ₹ 100
5 units → 5 × ₹ 100 = ₹ 500

Jimmy had ₹ 500 at first.

4 **Check**

Did you answer the question?
Is your answer correct?

$\frac{2}{5}$ of ₹ 500 = $\frac{2}{\not{5}_1} \times$ ₹ $\not{500}^{100}$
= ₹ 200

My answer is correct.

- ☑ 1. Understand
- ☑ 2. Plan
- ☑ 3. Answer
- ☑ 4. Check

Let's Do

1. 48 children went to the Science Centre. $\frac{3}{8}$ of them were girls. How many boys were there?

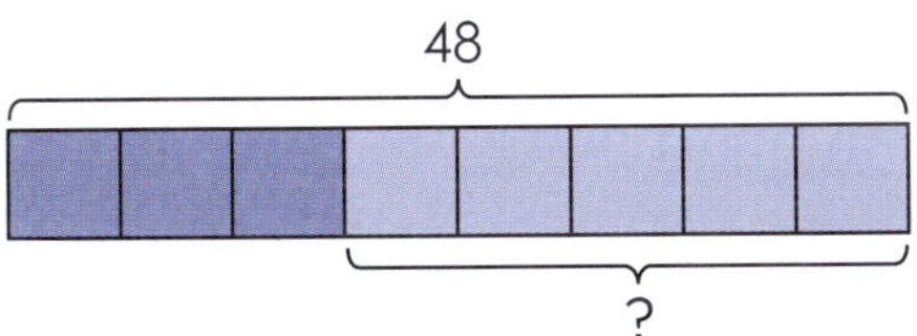

- ☐ 1. Understand
- ☐ 2. Plan
- ☐ 3. Answer
- ☐ 4. Check

8 units → ______

1 unit → ______

______ units → ______

There were ______ boys.

 ISBN 978-93-5103-031-7

Let's Learn

In a class of 40 students, 25 are boys. What fraction of the class are girls?

How many students are there in the class?
How many are boys? How many are girls?

Method 1

$40 - 25 = 15$

There are 15 girls.

$\frac{15}{40} = \square$

☐ of the class are girls.

Method 2

$\frac{25}{40} = \frac{5}{8}$

$\frac{5}{8}$ of the class are boys.

$1 - \frac{5}{8} = \square$

☐ of the class are girls.

- [x] 1. Understand
- [x] 2. Plan
- [x] 3. Answer
- [x] 4. Check

Let's Do

1. There were 84 people at a school carnival. 49 of them were children and the rest were adults. What fraction of the people at the carnival were adults?

How many people were at the carnival?
How many children were there?
How many adults were there?

- [ ] 1. Understand
- [ ] 2. Plan
- [ ] 3. Answer
- [ ] 4. Check

 ISBN 978-93-5103-031-7

Let's Learn

A box containing 9 packets of flour has a total weight of 7 kilograms. If the weight of each packet of flour is $\frac{8}{11}$ kilogram, find the weight of the empty box.

What is the weight of 1 packet of flour?
What is the weight of 9 packets of flour?

$$\frac{8}{11} \times 9 = \frac{72}{11}$$
$$= 6\frac{6}{11}$$

The weight of 9 packets of flour is $6\frac{6}{11}$ kilograms.

$$7 - 6\frac{6}{11} = 6\frac{11}{11} - 6\frac{6}{11}$$
$$= \frac{5}{11}$$

The weight of the empty box is $\frac{5}{11}$ kilogram.

$$6\frac{6}{11} + \frac{5}{11} = 6\frac{11}{11}$$
$$= 7$$

My answer is correct.

- ☑ 1. Understand
- ☑ 2. Plan
- ☑ 3. Answer
- ☑ 4. Check

Let's Do

1. Rohit is $\frac{7}{10}$ metre tall. His sister is twice as tall as him. His father is $\frac{2}{5}$ metre taller than his sister. How tall is Rohit's father?

How much taller is Rohit's sister than Rohit?
How much taller is his father than his sister?

- ☐ 1. Understand
- ☐ 2. Plan
- ☐ 3. Answer
- ☐ 4. Check

P/B Chapter 3: Exercise 21, pages 72–73

 ISBN 978-93-5103-031-7

Practice 7

Solve the word problems. Show your work clearly.

1. Kabir spent $\frac{1}{4}$ of his money on a comic book. If the comic book cost ₹ 20, how much money did he have at first?

2. In a class of 35 students, 21 students do not wear glasses. What fraction of the students wear glasses?

3. Steven has a rope 7 metres long. Carl's rope is $\frac{5}{6}$ metre shorter than Steven's rope. What is the total length of rope the boys have?

4. $\frac{1}{4}$ of the fruits at a stall are watermelons, $\frac{5}{12}$ are pears and the rest are apples. If there are 132 apples, how many fruits are there at the stall?

Mind stretcher

Let's Learn

There were 440 boys and girls in a school hall. After $\frac{5}{7}$ of the boys and $\frac{1}{3}$ of the girls left the hall, an equal number of boys and girls remained. How many boys were there in the hall at first?

1 Understand the problem.

What fraction of the boys and girls left the hall?
What fraction of the boys and girls remained?

2 Plan what to do.

I can **draw bar models** and **work backwards** to help me solve the problem.

 ISBN 978-93-5103-031-7

3 Work out the **Answer**.

$1 - \frac{5}{7} = \frac{2}{7}$

$\frac{2}{7}$ of the boys remained.

$1 - \frac{1}{3} = \frac{2}{3}$

$\frac{2}{3}$ of the girls remained.

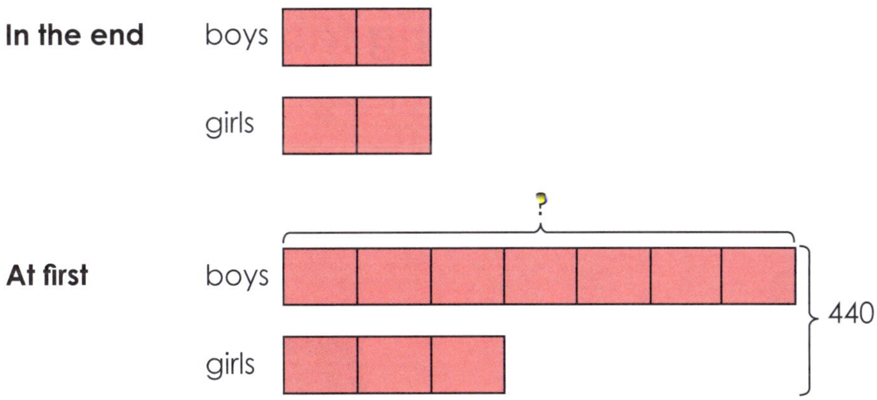

10 units → 440
1 unit → 440 ÷ 10 = 44
7 units → 7 × 44 = 308

There were 308 boys in the hall at first.

4 **Check**
Did you answer the question? Is your answer correct?

$\frac{2}{7} \times 308 = 88$

88 boys remained in the hall.

$440 - 308 = 132$

There were 132 girls at first.

$\frac{2}{3} \times 132 = 88$

88 girls remained in the hall.

My answer is correct.

☑ 1. Understand
☑ 2. Plan
☑ 3. Answer
☑ 4. Check

 ISBN 978-93-5103-031-7

4 Tables and Graphs

Lesson 1 Presenting Data

Completing and interpreting tables and bar graphs

Let's Learn

a) The weights of the recyclable items collected by students for Environment Week are shown below.

Picture It

clothes
38 kilograms

paper
43 kilograms

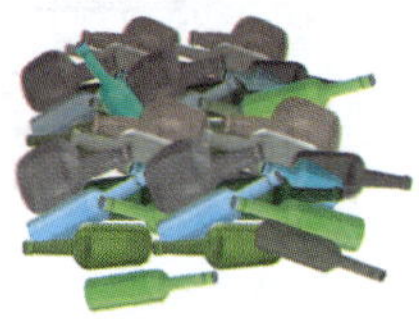

glass
39 kilograms

metal
40 kilograms

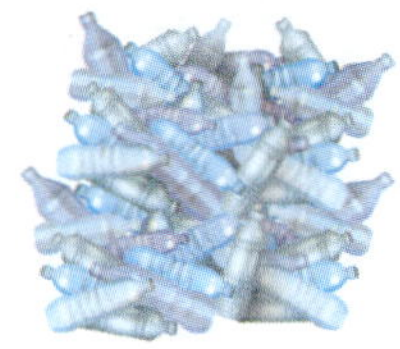

plastic
38 kilograms

We can present the data in a table.

Item	Weight
clothes	38 kg
glass	39 kg
plastic	38 kg
paper	43 kg
metal	40 kg

The weight of paper was the greatest among all the items collected.
The weights of clothes and plastic collected were the same.
1 kilogram more metal than glass was collected.

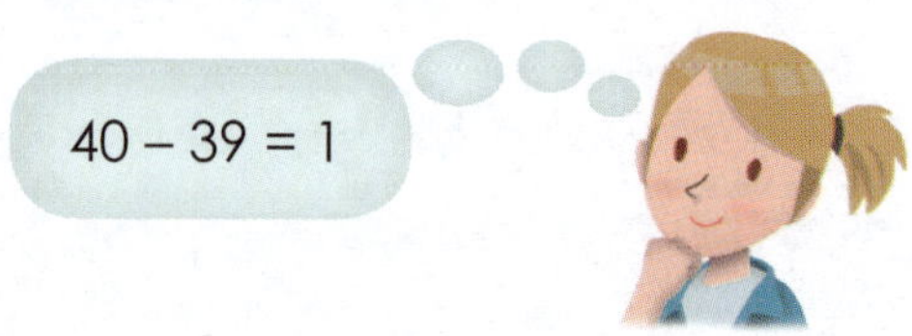

 ISBN 978-93-5103-031-7

b) We can also present the data in a bar graph.

Picture It

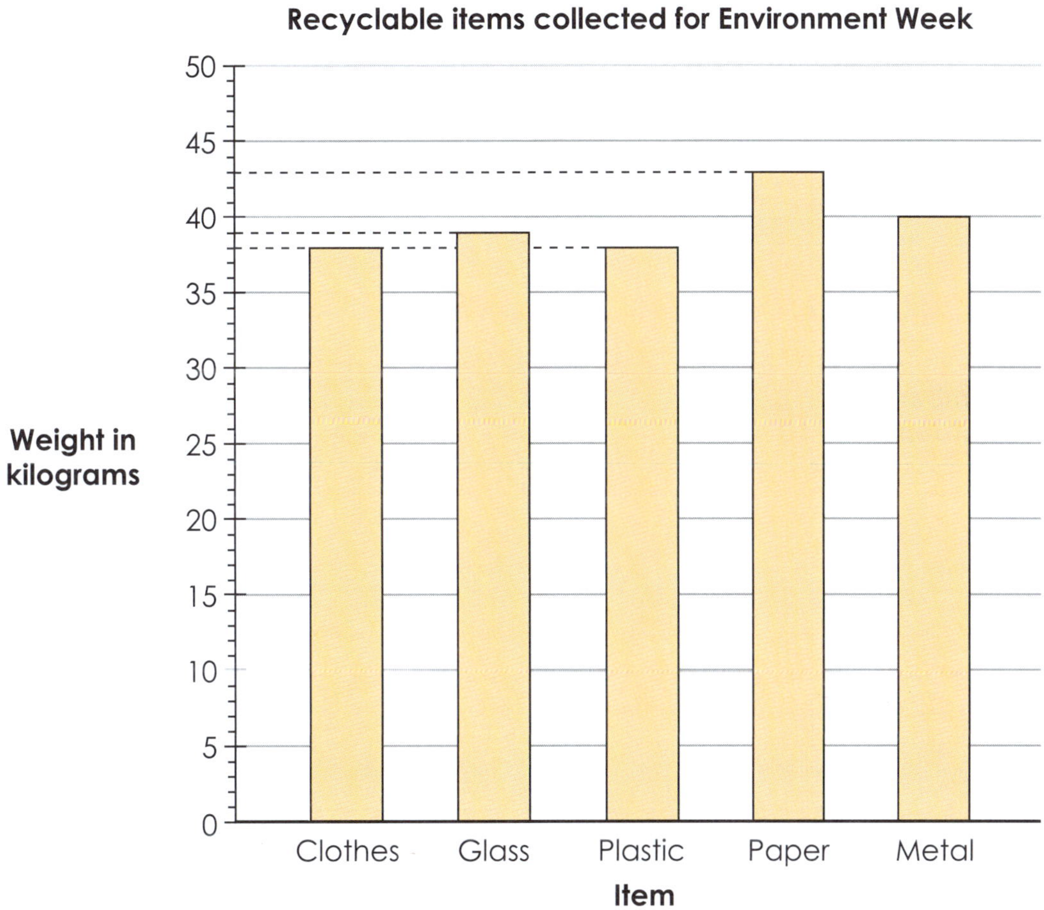

Let's Do

1. The table shows the number of orders for salads at a restaurant during lunch time.

Type of salad	Number of orders
chicken	16
tuna	8
green	10
egg	14

a) The most popular salad was ______________ salad.

b) There were ______ more orders for the egg salad than for the tuna salad.

 ISBN 978-93-5103-031-7

c) Complete the bar graph to show the data in the table on page 97.

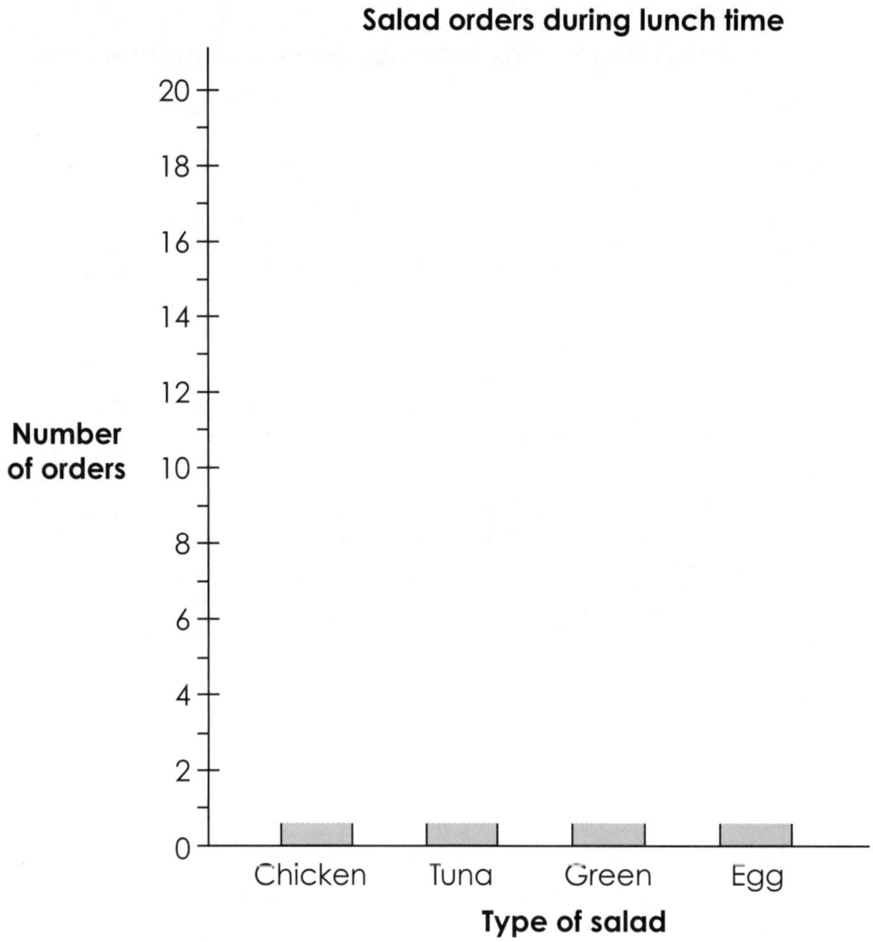

  ISBN 978-93-5103-031-7

2. The bar graph shows the number of cars sold by Mr. Iyer in six months.

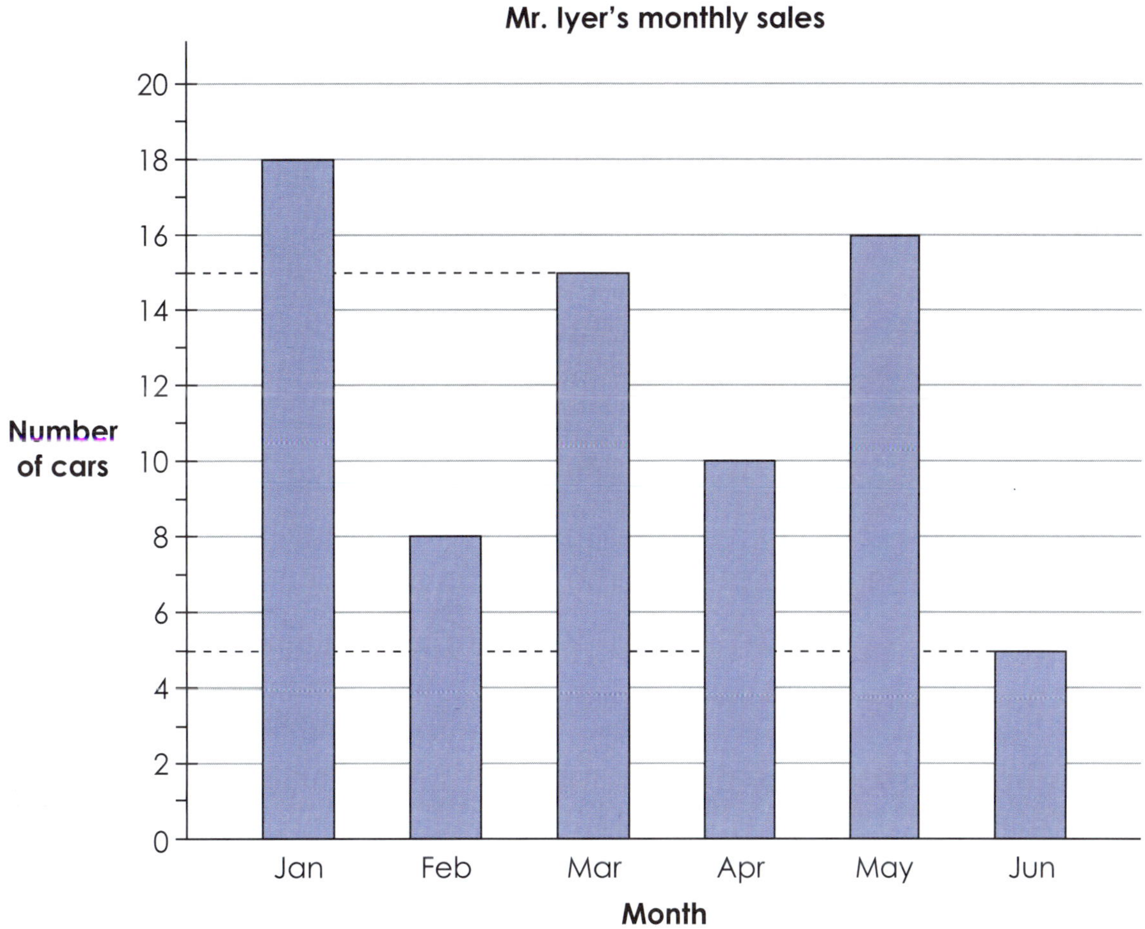

Fill in the blanks.

a) Mr. Iyer sold ______ cars in March.

b) He sold fewer than 10 cars in ______ and ______.

c) He sold the greatest number of cars in ______.

d) ______ more cars were sold in May than in April.

e) Half as many cars were sold in ______ as in May.

f) Complete the table to show the data in the bar graph.

Month	Jan	Feb	Mar	Apr	May	Jun
Number of cars sold						

P/B Chapter 4: Exercises 1–3, pages 74–79

 ISBN 978-93-5103-031-7

Solving problems using data given in tables

Let's Learn

The table shows the number of people who attended four courses in a community centre.

Course	Men	Women
art	14	11
computer	25	24
dancing	12	18
first aid	6	21

a) How many people attended the first aid course?

6 + 21 = 27

27 people attended the first aid course.

b) How many more women than men attended the dancing course?

18 – 12 = 6

____ more women than men attended the dancing course.

c) How many more people attended the computer course than the art course?

25 + 24 = 49

49 people attended the computer course.

14 + 11 = 25

25 people attended the art course.

49 – 25 = ____

____ more people attended the computer course than the art course.

 ISBN 978-93-5103-031-7

Let's Do

1. The table shows the number of children who took part in three different activities.

Activity	Boys	Girls
walkathon	56	50
swimming contest	63	66
carnival	45	47

Answer the questions.

a) How many children took part in the walkathon?

56 + 50 = ______

______ children took part in the walkathon.

b) How many more girls than boys took part in the swimming contest?

66 – ______ = ______

______ more girls than boys took part in the swimming contest.

c) How many more children took part in the swimming contest than in the carnival?

63 + 66 = ______

______ children took part in the swimming contest.

45 + 47 = ______

______ children took part in the carnival.

______ – ______ = ______

______ more children took part in the swimming contest than in the carnival.

P/B Chapter 4: Exercises 4–5, pages 80–84

 ISBN 978-93-5103-031-7

Completing tables using given data

Let's Learn

In a class of 22 boys and 20 girls, 8 boys wear glasses and 15 girls do not wear glasses.

	Number of boys	Number of girls	Total
Wearing glasses	8		
Not wearing glasses		15	
Total	22	20	42

We can complete the table using the given data.

a) 22 – 8 = 14

14 boys do not wear glasses.

There are 22 boys.
8 wear glasses.

b) 20 – 15 = 5

5 girls wear glasses.

There are 20 girls.
15 do not wear glasses.

c) 8 + 5 = ___

___ students wear glasses.

8 boys and 5 girls wear glasses.

d) 14 + 15 = ___

___ students do not wear glasses.

14 boys and 15 girls do not wear glasses.

 ISBN 978-93-5103-031-7

Let's Do

1. The table shows the number of books read by Ram and Karen from January to March.

Month	Ram	Karen	Total
January	7	4	11
February	9		12
March		8	
Total	20	15	35

Answer the questions.

a) How many books did Ram read in March?

20 – ______ – ______ = ______

Ram read ______ books in March.

Check the answer.

7 + 9 + ______ = 20

b) How many books did Karen read in February?

12 – ______ = ______

Karen read ______ books in February.

Check the answer.

4 + ______ + 8 = 15

c) How many books did Ram and Karen read in March?

______ + 8 = ______

Ram and Karen read ______ books in March.

Check the answer.

11 + 12 + ______ = 35

PB Chapter 4: Exercise 6, page 85

 ISBN 978-93-5103-031-7

Think About It

The table shows the number of red and blue beads used to make a necklace and a bracelet.

	Red beads	Blue beads	Total
Necklace	25		
Bracelet		11	
Total	31	18	

How many beads are used to make the necklace?

Ria

18 − 11 = 7

7 blue beads are used to make the necklace.

25 + 7 = 32

32 beads are used to make the necklace.

31 + 18 = 49

49 beads are used to make the necklace.

Sam

Who is correct? Explain why.

Practice 1

1. Miss Saba bought different fruits at a supermarket.

apples pears oranges peaches

a) Complete the table to show the given data.

Type of fruit	Number of fruits
apple	
pear	
orange	
peach	

 ISBN 978-93-5103-031-7

Fill in the blanks.

b) Miss Saba bought ____ apples.

c) She bought ____ more pears than oranges.

d) She bought twice as many ____ as peaches.

e) She bought ____ fruits altogether.

f) Complete the bar graph to show the data in the table.

Fruits bought by Miss Saba

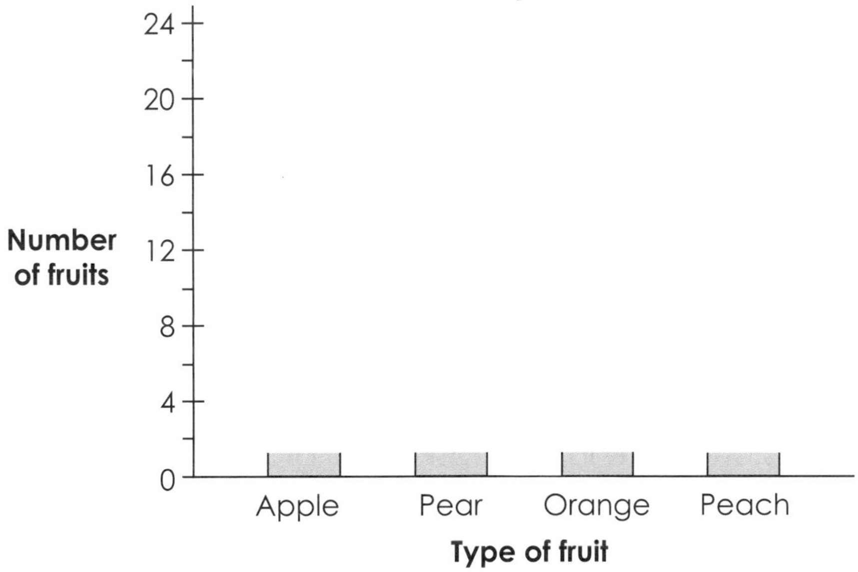

2. The table shows the number of coins Neena and Arun collected from two countries.

	Australia	U.S.	Total
Neena		28	48
Arun	15		
Total	35	55	90

Answer the questions.

a) How many Australian coins did Neena collect?

b) How many U.S. coins did Arun collect?

c) How many more U.S. coins than Australian coins did Neena and Arun collect altogether?

d) How many Australian and U.S. coins did Arun collect altogether?

e) How many more U.S. coins than Australian coins did Neena collect?

 ISBN 978-93-5103-031-7

Lesson 2 Problem Solving

Mind stretcher

Let's Learn

The table shows the number of boys and girls in three sports groups.

	Boys	Girls	Total
Basketball			24
Hockey	23		
Gymnastics	11	20	
Total			

There are twice as many boys as girls in the basketball group.
The total number of girls is 5 times the number of girls in the hockey group.

a) How many girls are there in the basketball group?

b) How many boys are there in the basketball group?

c) How many girls are there in the hockey group?

1 Understand the problem.

What is the total number of students in the basketball group?
How many boys are in the hockey group?

2 Plan what to do.

I can **draw bar models** to help me solve the problem.

3 Work out the **Answer**.

a)

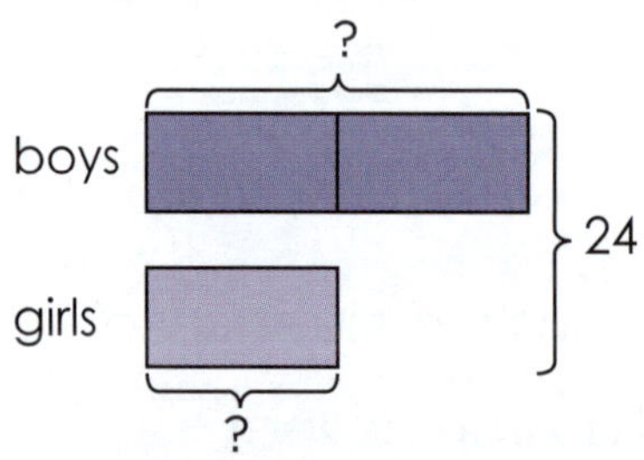

3 units → 24
1 unit → 24 ÷ 3 = 8
There are 8 girls in the basketball group.

 ISBN 978-93-5103-031-7

b) 2 units $\rightarrow 2 \times 8 = 16$
There are 16 boys in the basketball group.

c) Fill in the number of boys and girls in the basketball group.

	Boys	Girls	Total
Basketball	16	8	24
Hockey	23		
Gymnastics	11	20	
Total			

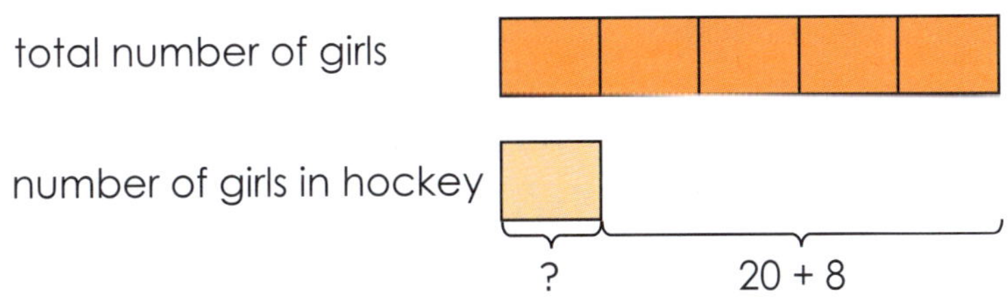

4 units $\rightarrow 20 + 8 = 28$
1 unit $\rightarrow 28 \div 4 = 7$
There are 7 girls in the hockey group.

4 Check

Did you answer the question?
Is your answer correct?

5 units $\rightarrow 5 \times 7 = 35$
There are 35 girls altogether.

$8 + 7 + 20 = 35$
My answer is correct.

- ☑ 1. Understand
- ☑ 2. Plan
- ☑ 3. Answer
- ☑ 4. Check

5 Angles

Lesson 1 Angle Measures

Naming angles

Let's Learn

a)

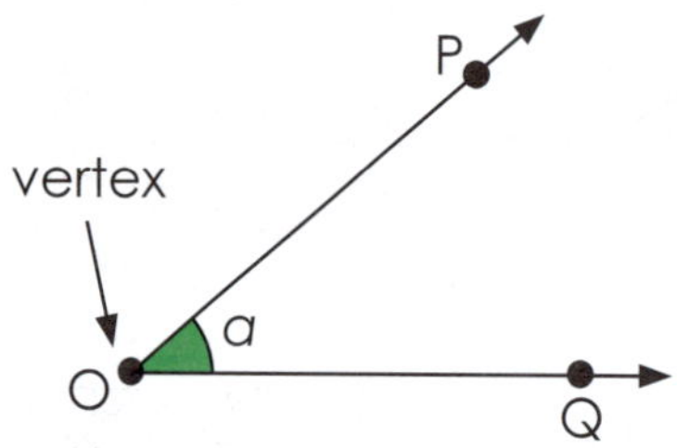

Rays OP and OQ meet at Point O to form an angle.
Point O is the **vertex** of the angle.
We name the angle as ∠POQ or ∠QOP.
The vertex is always the middle letter.
We can also name the angle as ∠*a*.

b) The angles in figures are also named in a similar way.

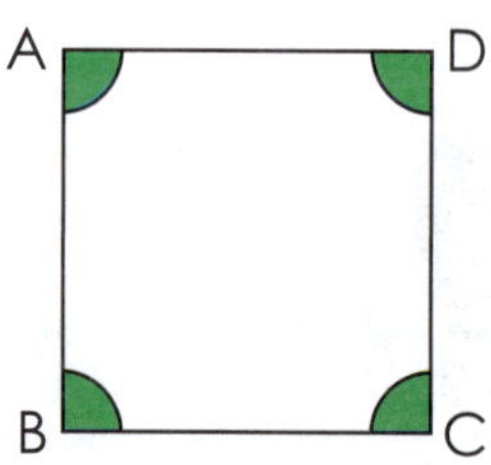

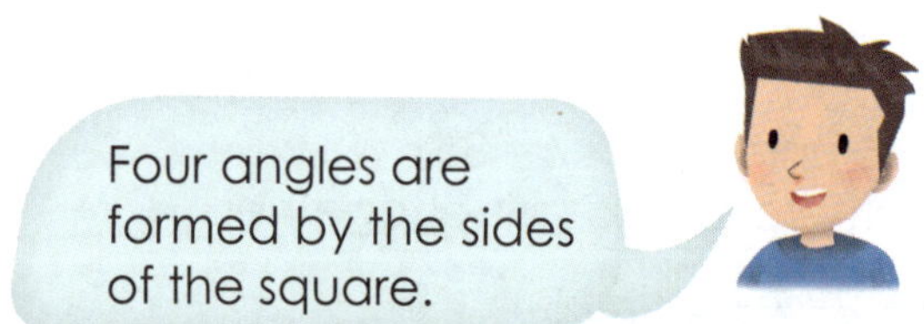

In the square, we name the angle at Vertex A as ∠BAD or ∠DAB.
Name the angles at vertices B, C and D.

Let's Do

1. Name the angles.

a)

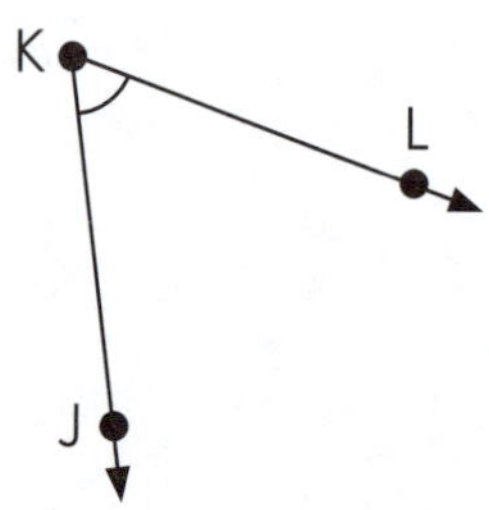

∠______

b)

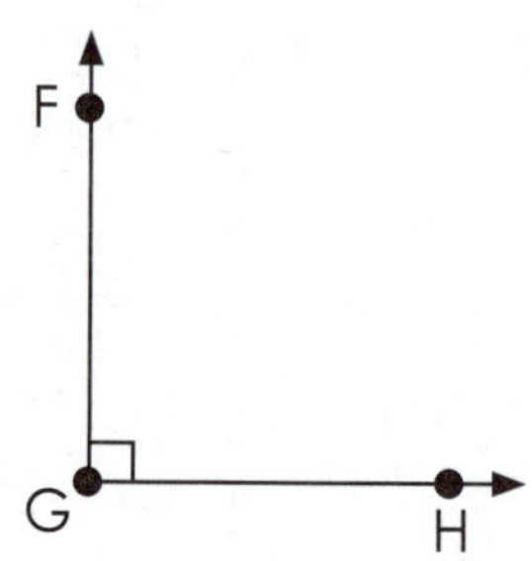

∠______

 ISBN 978-93-5103-031-7

2. Name the angles in another way.

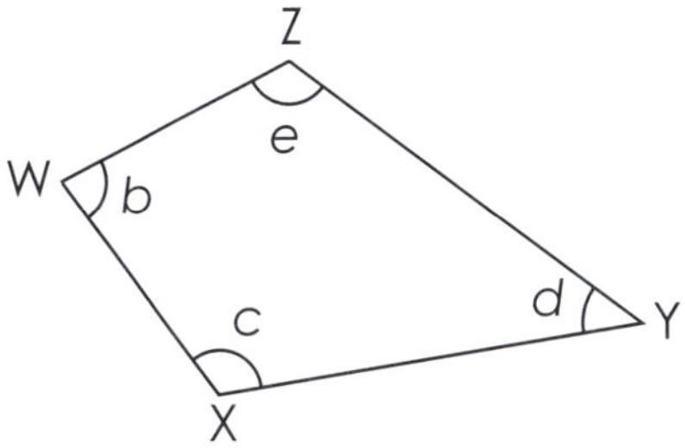

a) $\angle$WXY is also named as $\angle$_______.

b) $\angle$YZW is also named as $\angle$_______.

c) $\angle b$ is also named as $\angle$_______.

d) $\angle d$ is also named as $\angle$_______.

P/B Chapter 5: Exercise 1, pages 86–87

Measuring angles

Let's Learn

a) We measure angles in **degrees**.

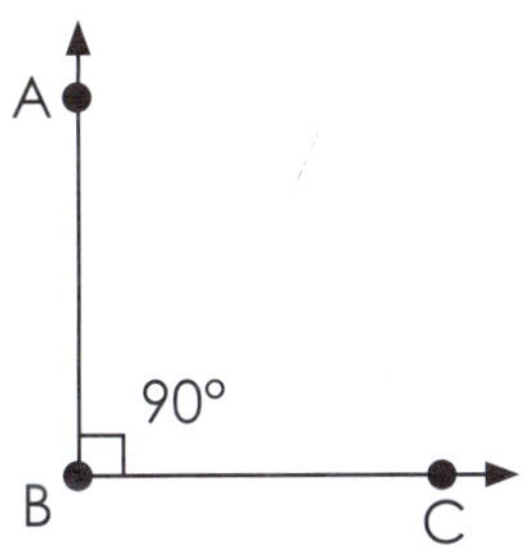

One right angle measures 90 degrees.
We write 90° for 90 degrees.

b) We use a protractor to measure an angle.

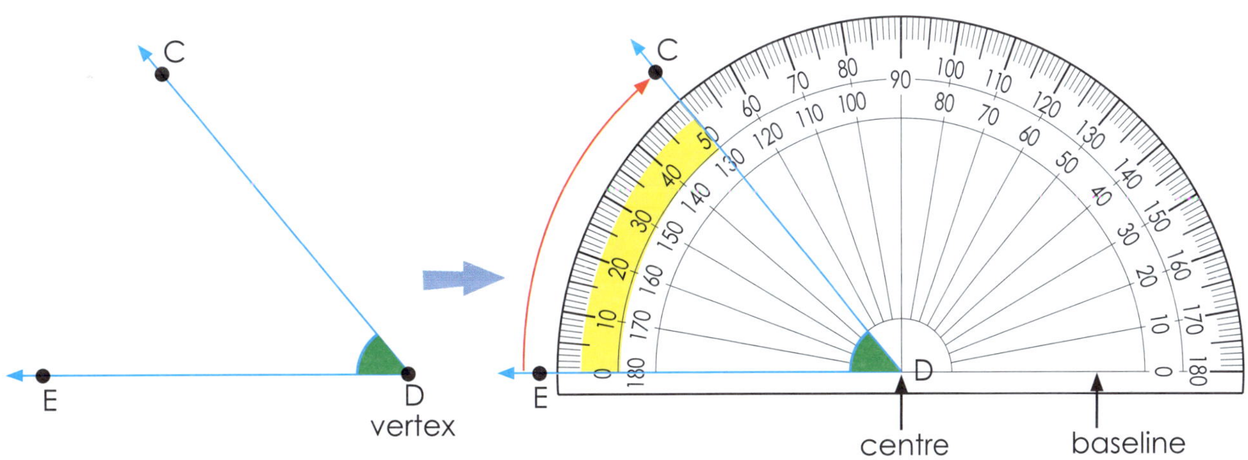

Step 1 Place the baseline of the protractor on Ray DE.

Step 2 Place the centre of the baseline at Vertex D.

Step 3 Read the angle measure from the scale.
Start reading from 0°. The measure of $\angle$CDE is 50°.

c) Measure ∠STU.

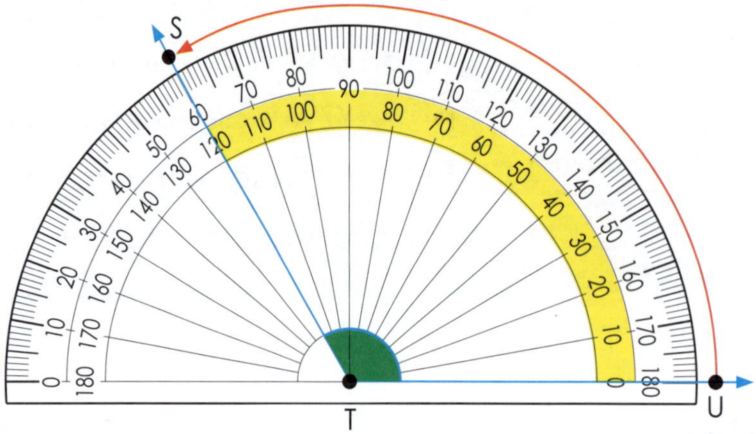

Step 1 Place the baseline of the protractor on Ray TU.

Step 2 Place the centre of the baseline at Vertex T.

Step 3 Read the angle measure from the scale.
Start reading from 0°.
The measure of ∠STU is ____.

∠STU is greater than a right angle.

Let's Do

1. Find the measure of each angle.

a)

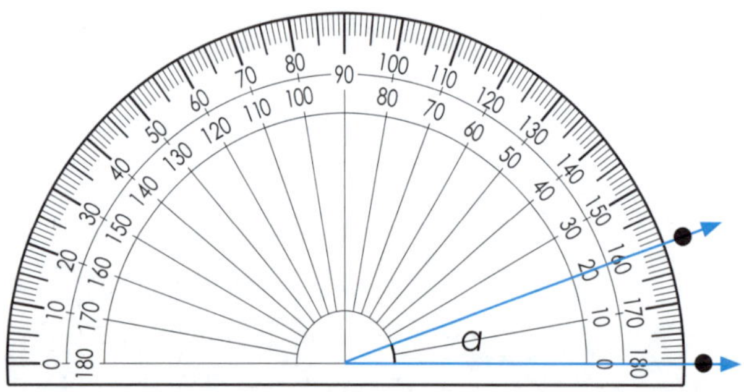

Measure of $\angle a$ = ______

b)

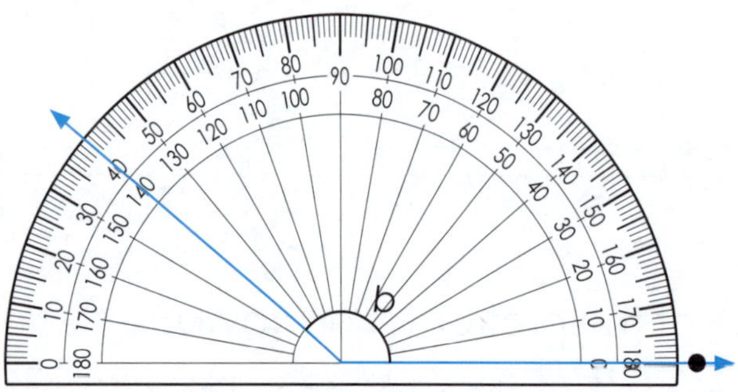

Measure of $\angle b$ = ______

 ISBN 978-93-5103-031-7

c)

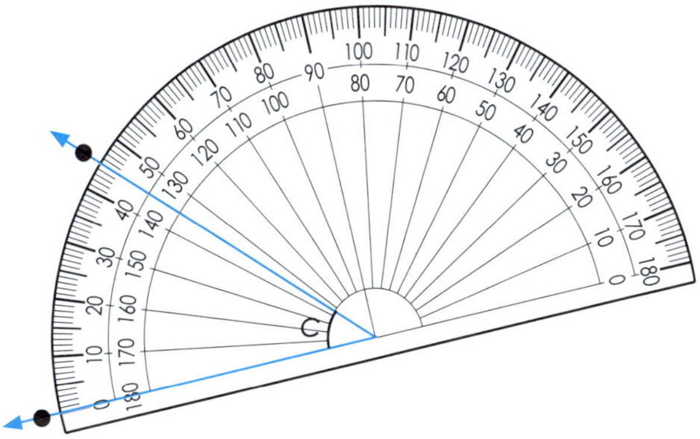

Measure of ∠c = ______

d)

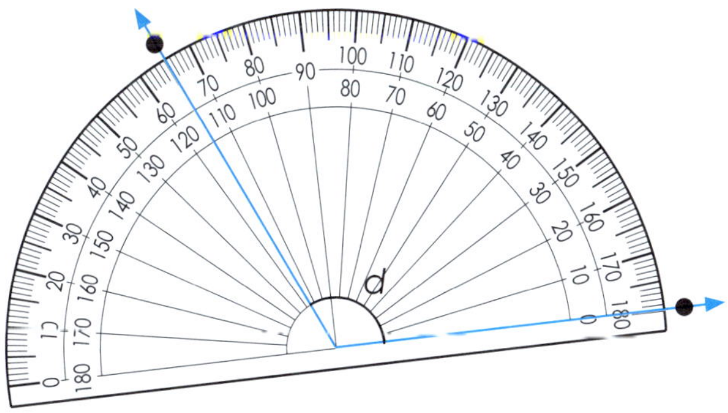

Measure of ∠*d* = ______

P/B Chapter 5: Exercise 2, pages 88–89

2. Estimate and then measure each angle.

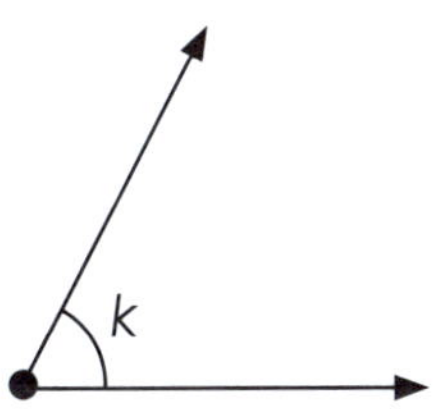

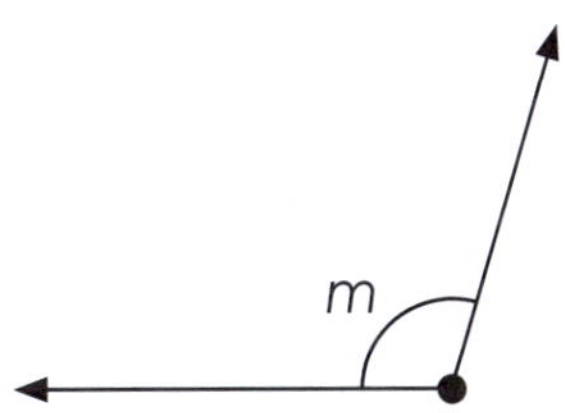

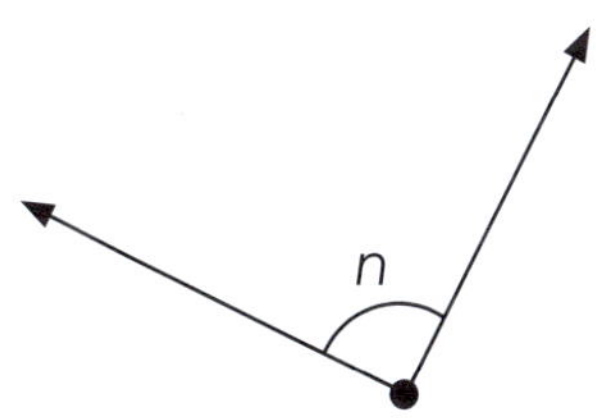

Angle	*k*	*m*	*n*
Estimate			
Measure			

P/B Chapter 5: Exercise 3, pages 90–91

 ISBN 978-93-5103-031-7

Drawing angles

Let's Learn

Maths Lab

Picture It

a) Draw ∠CAB with a measure of 35°.

Step 1 Draw Ray AB.

Step 2 Place the baseline of the protractor on Ray AB.
Place the centre of the baseline at Point A.
Mark Point C such that ∠CAB measures 35°.

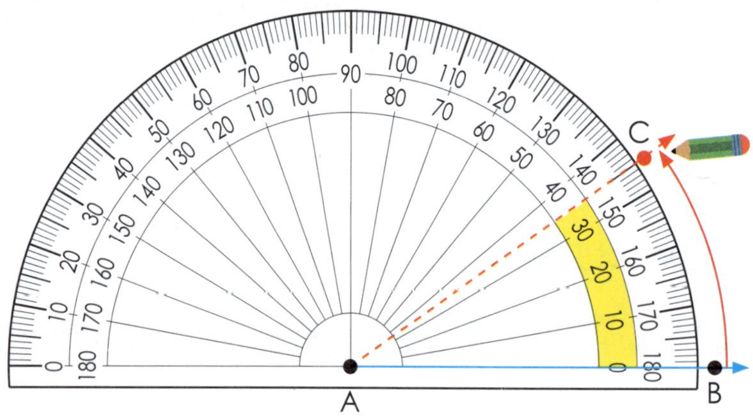

Step 3 Join Point C to Point A.
Mark the angle.

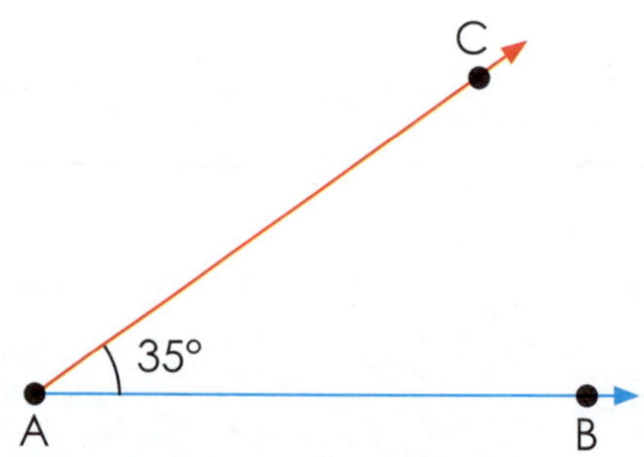

 ISBN 978-93-5103-031-7

b) Draw ∠POQ with a measure of 165°.

Step 1

Step 2

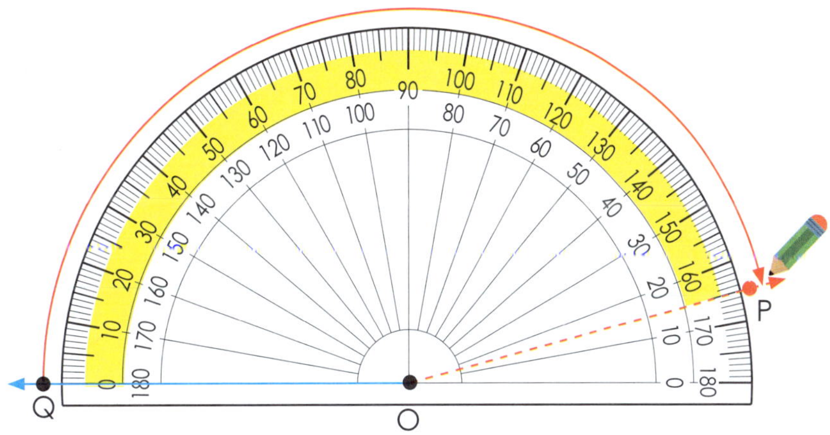

Step 3

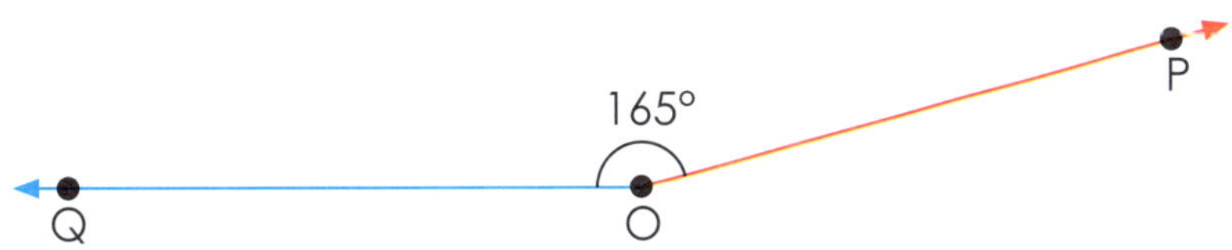

Let's Do

1. Join the end point of each ray to the correct dot to get the required angle measure. Use a protractor to help you. Then, label the angle.

   a) Measure of ∠p = 84°

   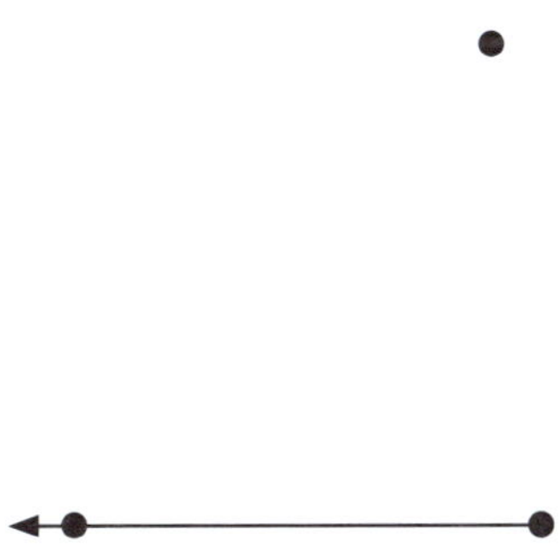

   b) Measure of ∠k = 154°

   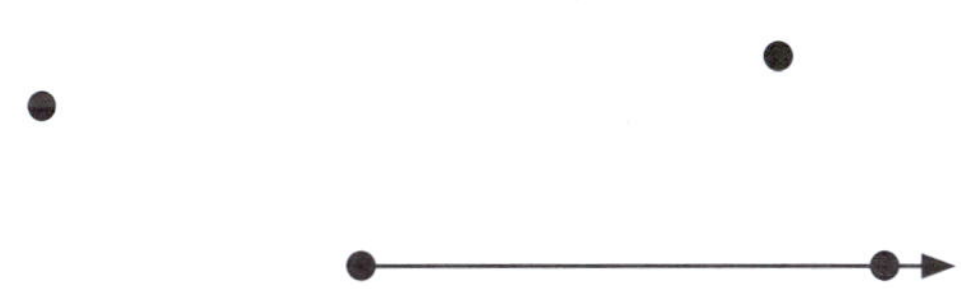

P/B Chapter 5: Exercise 4, pages 92–94

 ISBN 978-93-5103-031-7

Practice 1

1. Name each angle.

a)

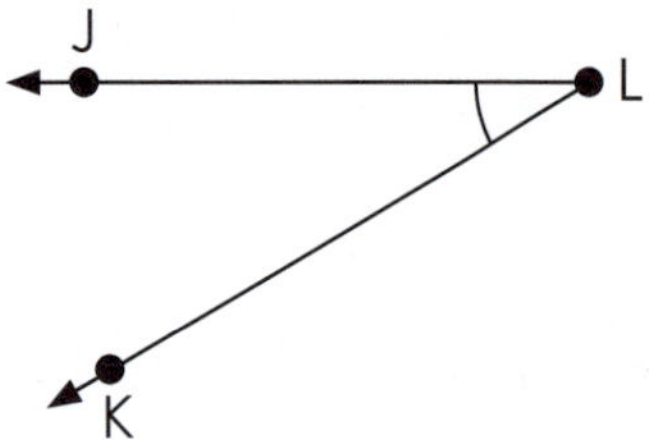

b)

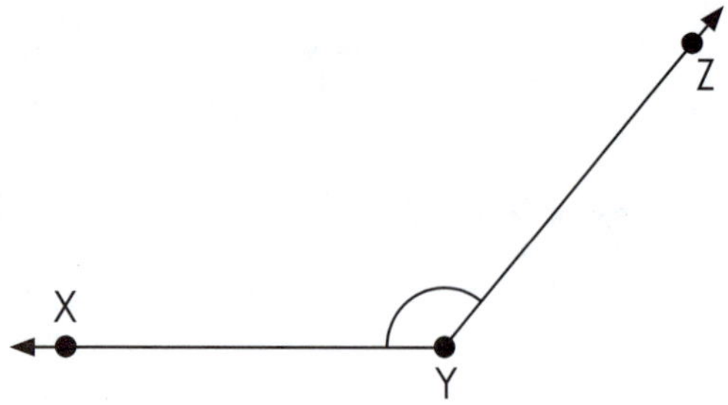

2. Find the measure of each angle.

a)

b)

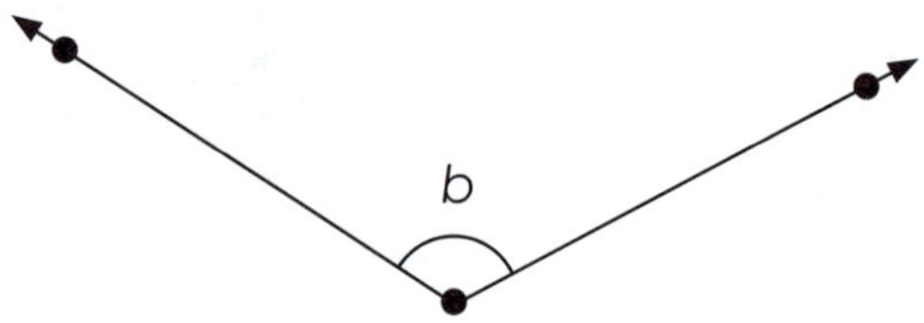

3. Draw an angle with a measure of

a) 60° b) 45° c) 125° d) 155°

4. Draw ∠ABC with a measure of 80°.

5. Draw ∠EFG with a measure of 145°.

Lesson 2 Turns and 8-point Compass

Relating turns to right angles

Let's Learn

Maths Lab

Picture It

One right angle

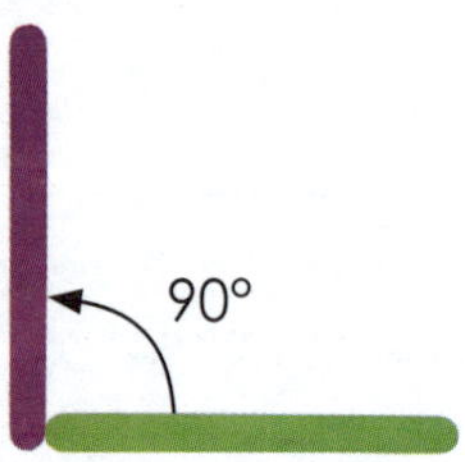

A $\frac{1}{4}$-turn measures 90°.

Two right angles

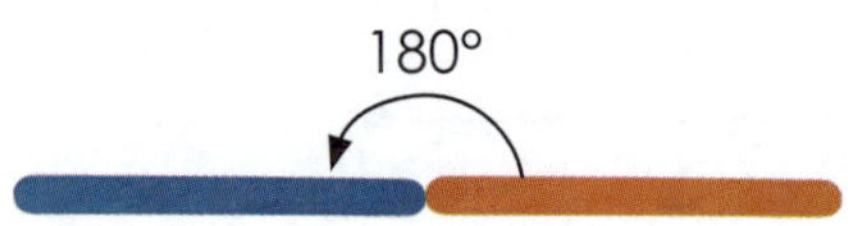

A $\frac{1}{2}$-turn measures 180°.

ISBN 978-93-5103-031-7

Three right angles

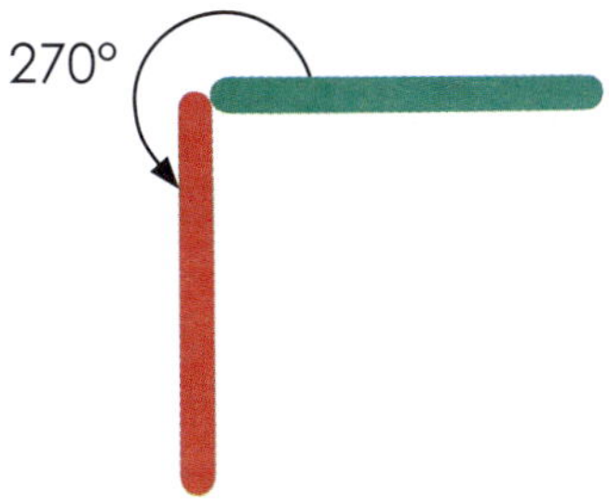

A $\frac{3}{4}$-turn measures 270°.

Four right angles

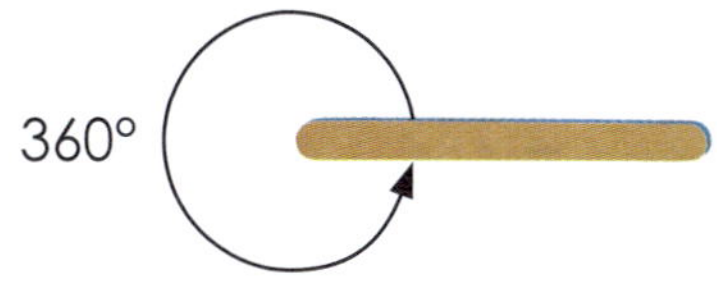

A complete turn measures 360°.

Let's Do

1. Fill in the blanks.
   a) ______ of a complete turn measures 270°.
   b) Two right angles make up a ______-turn.
   c) One complete turn is made up of ______ right angles.

P/B Chapter 5: Exercise 5, Page 95

Telling directions using the 8-point compass

Let's Learn

a) The 8-point compass shows direction.

Picture It

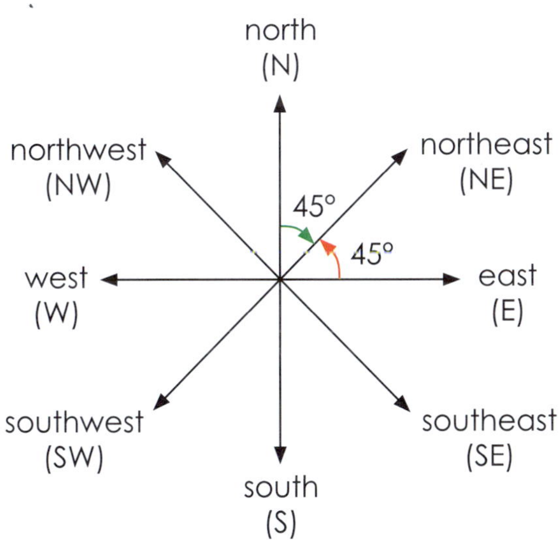

Northeast is 45° away from north and from east.
Southeast is 45° away from south and from east.
Southwest is 45° away from ____ and from ____.
Northwest is 45° away from ____ and from ____.

 ISBN 978-93-5103-031-7

b) This map shows the locations of places in a town.

Picture It

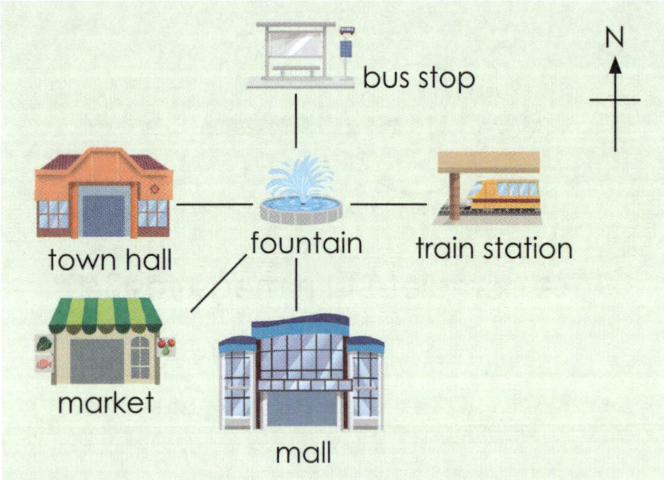

The bus stop is north of the fountain.

The ☐ is south of the fountain.

The market is ☐ of the fountain.

Let's Do

1. This map shows the locations of places in a town. Ganesh is standing at the fountain.

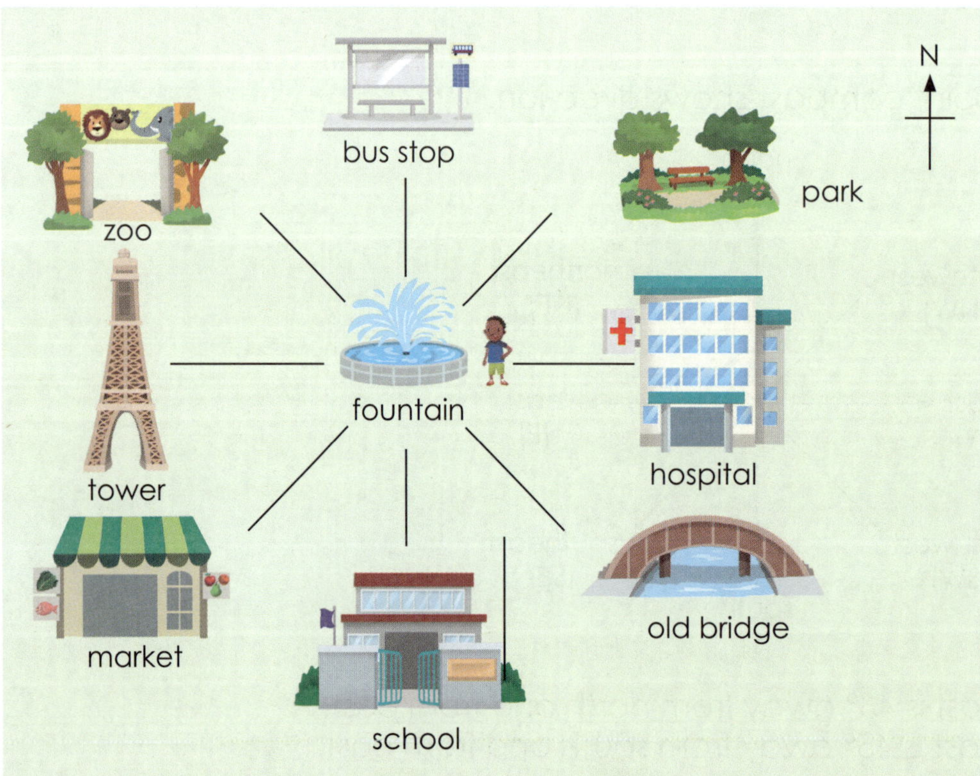

 ISBN 978-93-5103-031-7

a) The hospital is ________ of Ganesh.

b) The tower is ________ of Ganesh.

c) The ________ is south of Ganesh.

d) The ________ is northeast of Ganesh.

e) The ________ is southwest of Ganesh.

f) The old bridge is ______________________ of Ganesh.

P/B Chapter 5: Exercise 6, page 96

Let's Learn

Maya stands in a field and faces north (N).

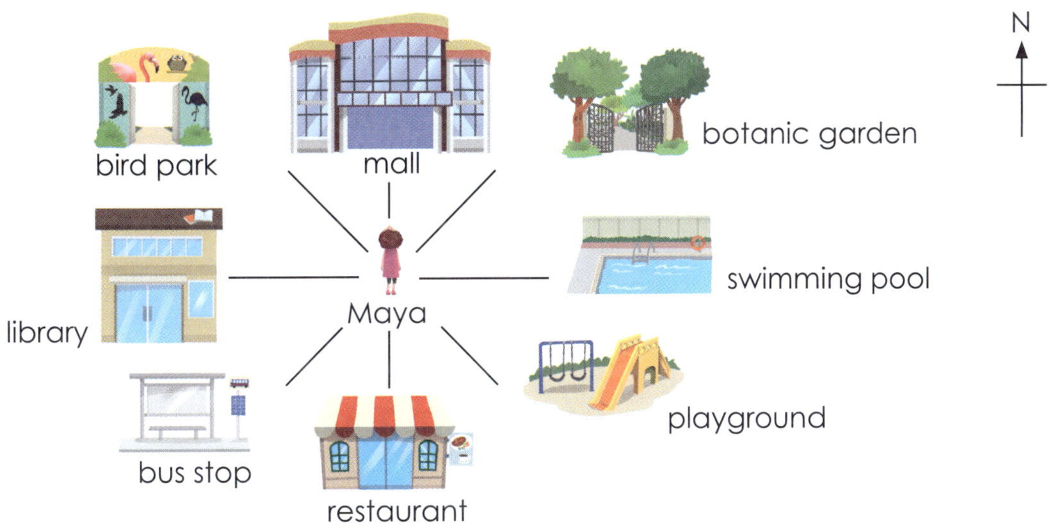

a) Maya turns 90° in the **clockwise** direction. She faces the swimming pool.

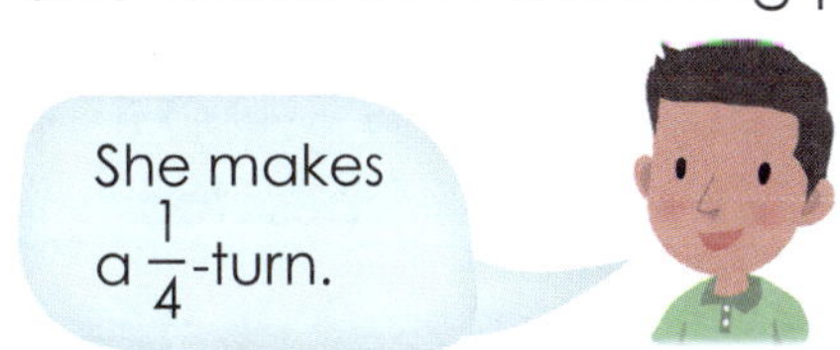

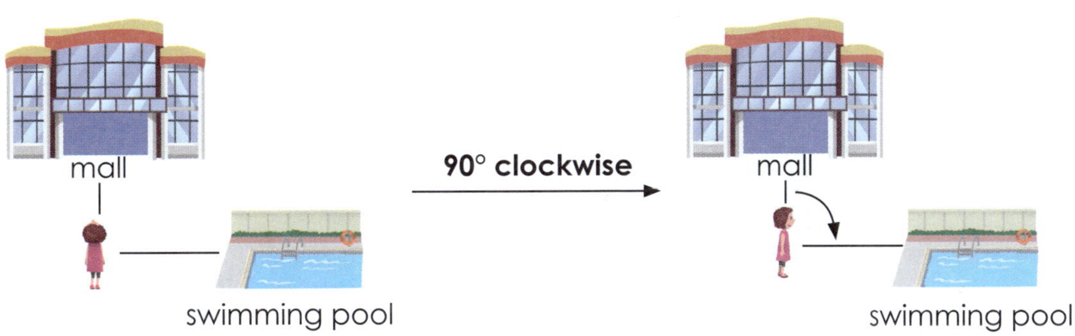

 ISBN 978-93-5103-031-7

b) Maya turns 180° in the **anticlockwise** direction. She faces the restaurant.

Maths Lab

Picture It

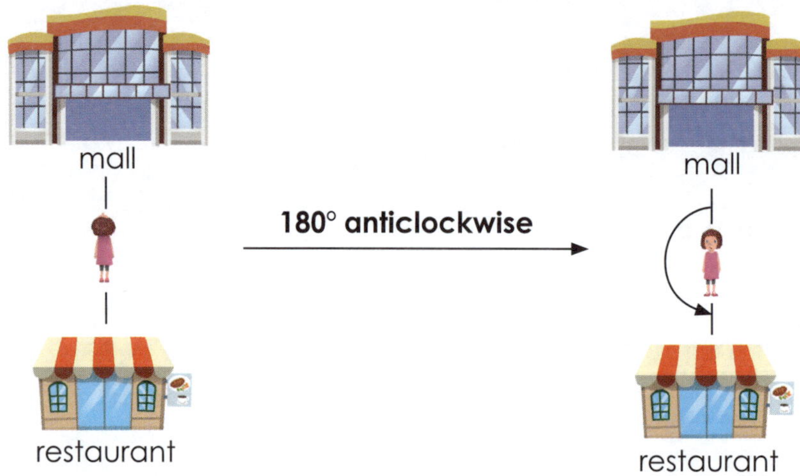

c) Maya turns 45° in the clockwise direction. She faces the botanic garden.

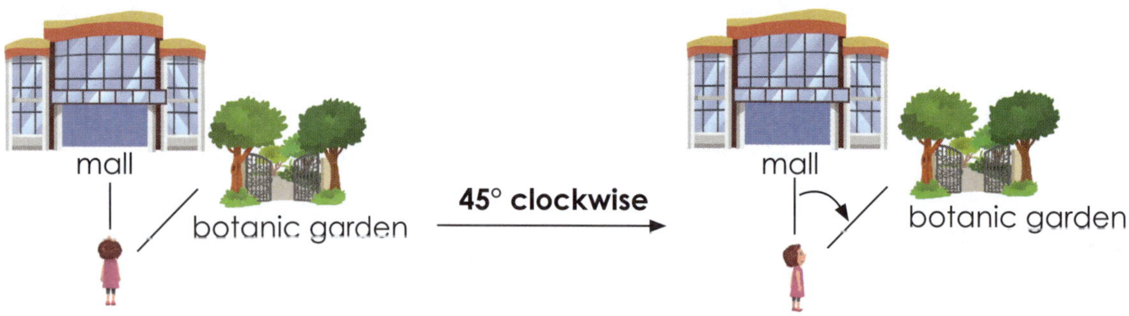

Let's Do

1. Colin is standing in the centre of the city park.

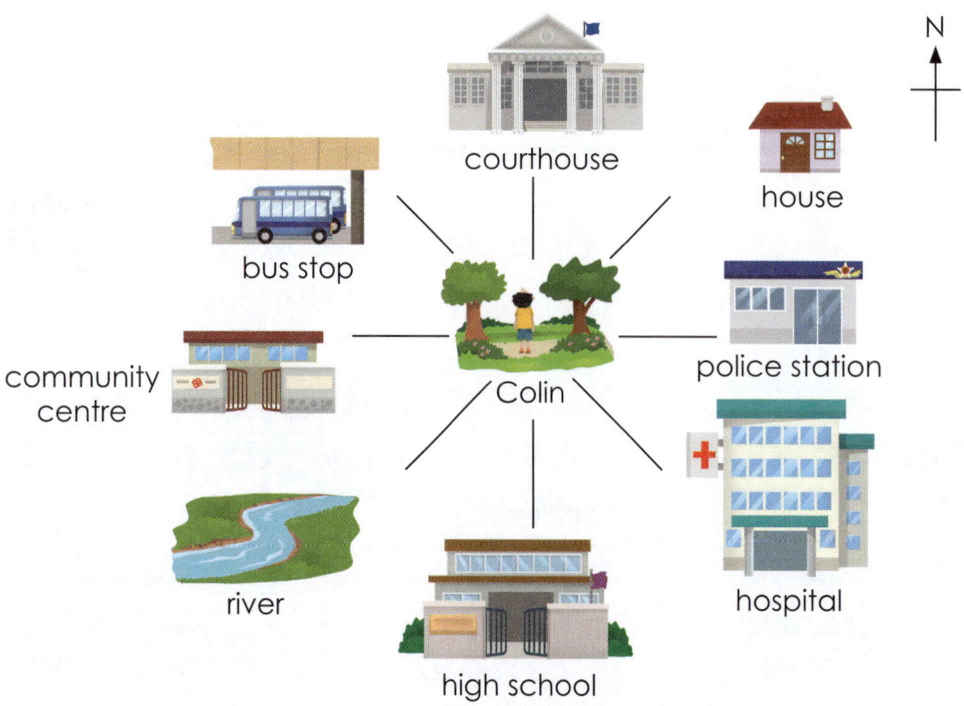

 ISBN 978-93-5103-031-7

a) Colin is facing north. If he turns 90° in the clockwise direction, he will face the ______________.

b) Colin is facing south. If he turns 270° in the anticlockwise direction, he will face the ______________.

c) Colin is facing southeast. If he turns ______________ in the anticlockwise direction, he will face the community centre.

d) Colin is facing ______________. If he turns 135° in the clockwise direction, he will face the bus stop.

P/B Chapter 5: Exercise 7, pages 97–98

Practice 2

1. Complete the table.

	Turn	Number of right angles	Angle measure
a)	a complete turn		
b)	$\frac{1}{2}$-turn		
c)	$\frac{1}{4}$-turn		
d)	$\frac{3}{4}$-turn		

2. a) What are the missing directions?

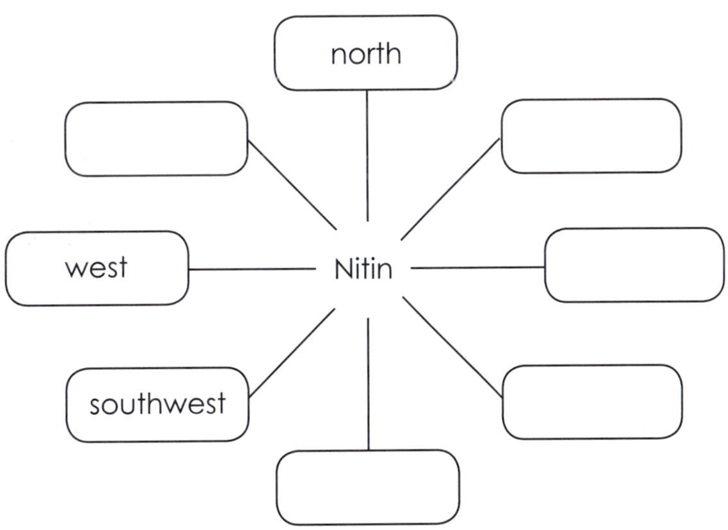

 ISBN 978-93-5103-031-7

b) Complete the table.

Nitin is facing	If Nitin turns	Nitin will be facing
north	90° clockwise	
east	135° clockwise	
south	____ anticlockwise	north
southwest	____ clockwise	west
northwest	270° clockwise	
	90° anticlockwise	northeast
	225° clockwise	east

Lesson 3 Problem Solving

Mind stretcher

Let's Learn

Tina wants to move from Point M to Point A along the gridlines. She cannot cross any of the black marked points.

Describe a possible route that Tina can take. Do not use more than five moves.

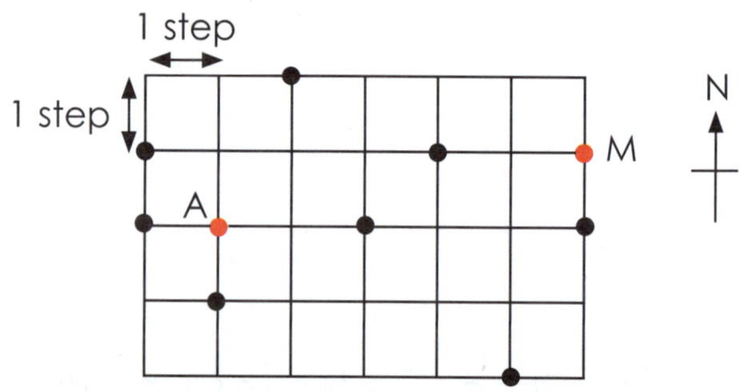

1 Understand the problem.

Where is Point M?
Where is Point A?
Which directions can Tina move in?

2 Plan what to do.

I can **make a list** of the directions Tina can move in.

 ISBN 978-93-5103-031-7

3 Work out the **Answer**.

Moves	Direction
1	1 step to the west
2	2 steps to the south
3	3 steps to the west
4	1 step to the north
5	1 step to the west

4 **Check**
Did you answer the question? Is your answer correct?

Trace the route on the map.
Tina can move from Point M to Point A without crossing the black marked points in five moves.

My answer is correct.

☑ **1. Understand**
☑ **2. Plan**
☑ **3. Answer**
☑ **4. Check**

 ISBN 978-93-5103-031-7

6 Perpendicular and Parallel Line Segments

Lesson 1 Drawing Perpendicular Line Segments

Using a protractor and a ruler to draw perpendicular line segments

Let's Learn

Maths Lab

Picture It

Step 1 Draw Line segment PQ. Mark a point on PQ and label it O.

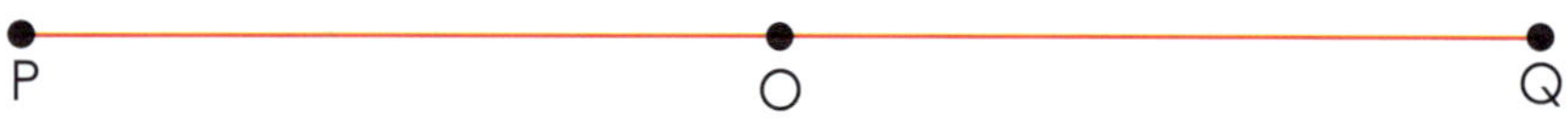

Step 2 Place the baseline of the protractor on PQ. Place the centre of the baseline at Point O. Mark Point R such that ∠POR measures 90°.

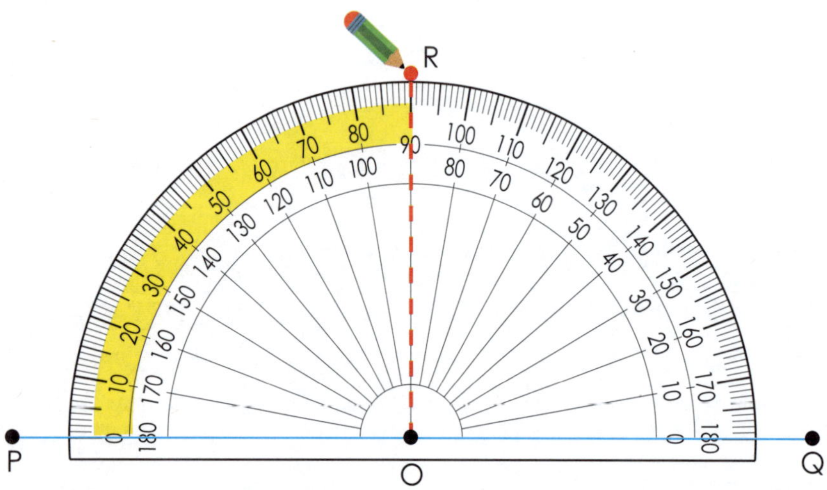

 ISBN 978-93-5103-031-7

Step 3 Join Point R to Point O. Mark the right angle.

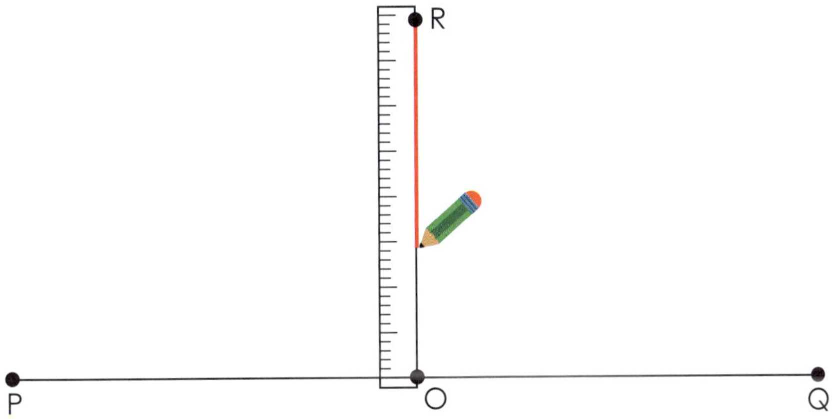

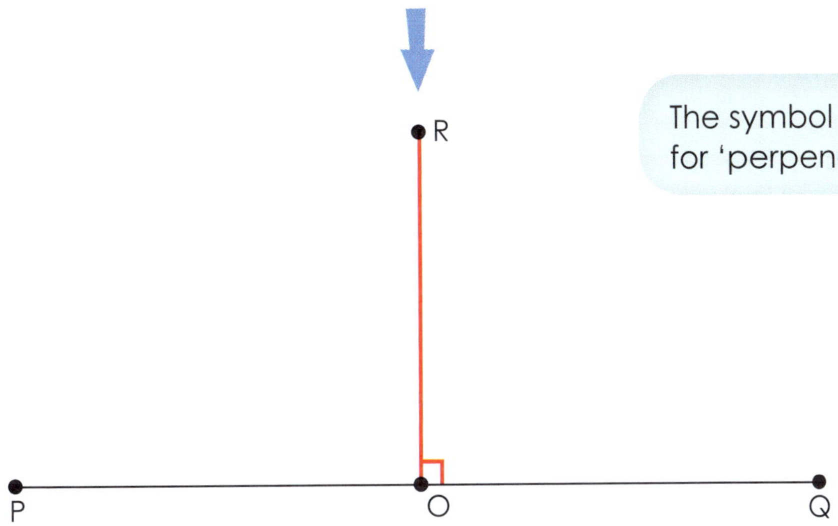

The symbol ⊥ stands for 'perpendicular to'.

PQ and RO are perpendicular line segments.
PQ ⊥ RO

Let's Do

1. Use a protractor and a ruler to draw a line segment perpendicular to the given line segment.

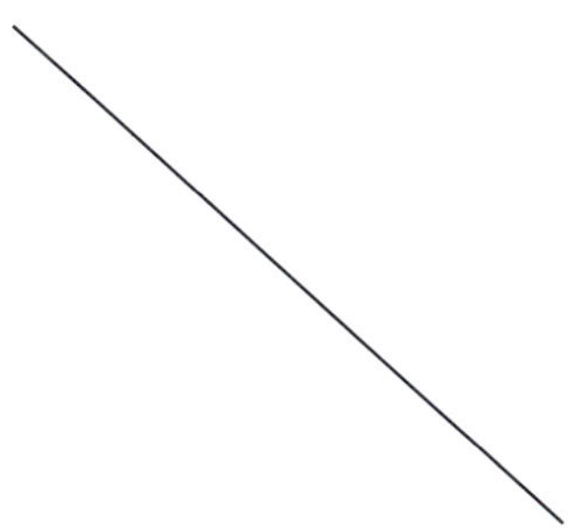

 ISBN 978-93-5103-031-7

Using a set square to draw perpendicular line segments

Let's Learn

Maths Lab

Picture It

a) Use a set square to draw a pair of perpendicular line segments.

Step 1 Draw Line segment AB. Place a set square against the line segment.

Step 2 Draw Line segment CD against the edge of the set square to meet Line segment AB. Mark the right angle.

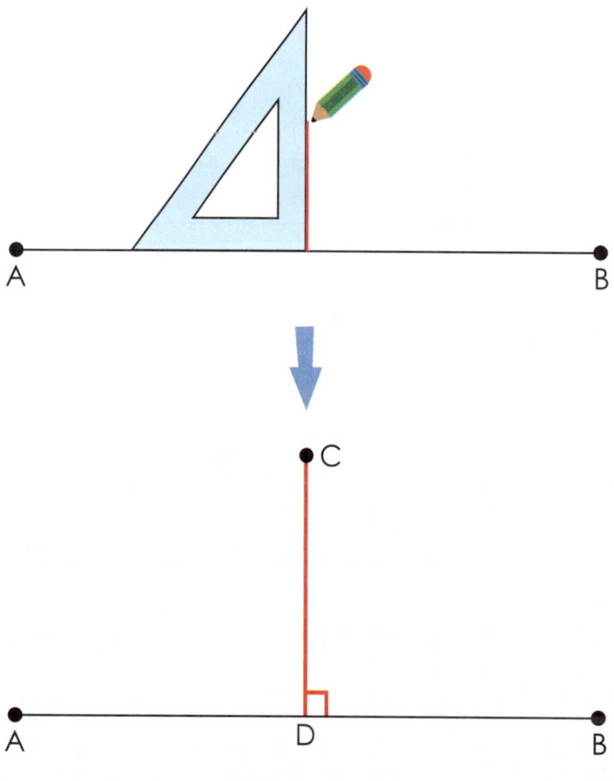

AB and CD are perpendicular line segments.

AB $\perp$ CD

 ISBN 978-93-5103-031-7

b) Use a set square to draw a line segment perpendicular to Line segment AB through Point P.

Step 1 Place a set square against Line segment AB and slide it along AB until the edge of the set square touches Point P.

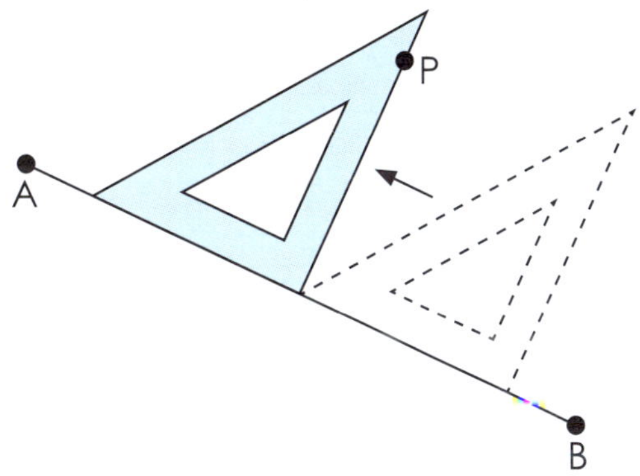

Step 2 Draw a line segment against the edge of the set square to meet Line segment AB at Point O.

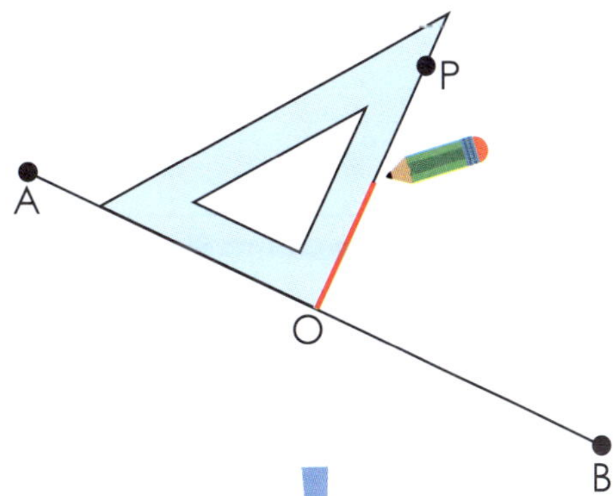

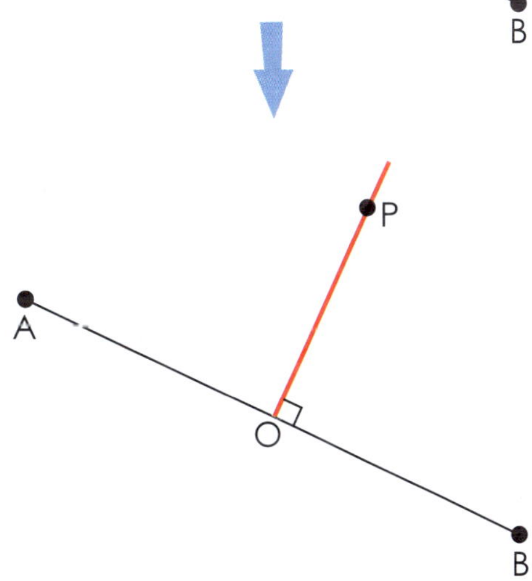

PO and AB are perpendicular line segments.
PO ⊥ AB

 ISBN 978-93-5103-031-7

Let's Do

1. Use a set square to draw a line segment perpendicular to

   a) the given line segment.

   b) the given line segment through Point P.

   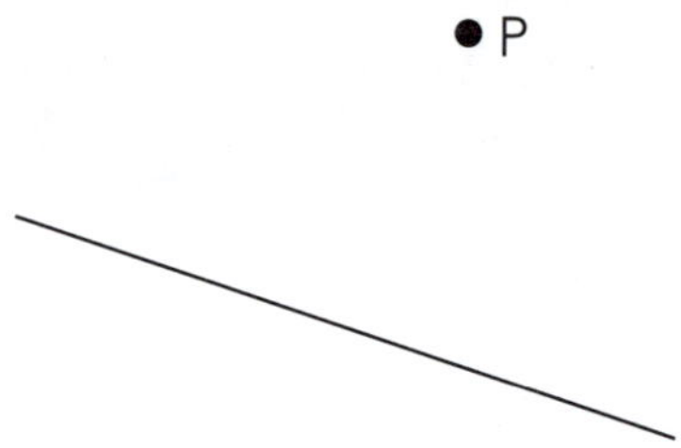

Chapter 6: Exercise 1, pages 99–100

Practice 1

1. Use a protractor and a ruler to draw a line segment perpendicular to the given line segment.

2. Use a set square to draw a line segment perpendicular to Line segment AB.

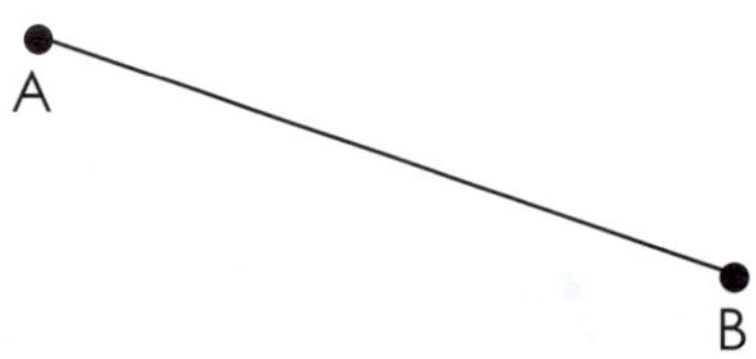

3. Use a set square to draw a line segment perpendicular to the given line segment through Point Y.

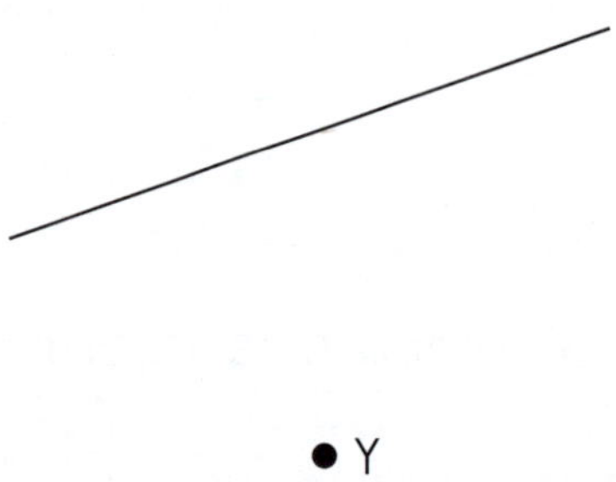

4. Draw a pair of perpendicular line segments.

 ISBN 978-93-5103-031-7

Lesson 2 Drawing Parallel Line Segments

Using a set square and a ruler to draw parallel line segments

Let's Learn

Maths Lab

Picture It

a) Use a set square and a ruler to draw a line segment parallel to Line segment AB.

Step 1 Place a set square against Line segment AB. Then, place a ruler against the base of the set square.

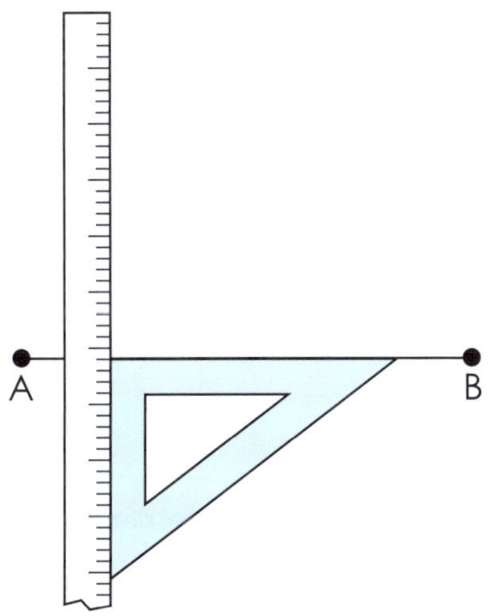

Step 2 Slide the set square along the ruler. Then, draw Line segment PQ against the edge of the set square.

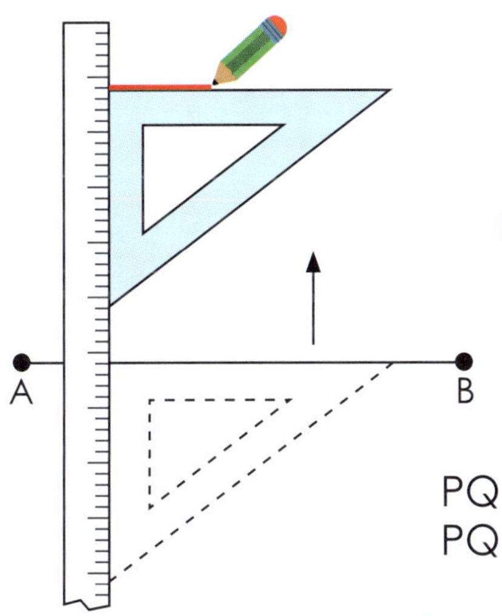

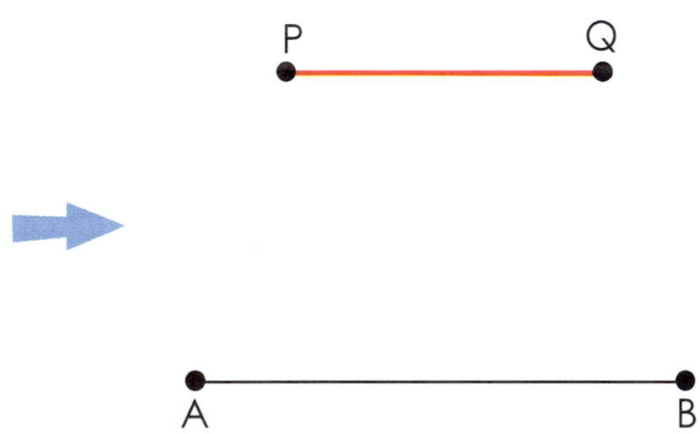

PQ and AB are parallel line segments.
PQ || AB

 ISBN 978-93-5103-031-7

b) Use a set square and a ruler to draw a line segment parallel to Line segment EF through Point P.

Maths Lab

Picture It

Step 1 Place a set square against Line segment EF. Then, place a ruler against the base of the set square.

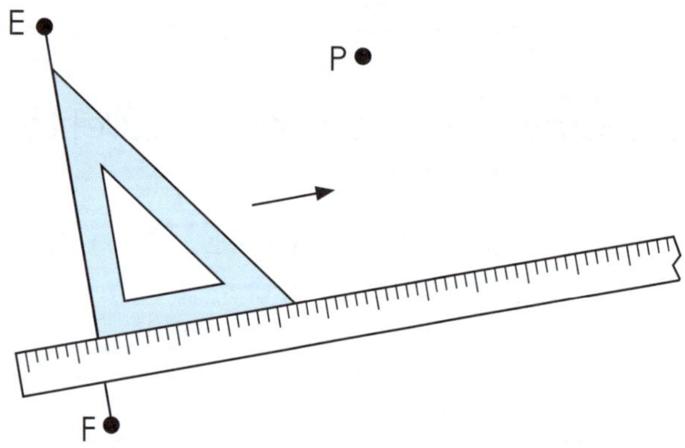

Step 2 Slide the set square along the ruler until it touches Point P. Then, draw Line segment PQ against the edge of the set square.

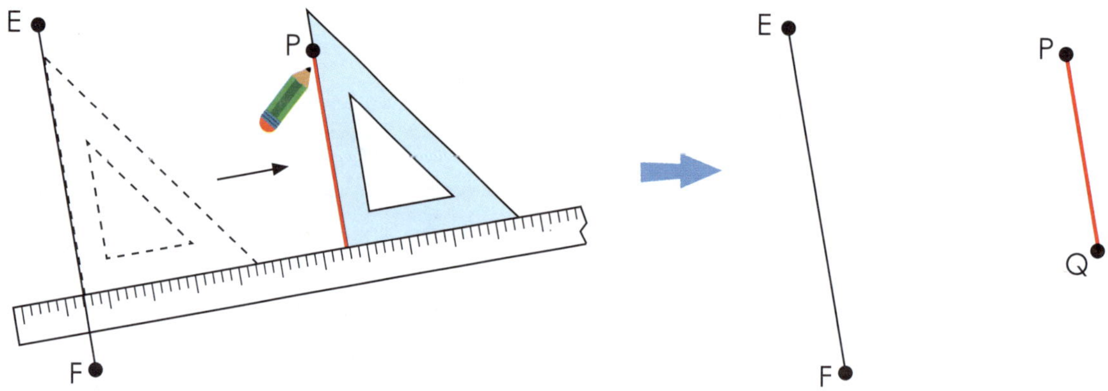

PQ and EF are parallel line segments.
PQ || EF

Let's Do

1. Use a set square and a ruler to draw a line segment parallel to

   a) the given line segment.

   b) the given line segment through Point D.

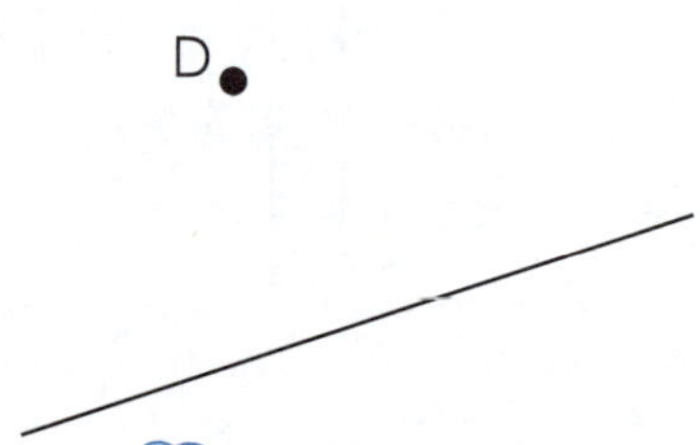

P/B Chapter 6: Exercise 2, page 101

  ISBN 978-93-5103-031-7

Think About It

Are the line segments parallel?

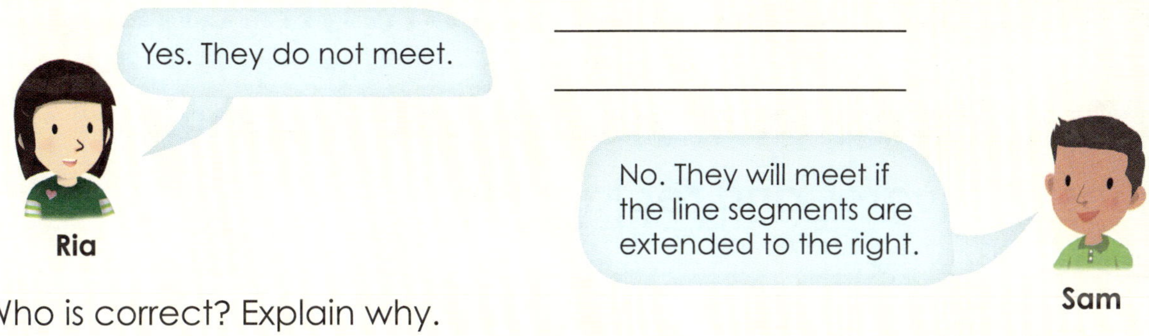

Who is correct? Explain why.

Practice 2

1. Using a set square and a ruler,

a) draw a line segment parallel to Line segment PQ.

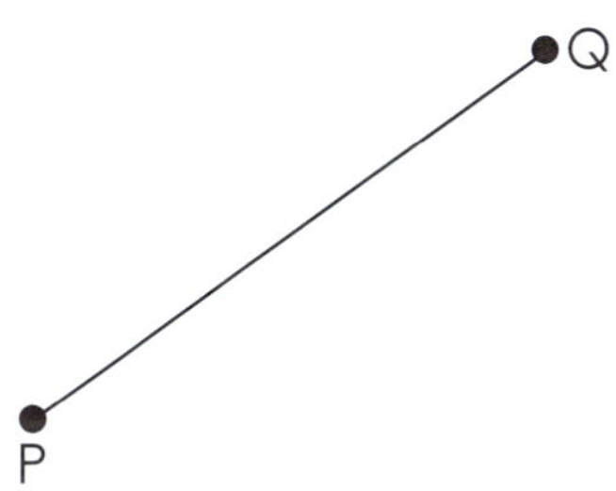

b) draw a line segment parallel to Line segment CD through Point P.

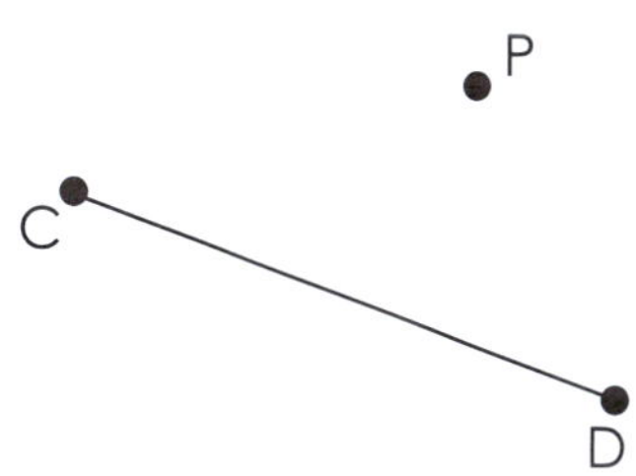

c) draw a line segment parallel to Line segment MN through Point A. Then, draw another line segment parallel to Line segment MN through Point B.

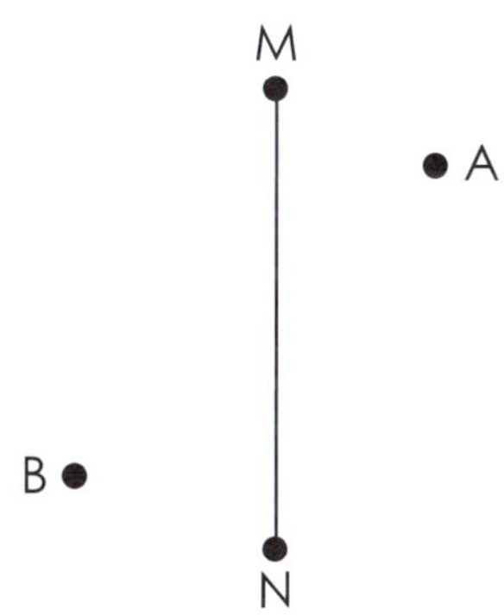

d) draw a pair of parallel line segments.

 ISBN 978-93-5103-031-7

7 Squares and Rectangles

Lesson 1 Properties of Squares and Rectangles

Properties of squares and rectangles

Let's Learn

a) Figure A is a square.

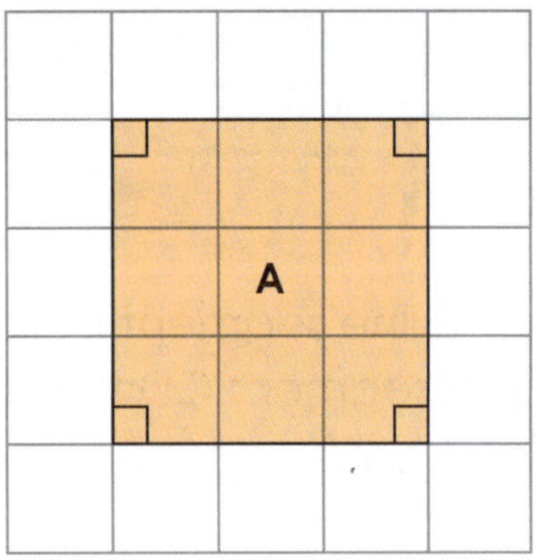

A square is a 4-sided figure.
It has 4 equal sides.
Its opposite sides are parallel.
It has 4 right angles.

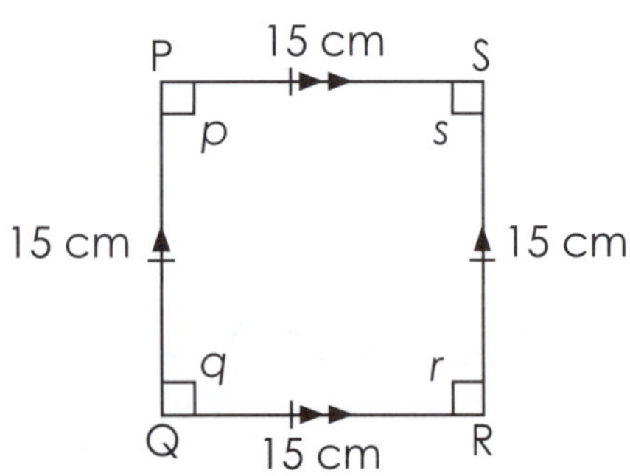

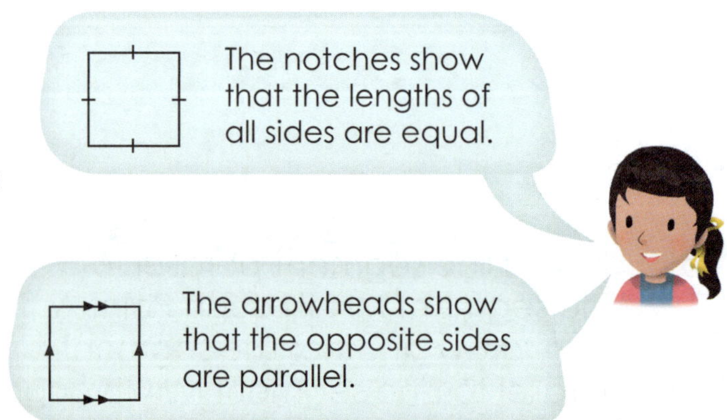

In Square PQRS, the length of each side is 15 centimetres.
PQ = QR = RS = SP

The square has 2 pairs of parallel sides.
PQ // SR and PS // QR

Measure of $\angle p$ = measure of $\angle q$ = measure of $\angle r$ = measure of $\angle s$ = 90°

 ISBN 978-93-5103-031-7

b) Figure B is a rectangle.

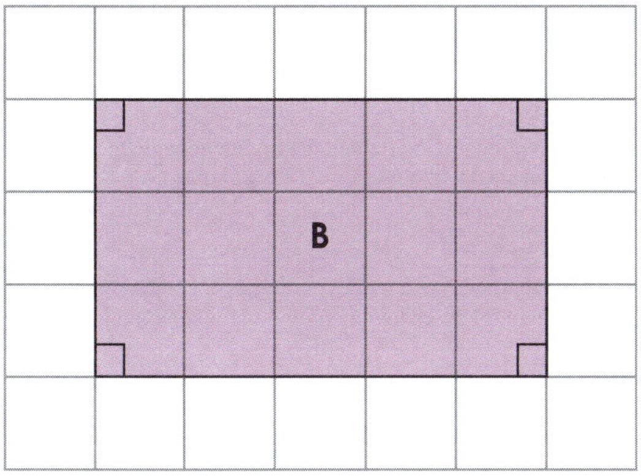

A rectangle is a 4-sided figure.
Its opposite sides are of equal length.
Its opposite sides are parallel.
It has 4 right angles.

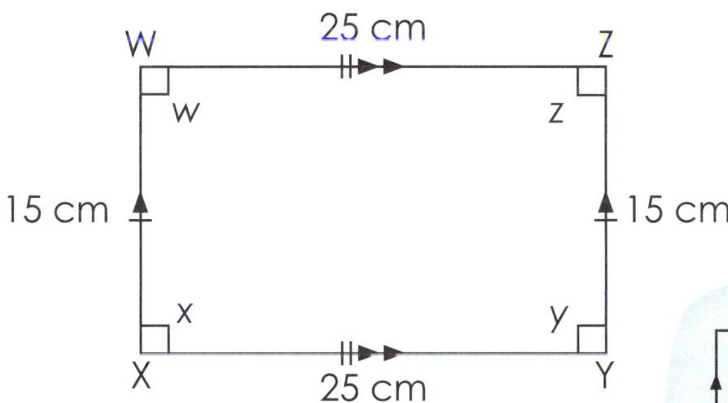

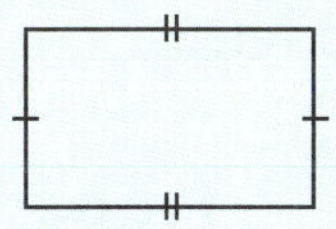

The notches show that the lengths of the opposite sides are equal.

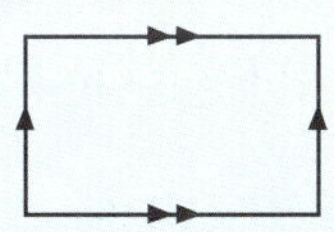

The arrowheads show that the opposite sides are parallel.

In Rectangle WXYZ, WZ and XY are 25 centimetres long and WX and ZY are 15 centimetres long.
WZ = XY and WX = ZY

The rectangle has 2 pairs of parallel sides.

WZ // ☐ and WX // ☐

Measure of $\angle w$ = measure of $\angle x$ = measure of $\angle y$ = measure of $\angle z$ = ☐

Think About It

Is a square a rectangle?

Ria

No. The length of a rectangle is always longer than its breadth. A square has 4 equal sides so it cannot be a rectangle.

Yes. The opposite sides of a square are of equal length and they are parallel. A square has 4 right angles. So, a square is a rectangle with 4 equal sides.

Sam

Who is correct? Explain why.

 ISBN 978-93-5103-031-7

Let's Do

1. Look at the shapes on the square grid.

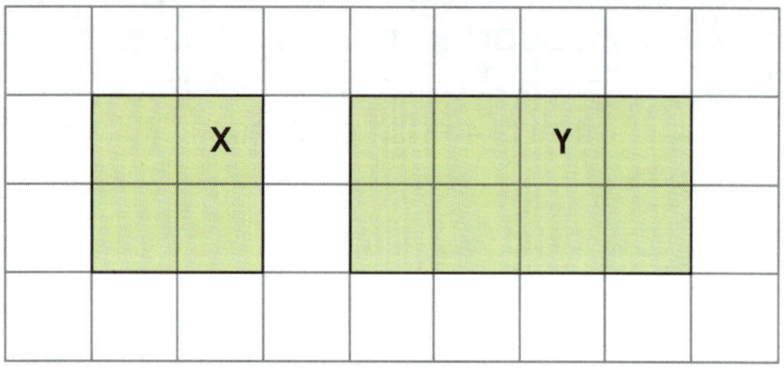

a) Complete the table.

Property	Shape X	Shape Y
It has 4 sides.	✓	✓
All sides are of equal length.		
Opposite sides are of equal length.		
All angles are right angles.		
Opposite sides are parallel.		

b) Use the table to identify the shapes.

Shape ______ is a square.

Shape ______ is a rectangle but not a square.

2. Write the lengths of the unknown sides.

a) ABCD is a rectangle.

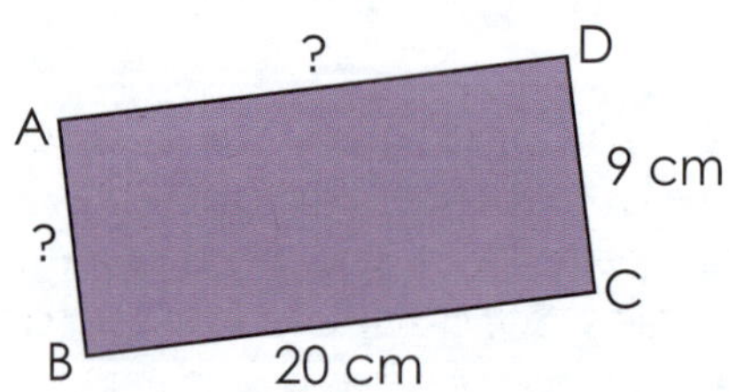

AD = ______ cm

AB = ______ cm

b) MNOP is a square.

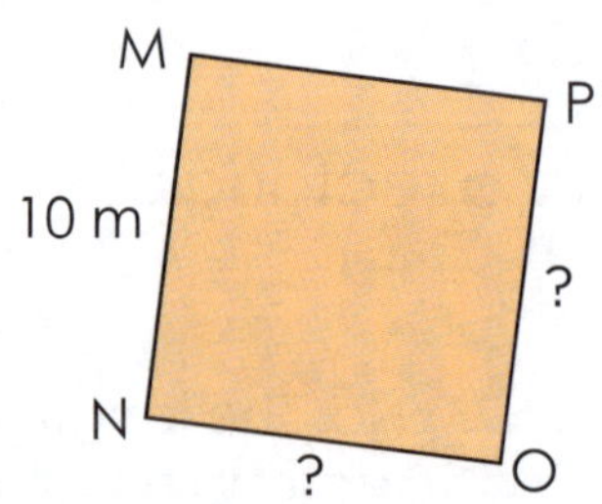

NO = ______ m

OP = ______ m

P/B Chapter 7: Exercise 1, pages 102–103

 ISBN 978-93-5103-031-7

Finding unknown angle measures

Let's Learn

Picture It a)

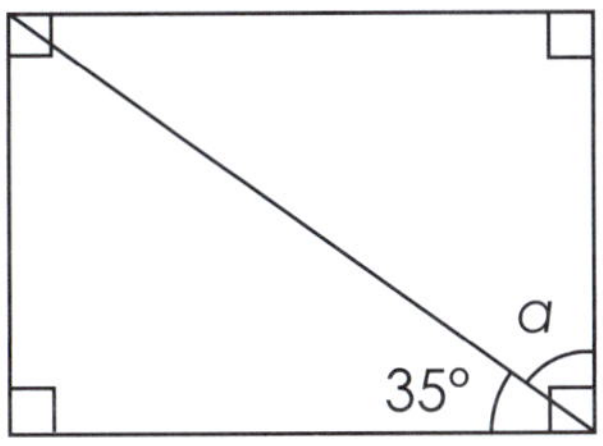

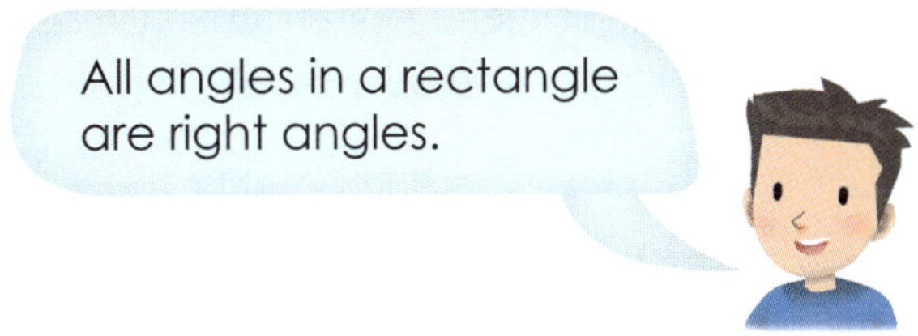

Measure of $\angle a = 90° - 35°$
$= 55°$

b)

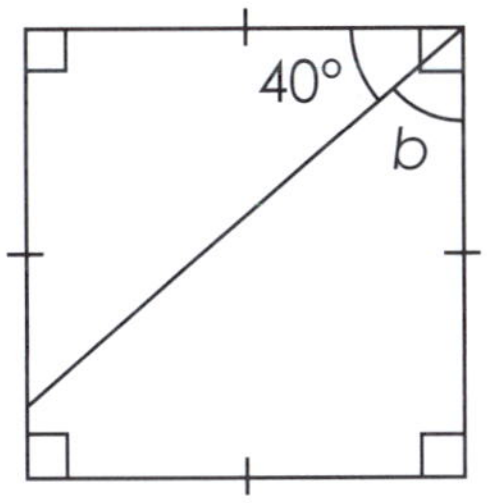

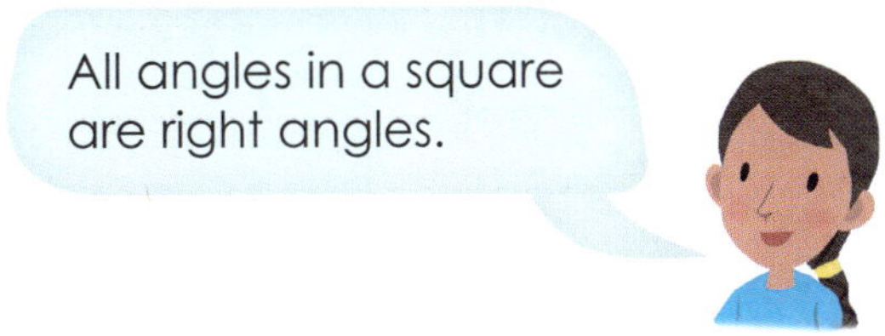

Measure of $\angle b = 90° -$ ☐
$=$ ☐

Let's Do

1. The figures are not drawn to scale. Find the measures of the unknown angles in the square and the rectangle.

a)

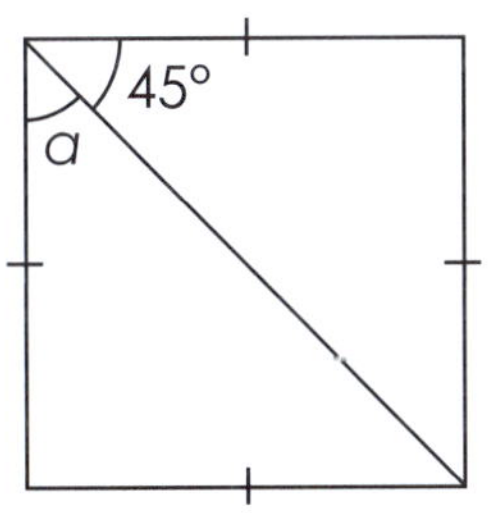

Measure of $\angle a$
= _______ – _______
= _______

b)

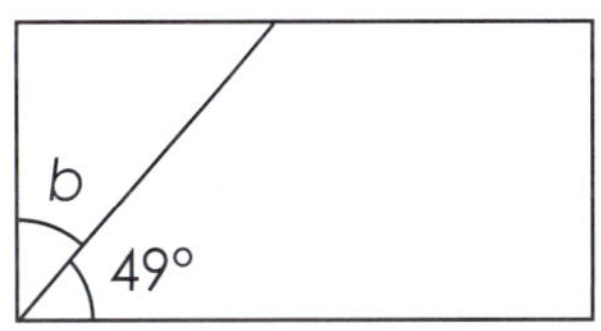

Measure of $\angle b$
= _______ – _______
= _______

P/B Chapter 7: Exercise 2, pages 104–105

 ISBN 978-93-5103-031-7

Finding unknown lengths

Let's Learn

a) Figure ABCDEF is made up of a square and a rectangle. What is the length of BC?

Picture It

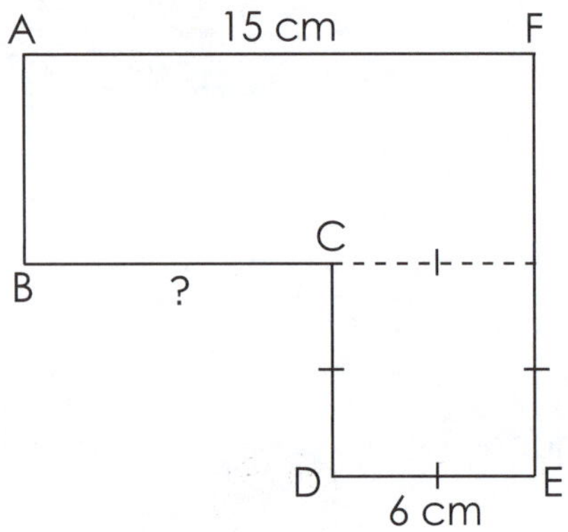

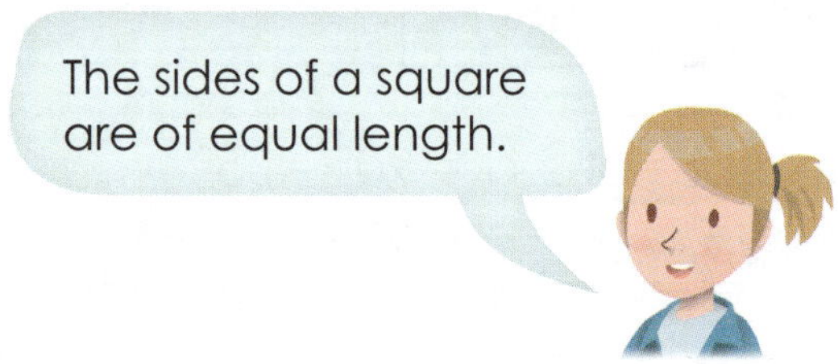

BC = 15 – 6
= 9 cm

The length of BC is 9 centimetres.

b) Figure PQRSTU is made up of two rectangles. What is the length of QR?

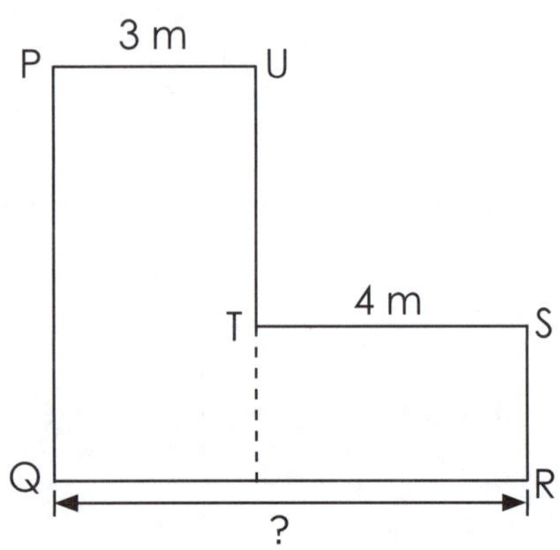

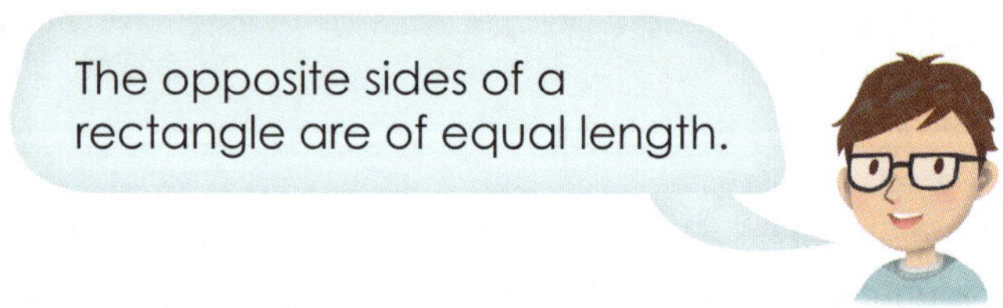

QR = 3 + ___
= ___ m

The length of QR is ___ metres.

 ISBN 978-93-5103-031-7

Let's Do

1. Figure ABCDEF is made up of a square and a rectangle.
   What is the length of AF?

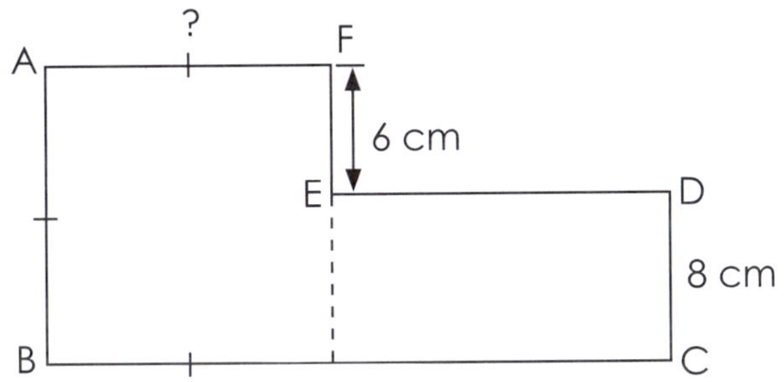

AB = ______ + ______

= ______ cm

AF = AB

= ______ cm

The length of AF is ______ centimetres.

P/B Chapter 7: Exercise 3, pages 106–107

Practice 1

The figures are not drawn to scale.

1. PQRS is a square.
   a) What is the measure of ∠a?
   b) What is the measure of ∠b?
   c) What is the length of QR?

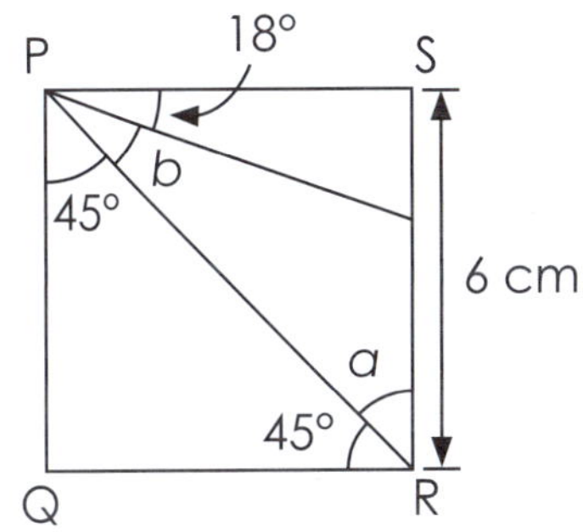

2. CDEF is a rectangle.
   a) What is the measure of ∠GEF?
   b) What is the measure of ∠CDG?
   c) What is the length of EF?

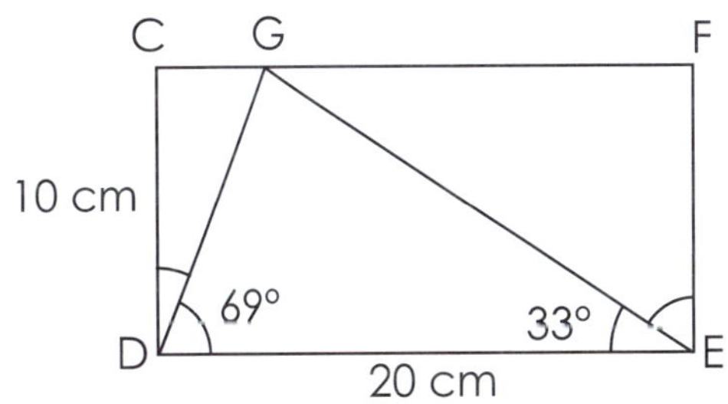

3. Figure KLMNOP is made up of a rectangle and a square.
   What are the lengths of NO and KL?

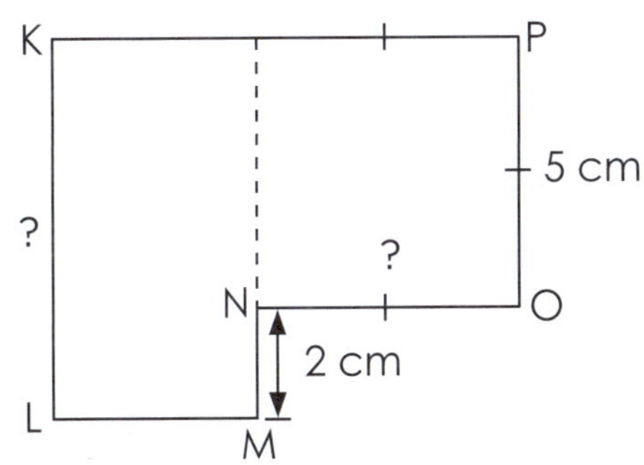

 ISBN 978-93-5103-031-7

Lesson 2 Drawing Four-sided Figures

Drawing rectangles

Let's Learn

Draw a rectangle ABCD in which AB = 5 centimetres and AD = 3 centimetres.

Maths Lab

Picture It

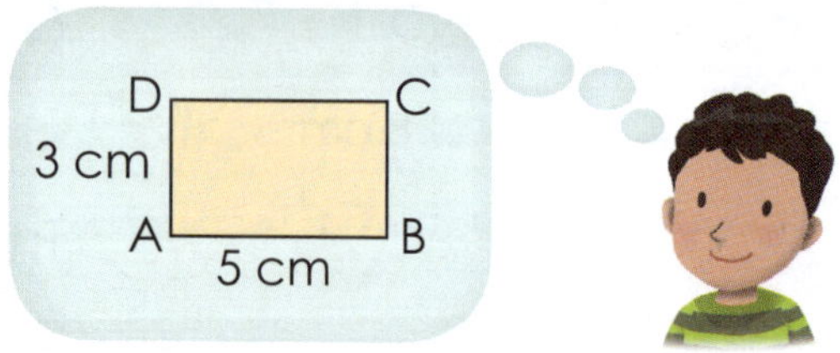

Step 1 Draw a line segment AB 5 centimetres long.

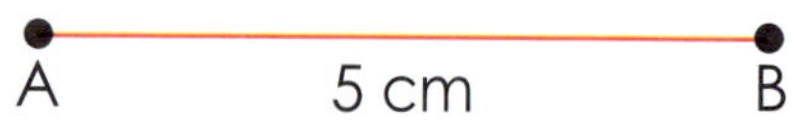

Step 2 Draw a line segment perpendicular to Line segment AB through Point A.

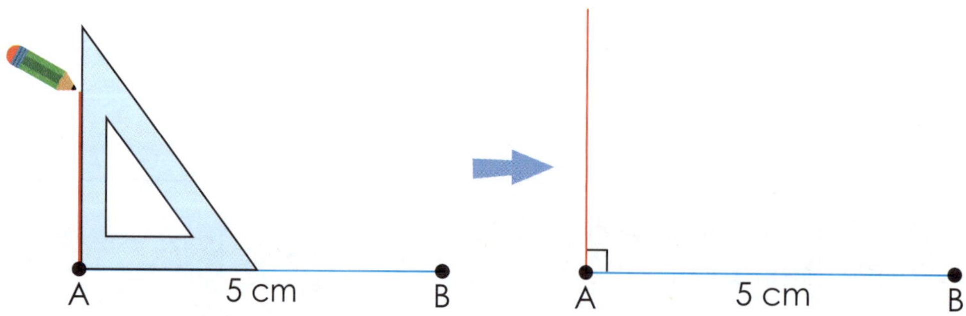

Step 3 Draw a line segment perpendicular to Line segment AB through Point B.

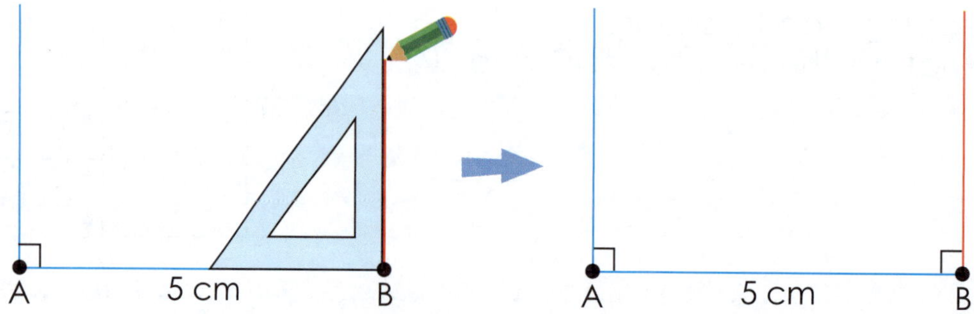

ISBN 978-93-5103-031-7

Step 4 Mark points C and D such that AD = 3 centimetres and BC = 3 centimetres. Then, join points C and D.

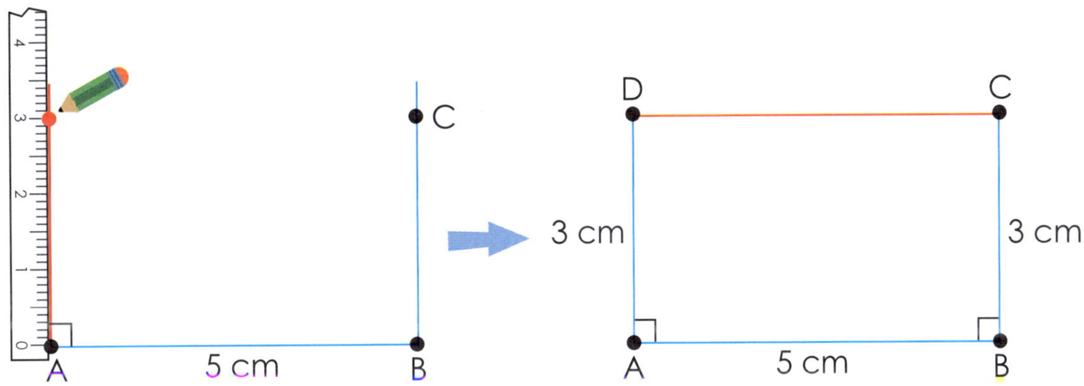

Let's Do

1. Draw a rectangle ABCD in which AB = 6 centimetres and BC = 5 centimetres.

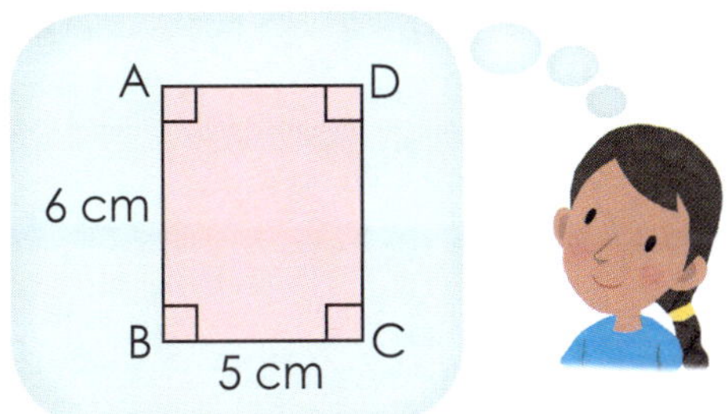

2. Draw a square CDEF of side 4 centimetres.

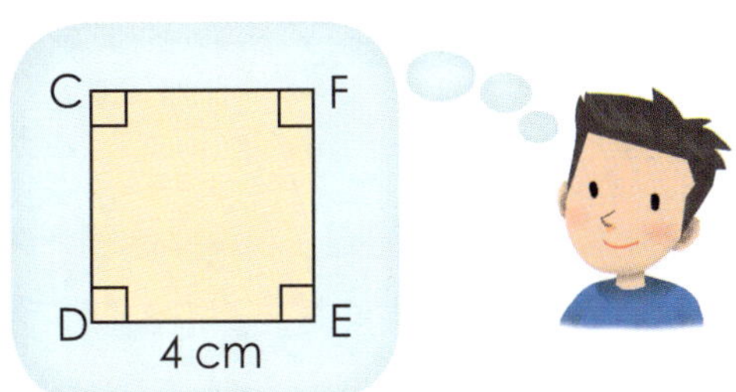

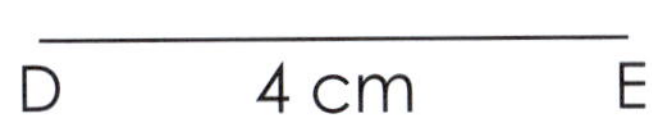

Chapter 7: Exercise 4, page 108

 ISBN 978-93-5103-031-7

Practice 2

1. Draw each figure with the given measurements.

a) ABCD is a rectangle.

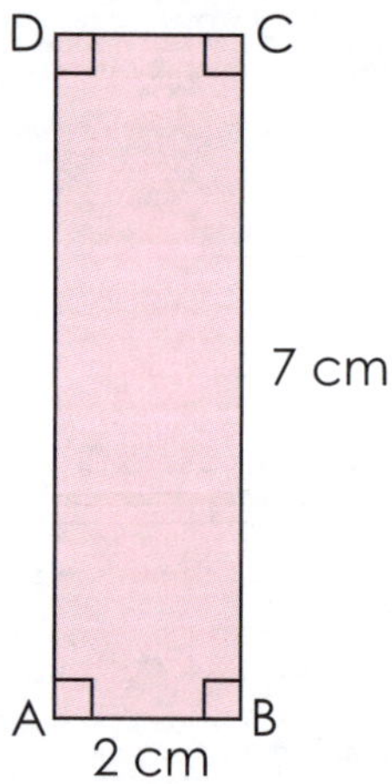

b) PQRS is a square.

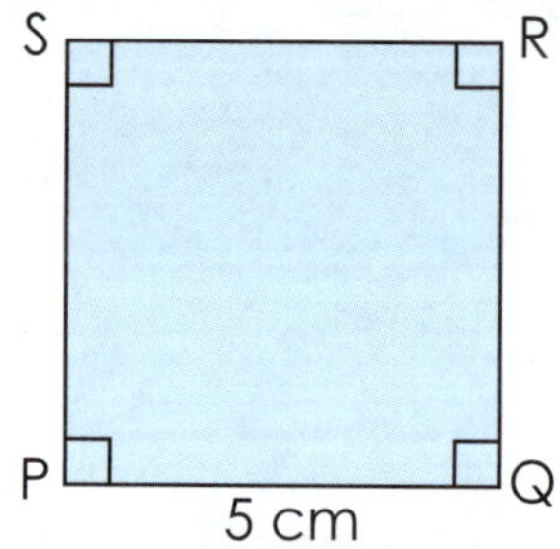

 ISBN 978-93-5103-031-7

8 Area and Perimeter

Lesson 1 Perimeter

Measuring perimeter

Let's Learn

a) Sue made these shapes on a geoboard.

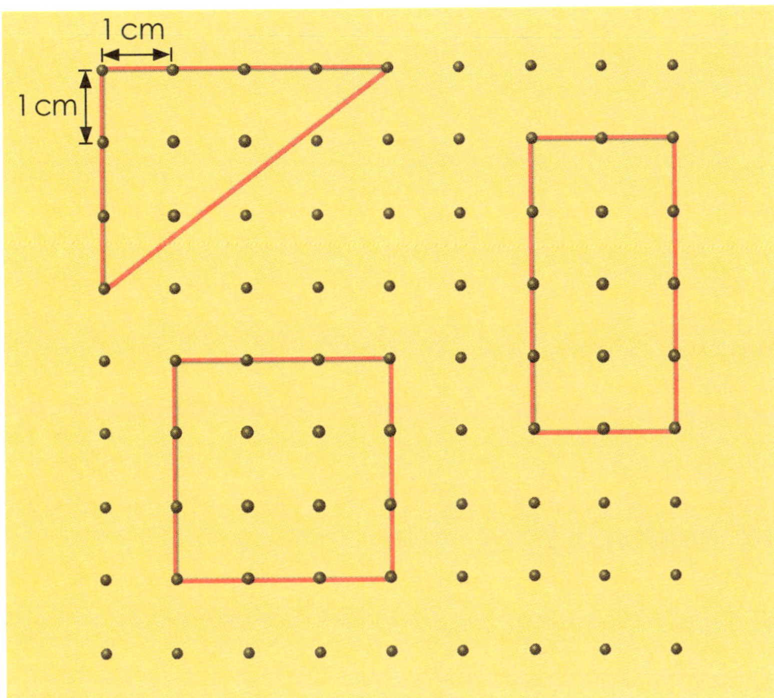

She used three strings to make these shapes.
Each string is 12 centimetres long.

The shapes are different, but they have the same **perimeter**.
The perimeter of a figure is the distance around the figure.
The perimeter of each shape is 12 centimetres.

b) Use a string and a ruler to measure the perimeter of each of these figures.

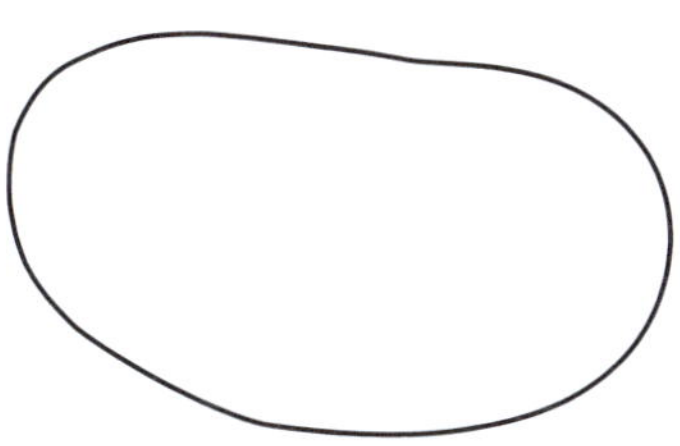

X

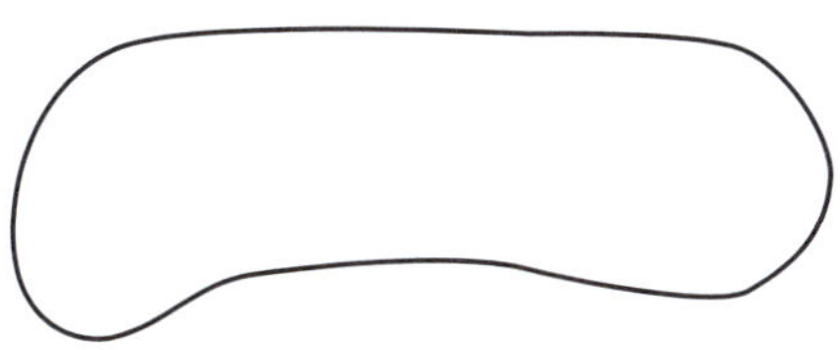

Y

Which figure has a longer perimeter?

 ISBN 978-93-5103-031-7

Let's Do

1. Fill in the blanks.

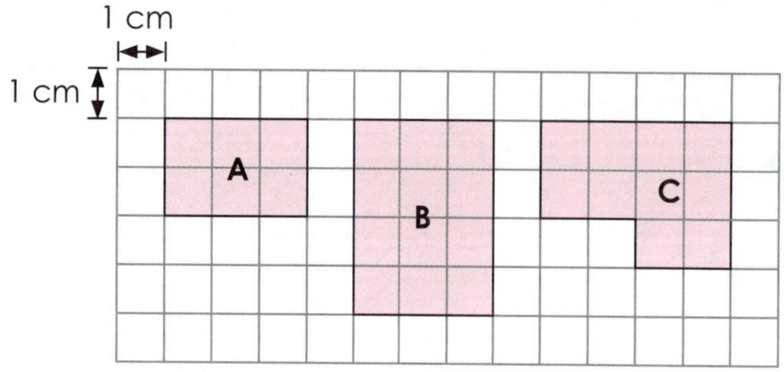

a) The perimeter of Figure A is ______ centimetres.

b) The perimeter of Figure B is ______ centimetres.

c) The perimeter of Figure C is ______ centimetres.

d) Figure ______ and Figure ______ have the same perimeter.

2. a) Measure the perimeter of your Mathematics coursebook in centimetres.

b) Measure the perimeter of your classroom in metres.

Comparing areas and perimeters

Let's Learn

a) These figures are made up of the same number of 1-centimetre squares.

Picture It

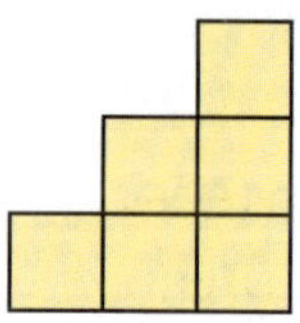

A

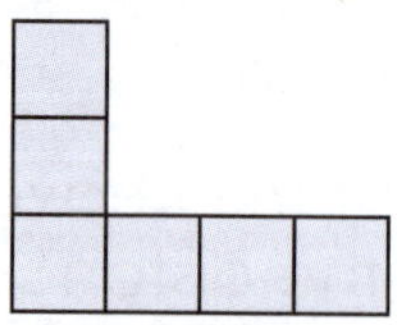

B

They have the same area.

The area of each figure is ☐ square centimetres.

They have different perimeters.

The perimeter of Figure A is ☐ centimetres.

The perimeter of Figure B is ☐ centimetres.

 ISBN 978-93-5103-031-7

b) These figures are made up of 1-metre squares.

C D E

They have different areas.

The area of Figure C is ___ square metres.

The area of Figure D is ___ square metres.

The area of Figure E is ___ square metres.

They have the same perimeter.

The perimeter of each figure is ___ metres.

Let's Do

1. These figures are made up of 1-centimetre squares.

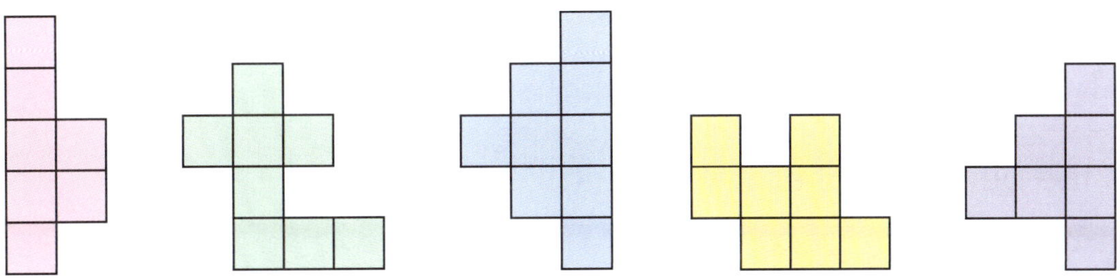

P Q R S T

a) Find the area and perimeter of each figure.

Figure	Area (cm^2)	Perimeter (cm)
P		
Q		
R		
S		
T		

Compare the areas and perimeters of the figures.

b) Figure ______ and Figure ______ have the same area but different perimeters.

c) Figure ______ and Figure ______ have the same perimeter but different areas.

d) Figure ______ and Figure ______ have the same area and perimeter.

P/B Chapter 8: Exercise 1, pages 109–110

 ISBN 978-93-5103-031-7

Finding perimeter of a figure

Let's Learn

Find the perimeter of each figure.

Picture It a)

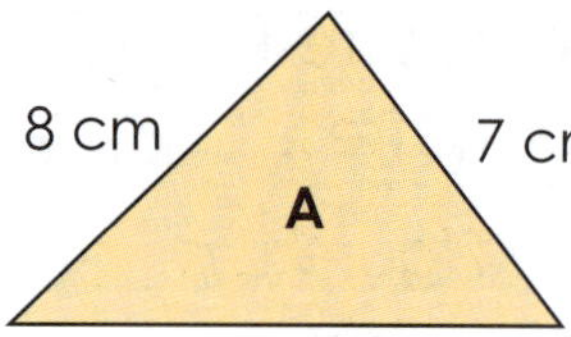

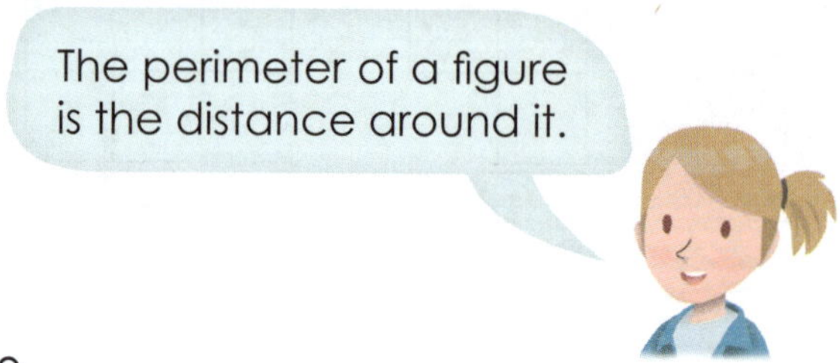

Perimeter of Figure A = 8 + 7 + 10
= 25 cm

b)

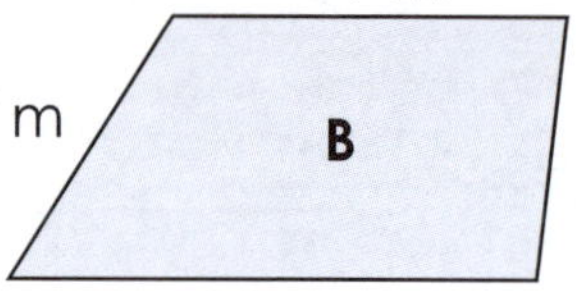

Perimeter of Figure B
= ____ + ____ + ____ + ____
= ____ m

Let's Do

1. Find the perimeter of each figure.

a)

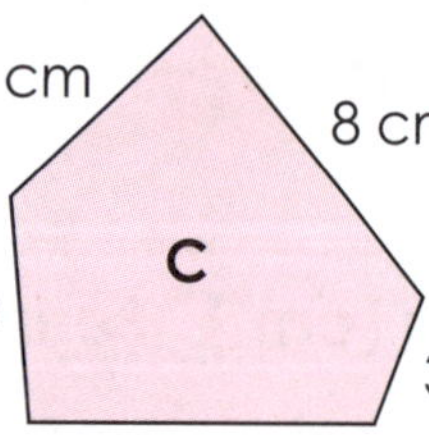

Perimeter
= ____ + ____ + ____ + ____ + ____
= ____ cm

b)

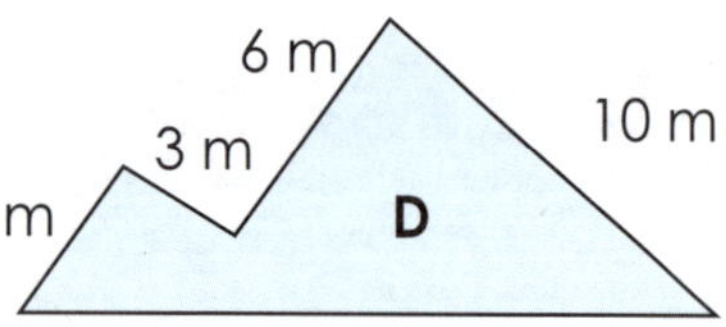

Perimeter
= ____ + ____ + ____ + ____ + ____
= ____ m

P/B Chapter 8: Exercise 2, page 111

Finding perimeter of squares and rectangles

Let's Learn

Picture It a) Each side of the square is 6 centimetres. Find its perimeter.

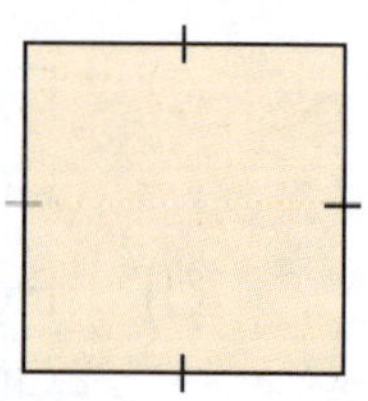

Method 1

Perimeter of square = 6 + 6 + 6 + 6
= ____ cm

 ISBN 978-93-5103-031-7

Method 2

Perimeter of square = 4 × Length of side
= 4 × ____ cm
= ____ cm

A square has 4 equal sides.

Perimeter of square = 4 × Length of side

b) The length of the rectangle is 12 centimetres. Its breadth is 4 centimetres. Find its perimeter.

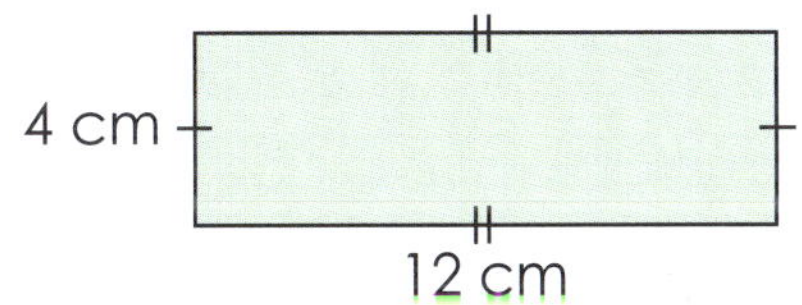

Method 1

Perimeter of rectangle
= Length + Breadth + Length + Breadth
= 12 + 4 + 12 + 4
= ____ cm

The opposite sides of a rectangle are equal.

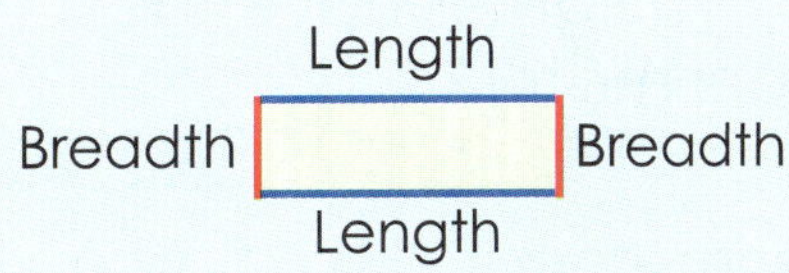

Method 2

Perimeter of rectangle
= 2 × Length + 2 × Breadth
= 2 × 12 cm + 2 × 4 cm
= 24 + 8
= ____ cm

Perimeter of rectangle = 2 × Length + 2 × Breadth

Let's Do

1. Each side of a square is 8 centimetres. Find its perimeter.

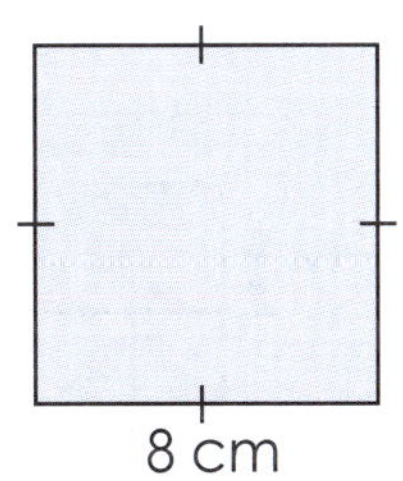

Method 1

Perimeter = ______ + ______ + ______ + ______
= ______ cm

Method 2

Perimeter = ______ × ______ cm
= ______ cm

 ISBN 978-93-5103-031-7

2. The length of a rectangle is 10 centimetres. Its breadth is 3 centimetres. Find its perimeter.

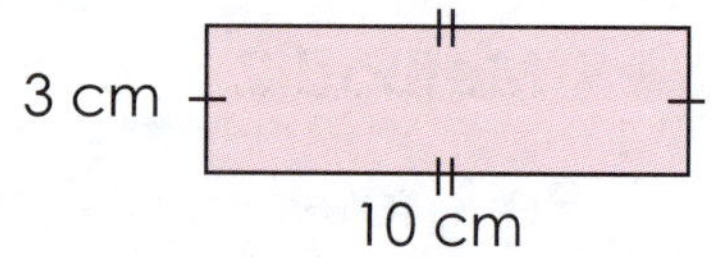

Method 1

Perimeter = ____ + ____

+ ____ + ____

= ____ cm

Method 2

Perimeter = 2 × ____ cm + 2 × ____ cm

= ____ cm + ____ cm

= ____ cm

P/B Chapter 8: Exercise 3, page 112

Practice 1

1. These figures are made up of 1-centimetre squares.
   a) Which two figures have the same area?
   b) Which two figures have the same perimeter?

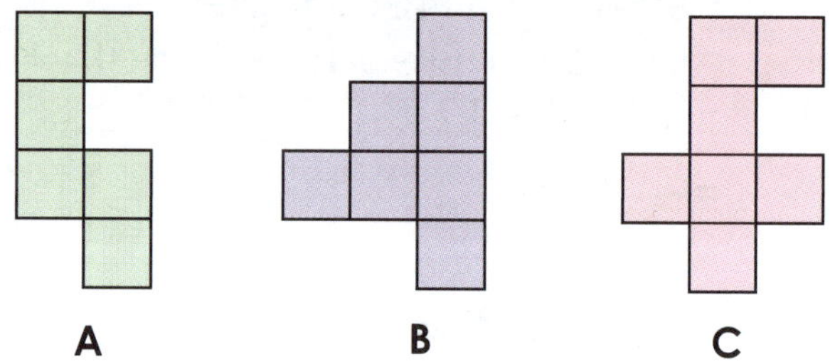

2. Find the perimeter of each figure.

a)

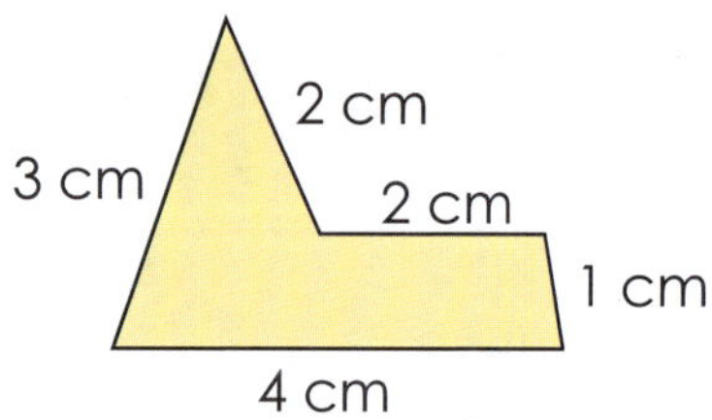

b)

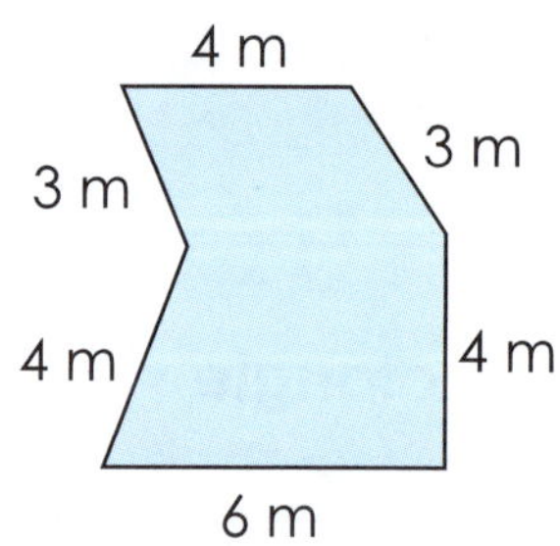

3. Find the perimeter of each rectangle.

a)

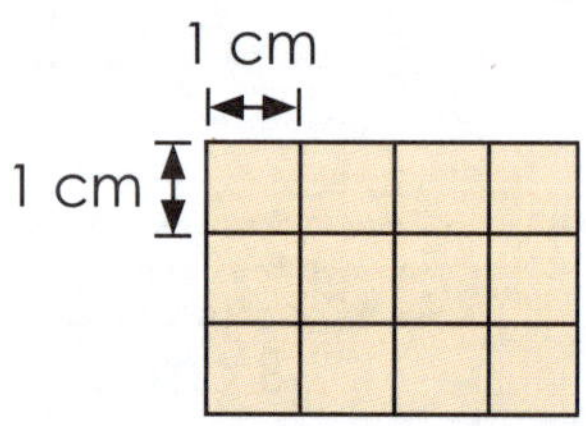

b)

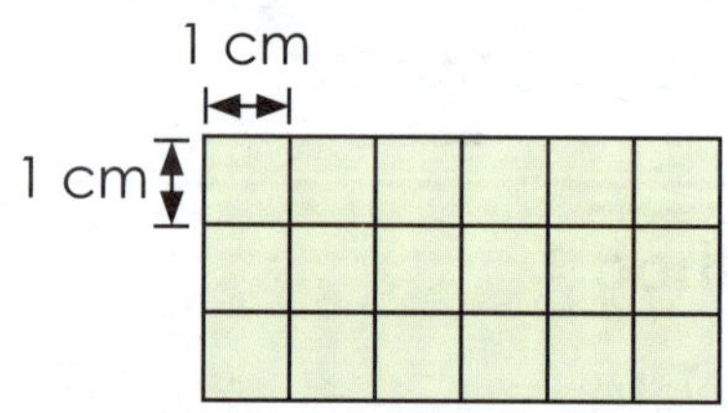

c)

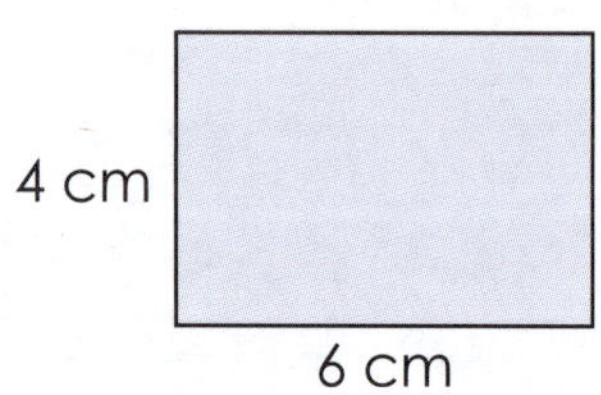

d)

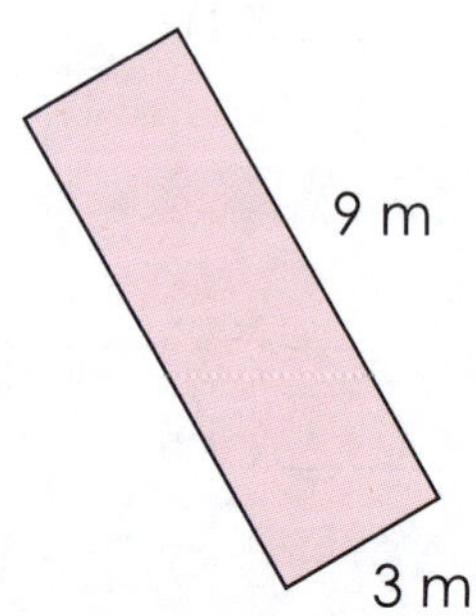

 ISBN 978-93-5103-031-7

Lesson 2 Area of a Rectangle

Finding area of a rectangle

Let's Learn

Picture It

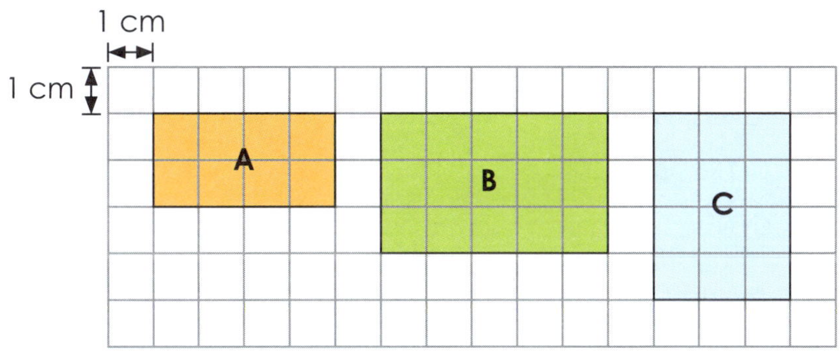

Rectangle	Length	Breadth	Number of squares	Area
A	4 cm	2 cm	8	8 cm^2
B	___ cm	___ cm	15	___ cm^2
C	___ cm	___ cm	12	___ cm^2

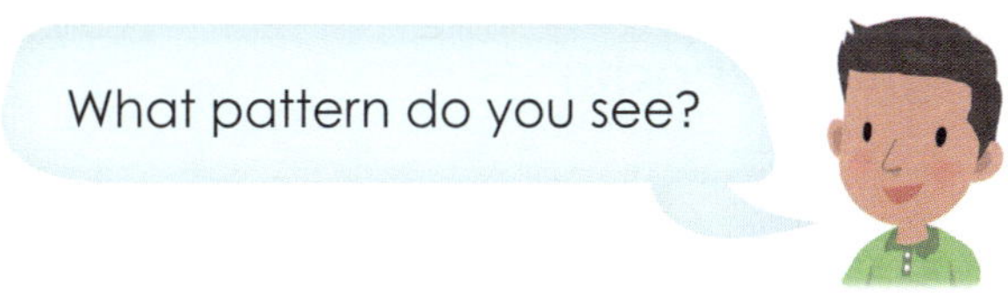

a)

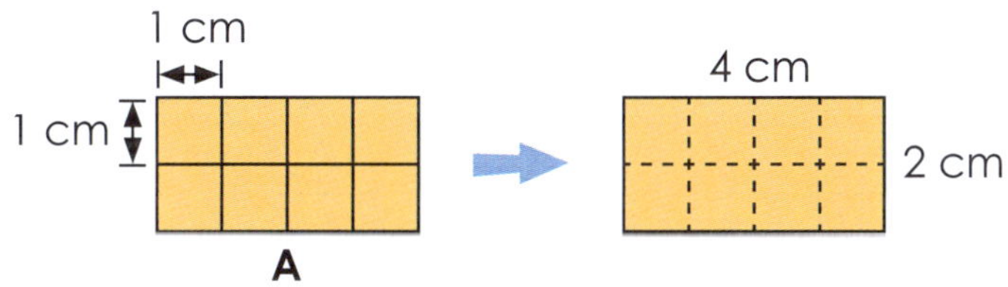

There are 2 rows of 1-centimetre squares in Rectangle A.
There are 4 squares in each row.

Area of Rectangle A = 4 cm × 2 cm
= 8 cm^2

 ISBN 978-93-5103-031-7

b)

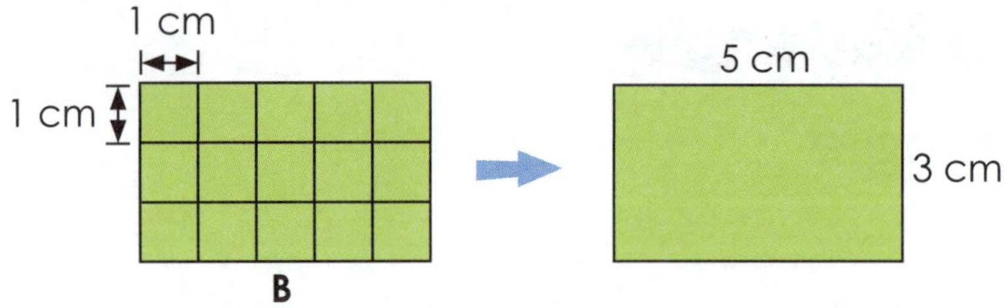

There are ___ rows of 1-centimetre squares in Rectangle B.

There are ___ squares in each row.

Area of Rectangle B = ___ cm × ___ cm

= ___ cm^2

c)

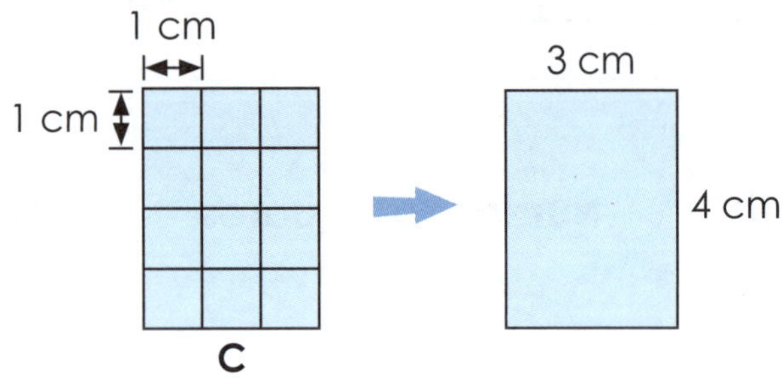

Area of Rectangle C = ___ cm × ___ cm

= ___ cm^2

Area of rectangle = Length × Breadth

Let's Do

1. Find the area of each rectangle.

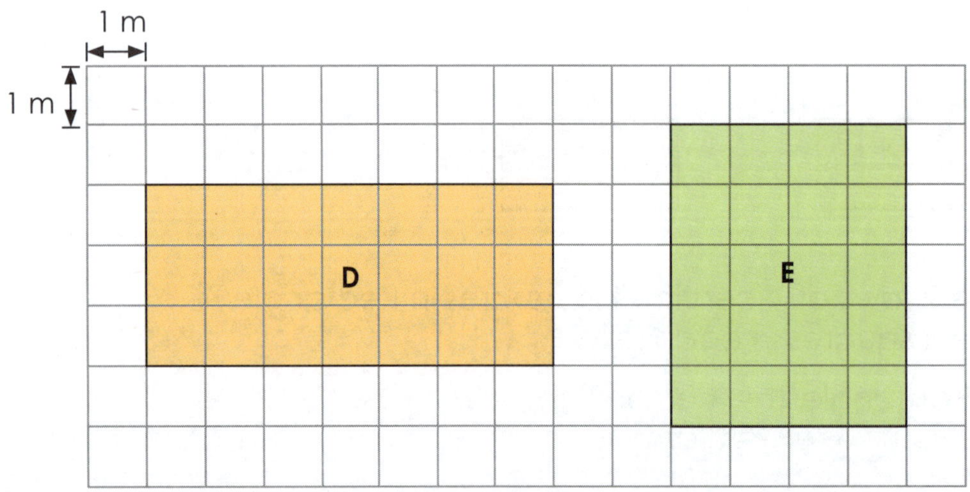

a) Area of Rectangle D

= ______ m × ______ m

= ______ m^2

b) Area of Rectangle E

= ______ m × ______ m

= ______ m^2

 ISBN 978-93-5103-031-7

Finding area of a square

Let's Learn

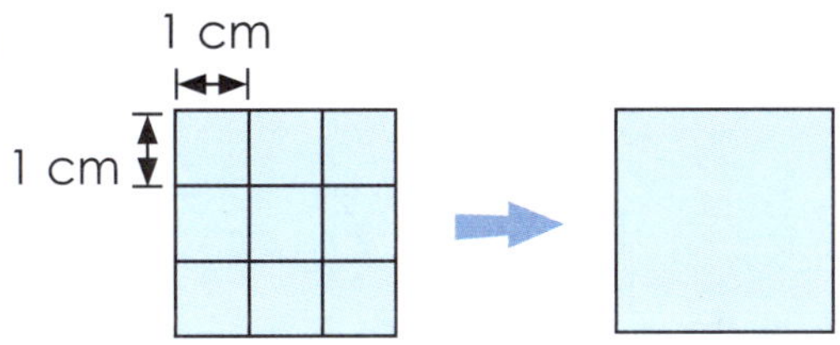

A square is a rectangle with 4 equal sides.
Area of rectangle = Length × Breadth
Area of square = Length × Length

Area of square = 3 cm × 3 cm
= ____ cm^2

Area of square = Length of side × Length of side

Let's Do

1. Find the area of a square of side 4 centimetres.

   Area of square = ______ cm × ______ cm
   = ______ cm^2

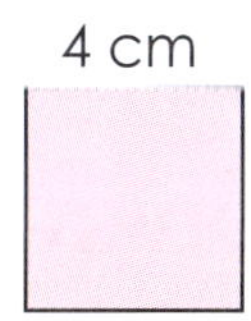

Chapter 8: Exercise 4, pages 113–116

Practice 2

1. Find the area of each square or rectangle.

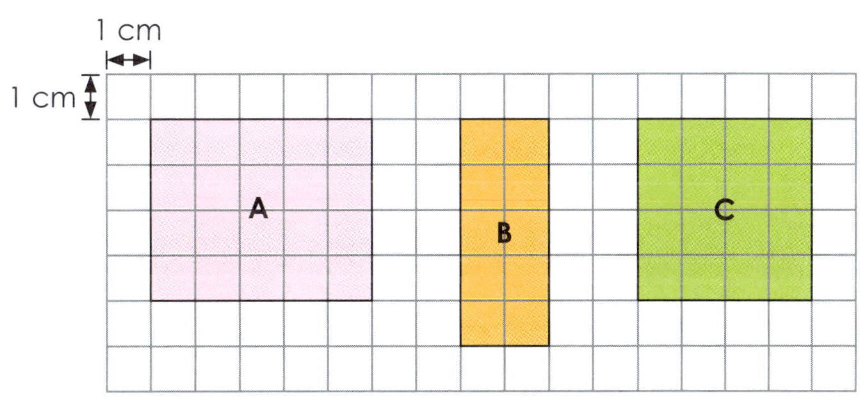

 ISBN 978-93-5103-031-7

2. Find the area of each square or rectangle.

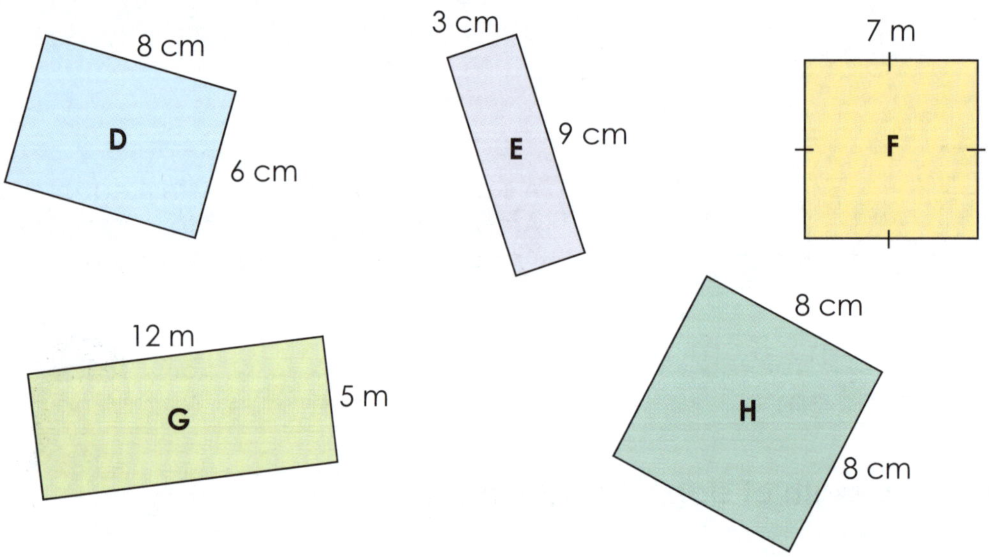

Lesson 3 Squares and Rectangles

Finding unknown side of a rectangle given its perimeter and a side

Let's Learn

The perimeter of a rectangle is 24 metres. Its length is 8 metres.
Find its breadth.

Picture It

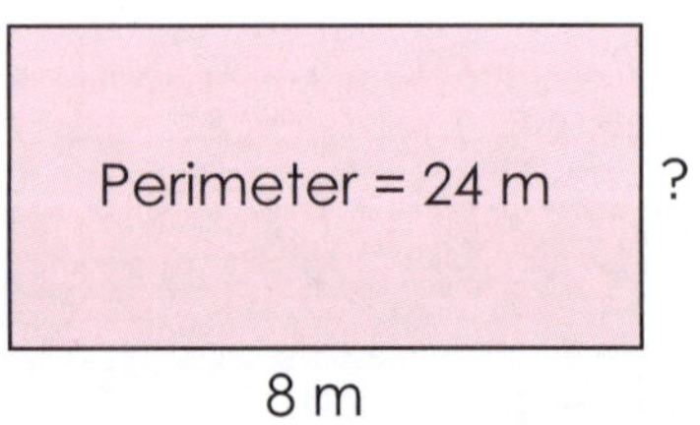

Perimeter = 24 m
Length + Breadth = 24 m ÷ 2
= 12 m

Length = 8 m
Breadth = 12 – 8
= 4 m

Its breadth is 4 metres.

Perimeter of rectangle
= Length + Breadth + Length + Breadth

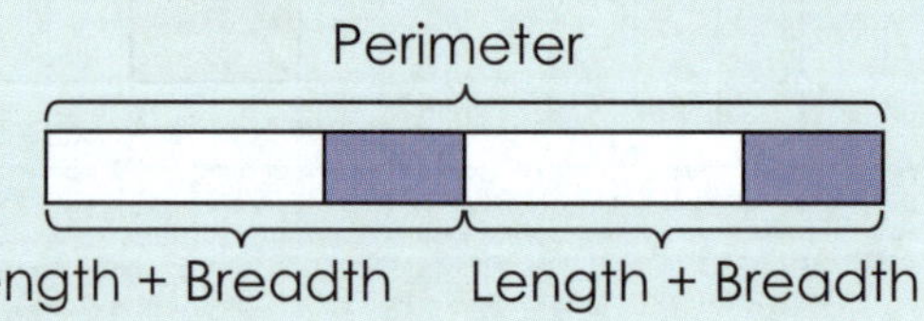

Perimeter ÷ 2 = Length + Breadth

 ISBN 978-93-5103-031-7

Let's Do

1. The perimeter of a rectangle is 38 centimetres. Its breadth is 6 centimetres.

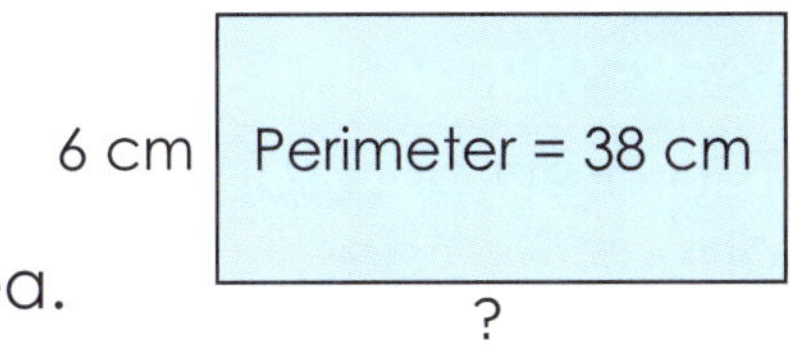

a) Find its length.

Length + Breadth

= ______ cm ◯ ______

= ______ cm

Length = ______ ◯ ______

= ______ cm

b) Find its area.

Area = ______ cm ◯ ______ cm

= ______ cm^2

Finding length of a side of a square given its perimeter

Let's Learn

The perimeter of a square is 20 metres. Find the length of one of its sides.

Picture It

Length of one side = 20 m ÷ 4

= ▭ m

The length of one of its sides is ▭ metres.

Perimeter of square
= 4 × Length of side
Perimeter ÷ 4 = Length of side

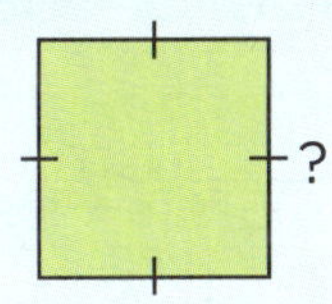

Let's Do

1. The perimeter of a square is 36 centimetres.

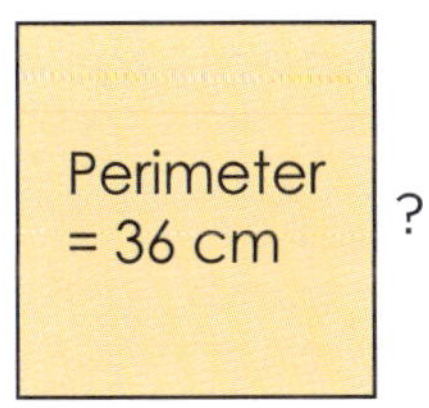

a) Find the length of one of its sides.

Length of one side = ______ cm ◯ ______

= ______ cm

b) Find the area of the square.

Area = ______ cm ◯ ______ cm

= ______ cm^2

P/B Chapter 8: Exercise 5, pages 117–118

 ISBN 978-93-5103-031-7

Finding length of a side of a square given its area

Let's Learn

The area of a square is 36 square centimetres. Find the length of one of its sides.

Picture It

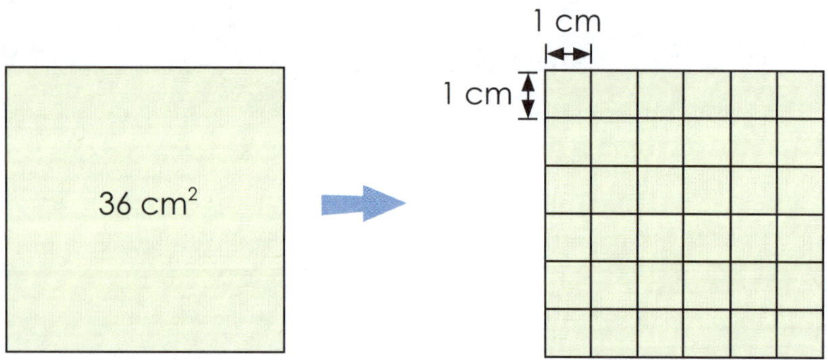

Area of square = Length × Length

$36\ cm^2 = 6\ cm \times 6\ cm$

Length of one side = ____ cm

The length of one of its sides is ____ centimetres.

Let's Do

1. The area of a square is 81 square centimetres.

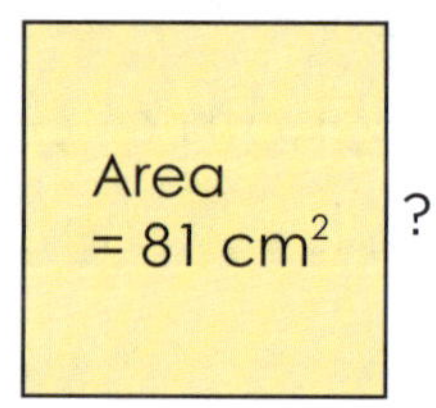

a) Find the length of one of its sides.

$81\ cm^2$ = ______ cm ◯ ______ cm

Length of one side = ______ cm

b) Find the perimeter of the square.

Perimeter = ______ ◯ ______ cm

= ______ cm

 ISBN 978-93-5103-031-7

Finding unknown side of a rectangle given its area and a side

Let's Learn

The area of a rectangle is 40 square centimetres. The length of the rectangle is 8 centimetres. Find its breadth.

Picture It

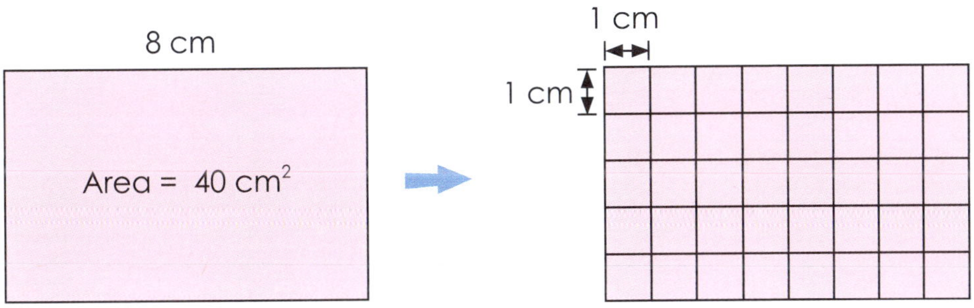

Area of rectangle = Length × Breadth

$40\ \text{cm}^2 = 8\ \text{cm} \times \text{Breadth}$

Breadth = (40 ÷ 8) cm

= ___ cm

Its breadth is ___ centimetres.

Let's Do

1. The area of a rectangle is 84 square centimetres. The breadth of the rectangle is 7 centimetres.

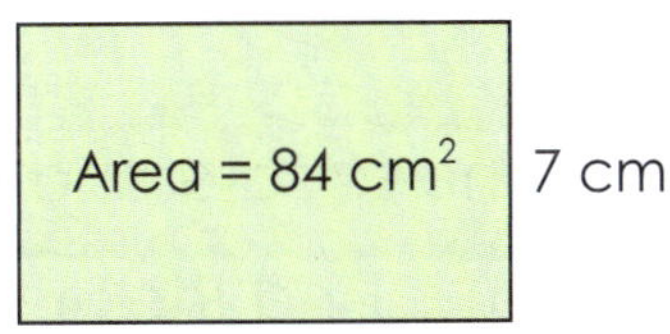

a) Find its length.

$84\ \text{cm}^2$ = ______ ◯ ______ cm

Length of rectangle = (______ ◯ ______) cm

= ______ cm

b) Find its perimeter.

Perimeter = ______ + ______ + ______ + ______

= ______ cm

P/B Chapter 8: Exercise 6, pages 119–120

ISBN 978-93-5103-031-7

Practice 3

1. Find the unknown side and the area of each square or rectangle.

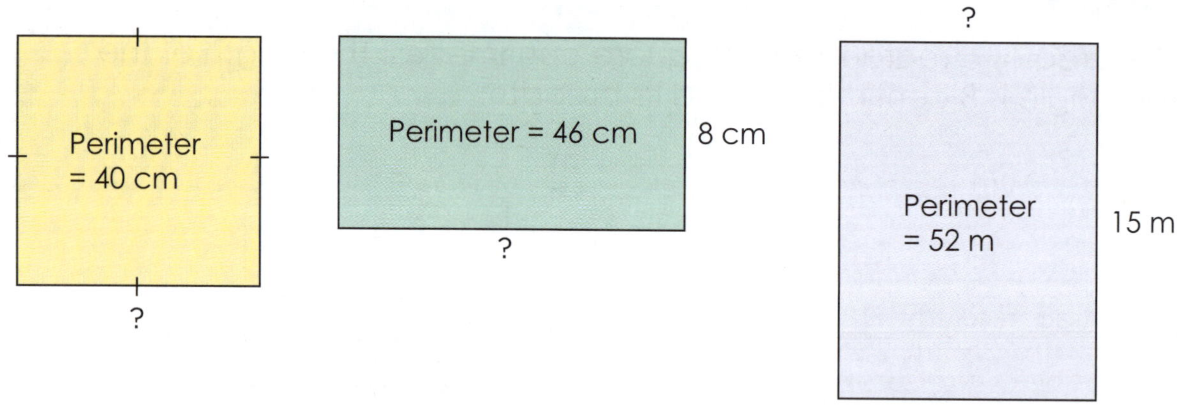

2. Find the unknown side and the perimeter of each square or rectangle.

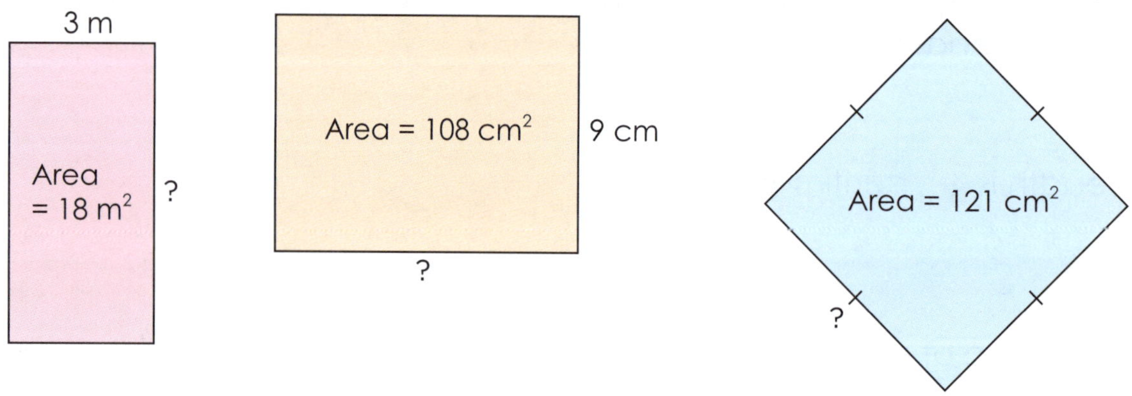

3. The square and the rectangle have the same perimeter.
   a) Find the length of the rectangle.
   b) Which has a bigger area, the square or the rectangle?

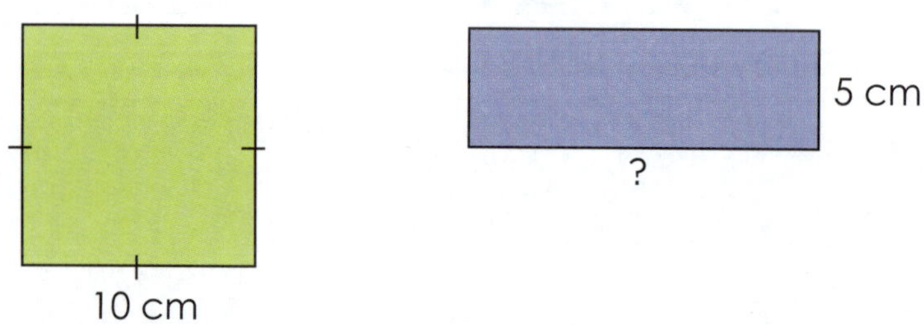

 ISBN 978-93-5103-031-7

Lesson 4 Composite Figures

Finding area and perimeter of composite figures on square grid

Let's Learn

Each figure is made up of two rectangles. Find the area and perimeter of each figure.

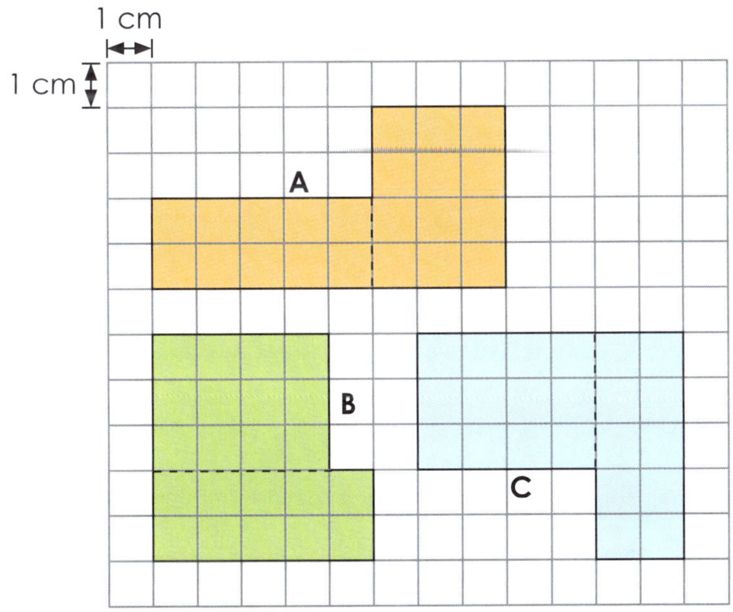

Figure	Area	Perimeter
A	$10 + 12 = 22$ cm^2	24 cm
B	$12 + 10 = 22$ cm^2	20 cm
C	___ + ___ = ___ cm^2	___ cm

Let's Do

1. Each figure is made up of two rectangles. Find the area and perimeter of each figure.

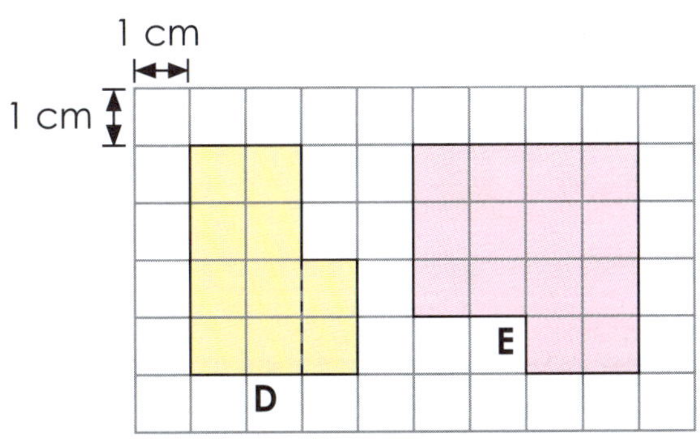

a) Figure D

Area = 8 + ____ = ____ cm^2

Perimeter = ____ cm

b) Figure E

Area = ____ + ____ = ____ cm^2

Perimeter = ____ cm

 ISBN 978-93-5103-031-7

Finding perimeter of composite figures

Let's Learn

a) Find the perimeter of the figure.

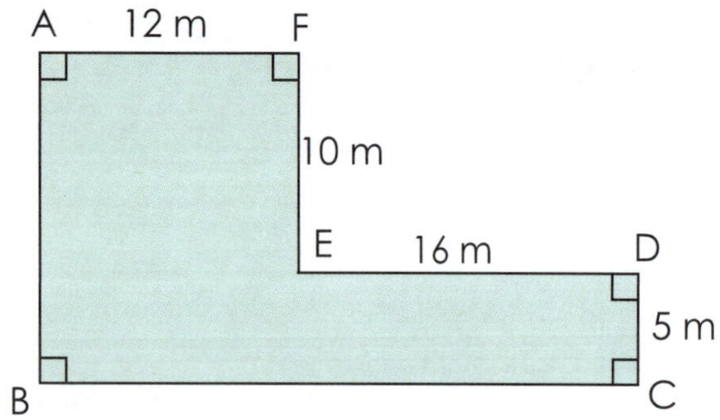

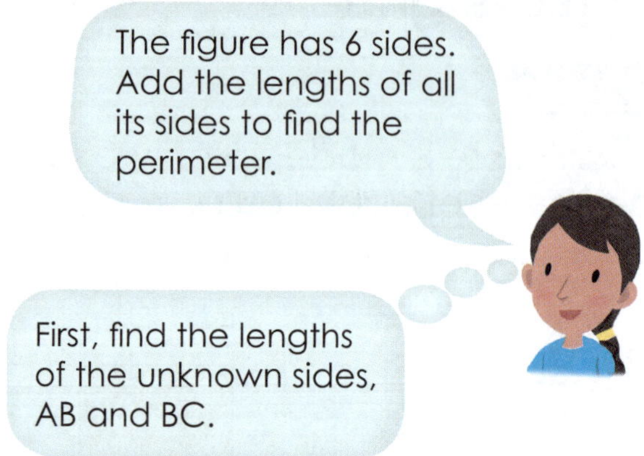

AB = 10 + 5 = 15 m
BC = 12 + 16 = 28 m

Perimeter = AB + BC + CD + DE + EF + FA
= 15 + 28 + 5 + 16 + 10 + 12
= ____ m

The perimeter of the figure is ____ metres.

b) Find the perimeter of the figure.

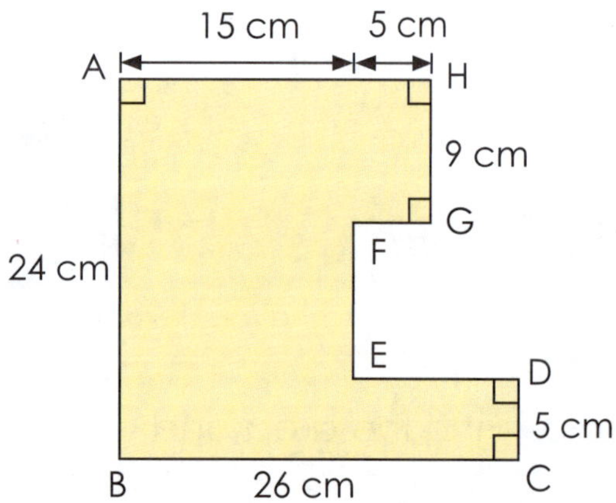

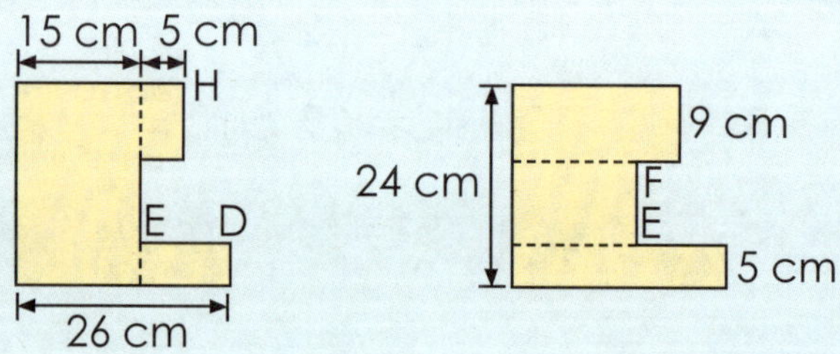

DE = 26 – 15 = ____ cm
HA = 15 + ____ = ____ cm
EF = 24 – 5 – 9 = ____ cm

Perimeter = AB + BC + CD + DE + EF + FG + GH + HA
= 24 + 26 + 5 + ____ + ____ + 5 + 9 + ____
= ____ cm

The perimeter of the figure is ____ centimetres.

 ISBN 978-93-5103-031-7

Let's Do

1. Find the perimeter of the figure.

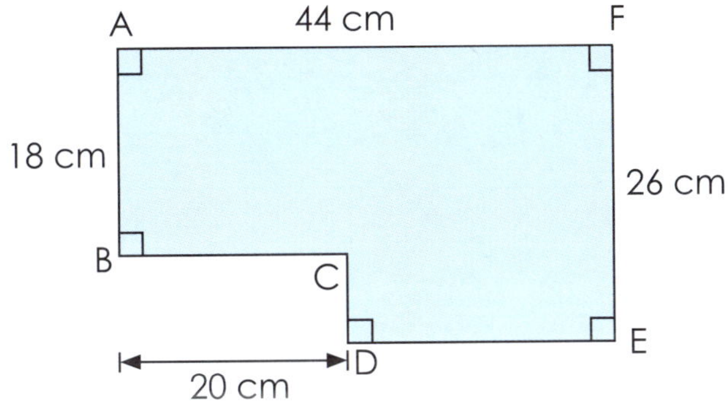

Perimeter = AB + BC + _______ + _______ + EF + FA

= 18 + 20 + _______ + _______ + 26 + 44

= _______ cm

P/B Chapter 8: Exercise 7, pages 121–122

Finding area of composite figures by adding areas of rectangles

Let's Learn

Find the area of the figure.

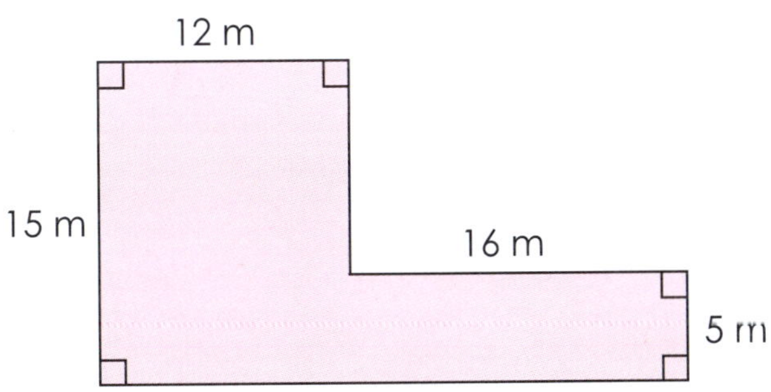

 ISBN 978-93-5103-031-7

Method 1

Picture It

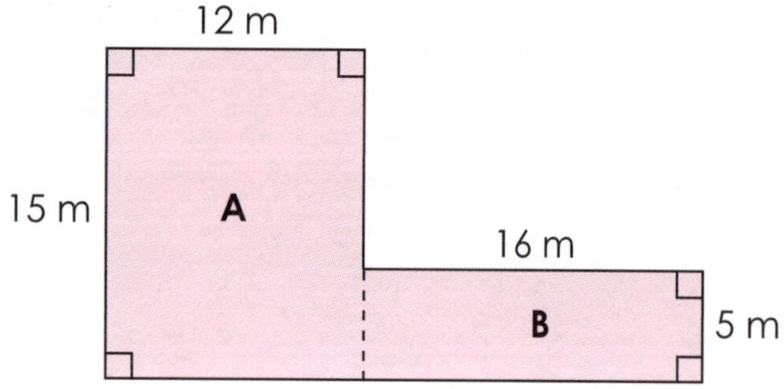

Area of figure = Area of Rectangle A + Area of Rectangle B

Area of Rectangle A = 15 m × 12 m
= 180 m^2

Area of Rectangle B = 16 m × 5 m
= 80 m^2

Area of figure = 180 + 80
= 260 m^2

Method 2

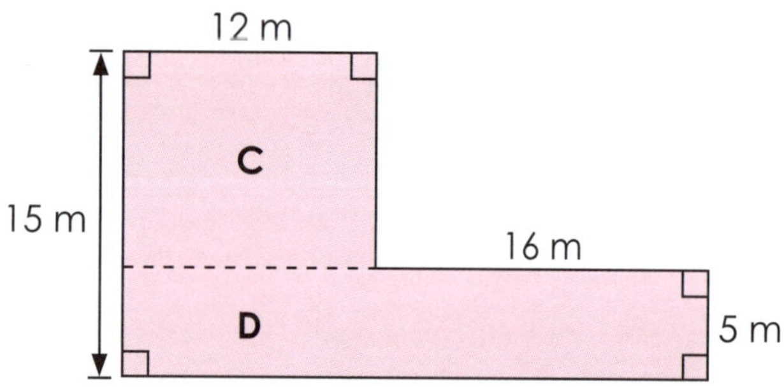

Area of figure = Area of Rectangle C + Area of Rectangle D

Area of Rectangle C = 12 m × ___ m
= ___ m^2

Area of Rectangle D = ___ m × 5 m
= ___ m^2

Area of figure = ___ + ___
= ___ m^2

Breadth of Rectangle C = 15 − ___
= ___ m

Length of Rectangle D = ___ + ___
= ___ m

Compare Methods 1 and 2.
Which method is easier? ___

 ISBN 978-93-5103-031-7

Let's Do

1. The figure is made up of two rectangles. Find its area.

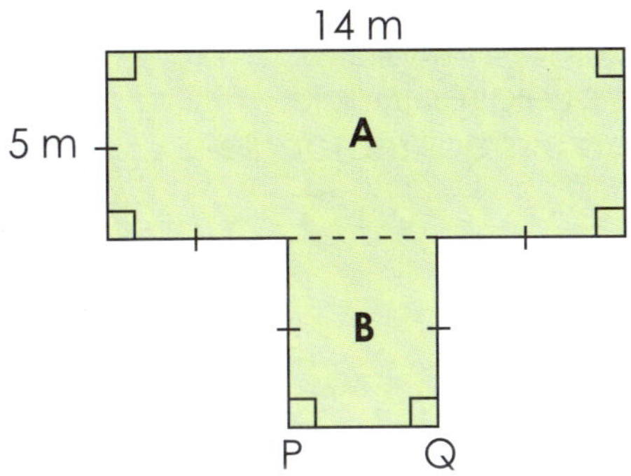

Area of the figure
= Area of rectangle A
+ Area of rectangle B

P/B Chapter 8: Exercise 8, page 123

Finding area of composite figures by subtracting areas of rectangles

Let's Learn

a) Find the area of the shaded figure.

Picture It

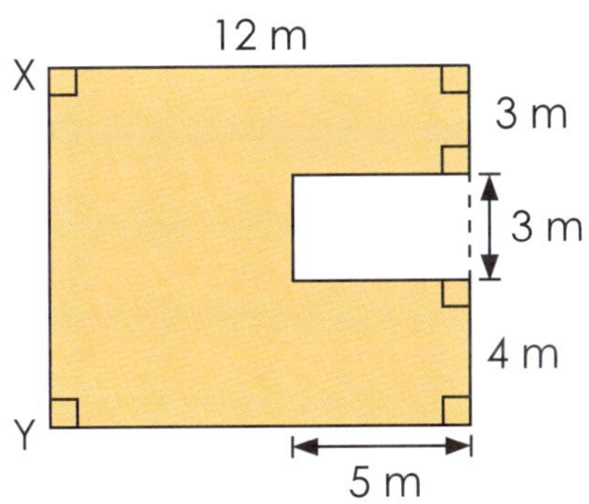

The big rectangle is made up of the shaded figure and a small rectangle.

Area of shaded figure = Area of big rectangle – Area of small rectangle

Area of big rectangle = $12 \text{ m} \times XY$
$= 12 \text{ m} \times 10 \text{ m}$
$= 120 \text{ m}^2$

XY = 3 + 3 + 4
= 10 m

Area of small rectangle = $5 \text{ m} \times 3 \text{ m}$
$= 15 \text{ m}^2$

Area of shaded figure = 120 – 15
$= 105 \text{ m}^2$

The area of the shaded figure is 105 square metres.

Think of another way to find the shaded area. Which method is easier?

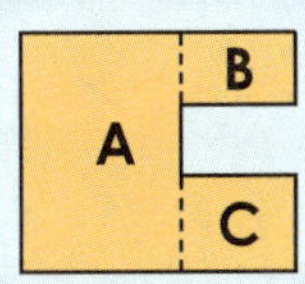

 ISBN 978-93-5103-031-7

b) The figure shows a rectangle with a border 1 metre wide around it. Find the area of the border.

Picture It

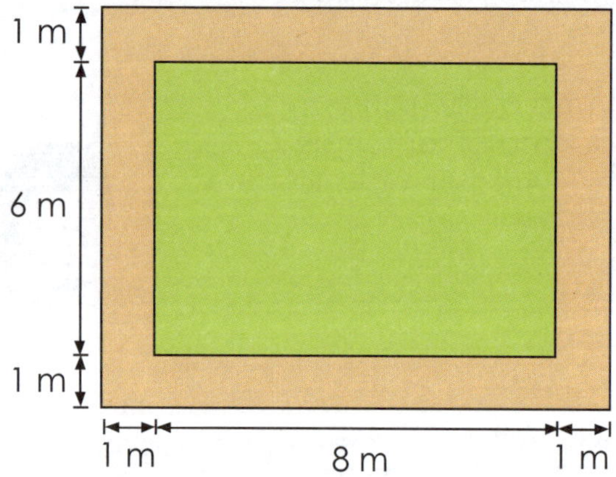

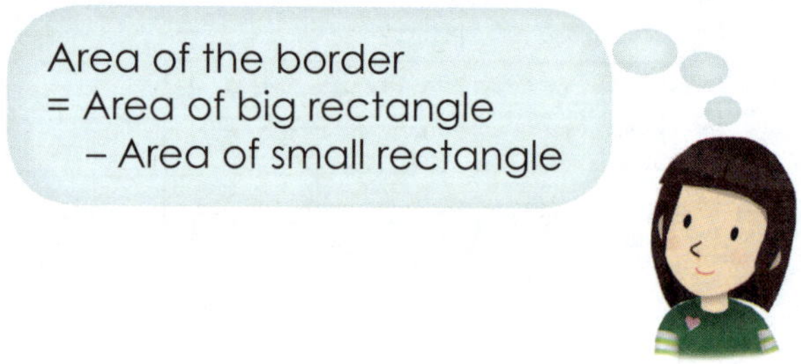

Area of big rectangle = 10 m × 8 m

= ___ m^2

Area of small rectangle = 8 m × 6 m

= ___ m^2

Area of border = ___ – ___

= ___ m^2

The area of the border is ___ square metres.

Let's Do

1. The figure shows a small rectangle in a big rectangle. Find the area of the shaded part of the big rectangle.

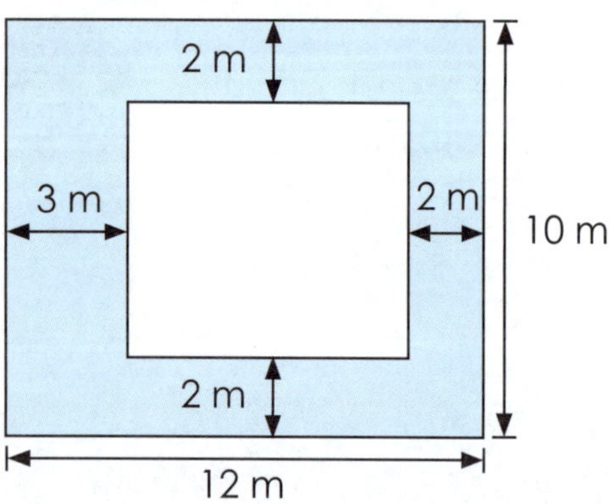

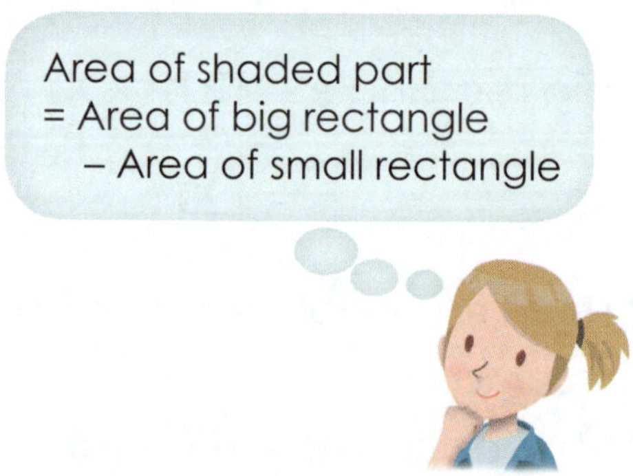

P/B Chapter 8: Exercise 9, pages 124–125

 ISBN 978-93-5103-031-7

Practice 4

1. Find the area and perimeter of each figure. All sides meet at right angles.

a)

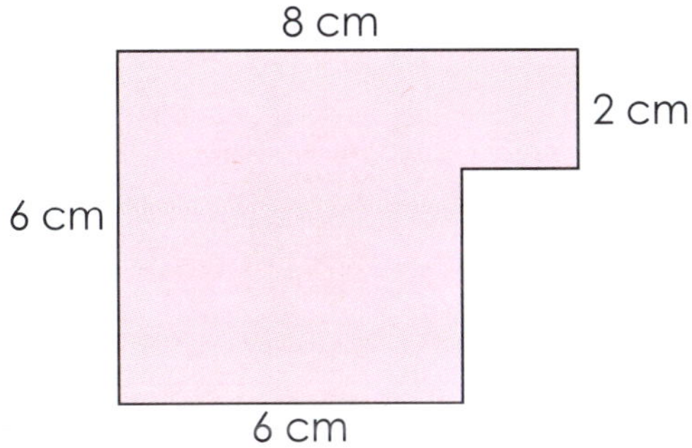

b)

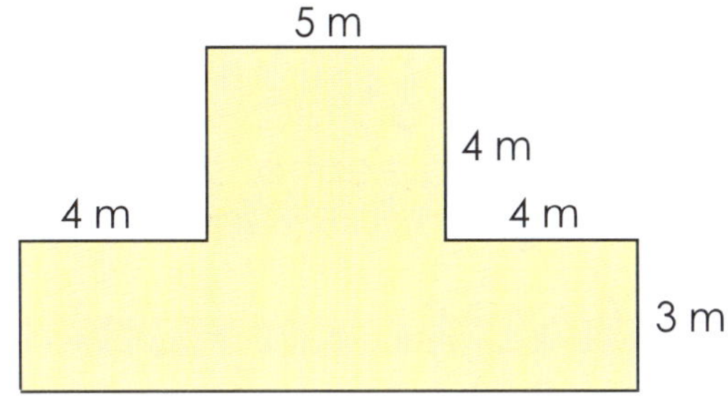

c)

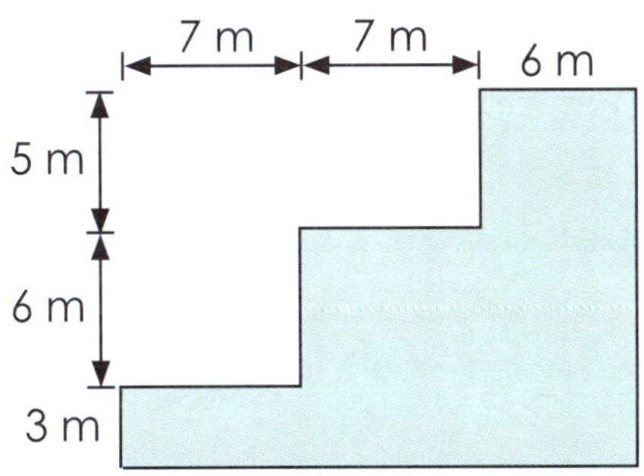

d)

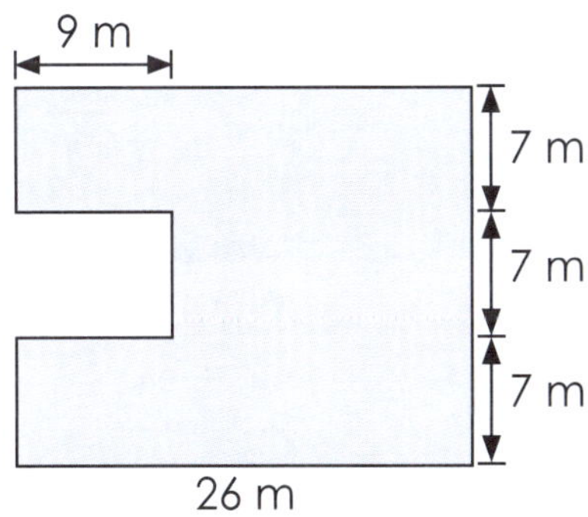

2. Each figure shows a small rectangle in a big rectangle. Find the area of the shaded part of each rectangle.

a)

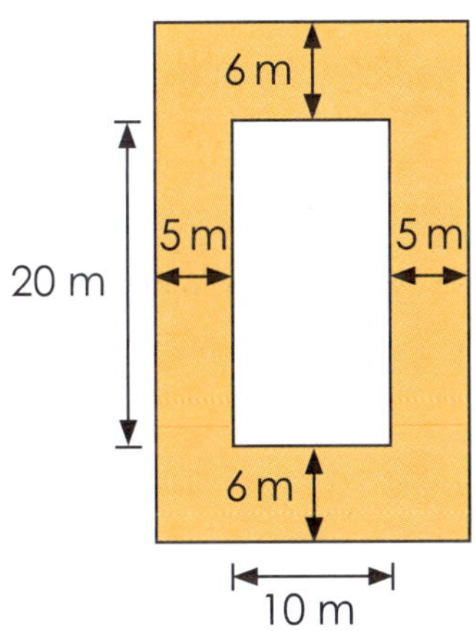

b)

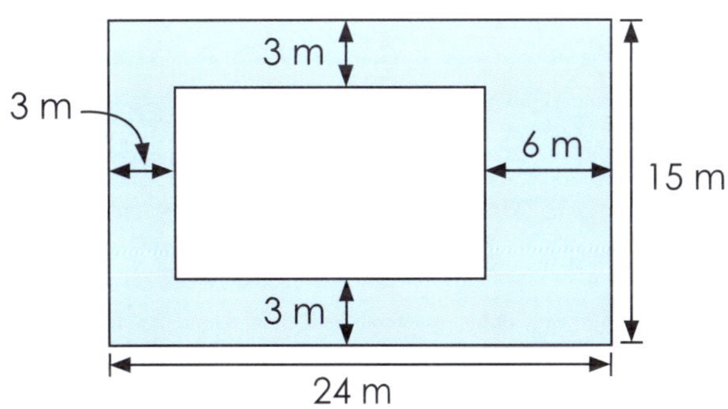

Lesson 5 Problem Solving

Word problems

Let's Learn

Mr. Pinto had a square garden. He built a rectangular greenhouse in the garden and planted grass in the remaining area.

a) What area of the garden was covered by grass?

b) If each square metre of grass cost ₹ 30, how much did it cost Mr. Pinto to plant grass in his garden?

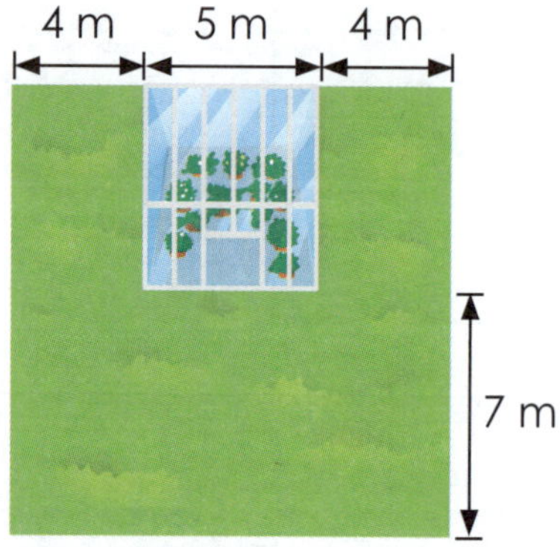

1 Understand the problem.

What measurements are given?
What do I have to find?

2 Plan what to do.

To find the area of the greenhouse, I have to find the unknown length of the greenhouse.

3 Work out the **Answer**.

a) Length of one side of the garden = 4 + 5 + 4
= 13 m

Unknown length of greenhouse = 13 – 7
= 6 m

Area of garden covered by grass
= Area of garden – Area of greenhouse

Area of garden = 13 m × 13 m
= 169 m^2

Area of greenhouse = 6 m × 5 m
= 30 m^2

Area of garden covered by grass = 169 – 30
= 139 m^2

139 square metres of the garden is covered by grass.

b) 139 × ₹ 30 = ₹ 4170

It cost Mr. Pinto ₹ 4170 to plant grass in his garden.

 ISBN 978-93-5103-031-7

4 Check

Did you answer the question? Is your answer reasonable?

Area of garden covered by grass < Area of garden
$139 < 169$

My answer is reasonable.

- ☑ 1. Understand
- ☑ 2. Plan
- ☑ 3. Answer
- ☑ 4. Check

Let's Do

1. Karen cuts out a square from a rectangular cardboard.

   a) What is the area of the remaining piece of cardboard?

   b) What is the perimeter of the remaining piece of cardboard?

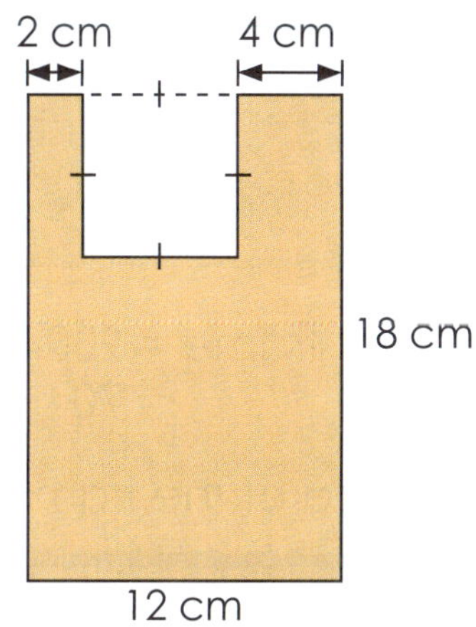

Area of remaining piece of cardboard
= Area of cardboard – Area of square

- ☐ 1. Understand
- ☐ 2. Plan
- ☐ 3. Answer
- ☐ 4. Check

ISBN 978-93-5103-031-7

Let's Learn

The frame around a square painting is 4 centimetres wide. Each side of the painting is 40 centimetres long. Find the area of the frame.

> What is the length of each side of the painting?
> How wide is the frame?

Area of frame = Area of big square – Area of small square

Length of one side of big square = 4 + 40 + 4
= 48 cm

Area of big square = 48 cm × 48 cm
= 2304 cm^2

Area of small square = 40 cm × 40 cm
= 1600 cm^2

Area of frame = 2304 – 1600
= 704 cm^2

The area of the frame is 704 square centimetres.

> The area of the frame is smaller than the area of the painting.
>
> My answer is reasonable.

- [x] **1. Understand**
- [x] **2. Plan**
- [x] **3. Answer**
- [x] **4. Check**

Let's Do

1. A rectangular flower bed measures 10 metres by 6 metres. It has a path 2 metres wide around it. Find the area of the path.

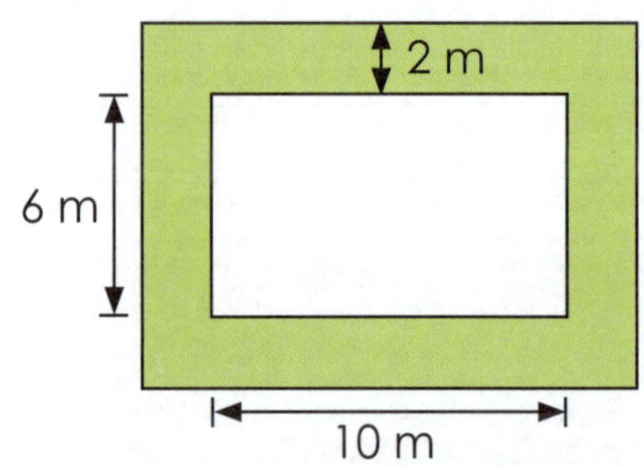

> What is the total length of the flower bed and the path?
> What is the total breadth?

- [ ] **1. Understand**
- [ ] **2. Plan**
- [ ] **3. Answer**
- [ ] **4. Check**

P/B Chapter 8: Exercise 10, pages 126–127

  ISBN 978-93-5103-031-7

Practice 5

Solve the word problems. Show your work clearly.

1. A rectangular piece of paper measures 60 centimetres by 46 centimetres. When it is placed on a table, it leaves a margin 4 centimetres wide all round it. What is the area of the tabletop not covered by the paper?

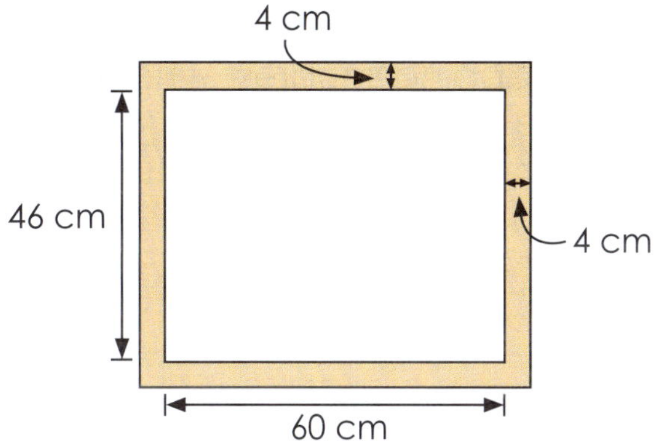

2. A rectangular carpet is placed on the floor of a rectangular room which measures 8 metres by 7 metres. It leaves a margin 1 metre wide around it. Find the area of the carpet.

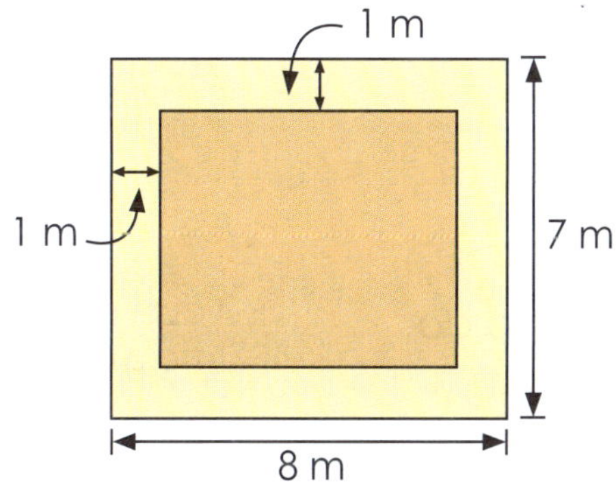

3. Mr. Lee wants to tile the floor area of his house. It costs ₹ 50 to tile each square metre of the floor area. How much will it cost to tile the entire floor area?

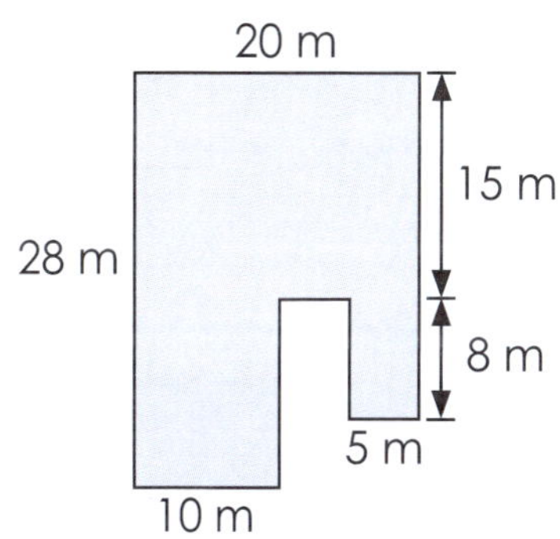

ISBN 978-93-5103-031-7

Mind stretcher

Let's Learn

The figure is made up of five identical overlapping squares. What is the area of the figure?

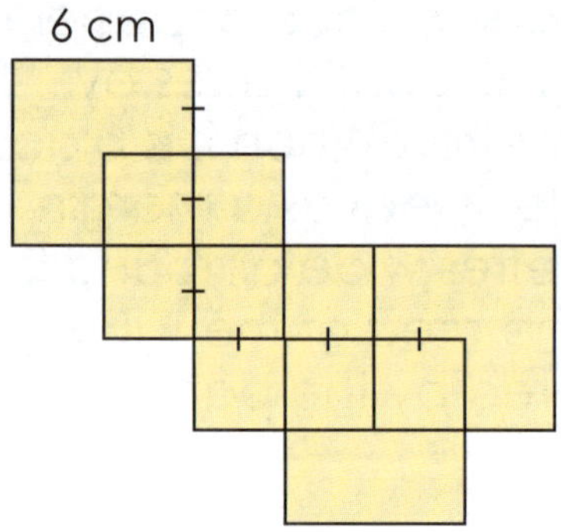

1 Understand the problem.

What is the length of each side of the square?
Do the squares overlap each other in a similar way?
Are the smaller squares identical?
What do I have to find out?

2 Plan what to do.

I can **draw lines** to divide the figure into smaller squares.

3 Work out the **Answer**.

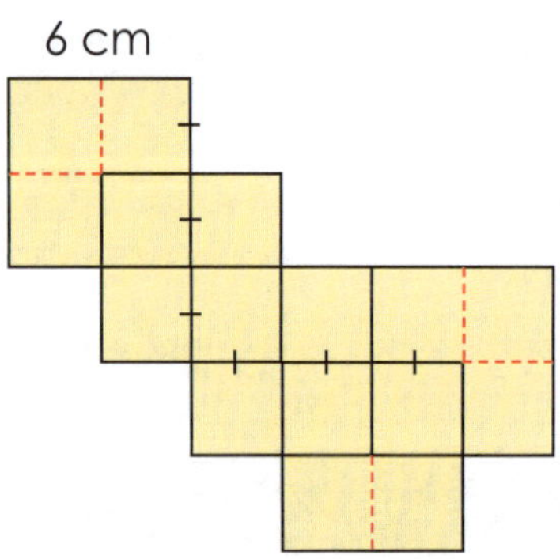

Area of small square
= 3 cm × 3 cm
= 9 cm^2

Area of 16 small squares
= 16 × 9 cm^2
= 144 cm^2

The area of the figure is 144 square centimetres.

4 Check
Did you answer the question?
Is your answer reasonable?

Area of big square = 6 cm × 6 cm = 36 cm^2
Total area of 5 big squares = 5 × 36 cm^2 = 180 cm^2
The area of the figure is less than the total area of 5 big squares.

My answer is reasonable.

☑ 1. Understand
☑ 2. Plan
☑ 3. Answer
☑ 4. Check

 ISBN 978-93-5103-031-7

9 Decimals

Lesson 1 Tenths

Reading and writing decimals smaller than 1

Let's Learn

a)

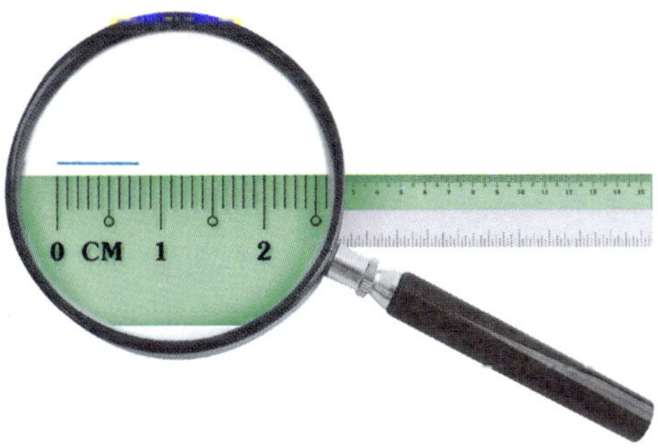

The length of the string is less than 1 centimetre.
It is 8 out of 10 equal parts of a centimetre.

The length of the string is $\frac{8}{10}$ centimetre or 0.8 centimetre.
Read 0.8 as **zero point eight**.

The weight of the loaf of bread is 0.8 kilogram.

The volume of water in the container is 0.8 litre.

 ISBN 978-93-5103-031-7

b) Divide 1 whole into 10 equal parts. Each part is $\frac{1}{10}$ or 0.1.

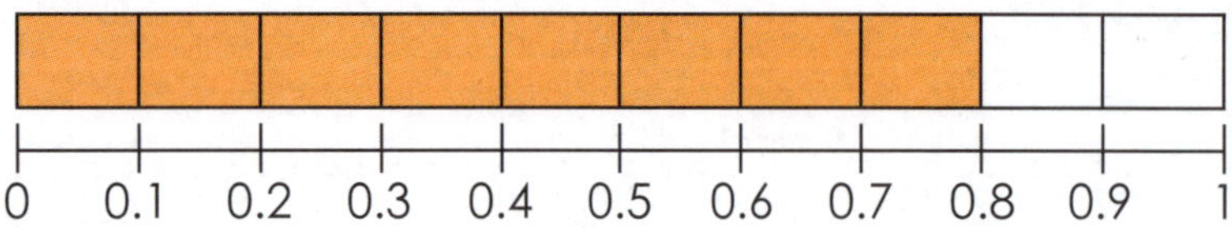

0.8 is 8 **tenths**.

Numbers like 0.1 and 0.8 are **decimals**.
The dot '.' in a decimal is called a **decimal point**.

c)

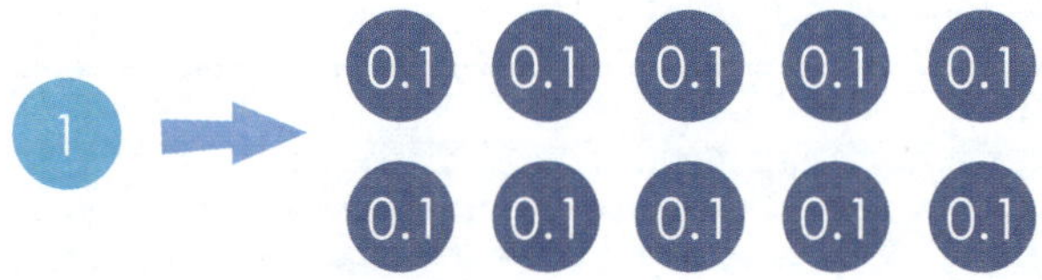

1 one = 10 tenths

Let's Do

1. Write a decimal for each of the following.

a)

4 tenths = ________

b)

6 tenths = ________

c)

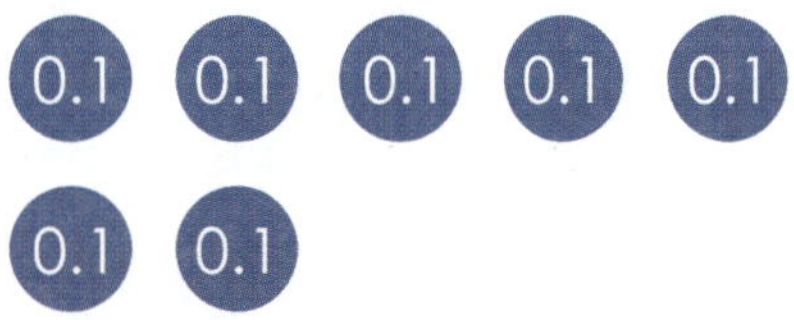

7 tenths = ________

d)

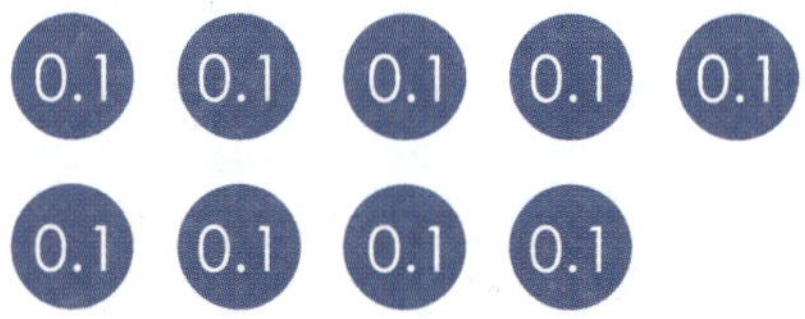

9 tenths = ________

Expressing fractions as decimals

Let's Learn

a)

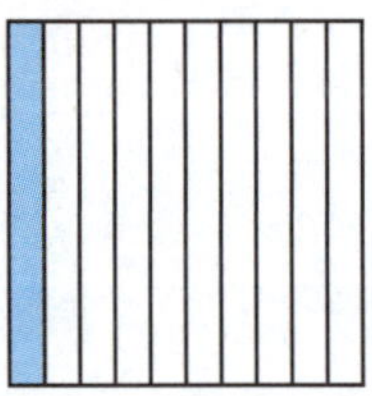

1 tenth

$\frac{1}{10} = 0.1$

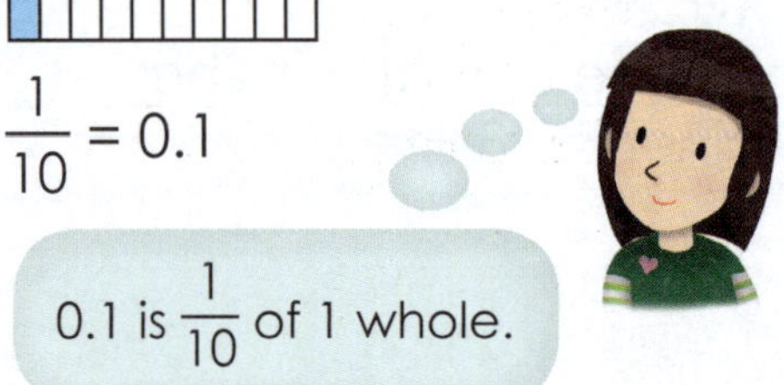

b)

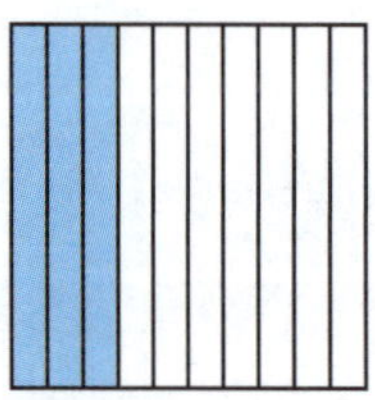

3 tenths

$\frac{3}{10} = 0.3$

 ISBN 978-93-5103-031-7

Let's Do

1. Express each fraction as a decimal.

a) 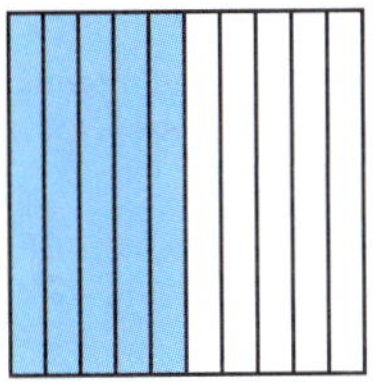

5 tenths

$\frac{5}{10}$ = ______

b) 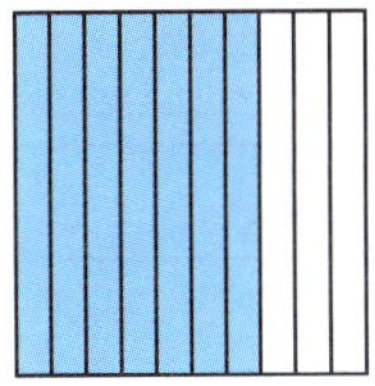

7 tenths

$\frac{7}{10}$ = ______

Expressing decimals as fractions with a denominator of 10

Let's Learn

a) Divide 1 metre into 10 equal parts. Each part is 0.1 metre.

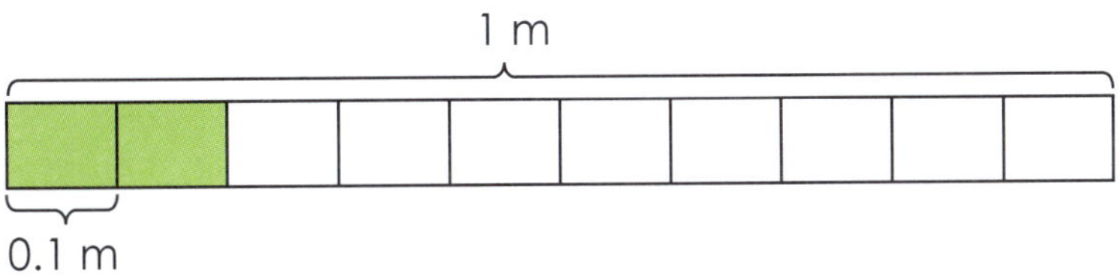

0.2 m = $\frac{2}{10}$ of 1 m

b) Divide 1 kilogram into 10 equal parts.

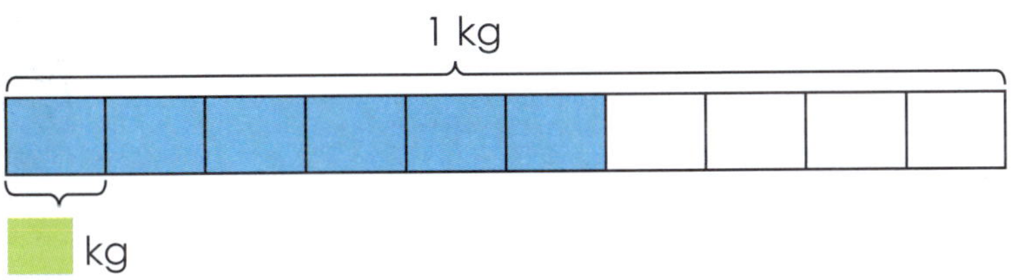

Each part is ☐ kilogram.

0.6 kg = $\frac{☐}{10}$ of 1 kg

Let's Do

1. Fill in the missing number.

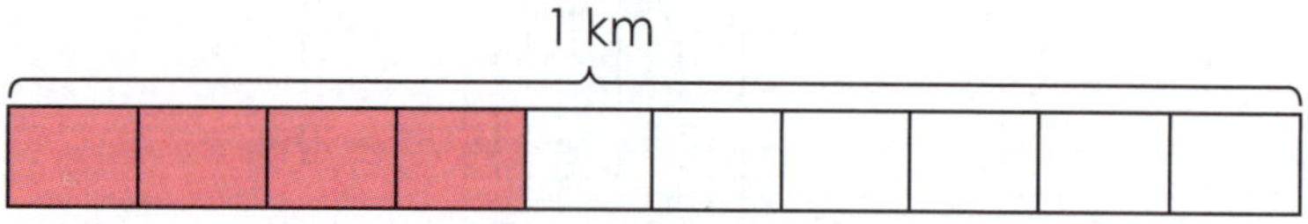

$0.4 \text{ km} = \frac{\square}{10}$ of 1 km

P/B Chapter 9: Exercise 1, pages 128–129

Reading and writing decimals greater than 1

Let's Learn

Picture It

The string is longer than 1 centimetre but shorter than 2 centimetres.

The length of the string is $1\frac{6}{10}$ centimetres or 1.6 centimetres.
1.6 is also a decimal.
Read 1.6 as **one point six**.

1.6 centimetres is 0.6 centimetre longer than 1 centimetre.

1.6 = 1 + 0.6

Let's Do

1. Write a decimal for each of the following.

   a)

The total volume of water in the containers is ______ litres.

 ISBN 978-93-5103-031-7

b) 

The weight of the watermelon is ______ kilograms.

Chapter 9: Exercise 2, page 130

Expressing mixed numbers as decimals

Let's Learn

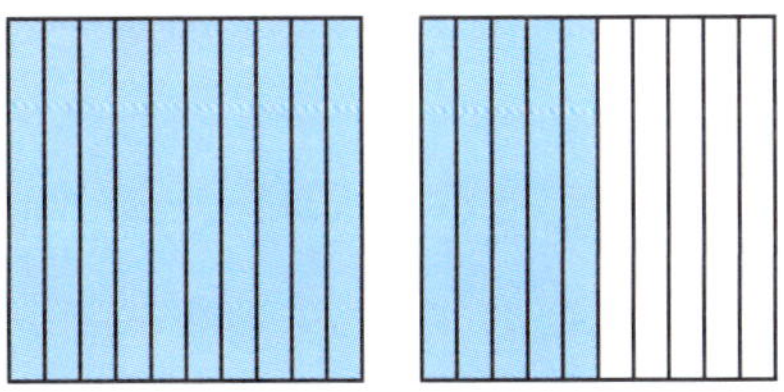

1 whole and 5 tenths

$1\frac{5}{10} = $ ▢

$$1\frac{5}{10} = 1 + \frac{5}{10}$$
$$= 1 + 0.5$$
$$= 1.5$$

Let's Do

1. Express each mixed number as a decimal.

a) $1\frac{1}{10} = $ ______

b) $3\frac{3}{10} = $ ______

Reading number lines

Let's Learn

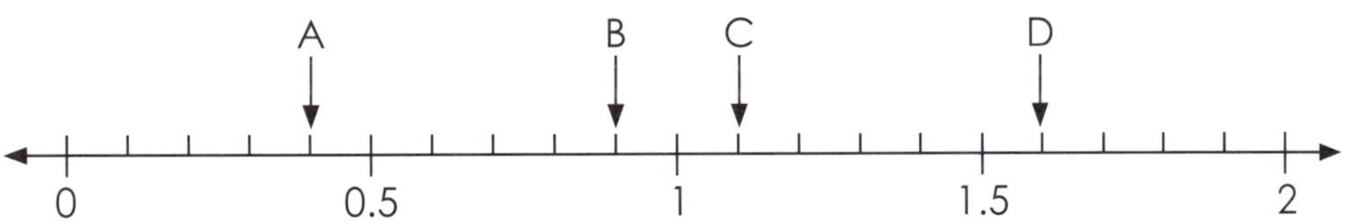

There are 10 equal intervals between 0 and 1.
Each interval stands for 0.1.

Point A stands for 0.4.
Point B stands for ▢.
Point C stands for 1.1.
Point D stands for ▢.

Count in steps of 0.1.
0.1, 0.2, 0.3, 0.4, ...

 ISBN 978-93-5103-031-7

Let's Do

1. Fill in the missing decimals.

a)

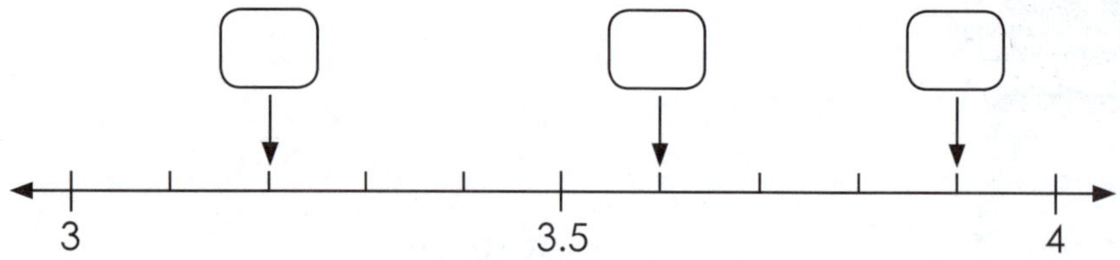

b)

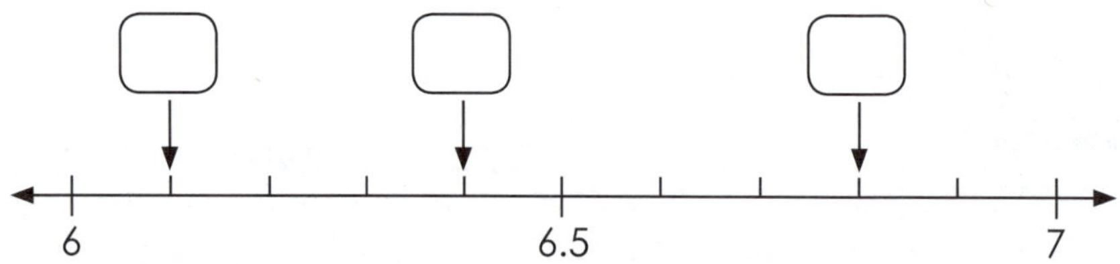

Expressing decimals as fractions or mixed numbers in their simplest form

Let's Learn

a) Express 0.2 as a fraction in its simplest form.

$$0.2 = \frac{2}{10} = \frac{1}{5}$$

$$\frac{2}{10} \xrightarrow{\div 2} \frac{1}{5} \quad (\text{numerator and denominator} \div 2)$$

b) Express 1.2 as a mixed number in its simplest form.

$$1.2 = 1\frac{2}{10} = 1\frac{1}{5}$$

$$1.2 = 1 + 0.2 = 1 + \frac{2}{10} = 1\frac{2}{10}$$

Let's Do

1. Express each decimal as a fraction or mixed number in its simplest form.

a) $0.8 = \frac{8}{10}$

$= \_\_\_\_\_\_$

b) $2.8 = \_\_\_\_\_\_$

$= \_\_\_\_\_\_$

PB Chapter 9: Exercise 3, pages 131–132

 ISBN 978-93-5103-031-7

Interpreting decimals in terms of tens, ones and tenths

Let's Learn

a)

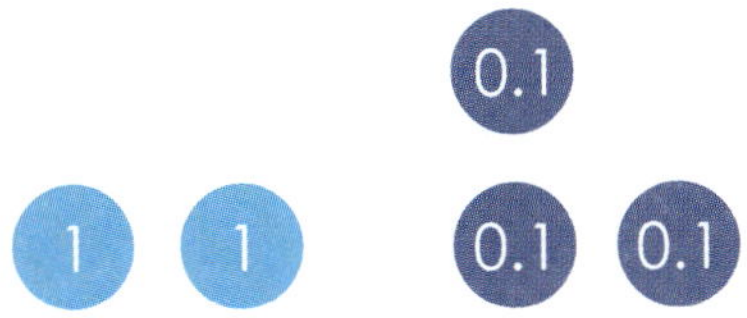

2 ones   3 tenths

2 + 0.3 = 2.3

b)

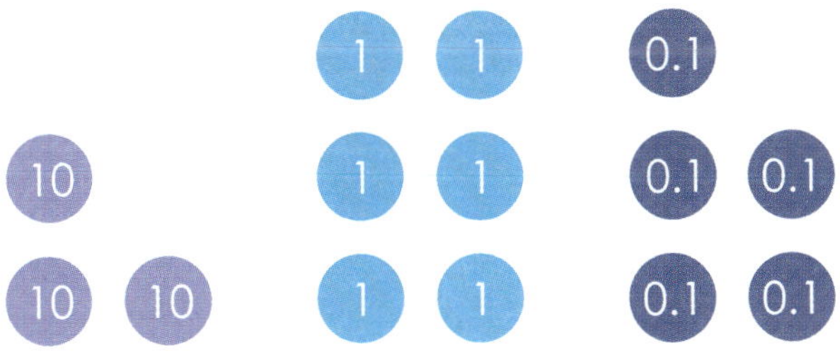

3 tens   6 ones   5 tenths

30 + 6 + 0.5 = 36.5

Let's Do

1. Fill in the blanks.

a)

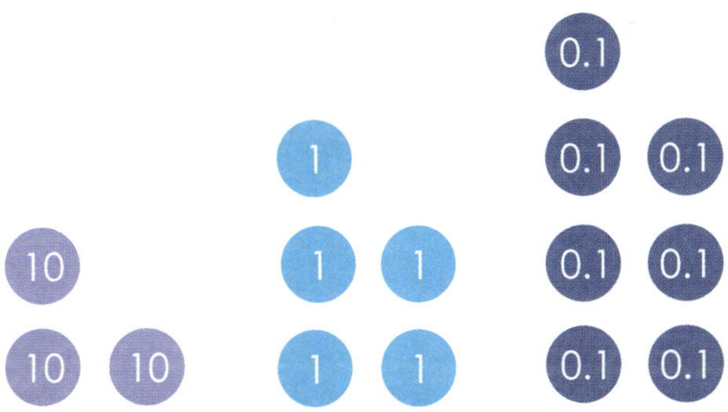

3 tens   5 ones   7 tenths

30 + 5 + 0.7 = ______

b) 50 + 0.4 = ______

Identifying values of digits

Let's Learn

Picture It

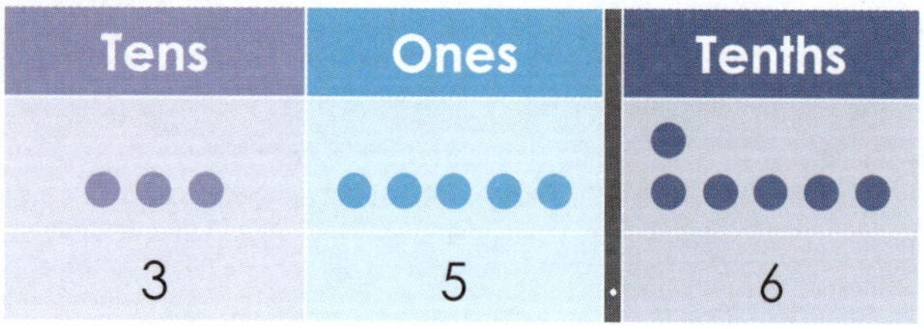

In 35.6, the digit 6 is in the tenths place.
The value of the digit 6 is 0.6.
The digit 6 stands for 0.6.

The digit ____ is in the tens place.

Its value is ____.

Let's Do

1. Read the table. Then, fill in the blanks.

Tens	Ones	Tenths
7	4	2

In 74.2,

a) the digit 7 stands for ______.

b) the digit ______ is in the ones place.

c) the value of the digit 2 is ______.

Writing tenths as decimals

Let's Learn

Picture It

a)

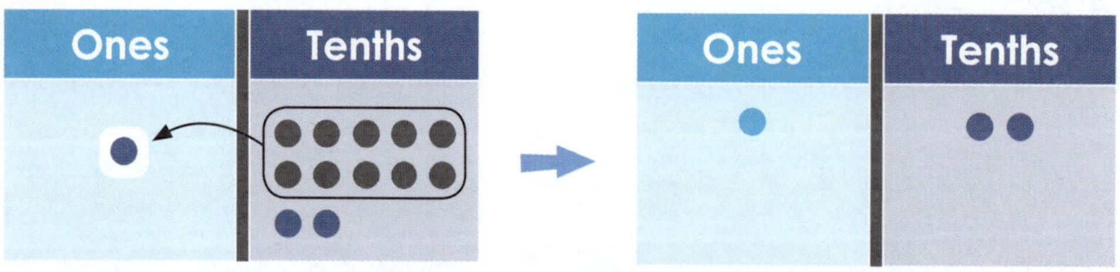

12 tenths = 1.2

12 tenths = 1 one + 2 tenths
= 1 + 0.2
= 1.2

 ISBN 978-93-5103-031-7

b)

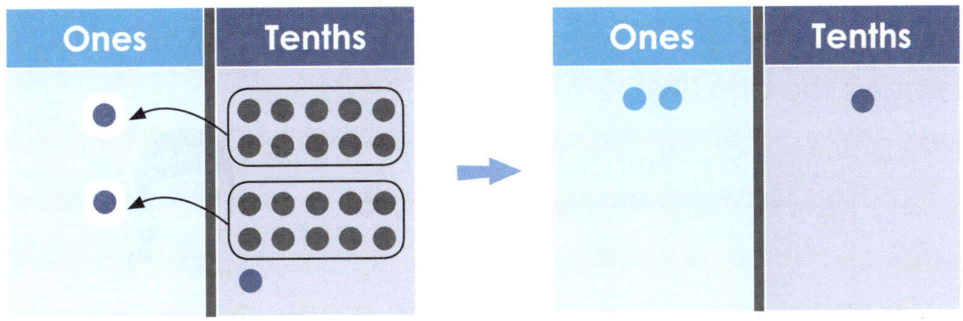

21 tenths = ▭

21 tenths = 2 ones + 1 tenth
= 2 + 0.1
= ▭

Let's Do

1. Write the decimals.

a) 34 tenths = ______

b) 52 tenths = ______

P/B Chapter 9: Exercise 4, page 133

Comparing and ordering decimals

Let's Learn

Compare 4.8, 6.4 and 6.

	Ones	Tenths
4.8	4	8
6.4	6	4
6	6	0

Write 6 as 6.0.

First, compare the ones.
4 ones is the smallest.

4.8 is the smallest number.

Then, compare the tenths of 6.4 and 6.
0 tenths is smaller than 4 tenths.

6 is smaller than 6.4.
6.4 is the greatest number.

Arranging the numbers in order from the smallest, we have:

4.8, 6, 6.4
(smallest)

 ISBN 978-93-5103-031-7

Let's Do

1. Which number is the greatest, 2.7, 4.8 or 8.5? ______

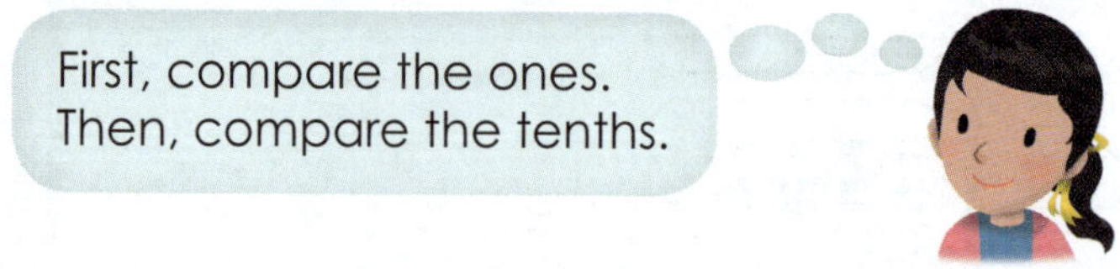

2. Arrange the numbers in order. Begin with the greatest.

   a) 3.1, 0.3, 3, 1.3 ____________________

   b) 7.2, 2.7, 9, 7.8 ____________________

P/B Chapter 9: Exercise 5, page 134

Practice 1

1. Write the decimals.

   a)

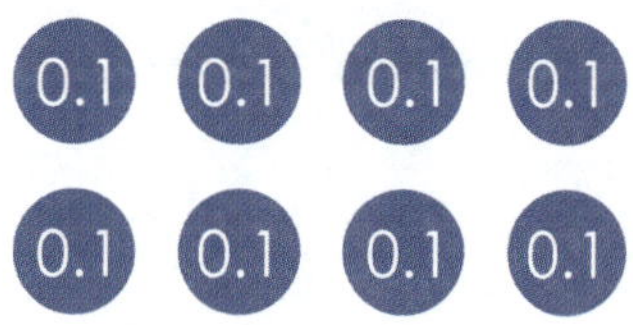

   8 tenths = ____

   b)

   $\frac{6}{10}$ = ____

   c)

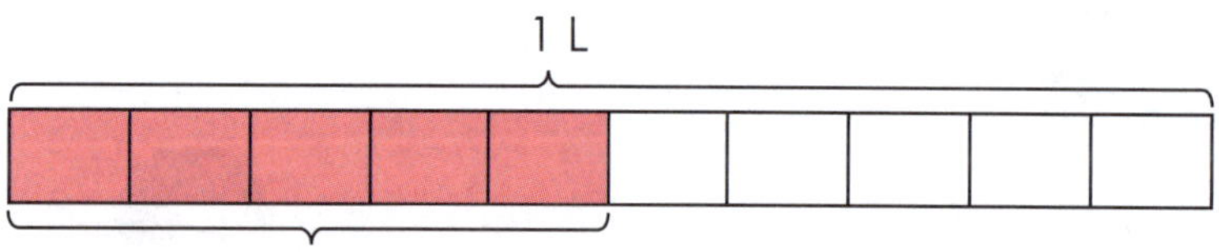

   ____ L

2. What is the total volume of water in the containers in litres?

3. Express each fraction or mixed number as a decimal.

   a) $\frac{3}{10}$ b) $\frac{9}{10}$ c) $1\frac{7}{10}$ d) $3\frac{2}{10}$

4. Express each decimal as a fraction or mixed number in its simplest form.

   a) 0.3 b) 0.5 c) 1.4 d) 3.6

 ISBN 978-93-5103-031-7

5. What number is represented by each letter?

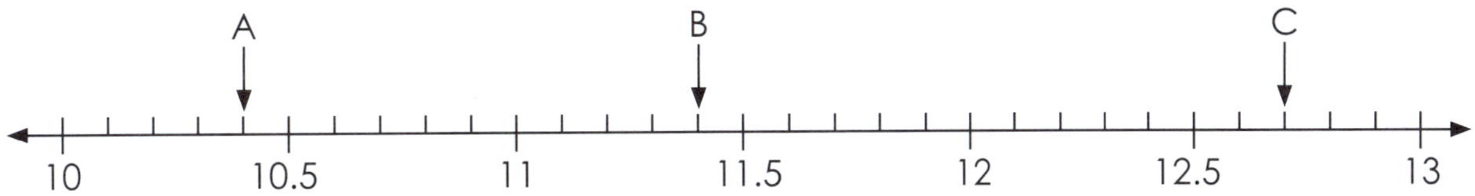

6. Find the value of each of the following.

a) 1 + 0.2 b) 20 + 5 + 0.4 c) 30 + 0.8

7.

Tens	Ones	Tenths
4	6	8

In 46.8,

a) which digit is in the tens place?

b) what is the value of the digit 8?

c) what does the digit 6 stand for?

8. Express each of the following as a decimal.

a) 47 tenths b) 65 tenths c) 84 tenths

9. Arrange the numbers in order. Begin with the smallest.

5.3, 5, 6.2, 6.8

Lesson 2 Hundredths

Reading and writing decimals

Let's Learn

a) The coloured part is longer than 0.3 metre.

Picture It

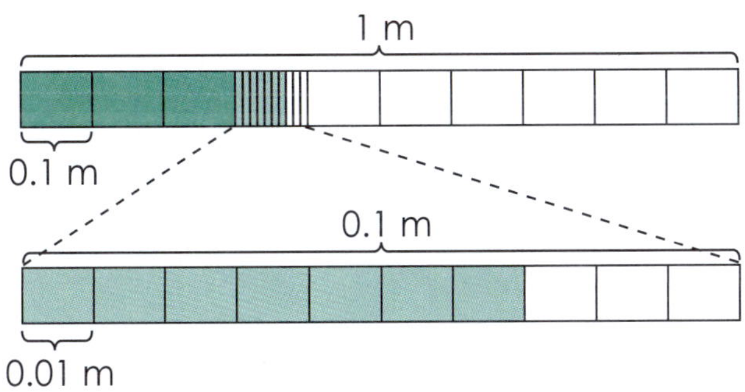

Divide 0.1 metre into 10 equal parts. Each part is 0.01 metre.

0.3 + 0.07 = 0.37

The length of the coloured part is 0.37 metre.

 ISBN 978-93-5103-031-7

b) Divide 1 whole into 100 equal parts.
Each part is $\frac{1}{100}$ or 0.01.

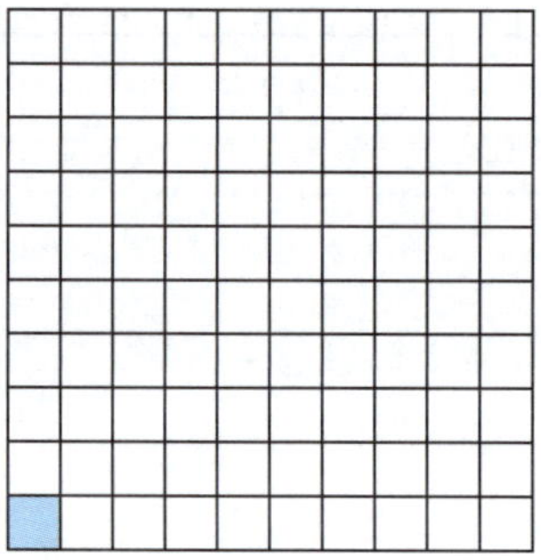

0.01 is 1 **hundredth**.
Read 0.01 as **zero point zero one**.

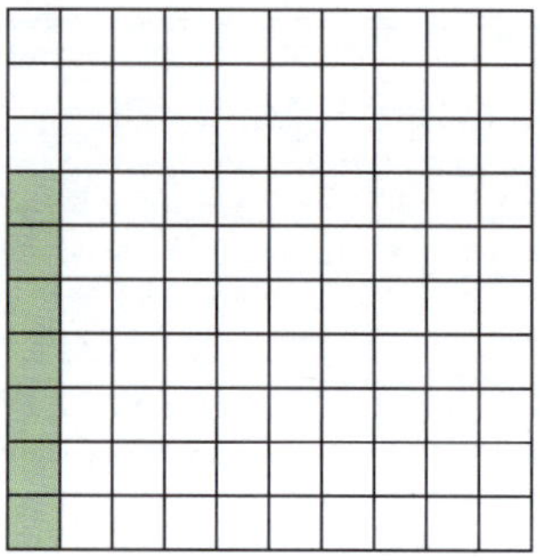

0.07 is 7 hundredths.

$0.07 = \frac{7}{100}$

Read 0.07 as **zero point zero seven**.

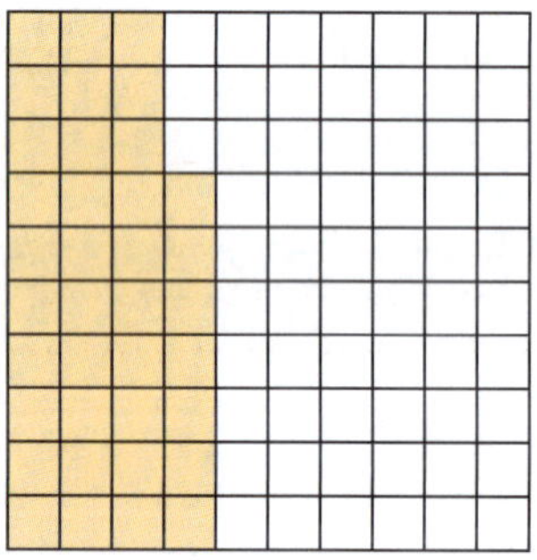

0.37 is 37 hundredths.

$0.37 = \frac{37}{100}$

Read 0.37 as **zero point three seven**.

0.37 is 3 tenths 7 hundredths.

$0.37 = \frac{3}{10} + \frac{7}{100}$

c)

1 tenth = 10 hundredths

Let's Do

1. Write a decimal for each of the following.

a)

3 hundredths = ______

b)

5 hundredths = ______

 ISBN 978-93-5103-031-7

Writing hundredths as decimals

Let's Learn

Maths Lab
Picture It

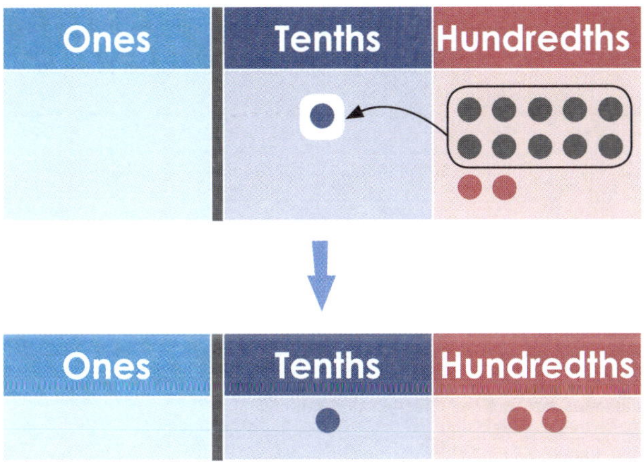

12 hundredths = 0.12

Let's Do

1. Write the decimals.

   a) 23 hundredths = ______ b) 45 hundredths = ______

Interpreting decimals in terms of tens, ones, tenths and hundredths

Let's Learn

a)

3 ones 2 hundredths

3 + 0.02 = 3.02

b)

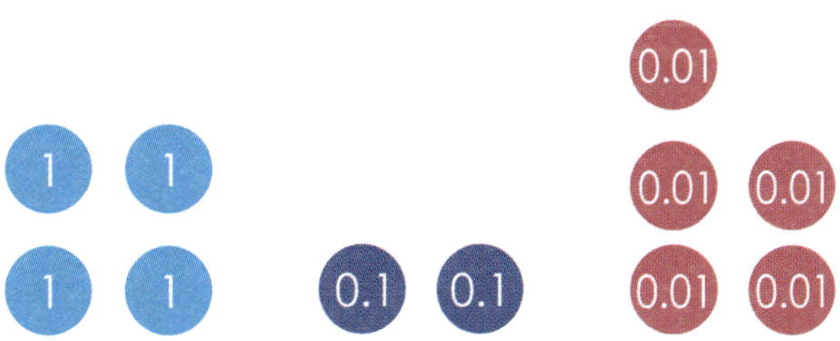

4 ones 2 tenths 5 hundredths

4 + 0.2 + 0.05 = 4.25

 ISBN 978-93-5103-031-7

Let's Do

1. Fill in the blanks.

   a) 2 + 0.8 + 0.04 = ______ b) 80 + 0.5 + 0.07 = ______

P/B Chapter 9: Exercise 6, pages 135–136

Identifying values of digits

Let's Learn

Picture It

Hundreds	Tens	Ones	Tenths	Hundredths
●●	●●●	●●●●	●●●●●	●●●●●●
2	3	4 .	5	6

In 234.56, the digit 2 stands for 200.
Its value is 200.

The digit 6 stands for 0.06.
Its value is 0.06.

The digit ___ is in the tenths place.

Its value is ___.

Let's Do

1. Read the table. Then, fill in the blanks.

Hundreds	Tens	Ones	Tenths	Hundredths
3	4	7 .	9	2

In 347.92,

a) the digit 9 is in the ______ place.

   Its value is ______.

b) the digit ______ is in the hundredths place.

   It stands for ______.

P/B Chapter 9: Exercise 7, page 137

 ISBN 978-93-5103-031-7

Expressing fractions and mixed numbers as decimals

Let's Learn

Picture It

a) 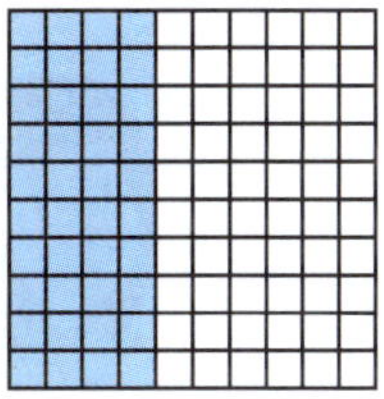

40 hundredths

$$\frac{40}{100} = 0.40$$
$$0.40 = 0.4$$

$$\frac{40}{100} = \frac{4}{10} = 0.4$$

b) 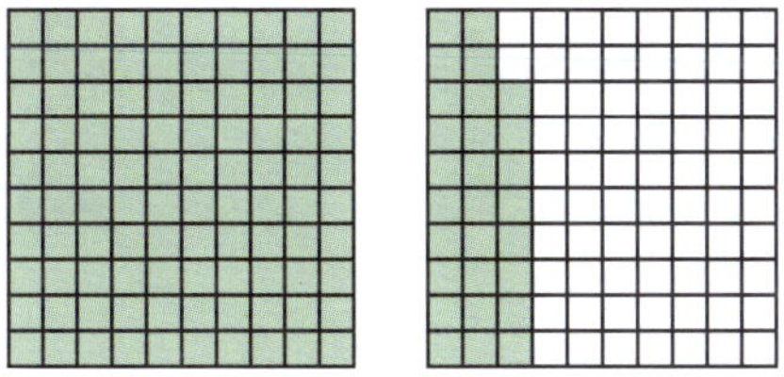

1 whole and 28 hundredths

$$1\frac{28}{100} = \square$$

$$1\frac{28}{100} = 1 + \frac{28}{100}$$
$$= 1 + 0.28$$
$$= 1.28$$

c) 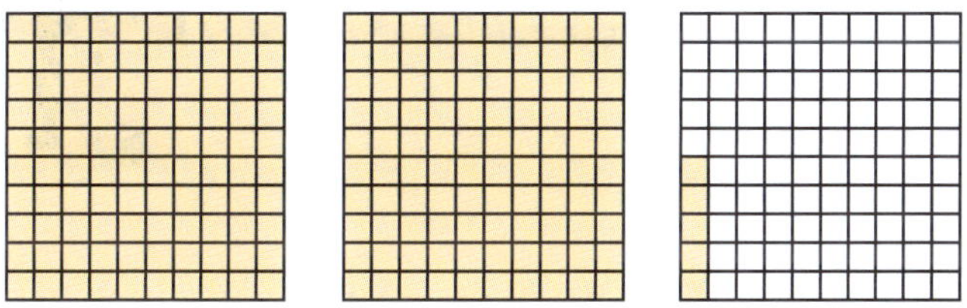

2 wholes and 5 hundredths

$$2\frac{5}{100} = \square$$

$$2\frac{5}{100} = 2 + \frac{5}{100}$$
$$= 2 + 0.05$$
$$= 2.05$$

Let's Do

1. Express each fraction or mixed number as a decimal.

a) $\frac{60}{100}$ = ______ b) $2\frac{48}{100}$ = ______ c) $3\frac{7}{100}$ = ______

PB Chapter 9: Exercise 8, pages 138–140

 ISBN 978-93-5103-031-7

Expressing amounts of money as decimals

Let's Learn

a) Express 10 paise in rupees.

$$10 \text{ p} = \frac{10}{100} \text{ of ₹ } 1$$

$$= ₹\ 0.10$$

$\frac{10}{100} = 0.10$
0.10 = 0.1
Write ₹ 0.10, not ₹ 0.1.

b) Express 3 rupees and 85 paise as a decimal.

3 rupees and 85 paise
- 3 rupees = ₹ 3
- 85 paise = ₹ 0.85

$\frac{85}{100} = 0.85$

3 rupees and 85 paise = ₹ 3.85

Let's Do

1. Express each amount of money as a decimal.

   a) 20 p = ₹ ______

   b) 45 p = ₹ ______

   c) 6 rupees and 50 paise = ₹ ______

   d) 8 rupees and 5 paise = ₹ ______

$\frac{20}{100} = 0.20$

Reading number lines

Let's Learn

Picture It

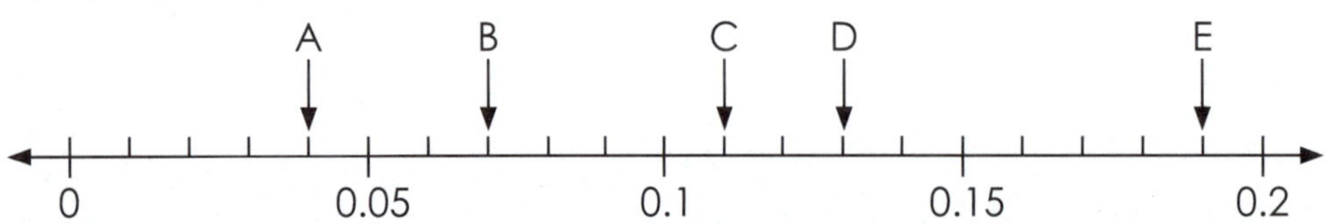

There are 10 equal intervals between 0 and 0.1.
Each interval stands for 0.01.

Point A stands for 0.04.
Point B stands for ____.
Point C stands for 0.11.
Point D stands for ____.
Point E stands for ____.

Count in steps of 0.01.
0.01, 0.02, 0.03, 0.04, ...

 ISBN 978-93-5103-031-7

Let's Do

1. Fill in the missing decimals.

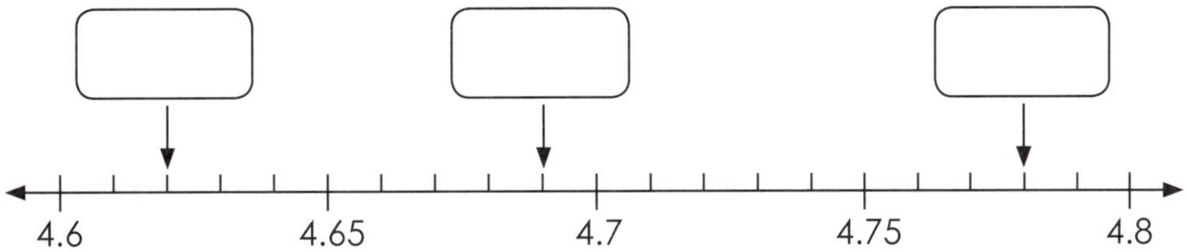

Finding 'more than' and 'less than'

Let's Learn

a) What number is 0.1 more than 412.34?

Picture It

412.**34** $\xrightarrow{+\,0.1}$ 412.**44**

0.1 more than 412.34 is 412.44.

b) What number is 0.1 less than 412.34?

412.**34** $\xrightarrow{-\,0.1}$ ▭

0.1 less than 412.34 is ▭.

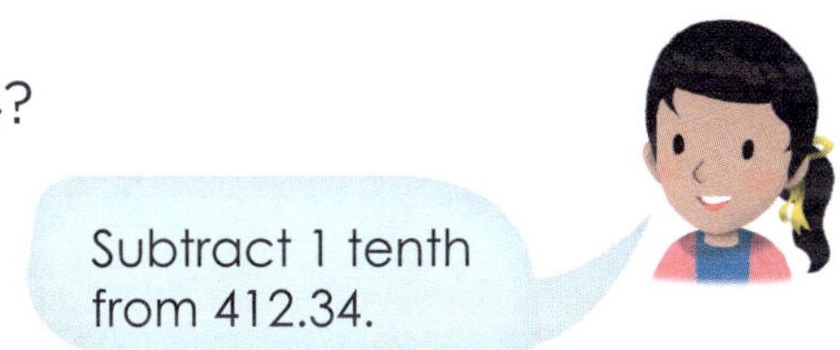

c) What number is 0.01 less than 123.48?

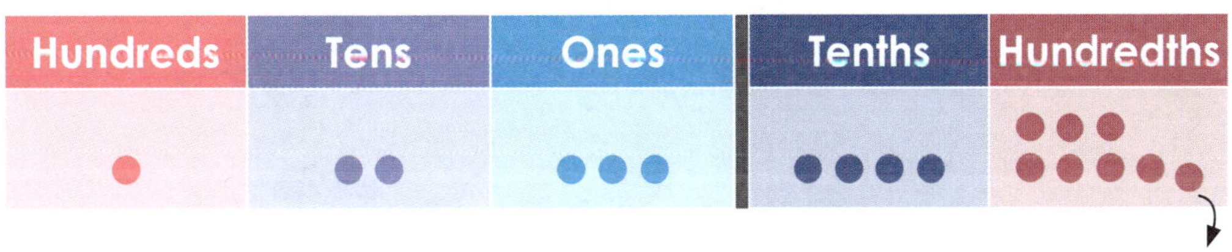

123.**48** $\xrightarrow{-\,0.01}$ 123.**47**

0.01 less than 123.48 is 123.47.

d) What number is 0.01 more than 123.48?

$123.4\mathbf{8} \xrightarrow{+0.01}$ ____

0.01 more than 123.48 is ____.

Add 1 hundredth to 123.48.

Let's Do

1. Fill in the blanks.

   a) 0.1 more than 31.25 is ______.

   b) 0.1 less than 42.57 is ______.

   c) 0.01 more than 125.83 is ______.

   d) 0.01 less than 248.91 is ______.

P/B Chapter 9: Exercise 9, pages 141–142

Expressing decimals as fractions or mixed numbers in their simplest form

Let's Learn

a) Express 0.25 as a fraction in its simplest form.

$$0.25 = \frac{25}{100} = \frac{1}{4}$$

25 hundredths is 25 out of 100 or $\frac{25}{100}$.

$$\frac{25}{100} \overset{\div 25}{\underset{\div 25}{=}} \frac{1}{4}$$

b) Express 1.84 as a mixed number in its simplest form.

$$1.84 = 1\frac{84}{100} = \text{____}$$

$$1.84 = 1 + 0.84 = 1 + \frac{84}{100} = 1\frac{84}{100}$$

Let's Do

1. Express each decimal as a fraction or mixed number in its simplest form.

   a) $0.06 = \frac{6}{100} =$ ______

   b) 0.28 = ______ = ______

   c) $2.05 = 2\frac{5}{100} =$ ______

   d) 3.65 = ______ = ______

 ISBN 978-93-5103-031-7

Expressing fractions and mixed numbers as decimals

Let's Learn

a) Express $\frac{3}{5}$ as a decimal.

$$\frac{3}{5} = \frac{6}{10}$$
$$= 0.6$$

$\frac{3}{5}$ can be changed to a fraction which has a denominator of 10.

$$\frac{3}{5} \underset{\times 2}{\overset{\times 2}{=}} \frac{6}{10}$$

b) Express $4\frac{9}{20}$ as a decimal.

$$\frac{9}{20} = \frac{\square}{100}$$
$$= \square$$
$$4\frac{9}{20} = \square$$

$\frac{9}{20}$ can be changed to a fraction which has a denominator of 100.

$$\frac{9}{20} \underset{\times 5}{\overset{\times 5}{=}} \frac{\square}{100}$$

Let's Do

1. Express each fraction or mixed number as a decimal.

a) $\frac{3}{4} = \frac{\square}{100} =$ ______

b) $\frac{7}{20} = \frac{\square}{100} =$ ______

c) $\frac{8}{25} = \frac{\square}{100} =$ ______

d) $1\frac{1}{2} = 1\frac{\square}{10} =$ ______

e) $2\frac{2}{5} = 2\frac{\square}{10} =$ ______

f) $3\frac{27}{50} = 3\frac{\square}{100} =$ ______

PB Chapter 9: Exercise 10, pages 143–144

 ISBN 978-93-5103-031-7

Comparing and ordering decimals

Let's Learn

a) Which is greater, 2.12 or 2.9?

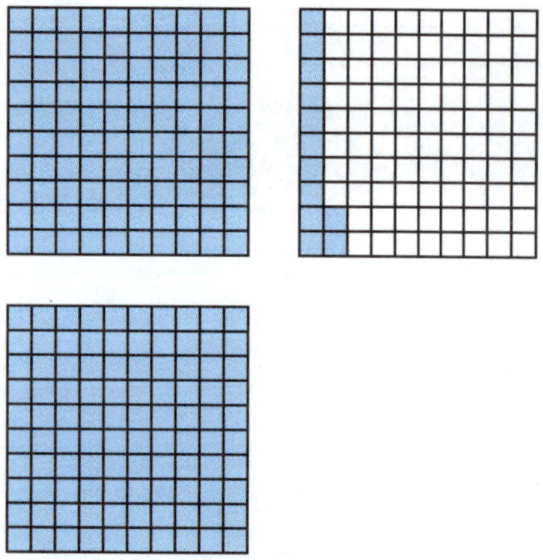

2.12

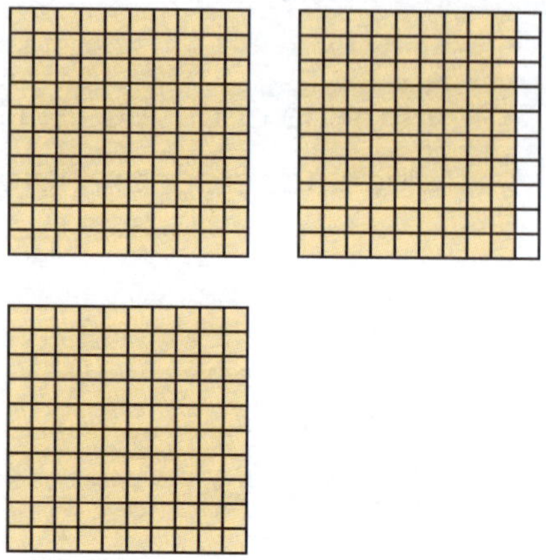

2.9

2.9 is greater than 2.12.
2.9 > 2.12

b) Compare 562.38, 562.41 and 56.97.

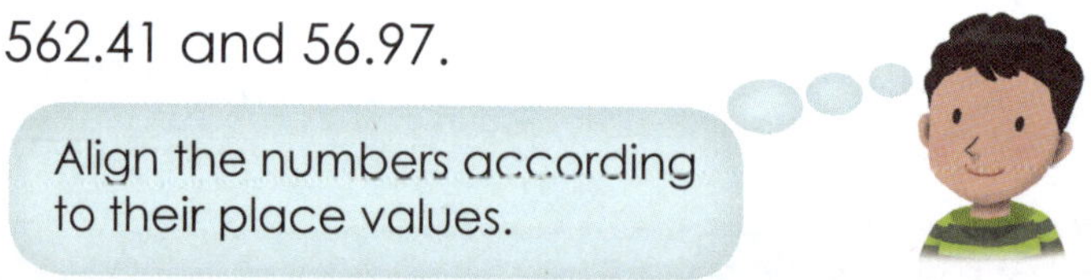

	Hundreds	Tens	Ones	Tenths	Hundredths
562.38	5	6	2	3	8
562.41	5	6	2	4	1
56.97		5	6	9	7

First, compare the hundreds.
0 hundreds is smaller than 5 hundreds.

56.97 is the smallest number.

Next, compare the tens and ones of 562.38 and 562.41.
They are the same.

Then, compare the tenths of 562.38 and 562.41.
3 tenths is smaller than 4 tenths.

562.38 is smaller than 562.41.
562.41 is the greatest number.

Arranging the numbers in order from the smallest, we have:

56.97, 562.38, 562.41
(smallest)

 ISBN 978-93-5103-031-7

Let's Do

1. Which is smaller, 1.68 or 2.35? ______

2. Which is greater, 89.67 or 243.5? ______

3. Arrange the numbers in order. Begin with the greatest.

   a) 2.02, 0.2, 0.02, 2.2 ________________________

   b) 74.5, 7.45, 7.8, 80.7 ________________________

P/B Chapter 9: Exercise 11, pages 145–146

Practice 2

1. Write the decimals.

   a) 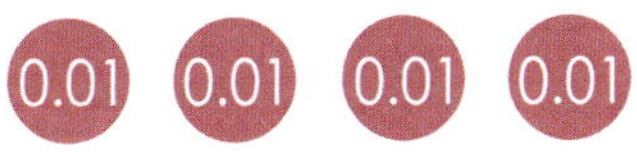

   4 hundredths = ____

   b) 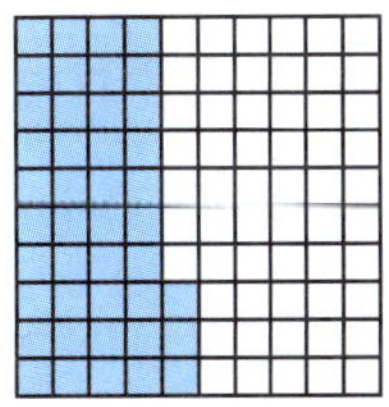

   $\frac{43}{100}$ = ____

2. Express each of the following as a decimal.

   a) 68 hundredths b) 72 hundredths c) 9 hundredths

3. What are the missing numbers?

   a) 8.07 = 8 + ____ b) 9.26 = 9 + ____ + 0.06

   c) 12.96 = 10 + ____ + 0.9 + 0.06 d) 6.38 = 6 + 0.3 + ____

   e) $5.14 = 5 + \frac{1}{10} + \frac{\square}{100}$ f) $3.04 = 3 + \frac{4}{\square}$

4. In 654.32,

   a) which digit stands for 600?

   b) which digit has a value of 0.3?

   c) which digit is in the tenths place?

   d) which digit is in the hundredths place?

 ISBN 978-93-5103-031-7

5. Express each fraction as a decimal.

a) $\frac{30}{100}$ b) $\frac{3}{100}$ c) $2\frac{18}{100}$ d) $3\frac{42}{100}$

6. Express each amount of money as a decimal.

a) 30 p
b) 50 p
c) 75 p
d) 95 p
e) 3 rupees and 50 paise
f) 5 rupees and 5 paise

7. What number is represented by each letter?

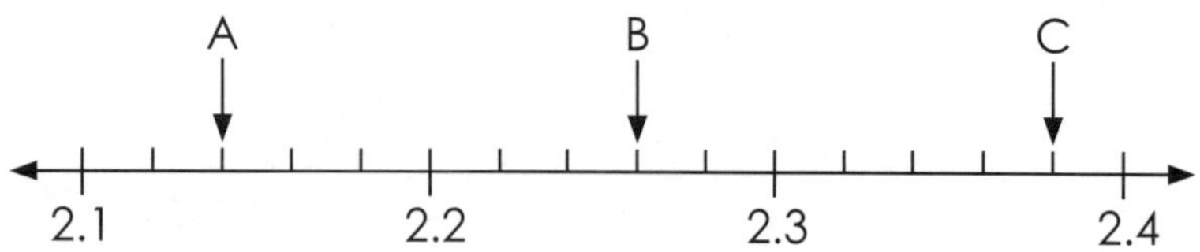

8. a) What number is 0.1 more than 20.08?
b) What number is 0.01 less than 20.08?
c) What number is 0.01 more than 35.09?

9. Express each decimal as a fraction or mixed number in its simplest form.

a) 0.08
b) 1.25
c) 4.45
d) 6.06

10. Express each fraction or mixed number as a decimal.

a) $\frac{1}{4}$
b) $\frac{3}{5}$
c) $5\frac{3}{4}$
d) $10\frac{17}{20}$

11. a) Which is greater, 42.6 or 42.06?
b) Which is longer, 2.38 m or 2.5 m?
c) Which is heavier, 32.6 kg or 3.26 kg?

12. Arrange the numbers in order. Begin with the greatest.

a) 3.03, 0.3, 0.03, 3.3
b) 63.5, 6.35, 6.4, 5.63

ISBN 978-93-5103-031-7

Lesson 3 Thousandths

Reading and writing decimals

Let's Learn

a) 0.001 is 1 **thousandth**.

$0.001 = \frac{1}{1000}$

Read 0.001 as **zero point zero zero one**.

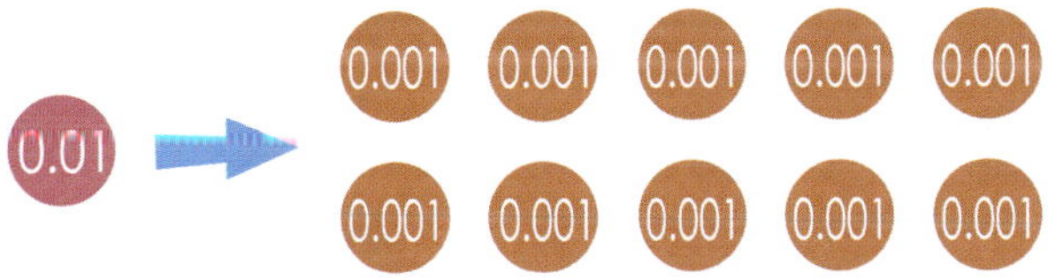

1 hundredth = 10 thousandths

$\frac{1}{100} = \frac{10}{1000}$

b)

0.123 is 123 thousandths.

$0.123 = \frac{123}{1000}$

Read 0.123 as **zero point one two three**.

0.123 is 1 tenth 2 hundredths 3 thousandths.

$0.123 = \frac{1}{10} + \frac{2}{100} + \frac{3}{1000}$

Let's Do

1. Write a decimal for each of the following.

a)

2 hundredths 4 thousandths = ______

b)

3 tenths 1 hundredth 5 thousandths = ______

c)

4 ones 2 thousandths = ______

 ISBN 978-93-5103-031-7

Interpreting decimals in terms of ones, tenths, hundredths and thousandths

Let's Learn

Picture It

Ones	Tenths	Hundredths	Thousandths
●●	●●●●	●	●●●

2 ones + 4 tenths + 1 hundredth + 3 thousandths
= 2 + 0.4 + 0.01 + 0.003
= 2.413

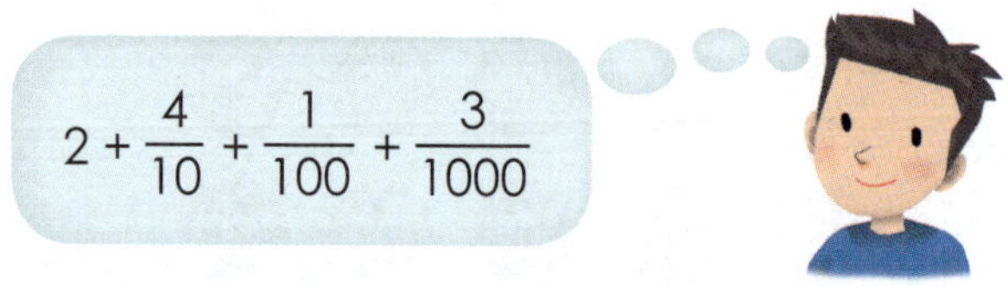

Let's Do

1. Fill in the blanks.

a) 30.125 = 30 + 0.1 + ______ + 0.005

b) $2.345 = 2 + \frac{\square}{10} + \frac{4}{\square} + \frac{5}{\square} = 2\frac{\square}{1000}$

P/B Chapter 9: Exercise 12, page 147

Identifying values of digits

Let's Learn

Picture It

Tens	Ones	Tenths	Hundredths	Thousandths
●●		●●●●	●●●	●●●●●
2	0	. 4	3	5

In 20.435, the digit 2 stands for 20.
Its value is 20.

The digit 0 is in the ones place.
Its value is 0.

The digit 5 is in the thousandths place.
Its value is 0.005.

The digit ___ is in the tenths place.
Its value is ___.

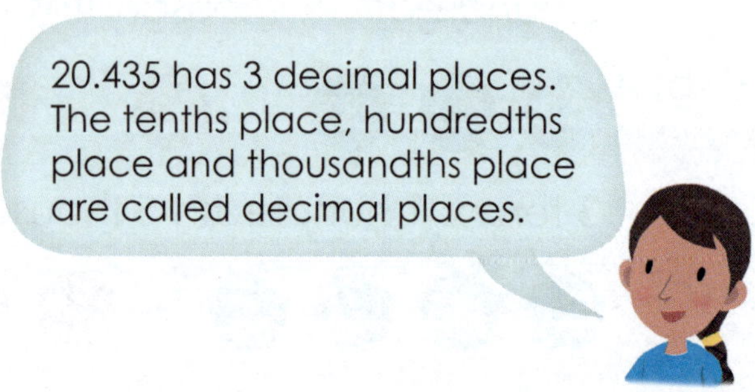

  ISBN 978-93-5103-031-7

Let's Do

1. Read the table. Then, fill in the blanks.

Hundreds	Tens	Ones	Tenths	Hundredths	Thousandths
4	2	6 .	5	0	8

In 426.508,

a) the digit 8 stands for ______.

b) the digit 0 is in the ______________ place.
Its value is ______.

c) the digit ______ is in the tenths place.
Its value is ______.

Chapter 9: Exercise 13, page 148

Expressing fractions and mixed numbers as decimals

Let's Learn

a) Express $\frac{8}{1000}$ as a decimal.

$\frac{8}{1000} = 0.008$

8 thousandths

b) Express $\frac{35}{1000}$ as a decimal.

$\frac{35}{1000} = 0.035$

35 thousandths

c) Express $2\frac{170}{1000}$ as a decimal.

$2\frac{170}{1000} = 2.17$

$$\begin{aligned} 2\frac{170}{1000} &= 2 + \frac{170}{1000} \\ &= 2 + 0.170 \\ &= 2.170 \\ &= 2.17 \end{aligned}$$

 ISBN 978-93-5103-031-7

Let's Do

1. Express each fraction or mixed number as a decimal.

a) $\frac{485}{1000} =$ ______ b) $\frac{64}{1000} =$ ______ c) $\frac{3}{1000} =$ ______

d) $5\frac{476}{1000} =$ ______ e) $2\frac{18}{1000} =$ ______ f) $3\frac{40}{1000} =$ ______

P/B Chapter 9: Exercise 14, page 149

Reading number lines

Let's Learn

Picture It

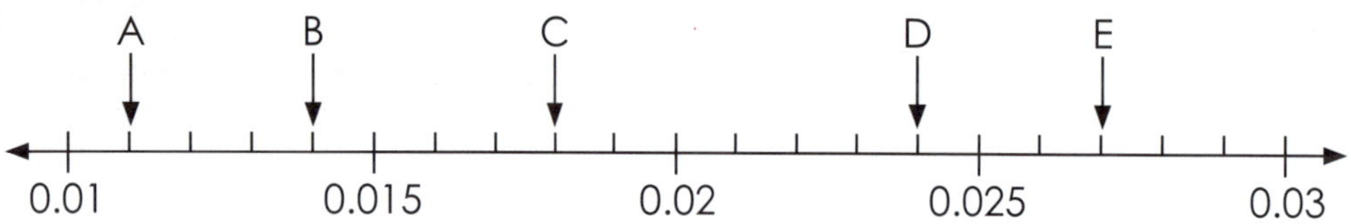

There are 10 equal intervals between 0.01 and 0.02.
Each interval stands for 0.001.

Point A stands for 0.011.

Point B stands for ▢.

Point C stands for ▢.

Point D stands for 0.024.

Point E stands for ▢.

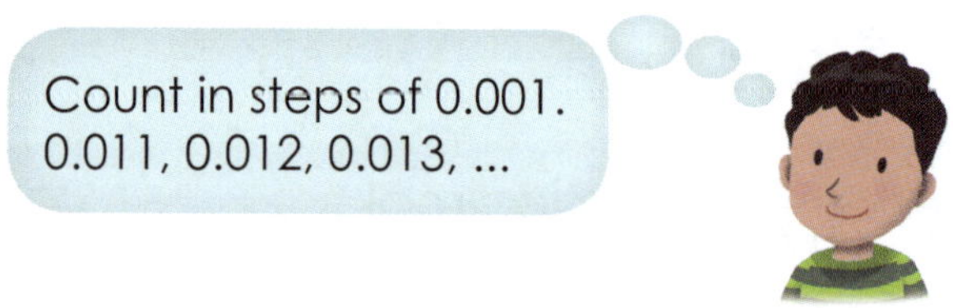

Let's Do

1. Fill in the missing decimals.

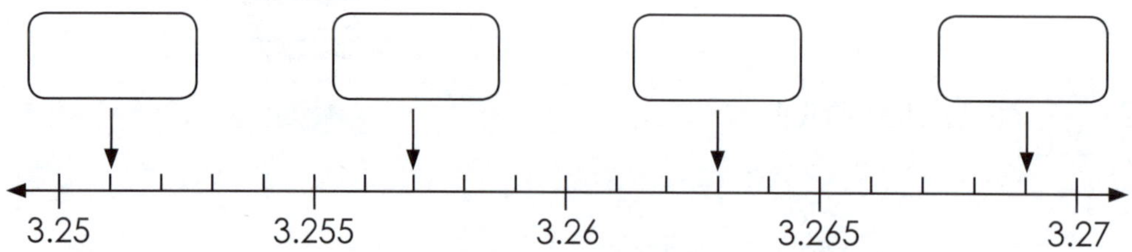

  ISBN 978-93-5103-031-7

Finding 'more than' and 'less than'

Let's Learn

a) What number is 0.001 more than 4.536?

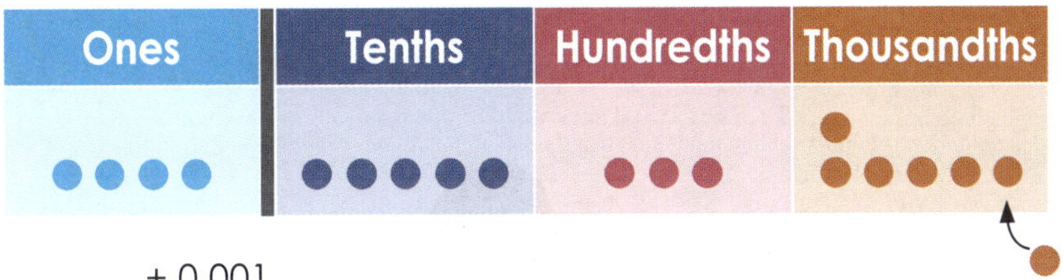

4.53**6** $\xrightarrow{+\ 0.001}$ 4.53**7**

0.001 more than 4.536 is 4.537.

b) What number is 0.01 less than 15.623?

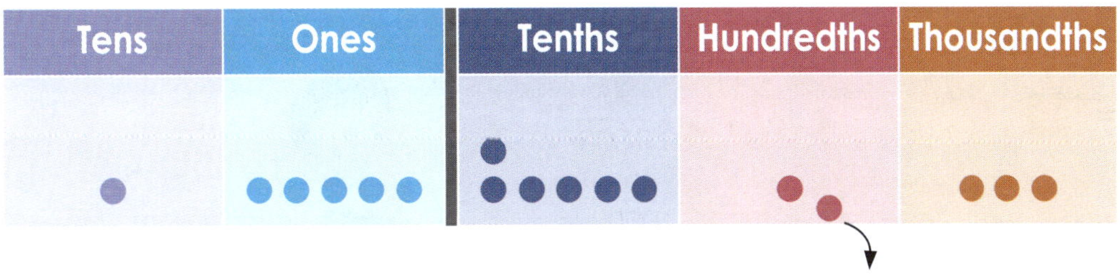

15.6**2**3 $\xrightarrow{-\ 0.01}$ 15.6**1**3

0.01 less than 15.623 is 15.613.

c) What number is 0.1 more than 15.623?

15.**6**23 $\xrightarrow{+\ 0.1}$

0.1 more than 15.623 is .

Let's Do

1. Fill in the blanks.

   a) 0.1 less than 27.148 is ______.

   b) 0.01 more than 27.148 is ______.

   c) 0.001 less than 27.148 is ______.

Chapter 9: Exercise 15, page 150

Expressing decimals as fractions or mixed numbers in their simplest form

Let's Learn

a) Express 0.052 as a fraction in its simplest form.

$$0.052 = \frac{52}{1000} = \frac{13}{250}$$

$$\frac{52}{1000} \overset{\div 4}{=} \frac{13}{250}$$

b) Express 2.045 as a mixed number in its simplest form.

$$2.045 = 2\frac{45}{1000} = \square$$

$$2.045 = 2 + 0.045 = 2 + \frac{45}{1000} = 2\frac{45}{1000}$$

Let's Do

1. Express each decimal as a fraction or mixed number in its simplest form.

a) $0.024 = \frac{24}{1000} =$ ______

b) $0.345 =$ ______ $=$ ______

c) $3.002 = 3\frac{2}{1000} =$ ______

d) $2.408 =$ ______ $=$ ______

P/B Chapter 9: Exercise 16, page 151

 ISBN 978-93-5103-031-7

Comparing and ordering decimals

Let's Learn

Compare 63.182, 63.187 and 6.319.

	Tens	Ones	Tenths	Hundredths	Thousandths
63.182	6	3 .	1	8	2
63.187	6	3 .	1	8	7
6.319		6 .	3	1	9

First, compare the tens.
0 tens is smaller than 6 tens.

6.319 is the smallest number.

Then, compare the ones, tenths and hundredths of 63.182 and 63.187.
They are the same.

Lastly, compare the thousandths of 63.182 and 63.187.
2 thousandths is smaller than 7 thousandths.

63.182 is smaller than 63.187.
63.187 is the greatest number.

Arranging the numbers in order from the smallest, we have:

6.319, 63.182, 63.187
(smallest)

Let's Do

1. Which is smaller, 52.071 or 52.08? ____________

2. Which is greater, 74.65 or 74.563? ____________

3. Arrange the numbers in order. Begin with the greatest.

   a) 0.32, 0.302, 0.032, 3.02 ____________________

   b) 2.139, 2.628, 2.045, 2.189 ____________________

 ISBN 978-93-5103-031-7

Comparing and ordering decimals and fractions

Let's Learn

Compare $\frac{4}{5}$, 0.652, 2 and 0.6.

To compare, express $\frac{4}{5}$ as a decimal.

$\frac{4}{5} = \frac{8}{10} = 0.8$

	Ones	Tenths	Hundredths	Thousandths
0.8	0 .	8	0	0
0.652	0 .	6	5	2
2	2 .	0	0	0
0.6	0 .	6	0	0

First, compare the ones.
2 ones is the greatest.

2 is the greatest number.

0.8 = 0.800
2 = 2.000
0.6 = 0.600

Next, compare the tenths of 0.8, 0.652 and 0.6.
8 tenths is greater than 6 tenths.
0.8 is greater than 0.652 and 0.6.

Then, compare the hundredths of 0.652 and 0.6.
5 hundredths is greater than 0 hundredths.
0.652 is greater than 0.6.

0.6 is the smallest number.

Arranging the numbers in order from the smallest, we have:

0.6, 0.652, 0.8, 2

0.6, 0.652, $\frac{4}{5}$, 2
(smallest)

 ISBN 978-93-5103-031-7

Let's Do

1. Arrange the numbers in order. Begin with the greatest.

   $7.231,\ \frac{7}{25},\ 1\frac{3}{4},\ 0.35$

   ____

   Express $\frac{7}{25}$ and $1\frac{3}{4}$ as decimals.

Chapter 9: Exercise 17, page 152

Practice 3

1. Write the decimals.

   a) 

   b) 

2. What are the missing numbers?

   a) $7.206 = 7 + \_\_\_\_ + 0.006$

   b) $6.805 = 6 + 0.8 + \_\_\_\_$

   c) $5.012 = 5 + \frac{1}{100} + \frac{\square}{1000}$

   d) $2.004 = 2 + \frac{4}{\square}$

3. What is the value of the digit 6 in each of the following numbers?

   a) 1.658 b) 6.185 c) 3.069 d) 5.746

4. What are the missing numbers?

   a) In 3.864, the digit ____ is in the thousandths place.

   b) In 49.73, the digit ____ is in the tenths place.

   c) In 12.58, the value of the digit 8 is ____.

   d) In 3.704, the value of the digit 4 is ____.

5. Express each fraction or mixed number as a decimal.

   a) $\frac{567}{1000}$ b) $\frac{49}{1000}$ c) $3\frac{7}{1000}$ d) $2\frac{9}{1000}$

 ISBN 978-93-5103-031-7

6. Express each of the following as a decimal.

a) $1 + \frac{7}{10} + \frac{3}{1000}$

b) $\frac{8}{100} + \frac{5}{1000}$

c) $5 + \frac{6}{100} + \frac{9}{1000}$

d) $10 + \frac{52}{1000}$

7. What number is represented by each letter?

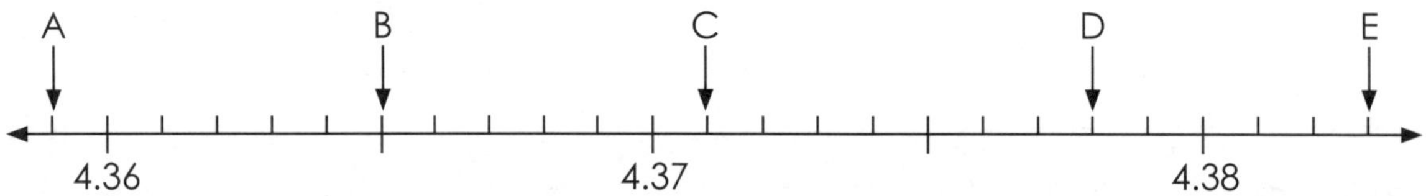

8. a) What number is 0.1 less than 5.609?

b) What number is 0.01 more than 2.809?

c) What number is 0.001 less than 13.521?

9. Express each decimal as a fraction or mixed number in its simplest form.

a) 0.145 b) 0.408 c) 4.506 d) 2.006

10. Fill in the blanks with **greater than**, **smaller than** or **equal to**.

a) $\frac{47}{1000}$ is ______ 0.047.

b) 0.205 is ______ $\frac{25}{1000}$.

c) $3\frac{3}{5}$ is ______ 3.69.

d) 2.8 is ______ $2\frac{4}{5}$.

e) 1.425 is ______ $1\frac{1}{4}$.

f) 0.87 is ______ $\frac{78}{100}$.

11. Arrange the numbers in order. Begin with the greatest.

a) 0.008, 0.09, 0.08, 0.009

b) 3.25, 3.205, 3.025, 3.502

c) 4.386, 4.683, 4.638, 4.9

d) 10, 9.932, 9.392, 9.923

ISBN 978-93-5103-031-7

Lesson 4 Rounding

Rounding decimals to the nearest whole number

Let's Learn

a) The height of the Petronas Towers in Malaysia is 451.9 metres.

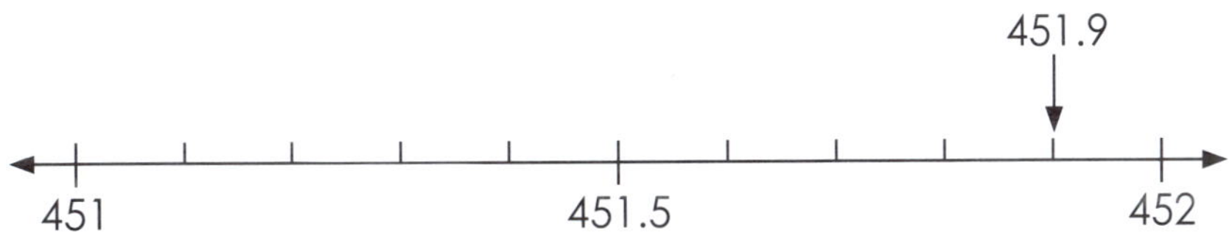

451.9 is between 451 and 452.
It is nearer to 452 than to 451.

451.9 is 452 when rounded to the nearest whole number.
$451.9 \approx 452$
The height of the Petronas Towers is about 452 metres.

b) John's weight is 37.42 kilograms.

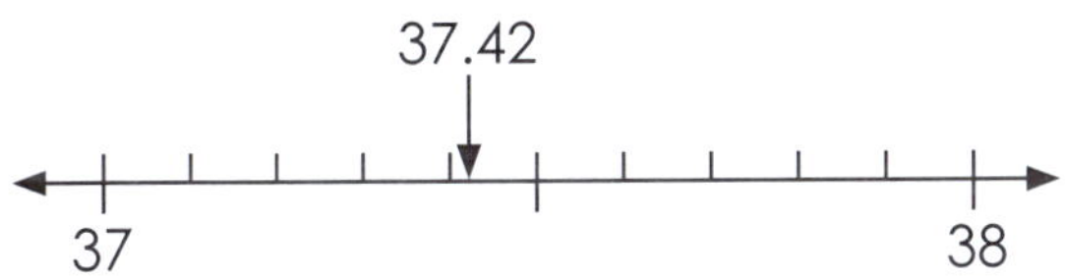

$37.42 \approx 37$
His weight is 37 kilograms when rounded to the nearest kilogram.

37.42 is less than halfway between 37 and 38.
It is rounded to 37.

c) A tank contains 24.5 litres of water.

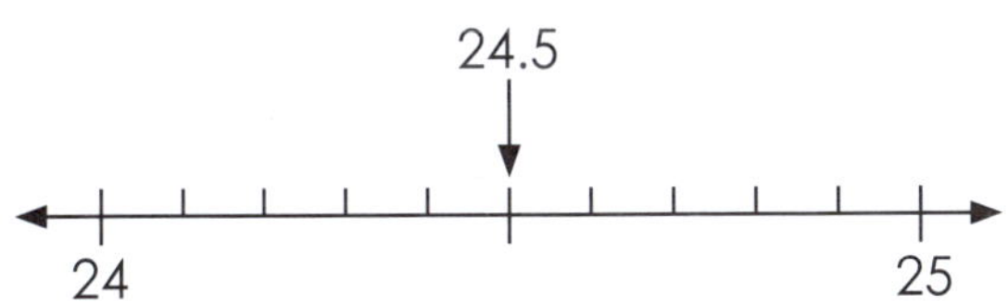

$24.5 \approx 25$
The volume of water in the tank is 25 litres when rounded to the nearest litre.

24.5 is halfway between 24 and 25.
Take 25 to be the nearest whole number.

 ISBN 978-93-5103-031-7

Let's Do

1. Round each decimal to the nearest whole number.

a) 4.2 ≈ ______ b) 13.9 ≈ ______ c) 29.5 ≈ ______

d) 5.45 ≈ ______ e) 15.64 ≈ ______ f) 18.52 ≈ ______

Chapter 9: Exercise 18, pages 153–154

Rounding decimals to 1 decimal place

Let's Learn

a) Round 3.18 metres to the nearest metre.

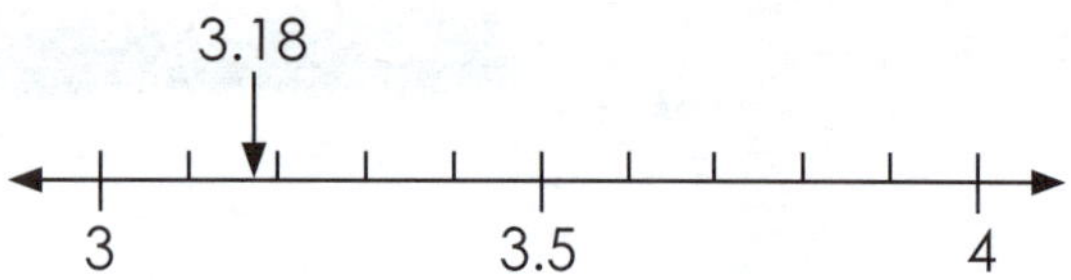

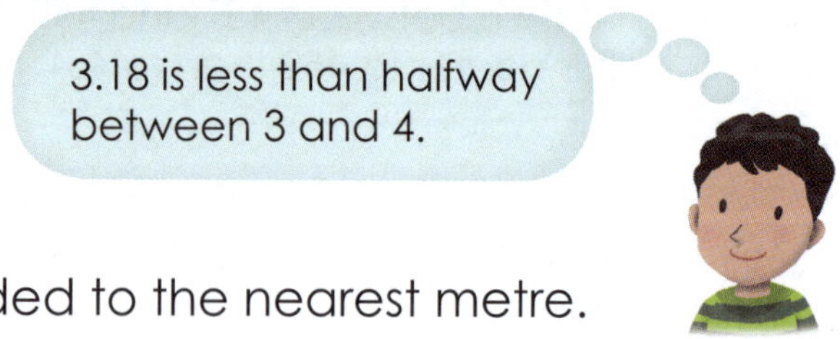

3.18 ≈ 3
3.18 metres is 3 metres when rounded to the nearest metre.

b) Round 3.18 metres to 1 decimal place.

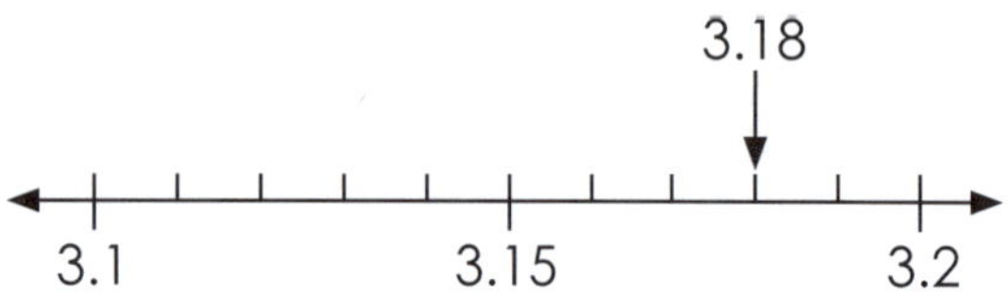

3.18 ≈ 3.2
3.18 metres is 3.2 metres when rounded to 1 decimal place.

c) Round 6.15 to the nearest whole number.

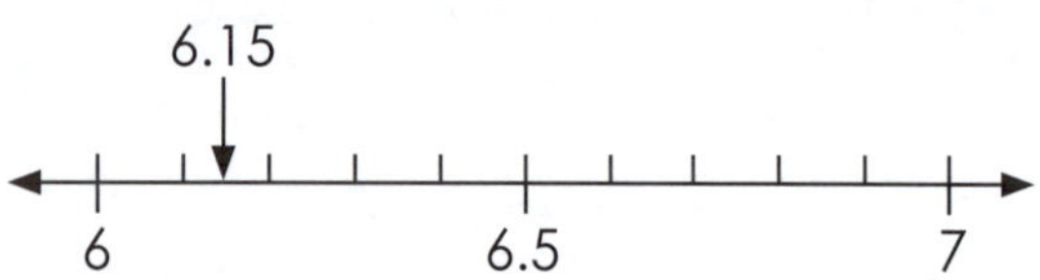

6.15 ≈ 6
6.15 is 6 when rounded to the nearest whole number.

d) Round 6.15 to 1 decimal place.

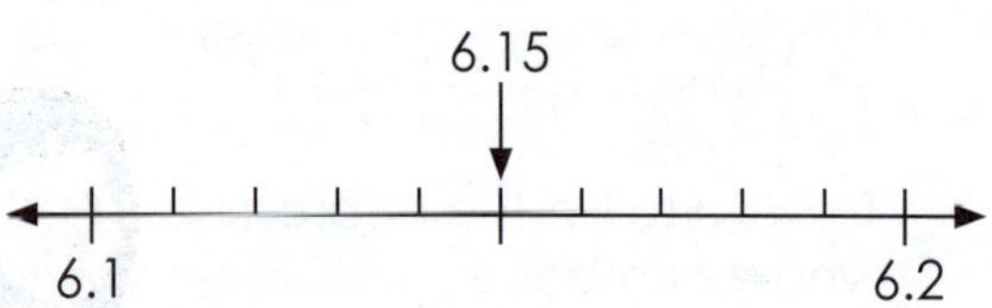

6.15 ≈ 6.2
6.15 is 6.2 when rounded to 1 decimal place.

 ISBN 978-93-5103-031-7

Let's Do

1. Round each decimal to 1 decimal place.

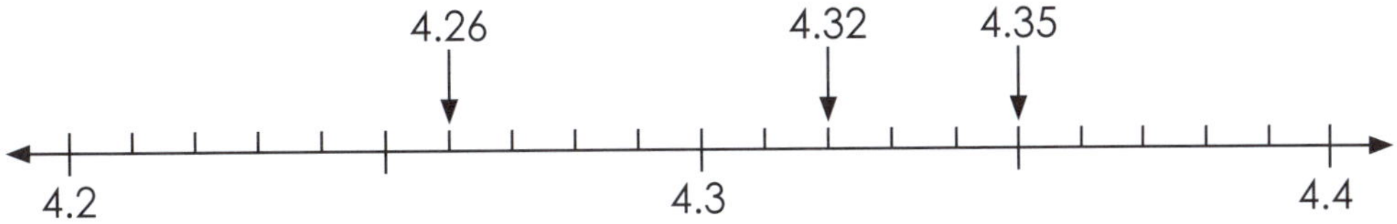

a) 4.26 ≈ ______ b) 4.32 ≈ ______ c) 4.35 ≈ ______

2. Round each decimal to 1 decimal place.

a) 0.91 ≈ ______ b) 2.45 ≈ ______ c) 7.08 ≈ ______

d) 24.55 ≈ ______ e) 18.01 ≈ ______ f) 10.96 ≈ ______

Chapter 9: Exercise 19, page 155

Think About It

Round 7.04 to 1 decimal place.

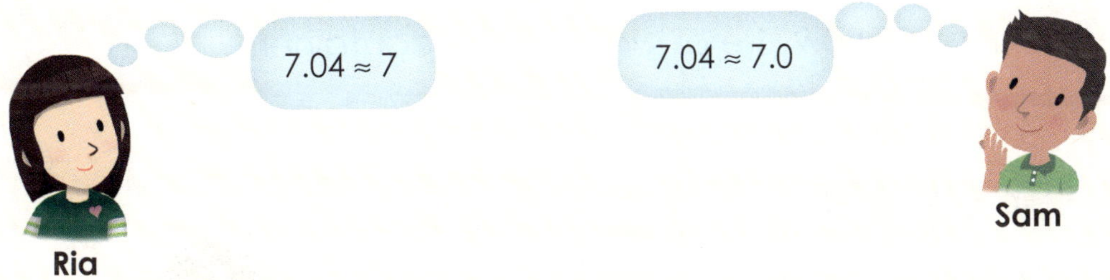

Who is correct? Explain why.

Practice 4

1. Round each decimal to the nearest whole number.

a) 3.2	b) 0.99	c) 12.8	d) 10.09
e) 3.95	f) 4.55	g) 10.28	h) 19.51

2. Round each decimal to 1 decimal place.

a) 0.82	b) 0.09	c) 2.65	d) 8.07
e) 10.89	f) 19.07	g) 20.55	h) 10.04

 ISBN 978-93-5103-031-7

10 The Four Operations of Decimals

Lesson 1 Addition

Adding tenths or hundredths without regrouping

Let's Learn

a) There is less than 1 litre of water in each container.

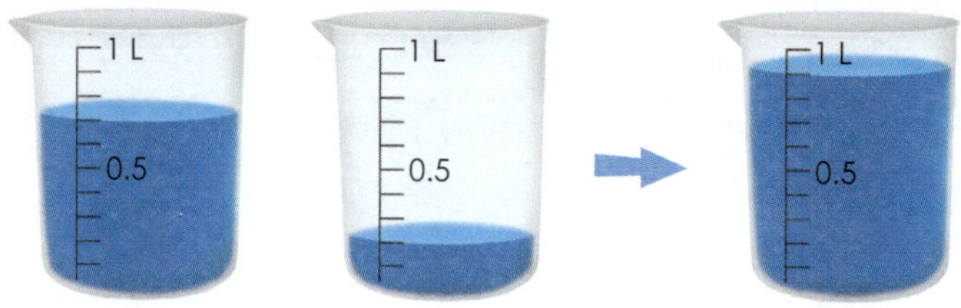

$0.7 + 0.2 = 0.9$

There is a total of 0.9 litre of water in the containers.

b) Add 0.4 and 0.3.

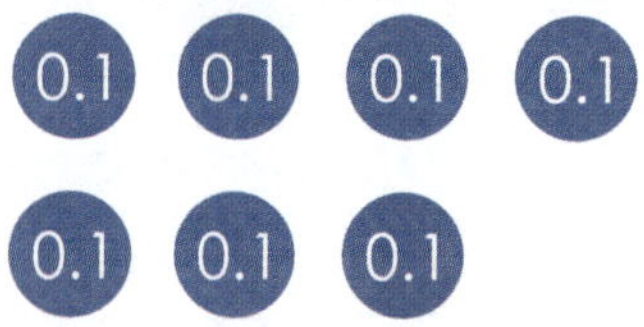

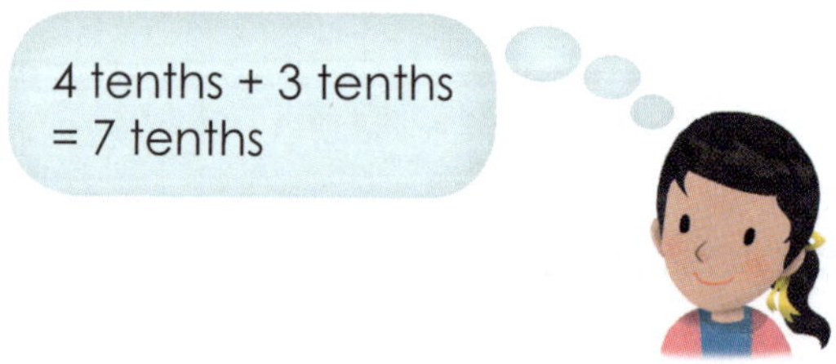

0.4 + 0.3 = ▢

c) Add 0.04 and 0.03.

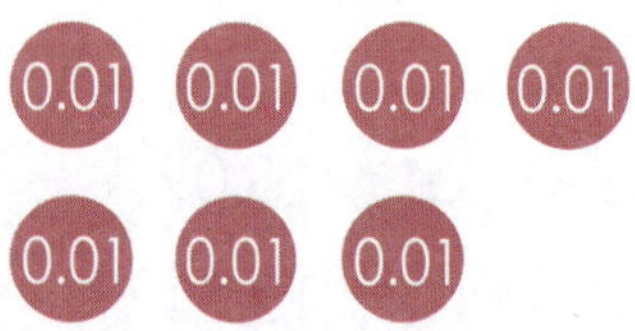

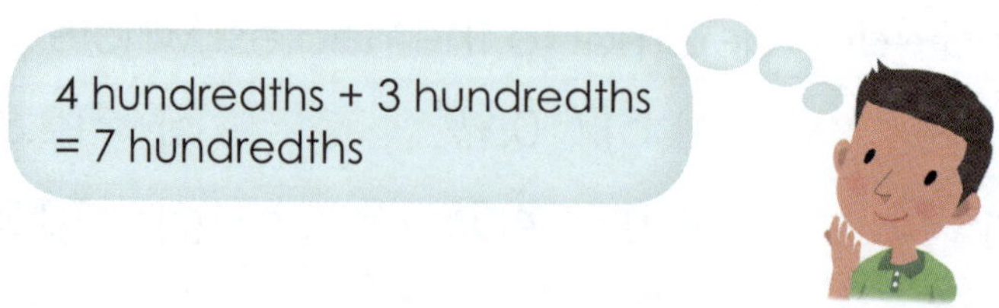

0.04 + 0.03 = ▢

Let's Do

1. Add.

a) 0.6 + 0.2 = ______ b) 0.02 + 0.04 = ______

 ISBN 978-93-5103-031-7

Adding tenths or hundredths with regrouping

Let's Learn

a) Add 0.7 and 0.6.

0.7 + 0.6 = ☐

Maths Lab

Picture It

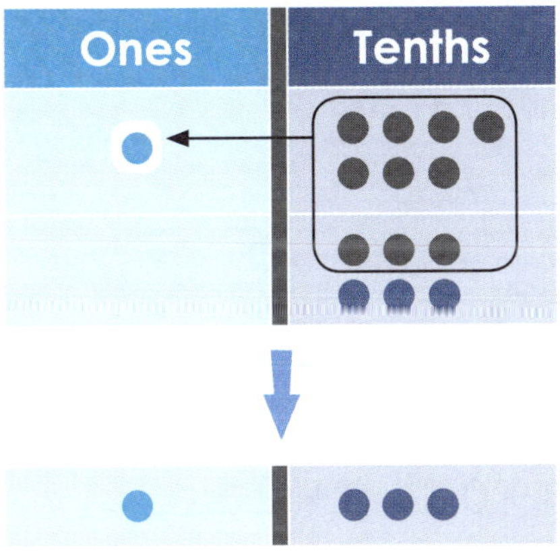

Add the tenths.

$$\begin{array}{r} {}^{1}\\ 0\,.\,7 \\ +\;0\,.\,6 \\ \hline 1\,.\,3 \\ \hline \end{array}$$

Align the decimal points.

7 tenths + 6 tenths
= 13 tenths
= 1 one 3 tenths

0.7 + 0.6 = 1.3

b) Add 0.07 and 0.06.

0.07 + 0.06 = ☐

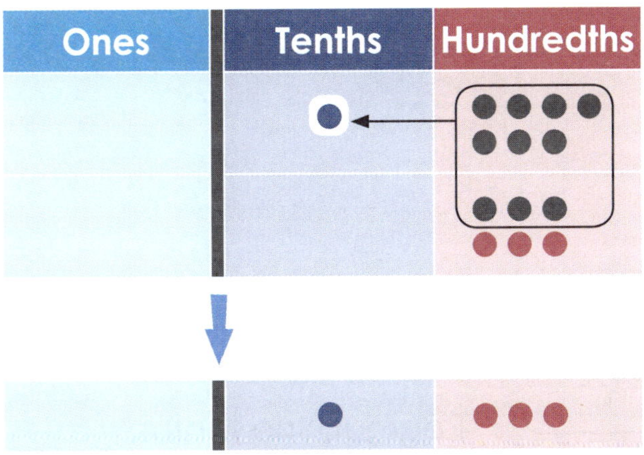

Add the hundredths.

$$\begin{array}{r} {}^{1}\;\; \\ 0\,.\,0\;7 \\ +\;0\,.\,0\;6 \\ \hline 0\,.\,1\;3 \\ \hline \end{array}$$

7 hundredths + 6 hundredths
= 13 hundredths
= 1 tenth 3 hundredths

0.07 + 0.06 = 0.13

Let's Do

1. Add.

a) $\begin{array}{r} 0\,.\,8 \\ +\;0\,.\,5 \\ \hline \square\,.\,\square \\ \hline \end{array}$ b) $\begin{array}{r} 0\,.\,3 \\ +\;0\,.\,9 \\ \hline \square\,.\,\square \\ \hline \end{array}$ c) $\begin{array}{r} 0\,.\,0\;7 \\ +\;0\,.\,0\;3 \\ \hline \square\,.\,\square\square \\ \hline \end{array}$ d) $\begin{array}{r} 0\,.\,0\;8 \\ +\;0\,.\,0\;9 \\ \hline \square\,.\,\square\square \\ \hline \end{array}$

PB Chapter 10: Exercise 1, pages 156–157

 ISBN 978-93-5103-031-7

Adding decimals with 1 decimal place with regrouping using number bonds

Let's Learn

Add 6.9 and 0.4.

6.9 + 0.4 = 6 + 1.3

= ▢

6.9 + 0.4

6 0.9

0.9 + 0.4 = 1.3

Let's Do

1. Add.

a) 2.8 + 0.7 = 2 + ______

2 ▢ = ______

b) 3.4 + 0.6 = 3 + ______

3 ▢ = ______

Adding decimals with 1 decimal place with regrouping using place values

Let's Learn

Add 3.6 and 1.8.

3.6 + 1.8 = ▢

Maths Lab

Picture It

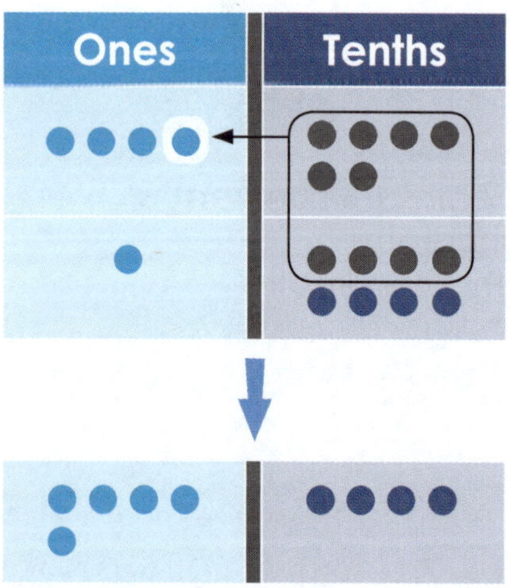

3.6 + 1.8 = 5.4

❶ Add the tenths.

```
   1
   3 . 6
 + 1 . 8
 -------
     . 4
```

6 tenths + 8 tenths = 14 tenths

Regroup the tenths.
14 tenths = 1 one 4 tenths

❷ Add the ones.

```
   1
   3 . 6
 + 1 . 8
 -------
   5 . 4
```


 ISBN 978-93-5103-031-7

Let's Do

1. Add.

a)
$$\begin{array}{r} 3.7 \\ +\ 2.3 \\ \hline \square.\square \end{array}$$

b)
$$\begin{array}{r} 8.4 \\ +\ 1.7 \\ \hline \square\square.\square \end{array}$$

c)
$$\begin{array}{r} 4.9 \\ +\ 1.8 \\ \hline \square.\square \end{array}$$

P/B Chapter 10: Exercise 2, pages 158–159

Adding decimals with 2 decimal places with regrouping using number bonds

Let's Learn

a) Add 0.42 and 0.9.

0.42 + 0.9 = 0.02 + 1.3

= ▢

0.42 + 0.9
/ \
0.4 0.02

0.4 + 0.9 = 1.3

b) Add 0.42 and 0.09.

0.42 + 0.09 = 0.4 + 0.11

= ▢

0.42 + 0.09
/ \
0.4 0.02

0.02 + 0.09 = 0.11

Let's Do

1. Add.

a) 0.56 + 0.4 = 0.06 + ______
(0.56 → ▢ and 0.06)
= ______

b) 0.84 + 0.3 = 0.04 + ______
(0.84 → ▢ and 0.04)
= ______

c) 0.37 + 0.03 = 0.3 + ______
(0.37 → 0.3 and ▢)
= ______

d) 0.97 + 0.06 = 0.9 + ______
(0.97 → 0.9 and ▢)
= ______

Adding decimals with 2 decimal places with regrouping of hundredths using place values

Let's Learn

Add 0.24 and 0.37.

0.24 + 0.37 = ▢

Maths Lab

Picture It

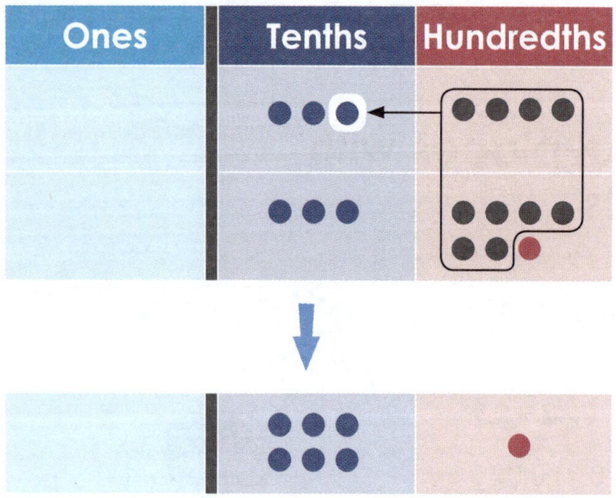

❶ Add the hundredths.

$$\begin{array}{r} {}^{1} \\ 0\,.\,2\,4 \\ +\;0\,.\,3\,7 \\ \hline 1 \\ \hline \end{array}$$

4 hundredths + 7 hundredths
= 11 hundredths

Regroup the hundredths.
11 hundredths
= 1 tenth 1 hundredth

❷ Add the tenths.

$$\begin{array}{r} {}^{1} \\ 0\,.\,2\,4 \\ +\;0\,.\,3\,7 \\ \hline 0\,.\,6\,1 \\ \hline \end{array}$$

0.24 + 0.37 = 0.61

Let's Do

1. Add.

a)
$$\begin{array}{r} 2\,.\,4\,6 \\ +\;0\,.\,0\,6 \\ \hline \\ \hline \end{array}$$

b)
$$\begin{array}{r} 0\,.\,6\,5 \\ +\;0\,.\,2\,5 \\ \hline \\ \hline \end{array}$$

c)
$$\begin{array}{r} 0\,.\,4\,6 \\ +\;0\,.\,3\,9 \\ \hline \\ \hline \end{array}$$

 ISBN 978-93-5103-031-7

Adding decimals with 2 decimal places with regrouping of tenths using place values

Let's Learn

Add 2.63 and 3.84.

2.63 + 3.84 = ▢

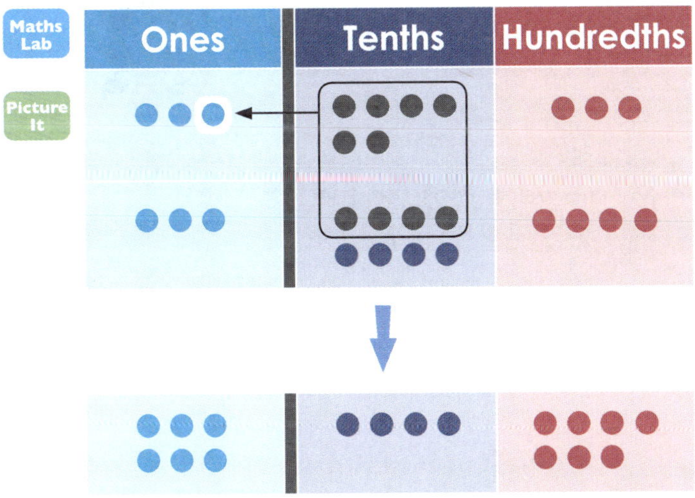

❶ Add the hundredths.

$$\begin{array}{r} 2\,.\,6\,3 \\ +\ 3\,.\,8\,4 \\ \hline 7 \\ \hline \end{array}$$

❷ Add the tenths.

$$\begin{array}{r} \scriptstyle 1\ \ \ \ \ \ \\ 2\,.\,6\,3 \\ +\ 3\,.\,8\,4 \\ \hline .\,4\,7 \\ \hline \end{array}$$

6 tenths + 8 tenths = 14 tenths

Regroup the tenths.
14 tenths = 1 one 4 tenths

❸ Add the ones.

$$\begin{array}{r} \scriptstyle 1\ \ \ \ \ \ \\ 2\,.\,6\,3 \\ +\ 3\,.\,8\,4 \\ \hline 6\,.\,4\,7 \\ \hline \end{array}$$

2.63 + 3.84 = 6.47

Let's Do

1. Add.

a) 25.48 + 7.64 = ______

$$\begin{array}{r} 2\,5\,.\,4\,8 \\ +\ \ \ 7\,.\,6\,4 \\ \hline \\ \hline \end{array}$$

b) 4.8 + 2.37 = ______

$$\begin{array}{r} 4\,.\,8\,0 \\ +\ 2\,.\,3\,7 \\ \hline \\ \hline \end{array}$$

PB Chapter 10: Exercises 3–4, pages 160–162

 ISBN 978-93-5103-031-7

Estimating sums

Let's Learn

a) Estimate the value of 34.26 + 10.82.

$34.26 + 10.82 \approx 34 + 11$
$= 45$

Note the change in symbol from ≈ to =.

Round each decimal to the nearest whole number.
$34.26 \approx 34$
$10.82 \approx 11$

b) Add 34.26 and 10.82.

$34.26 + 10.82 = 45.08$

My answer is close to the estimate. It is reasonable.

Let's Do

1. Estimate and then add.

a) $2.96 + 6.8 \approx$ ______ + ______
= ______

$$\begin{array}{r} 2.96 \\ +\ 6.80 \\ \hline \\ \hline \end{array}$$

b) $3.54 + 2.38 \approx$ ______ + ______
= ______

$$\begin{array}{r} 3.54 \\ +\ 2.38 \\ \hline \\ \hline \end{array}$$

P/B Chapter 10: Exercise 5, page 163

Solving word problems

Let's Learn

Peter paid ₹ 1.75 for a pencil and ₹ 5.40 for a pen. How much did he spend altogether?

Picture It

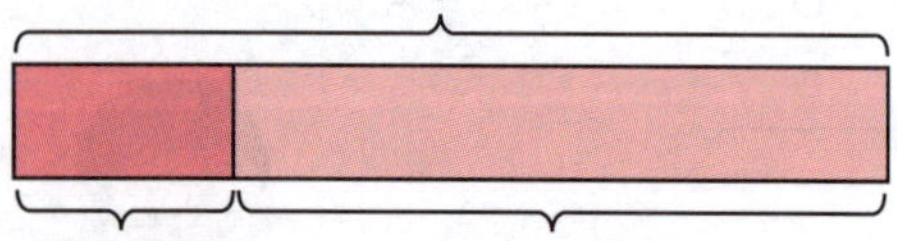

₹ 1.75 + ₹ 5.40 = ₹ 7.15

He spent ₹ 7.15 altogether.

₹ 1.75 + ₹ 5.40 ≈ ₹ 2 + ₹ 5
= ₹ 7
My answer is close to the estimate. It is reasonable.

 ISBN 978-93-5103-031-7

Let's Do

1. Mrs. Rao bought a papaya which weighed 1.87 kilograms. She also bought a watermelon which was 0.63 kilogram heavier than the papaya. What was the weight of the watermelon?

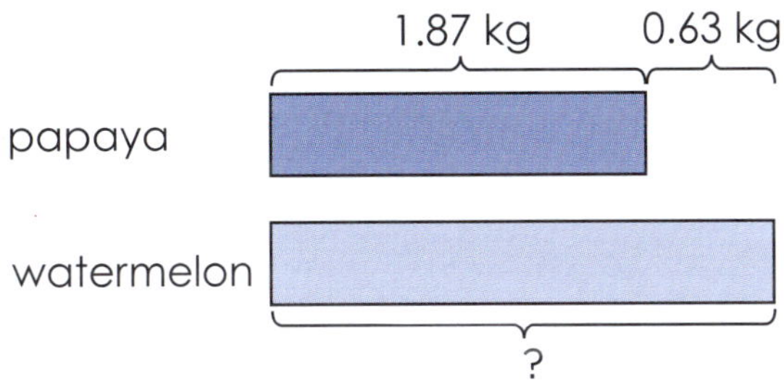

_______ + _______ = _______

The weight of the watermelon was _______ kilograms.

P/B Chapter 10: Exercise 6, page 164

Practice 1

1. Add.

a) 0.5 + 0.4	b) 0.8 + 0.9	c) 3.2 + 0.9
d) 0.02 + 0.08	e) 0.07 + 0.04	f) 0.76 + 0.5
g) 4.7 + 3.6	h) 0.58 + 0.24	i) 0.82 + 1.2
j) 40.29 + 8.45	k) 18.06 + 1.37	l) 26.29 + 13.73

2. Estimate and then add.

a) 1.85 + 5.7	b) 3.64 + 2.7	c) 3.2 + 3.98	d) 2.43 + 1.27
e) 8.92 + 4.16	f) 2.56 + 6.29	g) 1.08 + 6.5	h) 16.39 + 3.65

Solve the word problems. Show your work clearly.

3. After spending ₹ 3.60, Gopal had ₹ 16.80 left. How much money did he have at first?

4. Atul mixed 2.29 litres of orange juice and 1.76 litres of apple juice. What was the volume of the mixture?

5. Mrs. Kumar spent ₹ 15.75 on crayons. She spent ₹ 17.50 more on colour pencils than on crayons. How much did she spend on colour pencils?

 ISBN 978-93-5103-031-7

Lesson 2 Subtraction

Subtracting tenths from decimals smaller than 1 or from whole numbers

Let's Learn

a) There is more water in Container A than in Container B.

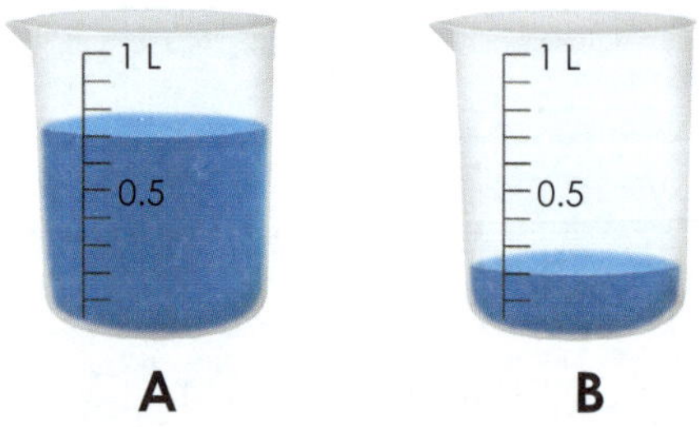

0.7 – 0.2 = 0.5

Container A has 0.5 litre more water than Container B.

b) Subtract 0.2 from 0.8.

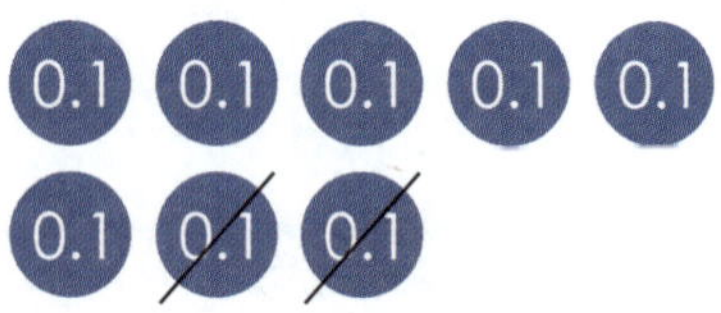

0.8 – 0.2 = ▢

c) Subtract 0.2 from 1.

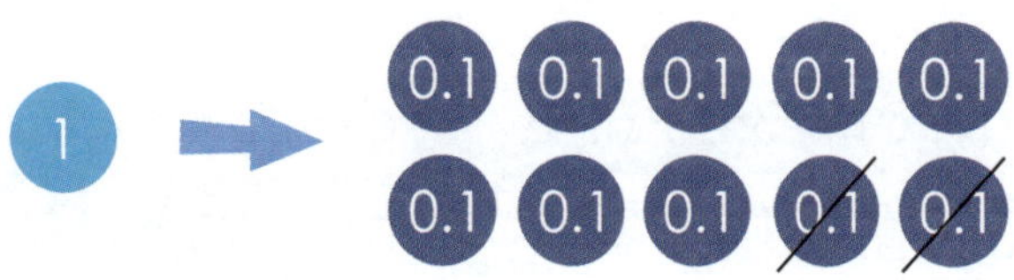

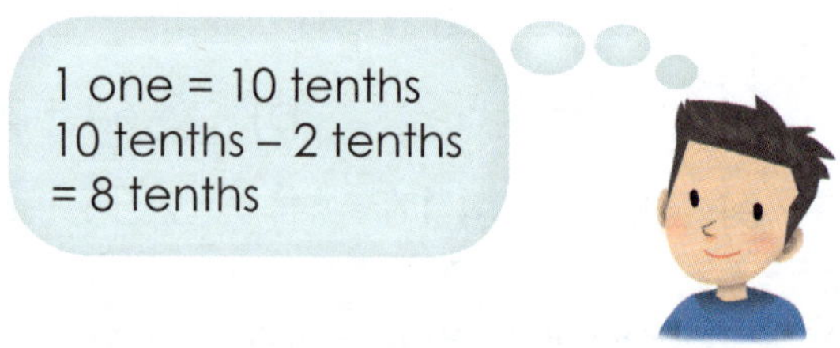

1 – 0.2 = ▢

d) Subtract 0.2 from 3.

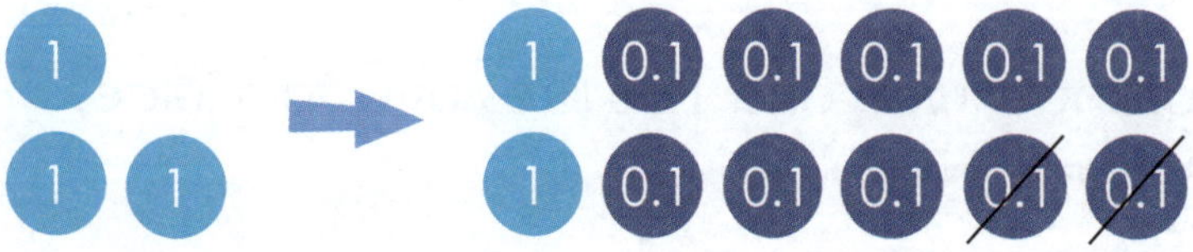

3 – 0.2 = ▢

 ISBN 978-93-5103-031-7

Let's Do

1. Subtract.

   a) $0.5 - 0.3 =$ ______ b) $0.9 - 0.2 =$ ______

   c) $1 - 0.4 =$ ______ d) $4 - 0.9 =$ ______

Subtracting tenths from decimals greater than 1

Let's Learn

Subtract 0.8 from 4.2.

$4.2 - 0.8 =$ ▭

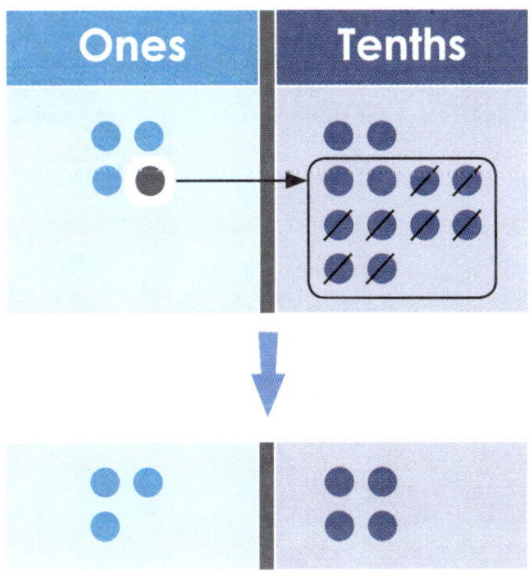

Subtract the tenths.

$$\begin{array}{r} \overset{3}{\not{4}}\ .\ {}^{1}2 \\ -\ 0\ .\ 8 \\ \hline 3\ .\ 4 \\ \hline \end{array}$$

Align the decimal points.

4 ones 2 tenths = 3 ones 12 tenths

3 ones 12 tenths – 8 tenths
= 3 ones 4 tenths

$4.2 - 0.8 = 3.4$

Let's Do

1. Subtract.

   a) $\begin{array}{r} 4\ .\ 7 \\ -\ 0\ .\ 6 \\ \hline \\ \hline \end{array}$ b) $\begin{array}{r} 1\ .\ 4 \\ -\ 0\ .\ 8 \\ \hline \\ \hline \end{array}$ c) $\begin{array}{r} 4\ .\ 0\ 5 \\ -\ 0\ .\ 5\ 0 \\ \hline \\ \hline \end{array}$

PB Chapter 10: Exercise 7, page 165

 ISBN 978-93-5103-031-7

Subtracting hundredths from decimals smaller than 1 or from whole numbers

Let's Learn

a) Subtract 0.06 from 0.08.

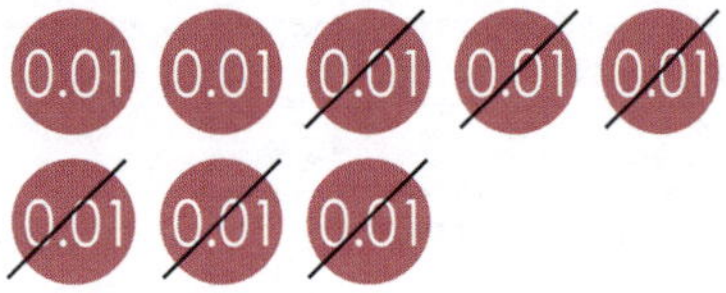

8 hundredths – 6 hundredths
= 2 hundredths

0.08 – 0.06 = ☐

b) Subtract 0.06 from 0.1.

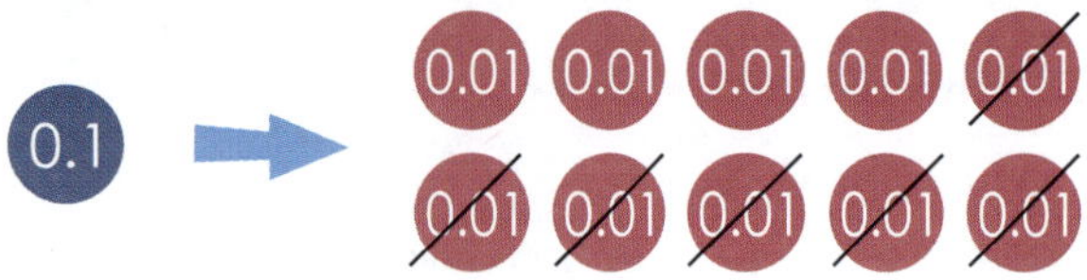

1 tenth = 10 hundredths

10 hundredths – 6 hundredths
= 4 hundredths

0.1 – 0.06 = ☐

c) Subtract 0.06 from 1.

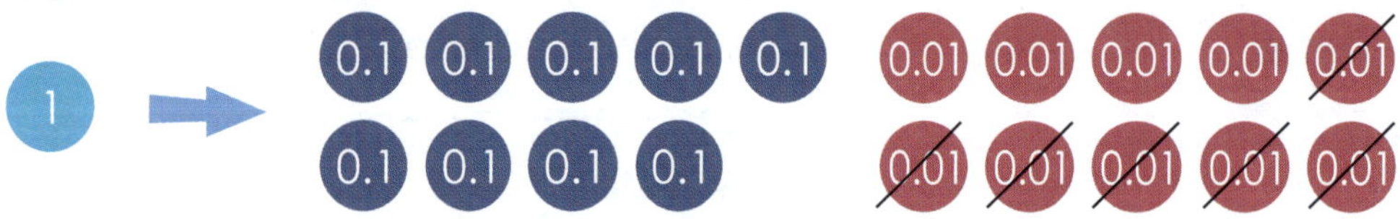

1 – 0.06 = ☐

1 one = 9 tenths 10 hundredths

9 tenths 10 hundredths – 6 hundredths
= 9 tenths 4 hundredths

Let's Do

1. Subtract.

a) 0.09 – 0.02 = ______

b) 0.49 – 0.02 = ______

c) 0.1 – 0.04 = ______

d) 0.3 – 0.04 = ______

e) 1 – 0.07 = ______

f) 2 – 0.07 = ______

 ISBN 978-93-5103-031-7

Subtracting decimals with 2 decimal places from whole numbers

Let's Learn

Subtract 0.23 from 1.

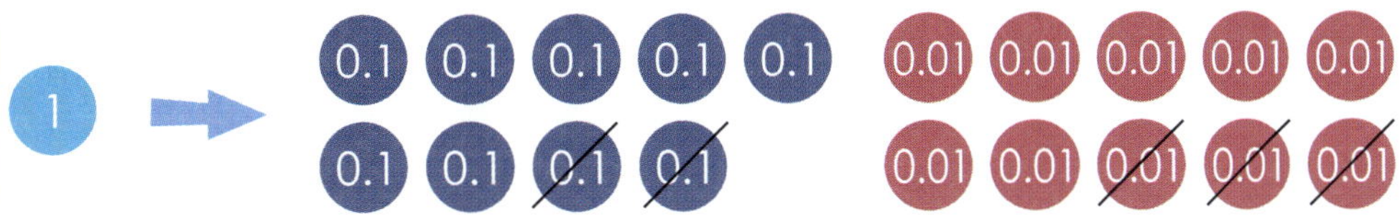

1 – 0.23 = ▢

1 one = 9 tenths 10 hundredths

9 tenths 10 hundredths – 2 tenths 3 hundredths
= 7 tenths 7 hundredths

Let's Do

1. Subtract.

a) 1 – 0.45 = ______ b) 4 – 0.86 = ______

c) 5 – 0.67 = ______ d) 7 – 0.72 = ______

Subtracting hundredths from decimals greater than 1

Let's Learn

Subtract 0.08 from 4.2.

4.2 – 0.08 = ▢

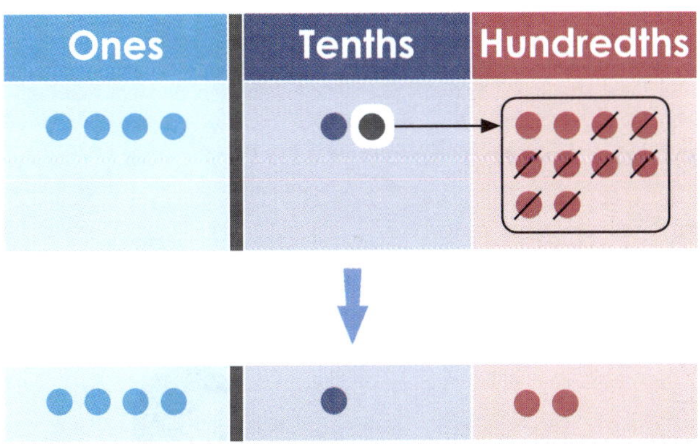

Subtract the hundredths.

```
     1
  4 .2̸ ¹0
– 0 . 0 8
---------
  4 . 1 2
```

Write 4.2 as 4.20 and align the decimal points.

4 ones 2 tenths = 4 ones 1 tenth 10 hundredths

4 ones 1 tenth 10 hundredths – 8 hundredths
= 4 ones 1 tenth 2 hundredths

4.2 – 0.08 = 4.12

 ISBN 978-93-5103-031-7

Let's Do

1. Subtract.

a) $\begin{array}{r} 3.29 \\ -\ 0.06 \\ \hline \\ \hline \end{array}$

b) $\begin{array}{r} 4.25 \\ -\ 0.09 \\ \hline \\ \hline \end{array}$

c) $\begin{array}{r} 6.20 \\ -\ 0.07 \\ \hline \\ \hline \end{array}$

P/B Chapter 10: Exercise 8, pages 166–167

Think About It

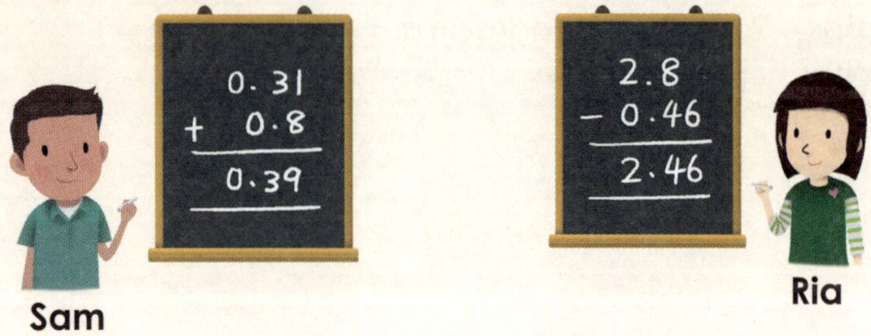

Are Sam and Ria correct? Explain why.

Subtracting decimals with 1 decimal place

Let's Learn

Subtract 2.7 from 6.

6 – 2.7 = ▢

Maths Lab

Picture It

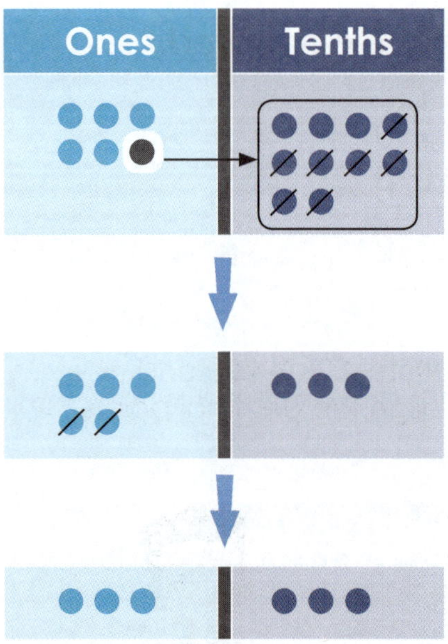

❶ Regroup the ones and tenths.
6 ones = 5 ones 10 tenths

Subtract the tenths.

$\begin{array}{r} \overset{5}{\not{6}}\,.\,^{1}0 \\ -\ 2\,.\,7 \\ \hline .\,3 \\ \hline \end{array}$

❷ Subtract the ones.

$\begin{array}{r} \overset{5}{\not{6}}\,.\,^{1}0 \\ -\ 2\,.\,7 \\ \hline 3\,.\,3 \\ \hline \end{array}$

6 – 2.7 = 3.3

 ISBN 978-93-5103-031-7

Let's Do

1. Subtract.

a)
$$\begin{array}{r} 4.9 \\ -\ 1.3 \\ \hline \\ \hline \end{array}$$

b)
$$\begin{array}{r} 5.2 \\ -\ 1.7 \\ \hline \\ \hline \end{array}$$

c)
$$\begin{array}{r} 8.0 \\ -\ 3.2 \\ \hline \\ \hline \end{array}$$

P/B Chapter 10: Exercise 9, page 168

Subtracting decimals up to 2 decimal places

Let's Learn

Subtract 2.53 from 4.27.

4.27 – 2.53 = ▢

Maths Lab

Picture It

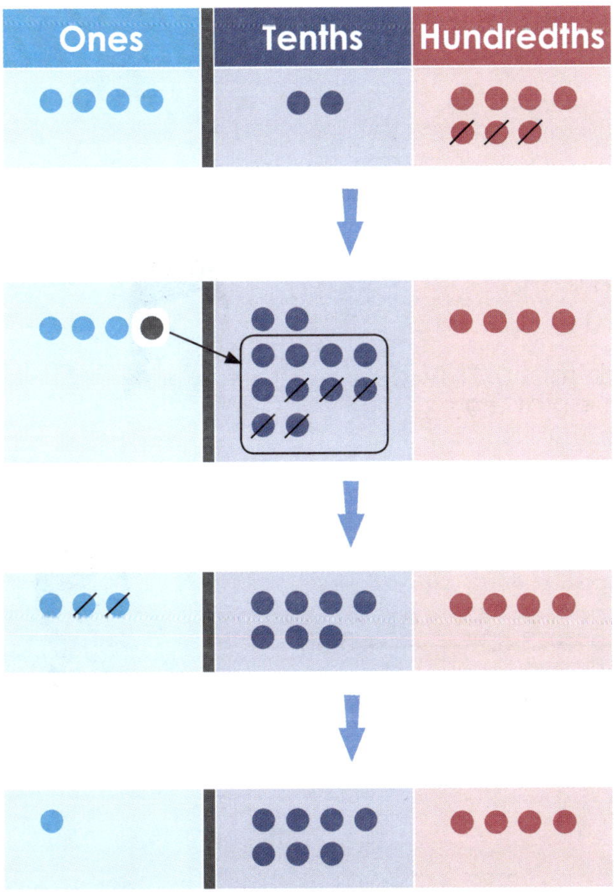

❶ Subtract the hundredths.

$$\begin{array}{r} 4.27 \\ -\ 2.53 \\ \hline 4 \\ \hline \end{array}$$

❷ Regroup the ones and tenths.
4 ones 2 tenths
= 3 ones 12 tenths

Subtract the tenths.

$$\begin{array}{r} \overset{3}{\not{4}}.{}^{1}27 \\ -\ 2.53 \\ \hline .74 \\ \hline \end{array}$$

❸ Subtract the ones.

$$\begin{array}{r} \overset{3}{\not{4}}.{}^{1}27 \\ -\ 2.53 \\ \hline 1.74 \\ \hline \end{array}$$

4.27 – 2.53 = 1.74

 ISBN 978-93-5103-031-7

Let's Do

1. Subtract.

a) $\begin{array}{r} 7.24 \\ -\ 3.50 \\ \hline \\ \hline \end{array}$ b) $\begin{array}{r} 5.00 \\ -\ 1.27 \\ \hline \\ \hline \end{array}$ c) $\begin{array}{r} 6.20 \\ -\ 3.54 \\ \hline \\ \hline \end{array}$

P/B Chapter 10: Exercise 10, pages 169–170

Adding or subtracting decimals close to whole numbers

Let's Learn

a) Add 4.28 and 2.99.

$4.28 + 2.99 = 7.28 - 0.01$
$= 7.27$

$2.99 = 3 - 0.01$

$4.28 \xrightarrow{+3} 7.28 \xrightarrow{-0.01} 7.27$

b) Add 8.99 and 0.99.

$8.99 + 0.99 = 10 - 0.02$
$= 9.98$

$8.99 = 9 - 0.01$
$0.99 = 1 - 0.01$

First, add 9 and 1.
$9 + 1 = 10$

Then, subtract 0.01 twice.
$10 - 0.01 - 0.01 = 9.98$

c) Subtract 1.99 from 5.62.

$5.62 - 1.99 = 3.62 + 0.01$
$= 3.63$

$1.99 = 2 - 0.01$

$5.62 \xrightarrow{-2} 3.62 \xrightarrow{+0.01} 3.63$

Let's Do

1. Find the value of

a) $3.87 + 1.99 =$ ______ $-$ ______
$=$ ______

$3.87 + 2 - 0.01$

  ISBN 978-93-5103-031-7

b) 3.99 + 5.99 = ______ − ______

= ______

c) 5.03 − 2.99 = ______ + ______

= ______

Chapter 10: Exercise 11, page 171

Estimating differences

Let's Learn

a) Estimate the value of 27.82 − 8.3.

$27.82 - 8.3 \approx 28 - 8$

$= 20$

Round each decimal to the nearest whole number.
$27.82 \approx 28$
$8.3 \approx 8$

b) Subtract 8.3 from 27.82.

$27.82 - 8.3 = 19.52$

My answer is close to the estimate.
It is reasonable.

Let's Do

1. Estimate and then subtract.

a) 7.23 − 4.6 ≈ ______ − ______

= ______

$$\begin{array}{r} 7.23 \\ -\ 4.60 \\ \hline \\ \hline \end{array}$$

b) 30.45 − 8.56 ≈ ______ − ______

= ______

$$\begin{array}{r} 30.45 \\ -\ 8.56 \\ \hline \\ \hline \end{array}$$

Chapter 10: Exercise 12, page 172

 ISBN 978-93-5103-031-7

Solving word problems

Let's Learn

Neena has a white ribbon that is 4.15 metres long. She also has a blue ribbon that is 1.9 metres long. How much longer is the white ribbon than the blue ribbon?

Picture It

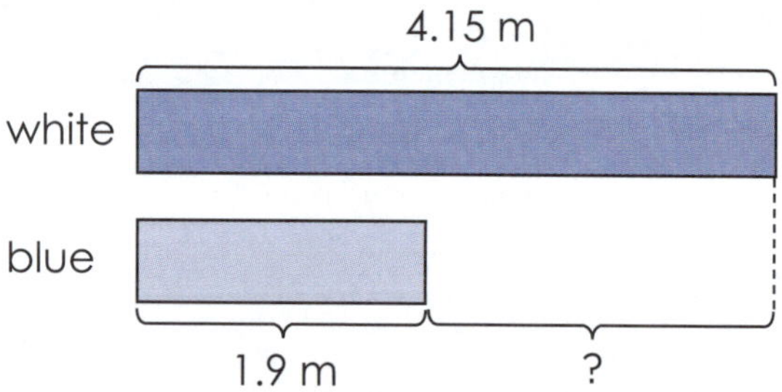

4.15 – 1.9 = 2.25

The white ribbon is 2.25 metres longer than the blue ribbon.

4.15 – 1.9 ≈ 4 – 2
= 2
My answer is close to the estimate. It is reasonable.

Let's Do

1. Mrs. Lee prepared two bottles of drinks for a picnic. One bottle contained 2.25 litres of orange juice and the other contained 0.37 litre less lemonade. How many litres of lemonade were there?

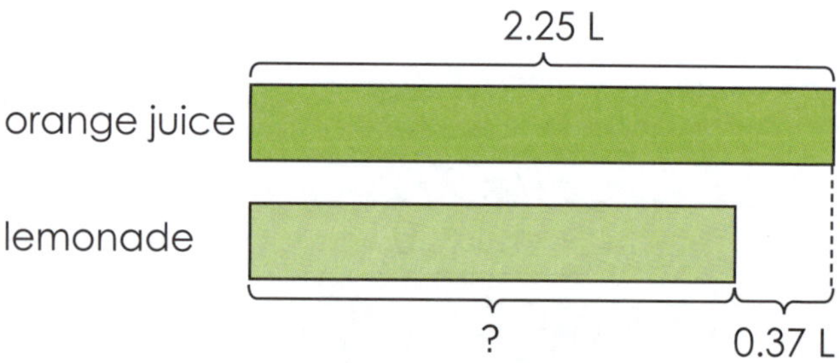

______ – ______ = ______

There were ______ litres of lemonade.

P/B Chapter 10: Exercise 13, page 173

Practice 2

1. Subtract.

a)	0.9 – 0.8	b)	2 – 0.4	c)	3.2 – 0.6	d)	1 – 0.05
e)	4 – 0.65	f)	6.8 – 4.3	g)	0.92 – 0.08	h)	1.46 – 0.59
i)	13.58 – 0.25	j)	24.5 – 2.27	k)	17.02 – 12.13	l)	39.45 – 2.8

 ISBN 978-93-5103-031-7

2. Add or subtract.

a) 10.99 + 6.32 b) 12.99 + 6.99 c) 16.04 – 4.99 d) 25.6 – 14.99

3. Estimate and then subtract.

a) 3.56 – 0.76 b) 9.31 – 4.8 c) 5.62 – 1.98

d) 25.6 – 3.38 e) 38.03 – 23.14 f) 49.45 – 3.9

Solve the word problems. Show your work clearly.

4. Hassan's weight was 42.5 kilograms three years ago. Now his weight is 38.6 kilograms. How many kilograms has he lost?

5. Trisha is 1.32 metres tall. She is 0.07 metre taller than May. How tall is May?

6. Aziz's time in a race was 14.5 seconds. Anil's time was 15.3 seconds. Who ran faster and by how much?

Lesson 3 Multiplication

Multiplying tenths or hundredths without regrouping

Let's Learn

a)

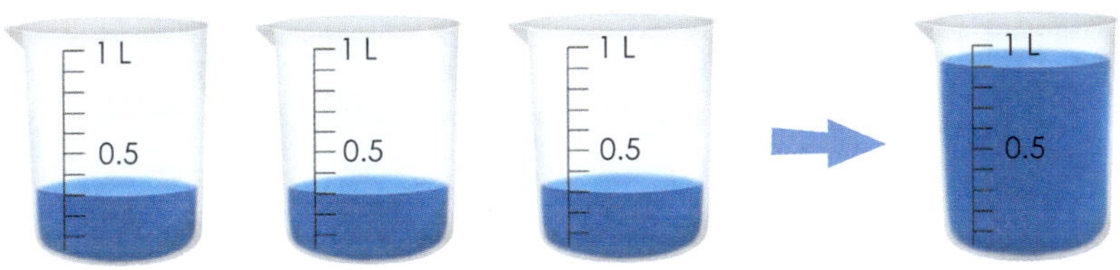

$0.3 \times 3 = 0.9$

There is a total of 0.9 litre of water in the containers.

b) Multiply 0.2 by 4.

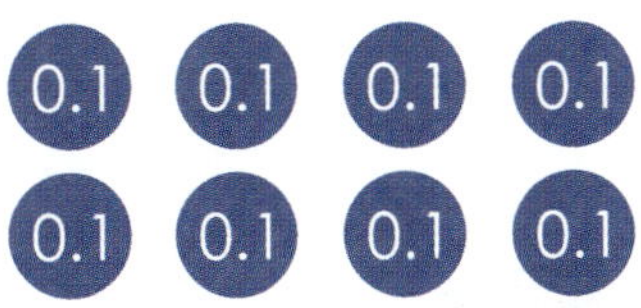

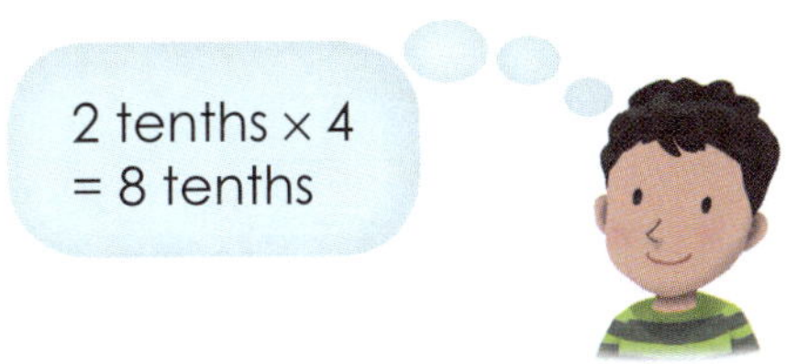

$0.2 \times 4 = 0.8$

 ISBN 978-93-5103-031-7

c) Multiply 0.02 by 4.

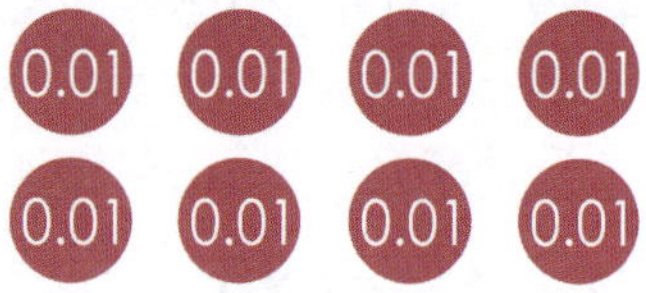

2 hundredths × 4
= 8 hundredths

$2 \times 4 = 8$
$0.2 \times 4 = 0.8$
$0.02 \times 4 = 0.08$

$0.02 \times 4 = 0.08$

Let's Do

1. Multiply.

a) $0.3 \times 2 =$ ______　　b) $0.03 \times 2 =$ ______

Multiplying tenths with regrouping

Let's Learn

a) Multiply 0.7 by 3.

$0.7 \times 3 = \square$

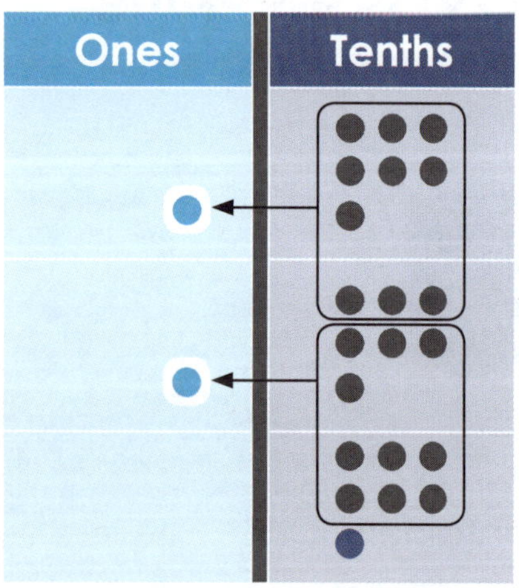

Multiply the tenths by 3.

$$\begin{array}{r} {}^{2}\\ 0.7 \\ \times\quad 3 \\ \hline 2.1 \\ \hline \end{array}$$

Align the decimal points.

7 tenths × 3 = 21 tenths
= 2 ones 1 tenth

$0.7 \times 3 = 2.1$

b) Multiply 0.6 by 5.

$0.6 \times 5 = \square$

6 tenths × 5 = 30 tenths
= 3 ones

 ISBN 978-93-5103-031-7

Let's Do

1. Multiply.

   a) $0.4 \times 7 =$ ______

   b) $0.5 \times 8 =$ ______

   c) ₹ $0.80 \times 4 =$ ₹ ______

$4 \times 7 =$ ______

$5 \times 8 =$ ______

$8 \times 4 =$ ______

Multiplying hundredths with regrouping

Let's Learn

a) Multiply 0.07 by 3.

$0.07 \times 3 = \square$

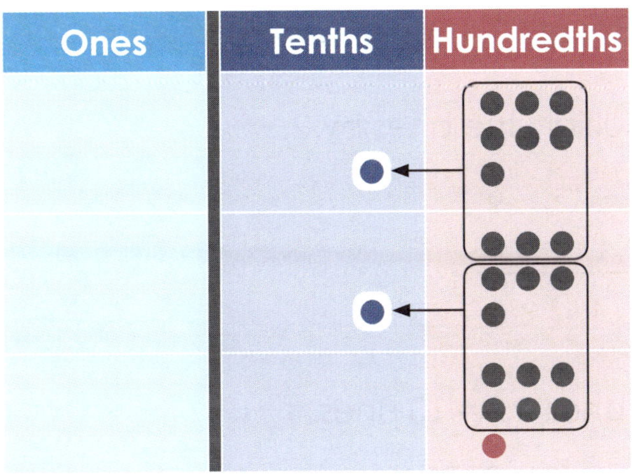

Multiply the hundredths by 3.

$$
\begin{array}{r}
\overset{2}{} \\
0\,.\,0\,7 \\
\times \quad \quad 3 \\
\hline
0\,.\,2\,1 \\
\hline
\end{array}
$$

7 hundredths × 3
= 21 hundredths
= 2 tenths 1 hundredth

$0.07 \times 3 = 0.21$

b) Multiply 0.06 by 5.

$0.06 \times 5 = \square$

6 hundredths × 5
= 30 hundredths
= 3 tenths

Let's Do

1. Multiply.

   a) $0.04 \times 7 =$ ______

   b) $0.05 \times 8 =$ ______

   c) ₹ $0.03 \times 8 =$ ₹ ______

$4 \times 7 =$ ______

$0.4 \times 7 =$ ______

PB Chapter 10: Exercise 14, pages 174–175

Multiplying decimals with 1 decimal place by 1-digit numbers

Let's Learn

Multiply 5.9 by 2.

$5.9 \times 2 = \square$

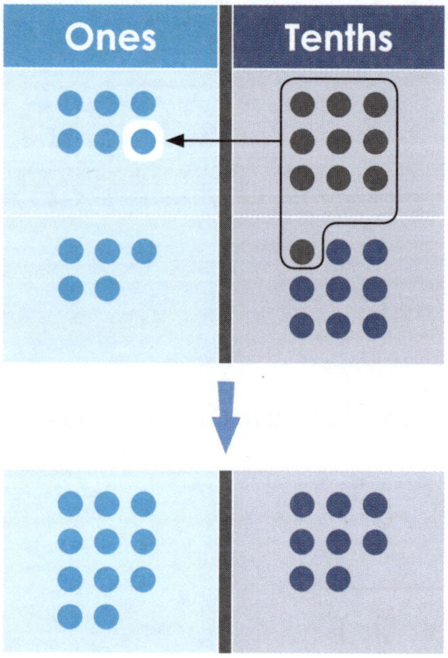

$5.9 \times 2 = 11.8$

1 Multiply the tenths by 2.

```
   1
   5 . 9
 ×     2
 -------
       8
 -------
```

9 tenths × 2 = 18 tenths

Regroup the tenths.
18 tenths = 1 one 8 tenths

2 Multiply the ones by 2.

```
     1
     5 . 9
 ×       2
 ---------
   1 1 . 8
 ---------
```

5 ones × 2 = 10 ones

Add the ones.
10 ones + 1 one = 11 ones

Regroup the ones.
11 ones = 1 ten 1 one

Let's Do

1. Multiply.

a)
```
   2 . 3
 ×     3
 -------

 -------
```

b)
```
   2 0 . 7
 ×       6
 ---------

 ---------
```

c)
```
   3 2 . 6
 ×       8
 ---------

 ---------
```

Chapter 10: Exercise 15, page 176

 ISBN 978-93-5103-031-7

Multiplying decimals with 2 decimal places by 1-digit numbers

Let's Learn

a) Multiply 0.25 by 3.

$0.25 \times 3 = \square$

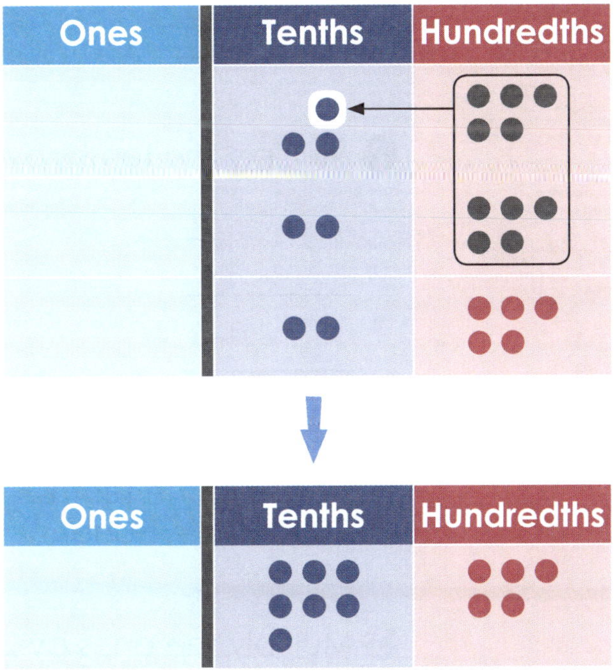

$0.25 \times 3 = 0.75$

❶ Multiply the hundredths by 3.

$$\begin{array}{r} \scriptstyle 1 \;\; \\ 0\,.\,2\;5 \\ \times \quad\;\; 3 \\ \hline 5 \\ \hline \end{array}$$

5 hundredths × 3
= 15 hundredths

Regroup the hundredths.
15 hundredths
= 1 tenth 5 hundredths

❷ Multiply the tenths by 3.

$$\begin{array}{r} \scriptstyle 1 \;\; \\ 0\,.\,2\;5 \\ \times \quad\;\; 3 \\ \hline 0\,.\,7\;5 \\ \hline \end{array}$$

2 tenths × 3 = 6 tenths

Add the tenths.
6 tenths + 1 tenth
= 7 tenths

ISBN 978-93-5103-031-7

b) Multiply 4.53 by 2.

$4.53 \times 2 = \square$

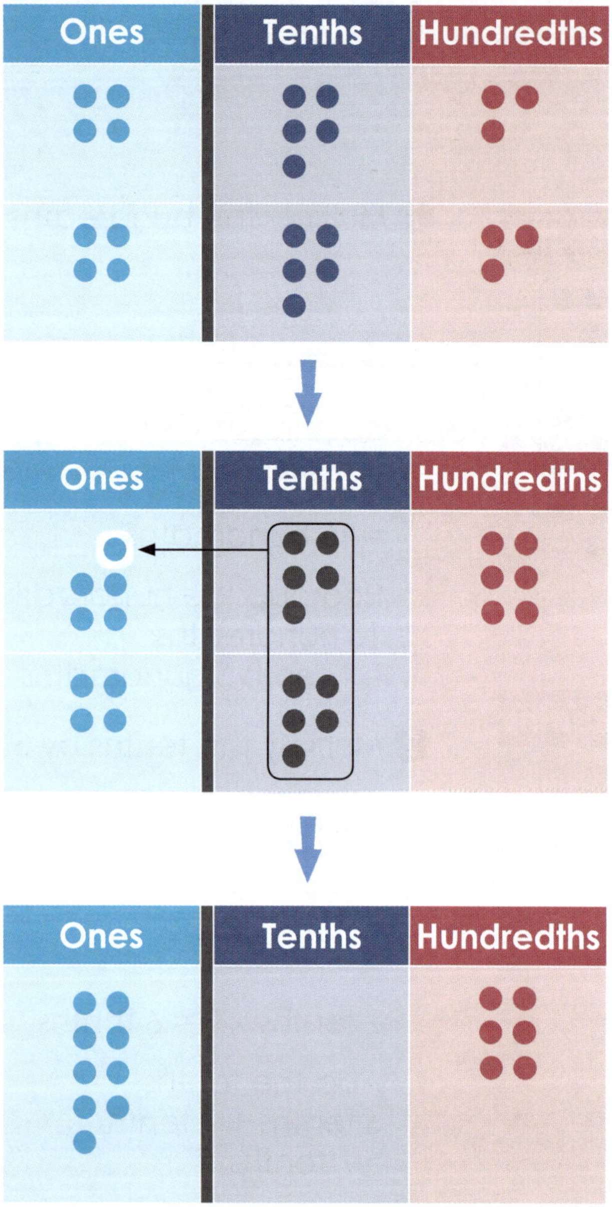

❶ Multiply the hundredths by 2.

$$\begin{array}{r} 4\,.\,5\,3 \\ \times \quad\;\; 2 \\ \hline 6 \\ \hline \end{array}$$

❷ Multiply the tenths by 2.

$$\begin{array}{r} {}^{1}\;\;\;\;\;\; \\ 4\,.\,5\,3 \\ \times \quad\;\; 2 \\ \hline .\,0\,6 \\ \hline \end{array}$$

5 tenths × 2 = 10 tenths

Regroup the tenths.
10 tenths = 1 one

❸ Multiply the ones by 2.

$$\begin{array}{r} {}^{1}\;\;\;\;\;\; \\ 4\,.\,5\,3 \\ \times \quad\;\; 2 \\ \hline 9\,.\,0\,6 \\ \hline \end{array}$$

4 ones × 2 = 8 ones

Add the ones.
8 ones + 1 one = 9 ones

$4.53 \times 2 = 9.06$

 ISBN 978-93-5103-031-7

c) Multiply 25.83 by 7.

$25.83 \times 7 = \square$

❶ Multiply the hundredths by 7.
3 hundredths × 7 = 21 hundredths

Regroup the hundredths.
21 hundredths = 2 tenths 1 hundredth

$$\begin{array}{r} {\scriptstyle 2} \\ 2\ 5\ .\ 8\ 3 \\ \times \qquad\quad 7 \\ \hline 1 \\ \hline \end{array}$$

❷ Multiply the tenths by 7.
8 tenths × 7 = 56 tenths

Add the tenths.
56 tenths + 2 tenths = 58 tenths

Regroup the tenths.
58 tenths = 5 ones 8 tenths

$$\begin{array}{r} {\scriptstyle 5\ \ 2} \\ 2\ 5\ .\ 8\ 3 \\ \times \qquad\quad 7 \\ \hline .\ 8\ 1 \\ \hline \end{array}$$

❸ Multiply the ones by 7.
5 ones × 7 = 35 ones

Add the ones.
35 ones + 5 ones = 40 ones

Regroup the ones.
40 ones = 4 tens

$$\begin{array}{r} {\scriptstyle 4\ \ 5\ \ \ 2} \\ 2\ 5\ .\ 8\ 3 \\ \times \qquad\quad 7 \\ \hline 0\ .\ 8\ 1 \\ \hline \end{array}$$

❹ Multiply the tens by 7.
2 tens × 7 = 14 tens

Add the tens.
14 tens + 4 tens = 18 tens

Regroup the tens.
18 tens = 1 hundred 8 tens

$$\begin{array}{r} {\scriptstyle 4\ \ 5\ \ \ 2} \\ 2\ 5\ .\ 8\ 3 \\ \times \qquad\quad 7 \\ \hline 1\ 8\ 0\ .\ 8\ 1 \\ \hline \end{array}$$

$25.83 \times 7 = 180.81$

Let's Do

1. Multiply.

a) $\begin{array}{r} 0\ .\ 2\ 6 \\ \times \qquad 4 \\ \hline \\ \hline \end{array}$

b) $\begin{array}{r} 3\ 4\ .\ 0\ 2 \\ \times \qquad\quad 3 \\ \hline \\ \hline \end{array}$

c) $\begin{array}{r} 4\ 8\ .\ 2\ 6 \\ \times \qquad\quad 6 \\ \hline \\ \hline \end{array}$

PB Chapter 10: Exercise 16, pages 177–180

 ISBN 978-93-5103-031-7

Estimating products

Let's Learn

a) Estimate the value of 6.84×9.

$$6.84 \times 9 \approx 7 \times 9$$
$$= 63$$

Round the decimal to the nearest whole number.
$6.84 \approx 7$

b) Multiply 6.84 by 9.

$6.84 \times 9 = 61.56$

My answer is close to the estimate.
It is reasonable.

Let's Do

1. Estimate and then multiply.

a) $3.9 \times 5 \approx$ ______ $\times 5$

= ______

$$\begin{array}{r} 3.9 \\ \times \quad 5 \\ \hline \\ \hline \end{array}$$

b) $29.73 \times 6 \approx$ ______ $\times$ ______

= ______

$$\begin{array}{r} 29.73 \\ \times \quad 6 \\ \hline \\ \hline \end{array}$$

P/B Chapter 10: Exercise 17, page 181

Solving word problems

Let's Learn

Rohit sold 6 lemons at ₹ 3.95 each. How much money did he collect altogether?

Picture It

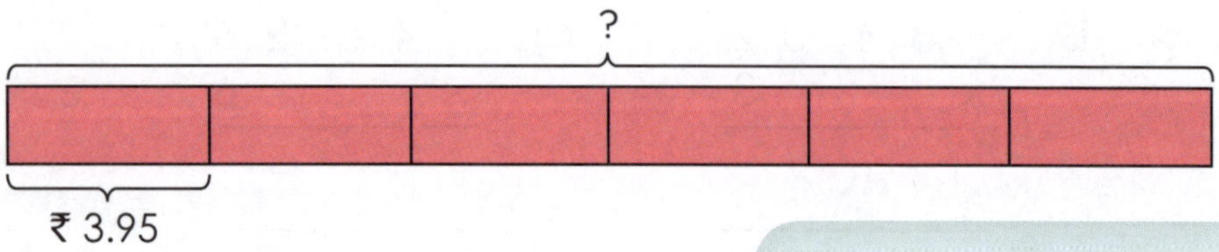

$₹\ 3.95 \times 6 = ₹\ 23.70$

He collected ₹ 23.70 altogether.

$₹\ 3.95 \times 6 \approx ₹\ 4 \times 6$
$= ₹\ 24$
My answer is close to the estimate.
It is reasonable.

 ISBN 978-93-5103-031-7

Let's Do

1. Mary saved ₹ 20.05. Seema saved 4 times as much as Mary.
   How much did Seema save?

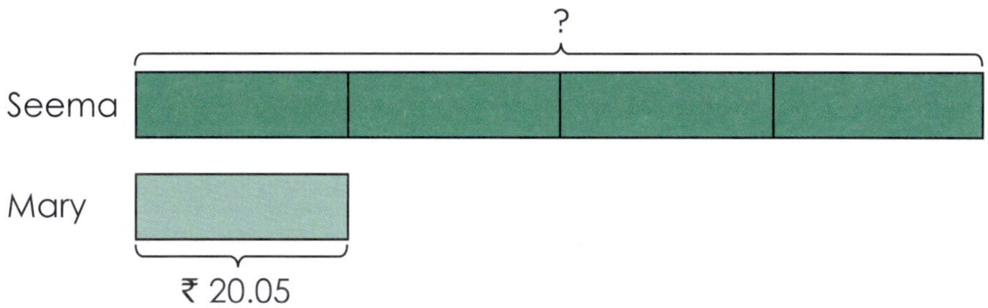

₹ ______ × ______ = ₹ ______

Seema saved ₹ ______

Chapter 10: Exercise 18, page 182

Practice 3

1. Multiply.

a)	0.4×9	b)	7×0.08	c)	0.31×6	d)	3×0.45
e)	4×8.2	f)	1.5×4	g)	5.29×3	h)	3.86×5
i)	8×3.29	j)	₹ 0.15×6	k)	₹ 4.05×4	l)	₹ 3.40×9

2. Estimate and then multiply.

a)	3.2×6	b)	2.48×3	c)	4.09×5
d)	9×4.36	e)	6×5.25	f)	1.94×7

Solve the word problems. Show your work clearly.

3. Roy used 8 tins of paint to paint his apartment. Each tin contained 5.5 litres of paint. How much paint did he use altogether?

4. One bottle of orange juice weighs 1.25 kilograms. What is the total weight of 6 such bottles of orange juice?

5. A pear costs ₹ 4.95. A pineapple costs 4 times as much as the pear. Find the cost of the pineapple.

6. A worker mixed 13.45 kilograms of cement with sand. The weight of sand used was 3 times the weight of the cement. How many kilograms of sand was used?

 ISBN 978-93-5103-031-7

Lesson 4 Division

Dividing tenths or hundredths without regrouping

Let's Learn

a)

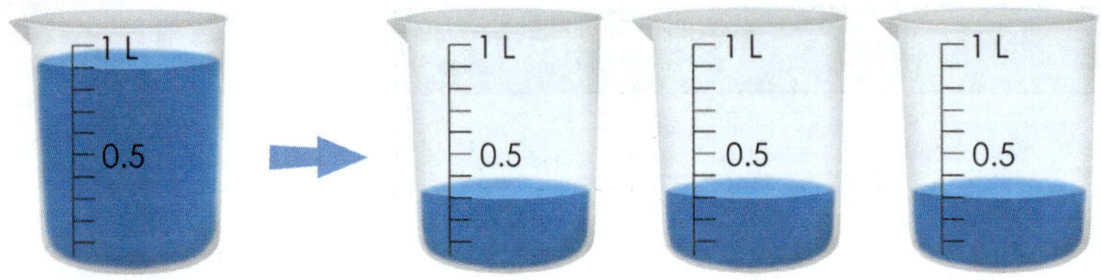

0.9 ÷ 3 = 0.3

There is 0.3 litre of water in each container.

b) Divide 0.6 by 2.

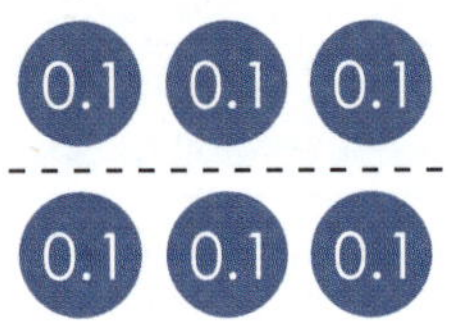

6 tenths ÷ 2
= 3 tenths

0.6 ÷ 2 = 0.3

c) Divide 0.06 by 2.

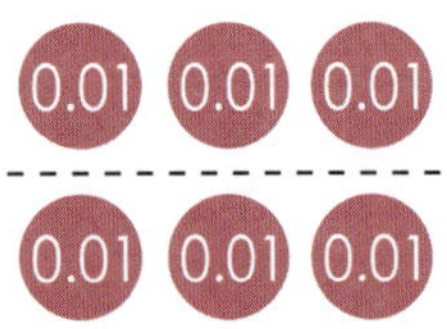

6 hundredths ÷ 2
= 3 hundredths

6 ÷ 2 = 3
0.6 ÷ 2 = 0.3
0.06 ÷ 2 = 0.03

0.06 ÷ 2 = 0.03

Let's Do

1. Divide.

a) 0.8 ÷ 4 = ______ b) 0.08 ÷ 4 = ______

 ISBN 978-93-5103-031-7

Dividing decimals and whole numbers by 1-digit numbers to get quotients in tenths

Let's Learn

a) Divide 1.8 by 3.

1.8 ÷ 3 = ▭

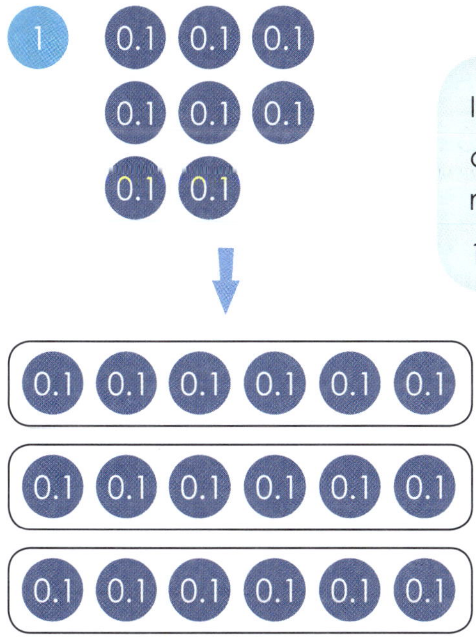

1.8 ÷ 3 = 0.6

1 Divide the ones by 3.

```
   0 .
3 ) 1 . 8
```

I do not have enough (1) to put a (1) each into 3 groups. So, I regroup the ones and tenths.

1 one 8 tenths = 18 tenths

Align the decimal points.

2 Divide the tenths by 3.

```
   0 . 6
3 ) 1 . 8   ← 1 one 8 tenths = 18 tenths
    1   8   ← 3 × 6 tenths = 18 tenths
    -----
        0
```

b) Divide 2 by 4.

2 ÷ 4 = ▭

2 ones = 20 tenths
20 tenths ÷ 4 = 5 tenths

Let's Do

1. Divide.

a) 3.5 ÷ 7 = ______

b) 3 ÷ 5 = ______

c) ₹ 4.20 ÷ 6 = ₹ ______

d) ₹ 5.40 ÷ 9 = ₹ ______

 ISBN 978-93-5103-031-7

Dividing decimals by 1-digit numbers to get quotients in hundredths

Let's Learn

a) Divide 0.18 by 3.

0.18 ÷ 3 = ▢

Maths Lab

Picture It

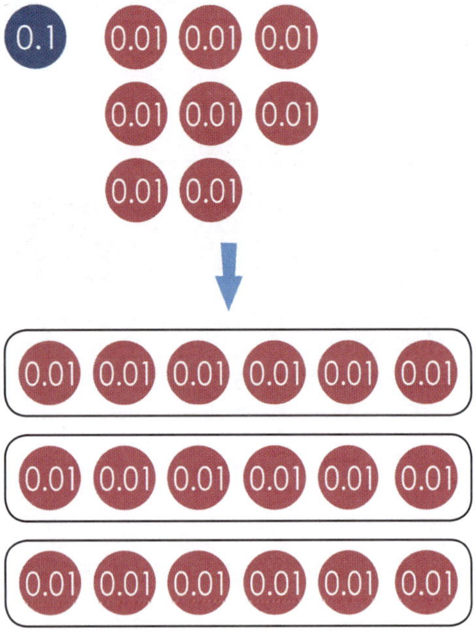

1 Divide the tenths by 3.

$$\begin{array}{r} 0.0 \\ 3\overline{)\,0.18} \end{array}$$

I do not have enough (0.1) to put a (0.1) each into 3 groups. So, I regroup the tenths and hundredths.

1 tenth 8 hundredths = 18 hundredths

2 Divide the hundredths by 3.

$$\begin{array}{r} 0.06 \\ 3\overline{)\,0.18} \\ 18 \\ \hline 0 \end{array}$$

← 1 tenth 8 hundredths = 18 hundredths

↖ 3 × 6 hundredths = 18 hundredths

0.18 ÷ 3 = 0.06

b) Divide 0.2 by 4.

0.2 ÷ 4 = ▢

2 tenths = 20 hundredths
20 hundredths ÷ 4
= 5 hundredths

Let's Do

1. Divide.

   a) 0.35 ÷ 7 = ______ b) 0.3 ÷ 5 = ______

   c) ₹ 0.30 ÷ 6 = ₹ ______ d) ₹ 0.45 ÷ 9 = ₹ ______

PB Chapter 10: Exercise 19, pages 183–184

 ISBN 978-93-5103-031-7

Dividing decimals with 2 decimal places by 1-digit numbers

Let's Learn

a) Divide 0.74 by 2.

0.74 ÷ 2 = ▢

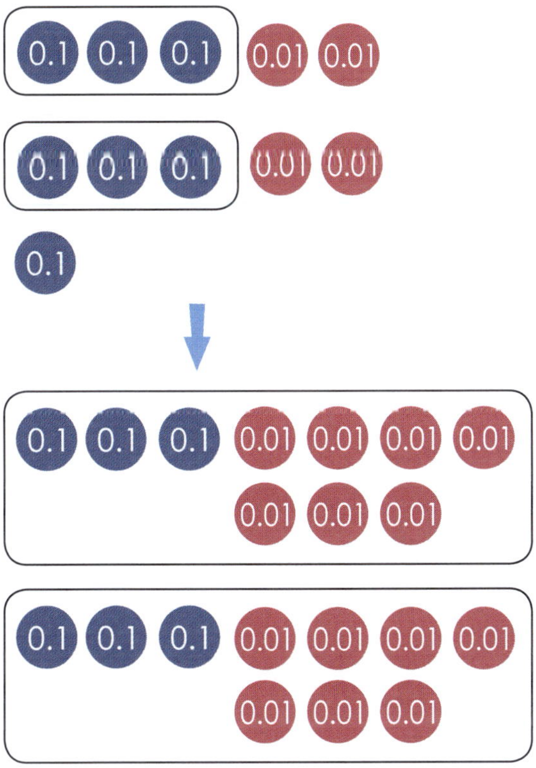

❶ Divide the tenths by 2.

```
    0 . 3
2 ) 0 . 7 4
        6      ← 2 × 3 tenths = 6 tenths
    -------
        1      ← remainder 1 tenth
```

❷ Divide the hundredths by 2.

```
    0 . 3 7
2 ) 0 . 7 4
        6        1 tenth 4 hundredths
    -------
        1 4  ↙   = 14 hundredths
        1 4  ←   2 × 7 hundredths
    -------
          0      = 14 hundredths
```

0.74 ÷ 2 = 0.37

b) Divide 4.35 by 3.

4.35 ÷ 3 = ▭

Maths Lab

Picture It

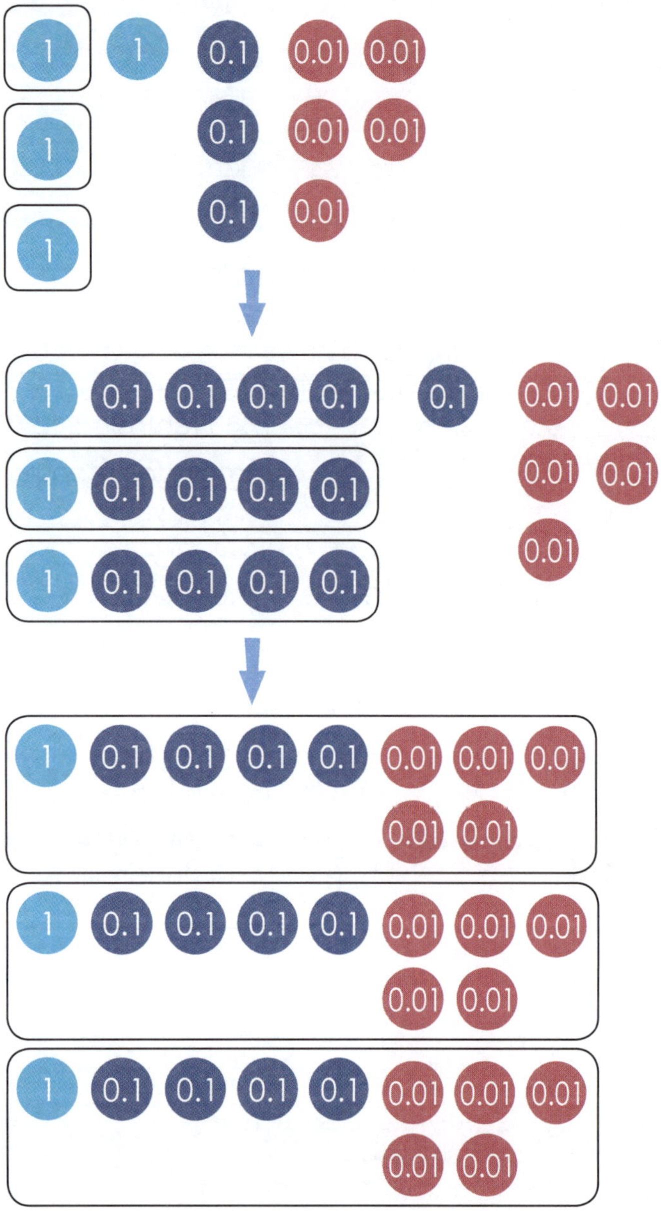

❶ Divide the ones by 3.

```
    1
3 ) 4 . 3 5
    3          ← 3 × 1 one = 3 ones
    1          ← remainder 1 one
```

❷ Divide the tenths by 3.

```
    1 . 4
3 ) 4 . 3 5
    3
    1   3      ← 1 one 3 tenths = 13 tenths
    1   2      ← 3 × 4 tenths = 12 tenths
        1      ← remainder 1 tenth
```

❸ Divide the hundredths by 3.

```
    1 . 4 5
3 ) 4 . 3 5
    3
    1   3
    1   2
        1 5    ← 1 tenth 5 hundredths = 15 hundredths
        1 5    ← 3 × 5 hundredths = 15 hundredths
          0
```

4.35 ÷ 3 = 1.45

Let's Do

1. Divide.

a) $4\overline{)\text{₹}0.60}$ b) $9\overline{)5.04}$ c) $8\overline{)\text{₹}18.40}$ d) $6\overline{)14.58}$

Chapter 10: Exercise 20, pages 185–188

 ISBN 978-93-5103-031-7

Dividing decimals and whole numbers with zero as a place holder

Let's Learn

a) Divide 5 by 4.

$5 \div 4 = \square$

❶ Divide the ones by 4.

```
    1
4 ) 5
    4    ← 4 × 1 one = 4 ones
    1    ← remainder 1 one
```

❷ Divide the tenths by 4.

```
    1 . 2
4 ) 5 . 0
    4
    1   0   ← 1 one = 10 tenths
        8   ← 4 × 2 tenths = 8 tenths
        2   ← remainder 2 tenths
```

❸ Divide the hundredths by 4.

```
    1 . 2 5
4 ) 5 . 0 0
    4
    1   0
        8
        2 0   ← 2 tenths = 20 hundredths
        2 0   ← 4 × 5 hundredths = 20 hundredths
          0
```

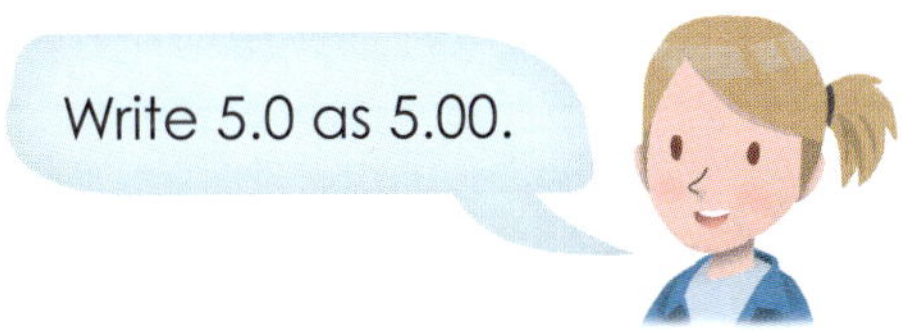

$5 \div 4 = 1.25$

b) Divide 2.1 by 6.

2.1 ÷ 6 = ▢

❶ Divide the ones by 6.

```
   0 .
6 ) 2 . 1
```

❷ Divide the tenths by 6.

```
   0 . 3
6 ) 2 . 1   ← 2 ones 1 tenth = 21 tenths
    1   8   ← 6 × 3 tenths = 18 tenths
   ------
        3   ← remainder 3 tenths
```

❸ Divide the hundredths by 6.

```
   0 . 3 5
6 ) 2 . 1 0
    1   8
   --------
        3 0  ← 3 tenths = 30 hundredths
        3 0  ← 6 × 5 hundredths = 30 hundredths
   --------
          0
```

2.1 ÷ 6 = 0.35

Let's Do

1. Divide.

a) 30.4 ÷ 5 = ______

5) 3 0 . 4

b) 12 ÷ 8 = ______

8) 1 2

 ISBN 978-93-5103-031-7

c) $25.5 \div 6 =$ ______

$6\overline{)25.5}$

d) $22 \div 8 =$ ______

$8\overline{)22}$

Chapter 10: Exercise 21, pages 189–190

Estimating quotients

Let's Learn

a) Estimate the value of $31.2 \div 8$.

$31.2 \div 8 \approx 32 \div 8$
$= 4$

Think of multiples of 8.
8, 16, 24, 32, 40, ...

31.2 is closer to 32 than to 40.
$31.2 \approx 32$

b) Divide 31.2 by 8.

$31.2 \div 8 = 3.9$

My answer is close to the estimate.
It is reasonable.

c) Estimate the value of $5.28 \div 6$.

$5.28 \div 6 \approx 5.4 \div 6$
$= 0.9$

Think of multiples of 6.
..., 42, 48, 54, 60
..., 4.2, 4.8, 5.4, 6.0

5.28 is closer to 5.4 than to 4.8.
$5.28 \approx 5.4$

d) Divide 5.28 by 6.

$5.28 \div 6 = 0.88$

My answer is close to the estimate.
It is reasonable.

 ISBN 978-93-5103-031-7

Let's Do

1. Estimate and then divide.

   a) $0.81 \div 3 \approx$ ______ $\div 3$

   $=$ ______

   $3\overline{)0.81}$

   b) $7.12 \div 8 \approx$ ______ $\div$ ______

   $=$ ______

   $8\overline{)7.12}$

   c) $46.35 \div 9 \approx$ ______ $\div$ ______

   $=$ ______

   $9\overline{)46.35}$

P/B Chapter 10: Exercise 22, page 191

Rounding quotients

Let's Learn

a) Find the value of $78.5 \div 4$ correct to the nearest whole number.

$$
\begin{array}{r}
19.6 \\
4\overline{)78.5} \\
4 \\
\hline
38 \\
36 \\
\hline
2\,5 \\
2\,4 \\
\hline
1
\end{array}
$$

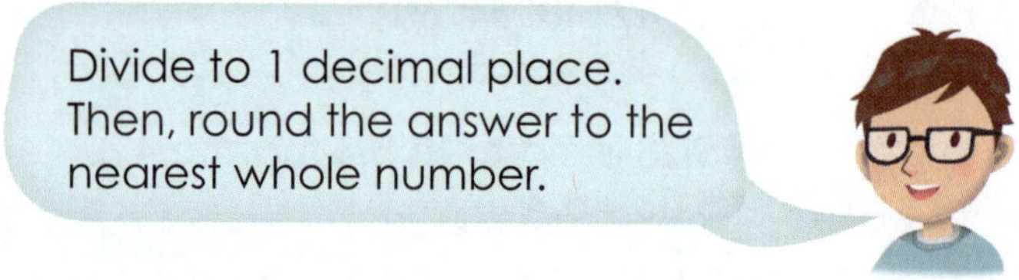

19.6 is 20 when rounded to the nearest whole number.
$78.5 \div 4 \approx 20$

 ISBN 978-93-5103-031-7

b) Find the value of 7 ÷ 3 correct to 1 decimal place.

```
    2.33
 3 )7.00
    6
    1 0
      9
      10
       9
       1
```

Divide to 2 decimal places. Then round the answer to 1 decimal place.

2.33 is ___ when rounded to 1 decimal place.

7 ÷ 3 ≈ ___

Let's Do

1. Find the value of 8 ÷ 6 correct to the nearest whole number.

   8 ÷ 6 ≈ ______

   ```
   6 )8
   ```

2. Find the value of 43.5 ÷ 8 correct to 1 decimal place.

   43.5 ÷ 8 ≈ ______

   ```
   8 )43.5
   ```

P/B Chapter 10: Exercise 23, page 192

 ISBN 978-93-5103-031-7

Solving word problems

Let's Learn

Lily bought 5 paper clips for ₹ 8. How much did each paper clip cost?

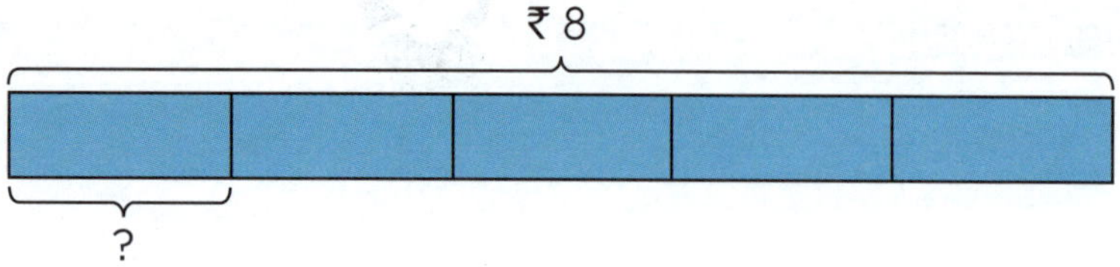

₹ 8 ÷ 5 = ₹ 1.60

Each paper clip cost ₹ 1.60.

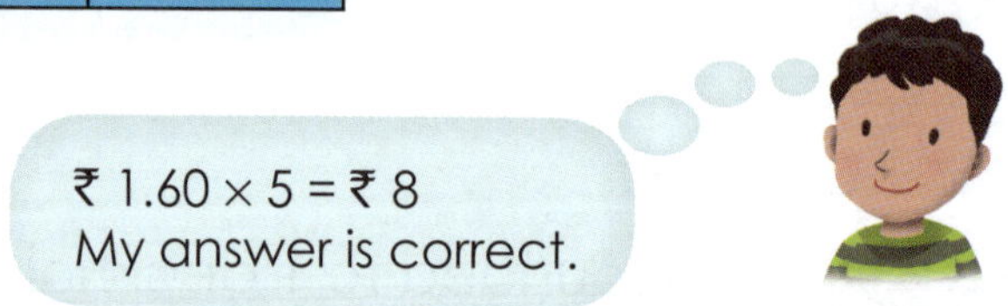

Let's Do

1. Noor has ₹ 5.40. She has 3 times as much money as Divya. How much money does Divya have?

   ₹ _______ ÷ _______ = ₹ _______

   Divya has ₹ _______.

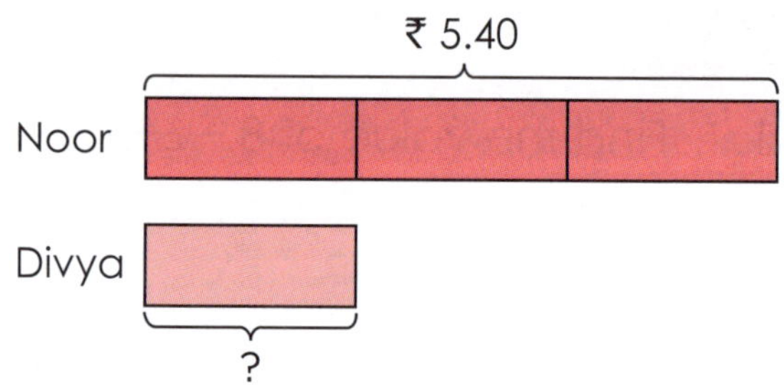

P/B Chapter 10: Exercise 24, page 193

Practice 4

1. Divide.

a)	3.6 ÷ 6	b)	6.4 ÷ 8	c)	0.84 ÷ 4	d)	0.77 ÷ 7
e)	0.45 ÷ 3	f)	3.55 ÷ 5	g)	25.6 ÷ 8	h)	2.94 ÷ 7
i)	6.8 ÷ 5	j)	8 ÷ 5	k)	15 ÷ 6	l)	24.4 ÷ 8

2. Divide.

   a) ₹ 0.90 ÷ 6 b) ₹ 4.20 ÷ 7 c) ₹ 6.80 ÷ 8

3. Estimate and then divide.

   a) 5.9 ÷ 2 b) 23.94 ÷ 6 c) 35.04 ÷ 4

4. Divide. Express your answer correct to the nearest whole number.

   a) 20 ÷ 3 b) 38 ÷ 7 c) 109 ÷ 8

5. Divide. Express your answer correct to 1 decimal place.

   a) 4 ÷ 7 b) 5 ÷ 9 c) 7.9 ÷ 4

 ISBN 978-93-5103-031-7

Solve the word problems. Show your work clearly.

6. Mrs. Faizal poured 6 litres of syrup equally into 4 bottles. How much syrup was there in each bottle?

7. A ribbon 6.75 metres long is cut into 5 equal pieces. How long is each piece?

8. Mr. Singh's weight is 67.4 kilograms. He is 4 times as heavy as his son. What is his son's weight?

9. 8 girls shared the cost of a birthday present equally. The birthday present cost ₹ 34.80. How much did each girl pay?

Lesson 5 Problem Solving

Word problems

Let's Learn

Radha used 4 packets of flour to make 5 cakes of the same size. Each packet of flour had a weight of 1.35 kilograms. How much flour did she use for each cake?

1 **Understand** the problem.

How many packets of flour did Radha use?
How many cakes did she make?
What is the weight of each packet of flour?

2 **Plan** what to do.

First, I find the total weight of flour used. Then, I divide the total weight of flour used by the number of cakes.

3 Work out the **Answer**.

$1.35 \times 4 = 5.4$
Radha used 5.4 kilograms of flour altogether.

$5.4 \div 5 = 1.08$
She used 1.08 kilograms of flour for each cake.

4 **Check**
Did you answer the question?
Is your answer reasonable?

She used less than 1 packet of flour for each cake.

Each packet of flour had a weight of 1.35 kilograms.

$1.08 < 1.35$
My answer is reasonable.

☑ 1. Understand
☑ 2. Plan
☑ 3. Answer
☑ 4. Check

 ISBN 978-93-5103-031-7

Let's Do

1. Patrick bought 5 litres of orange juice. After filling up 5 bottles of the same size with orange juice, he had 0.25 litre of orange juice left. Find the amount of orange juice in each bottle.

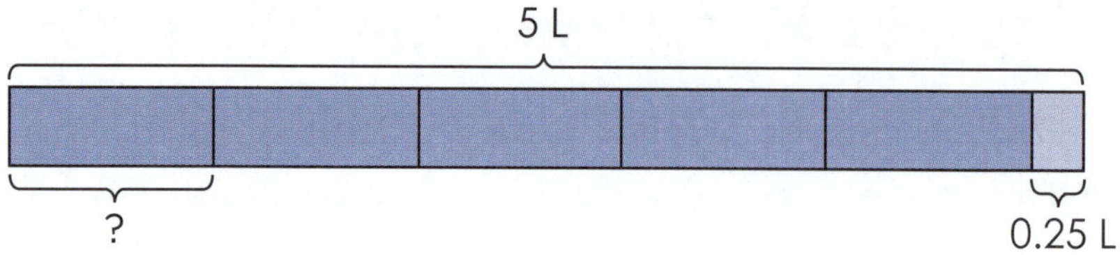

- ☐ 1. Understand
- ☐ 2. Plan
- ☐ 3. Answer
- ☐ 4. Check

P/B Chapter 10: Exercise 25, pages 194–195

Practice 5

Solve the word problems. Show your work clearly.

1. Neeta needs to buy 7 pencils and 2 notebooks. Estimate the cost of all the items if each pencil costs ₹ 3.40 and each notebook costs ₹ 25.75. Does Neeta have enough money if she has ₹ 100?

2. A painter mixed 1.46 litres of black paint with 0.8 litre of white paint to get grey paint. Then he used 0.96 litre of the grey paint. How much grey paint was he left with?

3. Hassan bought 4 stamps and a glue stick. Each stamp cost ₹ 1.95 and the glue stick cost ₹ 19.55. How much did he spend altogether?

4. Mrs. Jones bought 5 erasers. Each eraser cost ₹ 2.35. She gave the cashier ₹ 20. How much change did she receive?

5. Mala and Alice shared the cost of lunch equally. The lunch cost ₹ 46.70. How much money did Alice have left if she had ₹ 34.35 at first?

6. Alan paid ₹ 8.25 for a sharpener and a pen. The sharpener cost twice as much as the pen. Find the cost of the sharpener.

7. Neeraj bought a few books from a bookstore. Prepare a bill to show how much he needs to pay for each item and how much he needs to pay in total.

BEST
STATIONERS

Date................

Items	Quantity	Price per book	Total
Comics	4	₹ 4.50	______
Exercise books	3	₹ 25.00	______
Art and craft books	2	₹ 38.75	______
		Grand Total	______

 ISBN 978-93-5103-031-7

Mind stretcher

Let's Learn

There were 165.3 kilograms of rice in Warehouse X and 201.1 kilograms of rice in Warehouse Y. Some rice was transferred from Warehouse Y to Warehouse X. In the end, there was 4 times as much rice in Warehouse X as in Warehouse Y. How many kilograms of rice were transferred?

1 Understand the problem.

How many kilograms of rice were there in Warehouse X at first?
How many kilograms of rice were there in Warehouse Y at first?
Did the total amount of rice in the two warehouses change?

2 Plan what to do.

First, I find the total amount of rice in the two warehouses.
Then, I **draw a bar model** to help me solve the problem.

3 Work out the **Answer**.

165.3 + 201.1 = 366.4
There were 366.4 kilograms of rice in the two warehouses altogether.

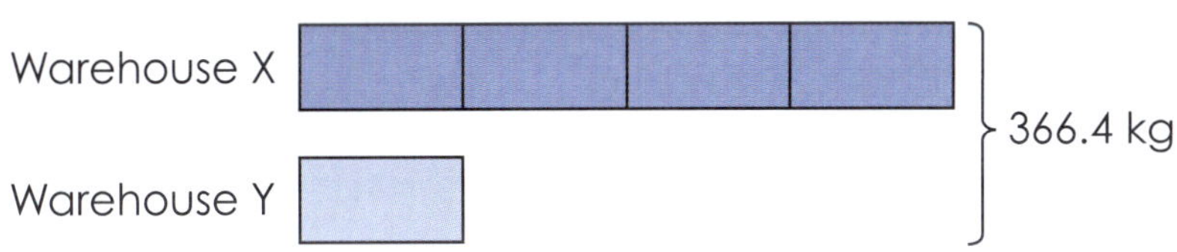

5 units → 366.4 kg
1 unit → 366.4 kg ÷ 5 = 73.28 kg

There were 73.28 kilograms of rice in Warehouse Y in the end.

201.1 – 73.28 = 127.82 kg

127.82 kilograms of rice were transferred.

4 Check
Did you answer the question?
Is your answer correct?

4 units → 4 × 73.28 kg = 293.12 kg
There were 293.12 kilograms of rice in Warehouse X in the end.

293.12 – 165.3 = 127.82 kg
127.82 kilograms of rice were transferred to Warehouse X.

My answer is correct.

☑ **1. Understand**
☑ **2. Plan**
☑ **3. Answer**
☑ **4. Check**

 ISBN 978-93-5103-031-7

11 Measures

Lesson 1 Multiplication

Multiplying without regrouping

Let's Learn

What is the total weight of the 3 parcels?

1 kg 200 g **1 kg 200 g** **1 kg 200 g**

1 kg 200 g × 3
- 1 kg × 3 = 3 kg
- 200 g × 3 = 600 g

1 kg 200 g
- 1 kg
- 200 g

The total weight of the 3 parcels is ___ kilograms ___ grams.

Let's Do

1. Multiply 1 litre 80 millilitres by 5.

   1 L 80 ml × 5
   - 1 L × 5 = ______ L
   - 80 ml × 5 = ______ ml

   1 L 80 ml × 5 = ______ L ______ ml

 ISBN 978-93-5103-031-7

Multiplying with regrouping

Let's Learn

a) The distance around a track in a park was 1 kilometre 300 metres. Jai ran round the track 4 times. How far did he run?

1 km 300 m × 4 → 1 km × 4 = 4 km; 300 m × 4 = 1200 m

1 km 300 m → 1 km; 300 m

1 km 300 m × 4 = 4 km 1200 m
= 5 km 200 m

1200 m = 1000 m + 200 m
= 1 km 200 m

Jai ran 5 kilometres 200 metres.

b) Alka filled an empty tank completely with 5 buckets of water. Each bucket contained 2 litres 400 millilitres of water. What was the capacity of the tank?

2 L 400 ml × 5 → 2 L × 5 = ____ L; 400 ml × 5 = ____ ml

2 L 400 ml → 2 L; 400 ml

2 L 400 ml × 5 = ____ L ____ ml
= ____ L

The capacity of the tank is the amount of water it can hold.

The capacity of the tank was ____ litres.

Let's Do

1. Multiply 1 metre 50 centimetres by 4.

1 m 50 cm × 4 → 1 m × 4 = ______ m; 50 cm × 4 = ______ cm

1 m 50 cm × 4 = ______ m ______ cm
= ______ m

P/B Chapter 11: Exercise 1, pages 196–197

 ISBN 978-93-5103-031-7

Practice 1

1. Multiply.

a)	1 cm 2 mm × 3	b)	2 kg 300 g × 2	c)	3 L 50 ml × 4
d)	4 km 5 m × 5	e)	2 m 60 cm × 4	f)	3 km 400 m × 3
g)	4 L 800 ml × 3	h)	5 kg 750 g × 5		

Solve the word problems. Show your work clearly.

2. Alice has 6 bags of flour. Each bag contains 2 kilograms 250 grams of flour. What is the total weight of flour that Alice has?

3. Ram drinks 2 litres 300 millilitres of water a day. How much water does he drink in 5 days?

4. Roger cycles every day. If he cycles 3 kilometres 650 metres a day, find the total distance he cycles in a week.

Lesson 2 Division

Dividing without regrouping

Let's Learn

The total weight of 5 similar packets of flour is 5 kilograms 650 grams. Find the weight of each packet of flour.

5 kg 650 g ÷ 5
- 5 kg ÷ 5 = 1 kg
- 650 g ÷ 5 = 130 g

5 kg 650 g
- 5 kg
- 650 g

The weight of each packet of flour is ___ kilogram ___ grams.

Let's Do

1. Divide 6 litres 540 millilitres by 6.

6 L 540 ml ÷ 6
- 6 L ÷ 6 = ______ L
- 540 ml ÷ 6 = ______ ml

6 L 540 ml ÷ 6 = ______ L ______ ml

 ISBN 978-93-5103-031-7

Dividing with regrouping

Let's Learn

a) Jane cut a ribbon 5 metres 20 centimetres long into 4 equal pieces. What was the length of each piece of ribbon?

5 m 20 cm = 4 m 120 cm

> 5 cannot be divided by 4 easily. Change 5 metres to 4 metres 100 centimetres.
>
> 5 m = 4 m + 1 m
> = 4 m 100 cm

4 m 120 cm ÷ 4
- 4 m ÷ 4 = 1 m
- 120 cm ÷ 4 = 30 cm

5 m 20 cm ÷ 4 = 4 m 120 cm ÷ 4
= 1 m 30 cm

The length of each piece of ribbon was 1 metre 30 centimetres.

b) Divide 7 kilograms 300 grams by 5.

7 kg 300 g = 5 kg 2300 g

> 7 cannot be divided by 5 easily. Change 7 kilograms to 5 kilograms 2000 grams.
>
> 7 kg = 5 kg + 2 kg
> = 5 kg 2000 g

5 kg 2300 g ÷ 5
- 5 kg ÷ 5 = ___ kg
- 2300 g ÷ 5 = ___ g

7 kg 300 g ÷ 5 = 5 kg 2300 g ÷ 5
= ___ kg ___ g

Let's Do

1. Divide 3 kilometres 500 metres by 2.

3 km 500 m = 2 km ______ m

2 km ______ m ÷ 2
- 2 km ÷ 2 = ______ km
- ______ m ÷ 2 = ______ m

3 km 500 m ÷ 2 = ______ km ______ m

2. Divide 6 litres 200 millilitres by 4.

6 L 200 ml = ______ L ______ ml

______ L ______ ml ÷ 4 → ______ L ÷ 4 = ______ L; ______ ml ÷ 4 = ______ ml

6 L 200 ml ÷ 4 = ______ L ______ ml

Dividing by changing compound units to a smaller unit

Let's Learn

Mark poured 3 litres 200 millilitres of milk equally into 8 glasses. What was the volume of milk in each glass?

First, express 3 litres 200 millilitres in millilitres.

3 L 200 ml = 3 L + 200 ml
= 3000 ml + 200 ml
= 3200 ml

Then, divide the millilitres by 8.

3200 ml ÷ 8 = 400 ml

The volume of milk in each glass was ______ millilitres.

Let's Do

1. Divide 5 kilograms 600 grams by 7.

5 kg 600 g = ______ g

______ g ÷ 7 = ______ g

5 kg 600 g ÷ 7 = ______ g

P/B Chapter 11: Exercise 2, pages 198–199

Practice 2

1. Divide.

a) 4 L 240 ml ÷ 2 b) 6 kg 360 g ÷ 3 c) 5 km 300 m ÷ 2

d) 7 m 50 cm ÷ 3 e) 11 L 420 ml ÷ 4 f) 3 cm 6 mm ÷ 6

g) 4 km 585 m ÷ 7 h) 5 L 40 ml ÷ 9

 ISBN 978-93-5103-031-7

Solve the word problems. Show your work clearly.

2. Mala bought 3 kilograms 570 grams of kidney beans. She packed them equally into 3 bags. What was the weight of the kidney beans in each bag?

3. A team of 4 girls took part in a relay walkathon. They walked a total distance of 6 kilometres 420 metres. If the girls each walked an equal distance, how far did each of them walk?

4. The capacity of a jug was 6 litres 40 millilitres. Mohan poured 8 equal glasses of water into the jug and filled it completely. What was the volume of water in each glass?

Lesson 3 Problem Solving

Word problems

Let's Learn

The weight of a papaya is 1 kilogram 800 grams. A watermelon is 3 times as heavy as the papaya.

a) What is the weight of the watermelon?
b) What is the total weight of the two fruits?

1 Understand the problem.

What is the weight of the papaya?
Which fruit is heavier?
What do I have to find?

2 Plan what to do.

I multiply to find the weight of the watermelon.

3 Work out the **Answer**.

a) 1 kg 800 g × 3
- 1 kg × 3 = 3 kg
- 800 g × 3 = 2400 g

1 kg 800 g × 3 = 3 kg 2400 g
= 5 kg 400 g

The weight of the watermelon is 5 kilograms 400 grams.

 ISBN 978-93-5103-031-7

b) 1 kg 800 g + 5 kg 400 g = 6 kg 1200 g
= 7 kg 200 g

The total weight of the two fruits is
7 kilograms 200 grams.

4 Check
Did you answer the question?
Is your answer correct?

Weight of watermelon
= 7 kg 200 g – 1 kg 800 g
= 6 kg 1200 g – 1 kg 800 g
= 5 kg 400 g

Weight of papaya
= 5 kg 400 g ÷ 3
= 3 kg 2400 g ÷ 3
= 1 kg 800 g

My answer is correct.

☑ 1. **Understand**
☑ 2. **Plan**
☑ 3. **Answer**
☑ 4. **Check**

Let's Do

1. Mrs. Lee used two packets of flour to make 8 pies. One packet contained 1 kilogram 240 grams of flour and the other contained 1 kilogram 160 grams of flour. If she used the same amount of flour for each pie, how much flour did she use for each pie?

How much flour did Mrs. Lee use?
How many pies did she make?
What do I have to find first?

☐ 1. **Understand**
☐ 2. **Plan**
☐ 3. **Answer**
☐ 4. **Check**

PB Chapter 11: Exercise 3, pages 200–201

Practice 3

Solve the word problems. Show your work clearly.

1. Mary bought 4 rolls of ribbon each of length 3 metres 50 centimetres. She used all the ribbon to wrap 2 presents. If she used an equal length of ribbon to wrap each present, how much ribbon did she use for each present?

2. A lump of dough 3 kilograms 60 grams was divided into two portions. The bigger portion was 3 times as heavy as the smaller portion. How much heavier was the bigger portion than the smaller portion?

 ISBN 978-93-5103-031-7

Mind stretcher

Let's Learn

There are 24 lamp posts along a street. Every two lamp posts are 1 metre 95 centimetres apart from each other. What is the distance between the first and the last lamp post?

1 Understand the problem.

How many lamp posts are there?
What is the distance between two lamp posts?

2 Plan what to do.

I can **draw a picture** to help me solve the problem.

3 Work out the **Answer**.

If there is 1 lamp post, there are 0 intervals.

If there are 2 lamp posts, there is 1 interval.

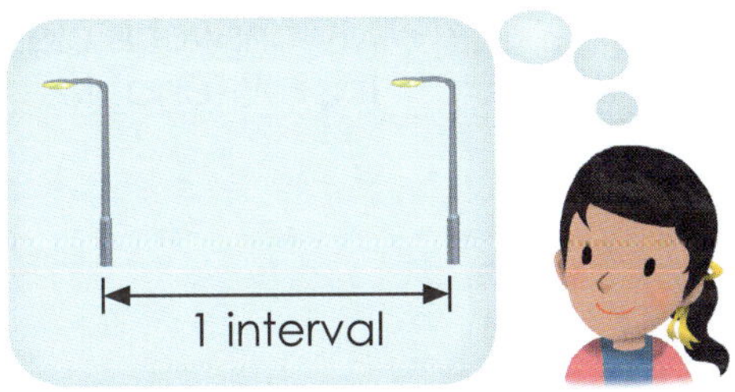

 ISBN 978-93-5103-031-7

If there are 3 lamp posts, there are 2 intervals.

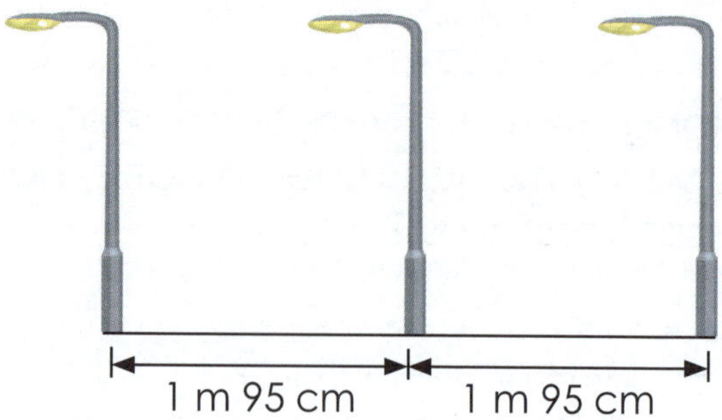

There are 24 lamp posts. So, there are 23 intervals between the first and the last lamp post.

1 m 95 cm × 23 → 1 m × 23 = 23 m; 95 cm × 23 = 2185 cm

1 m 95 cm × 23 = 23 m 2185 cm
= 44 m 85 cm

The distance between the first and the last lamp post is 44 metres 85 centimetres.

4 Check
Did you answer the question? Is your answer reasonable?

1 m 95 cm = 195 cm
≈ 200 cm

200 cm × 23 ≈ 200 × 20
= 4000 cm
= 40 m

My answer is close to 40 metres.
It is reasonable.

☑ **1. Understand**
☑ **2. Plan**
☑ **3. Answer**
☑ **4. Check**

 ISBN 978-93-5103-031-7

12 Symmetry

Lesson 1 Symmetric Figures

Identifying and making symmetric figures

Let's Learn

a) Many things around us have **symmetry**.

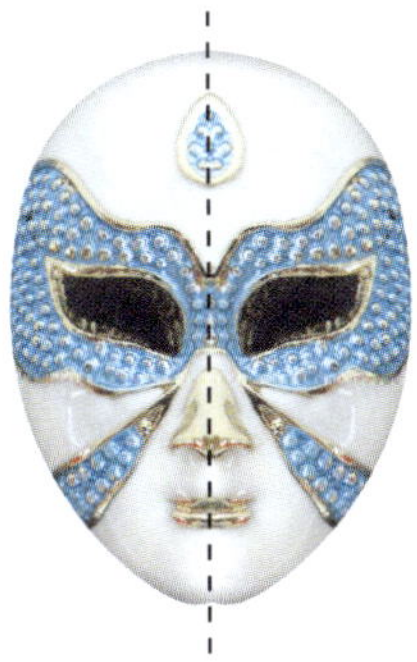

These are **symmetric figures**.
The dotted line in each figure is a **line of symmetry**.
When the figure is folded along this line, the two halves match exactly.

 ISBN 978-93-5103-031-7

b) Fold a piece of paper. Cut out a figure as shown.

Maths Lab

Picture It

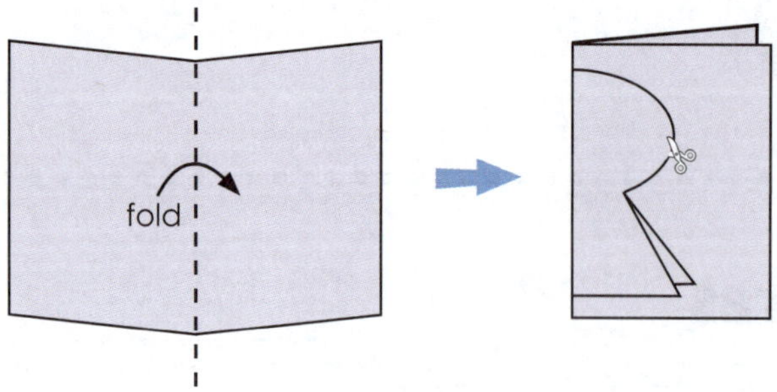

Unfold the figure. You will get a symmetric figure.

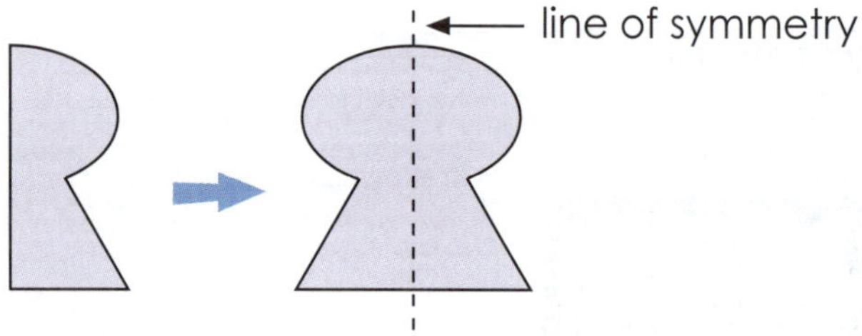

The fold line is a line of symmetry.

Let's Do

1. Trace these figures on folded sheets of paper. Then, cut out these symmetric figures.

a) 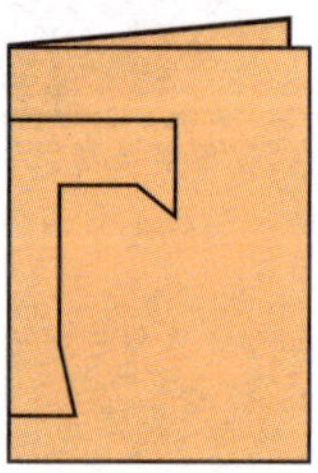

b) 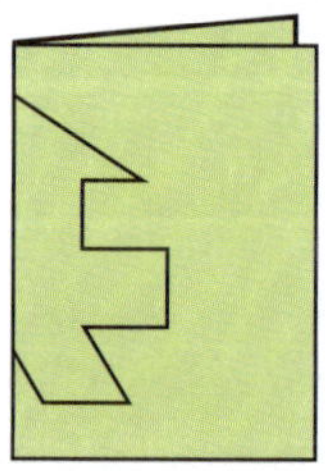

2. Circle the symmetric figures.

a) 

b) 

c) 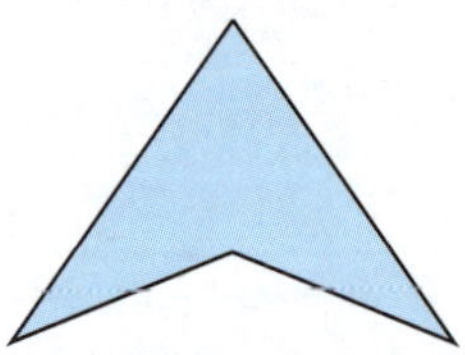

d) 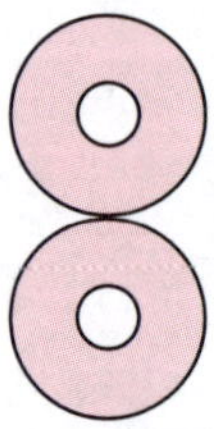

P/B Chapter 12: Exercise 1, pages 202–203

 ISBN 978-93-5103-031-7

Identifying lines of symmetry

Let's Learn

Maths Lab

Picture It

a) Fold a rectangle along the dotted line as shown.

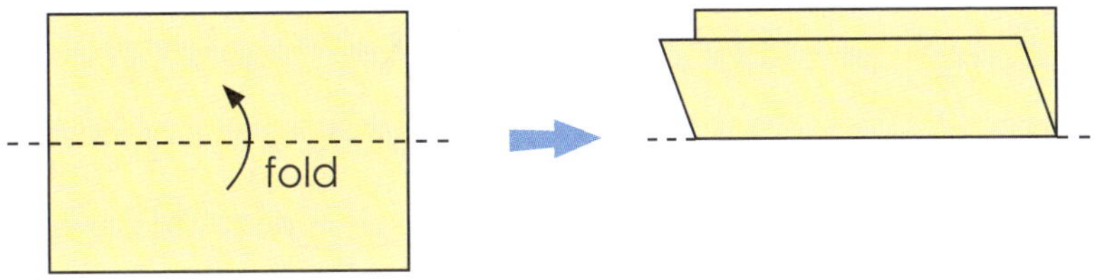

The two halves match exactly when folded along the dotted line. The dotted line is a line of symmetry of the rectangle.

b) Now fold the rectangle along the dotted line as shown.

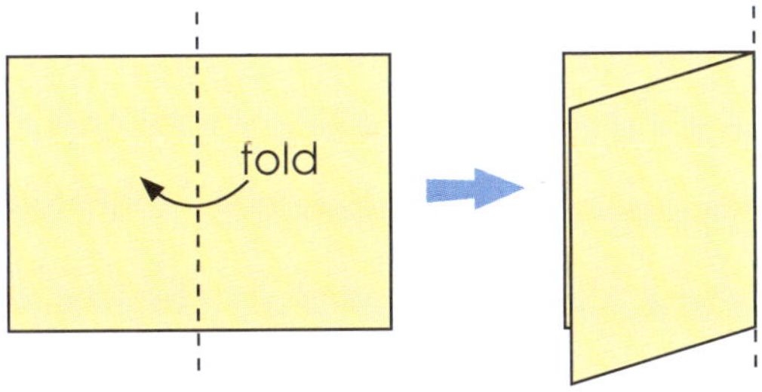

The two halves match exactly when folded along the dotted line. The dotted line is another line of symmetry of the rectangle.

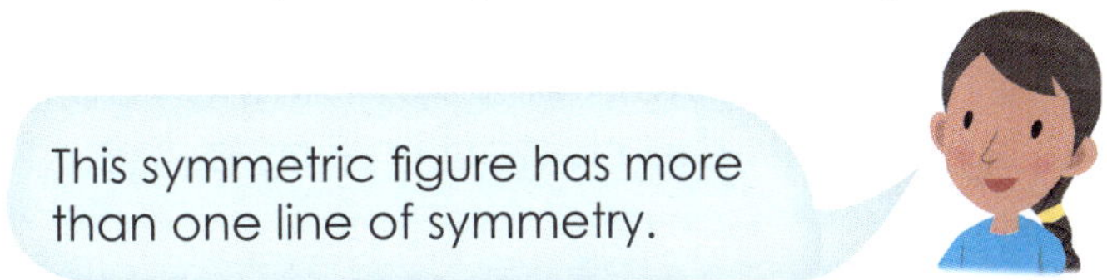

c) Now fold the rectangle along the dotted line as shown.

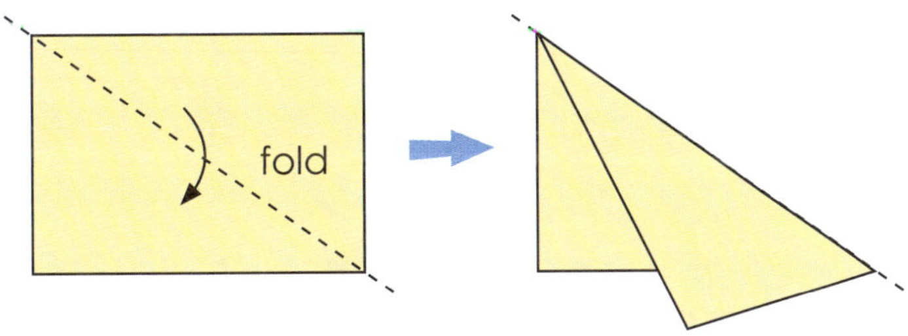

The two halves do not match exactly when folded along the dotted line. The dotted line is not a line of symmetry of the rectangle.

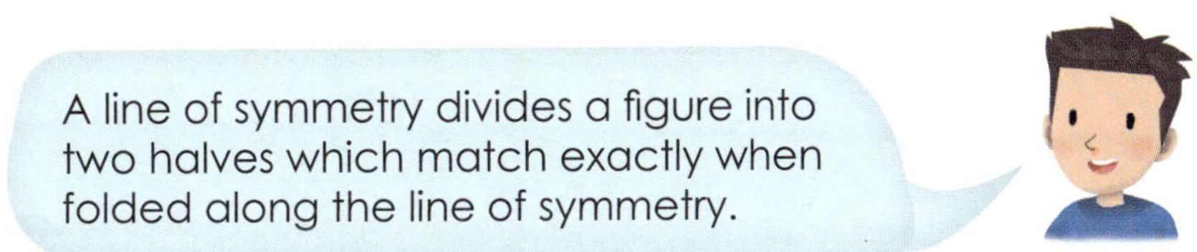

 ISBN 978-93-5103-031-7

Let's Do

1. Is the dotted line in each figure a line of symmetry? Fill in the blanks with **Yes** or **No**.

a) 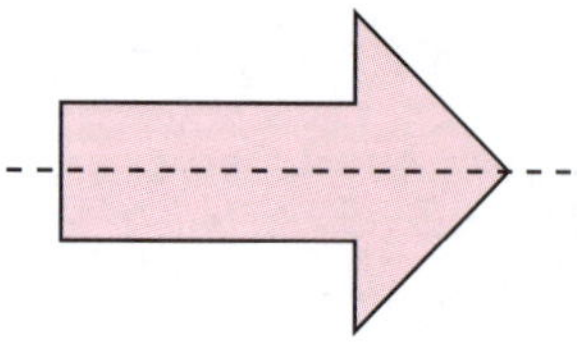 ______

b) 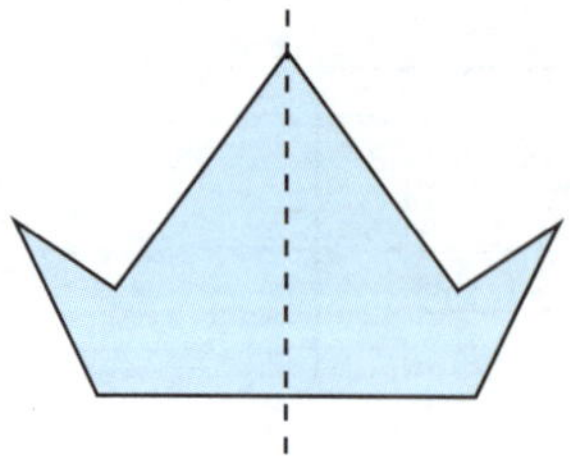 ______

c) 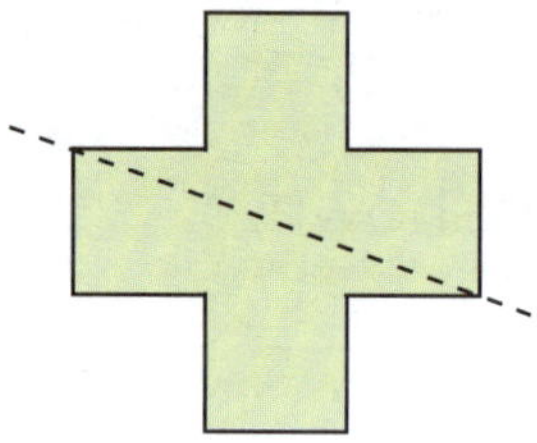 ______

d) 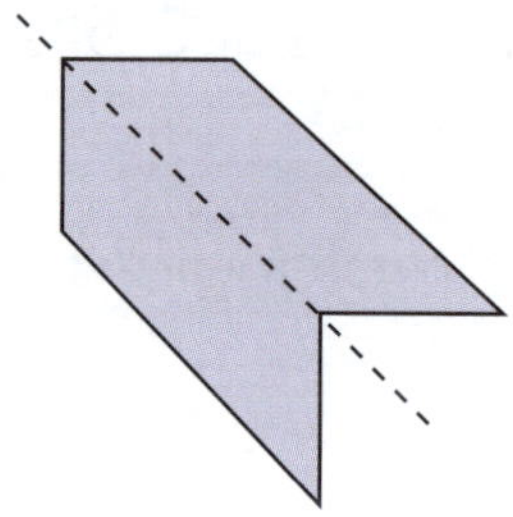 ______

P/B Chapter 12: Exercise 2, pages 204–205

Completing symmetric figures

Let's Learn

The figure on the left is half of a symmetric figure. We can complete the symmetric figure with the dotted line as a line of symmetry.

Picture It

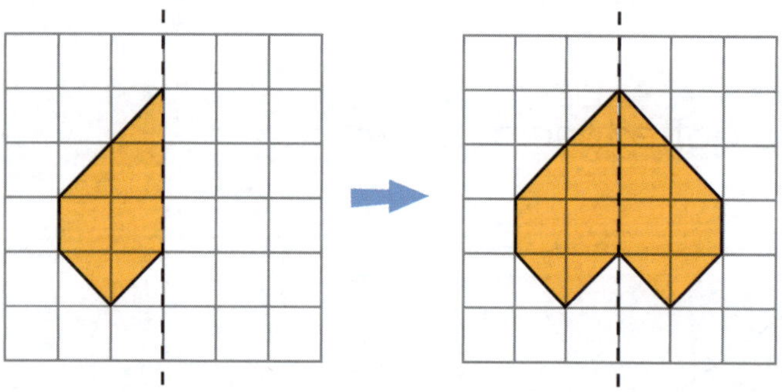

Check that your figure is symmetric by folding it along the line of symmetry.

ISBN 978-93-5103-031-7

Let's Do

1. Each figure below is half of a symmetric figure. Complete each symmetric figure with the dotted line as a line of symmetry.

a) 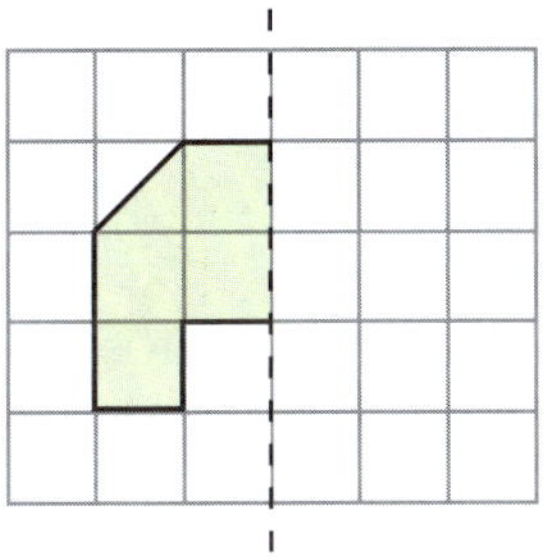

b) 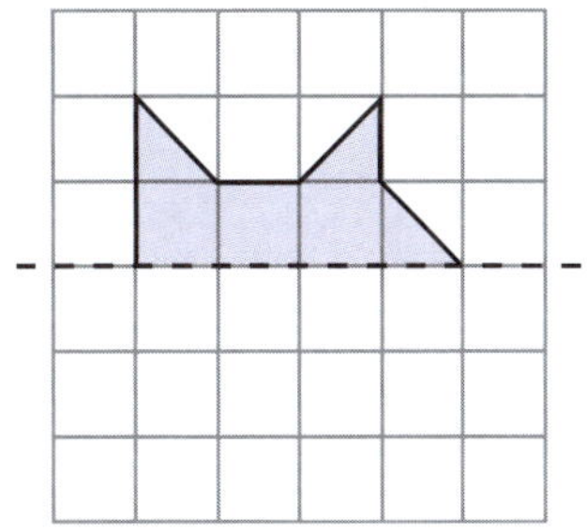

P/B Chapter 12: Exercise 3, pages 206–207

Making symmetric patterns

Let's Learn

The figure on the left shows half of a symmetric pattern. We can shade the squares on the other half of the grid to form a symmetric pattern.

Picture It

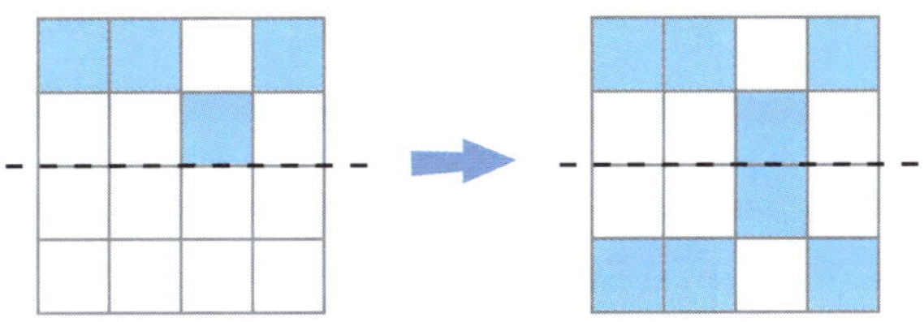

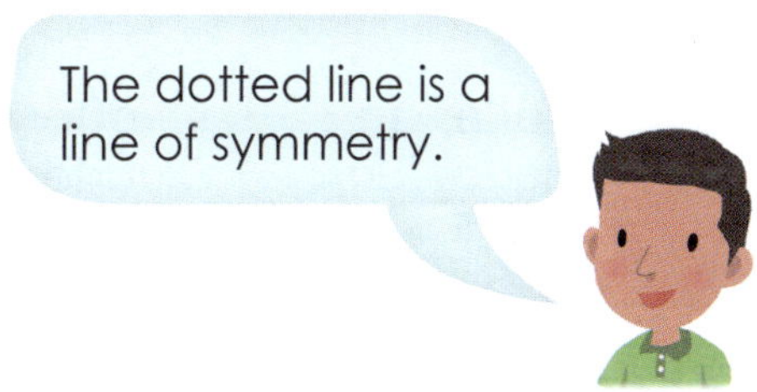

Let's Do

1. Each figure below is half of a symmetric pattern. Complete each symmetric pattern with the dotted line as a line of symmetry.

a) 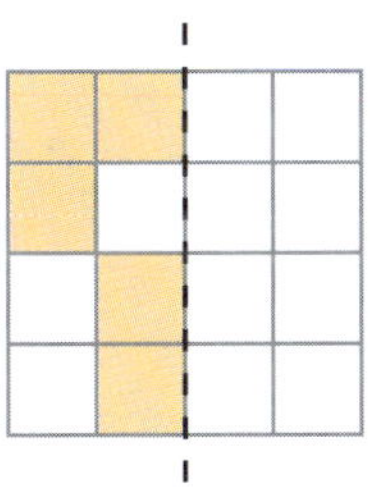

b) 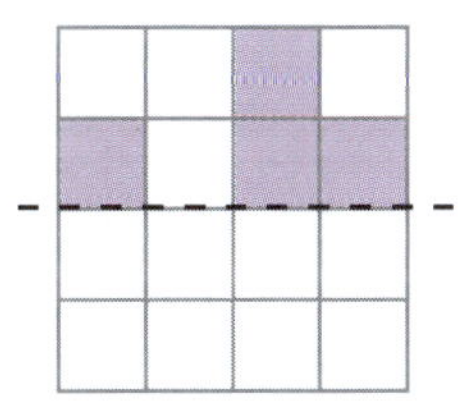

P/B Chapter 12: Exercise 4, page 208

 ISBN 978-93-5103-031-7

Rotational symmetry

Let's Learn

Maths Lab a) Rotate this figure using four quarter turns.

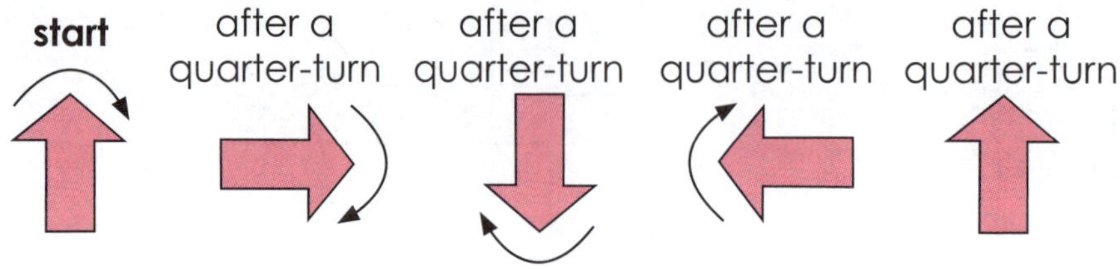

This figure looks exactly the same as the original only after it has completed a full-turn.

4 quarter-turns make a full-turn.

Maths Lab b) Some figures look the same as the original more than once during a full-turn.

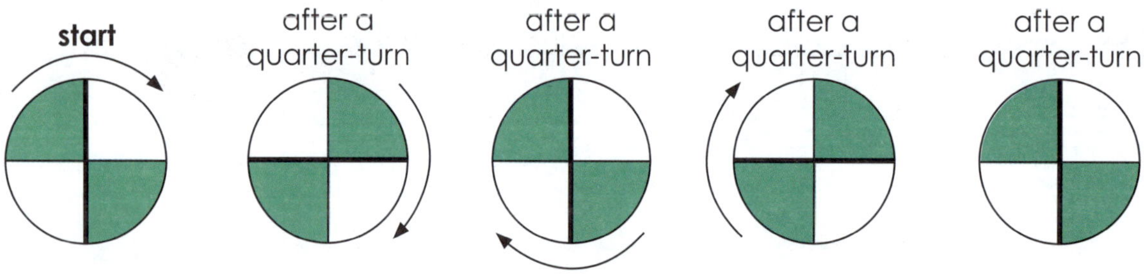

This figure looks exactly the same as the original after a half-turn and after a full-turn.

When a figure looks exactly the same more than once during a full-turn, we say that it has **rotational symmetry**.

2 quarter-turns make a half-turn.

The arrow in (a) does not have rotational symmetry.

 ISBN 978-93-5103-031-7

Let's Do

1. Each of these figures is rotated through four quarter-turns until it completes a full-turn. Tick the box next to the figure(s) with rotational symmetry.

   a) 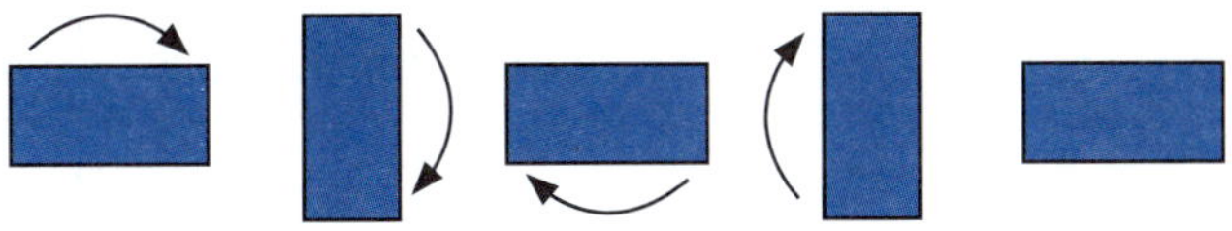 ☐

   b) 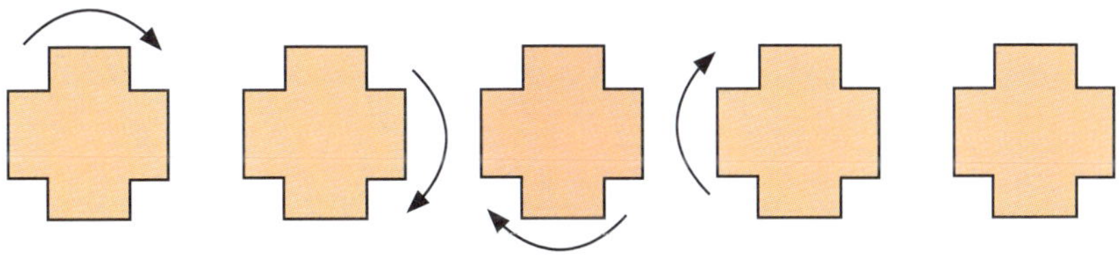 ☐

   c) 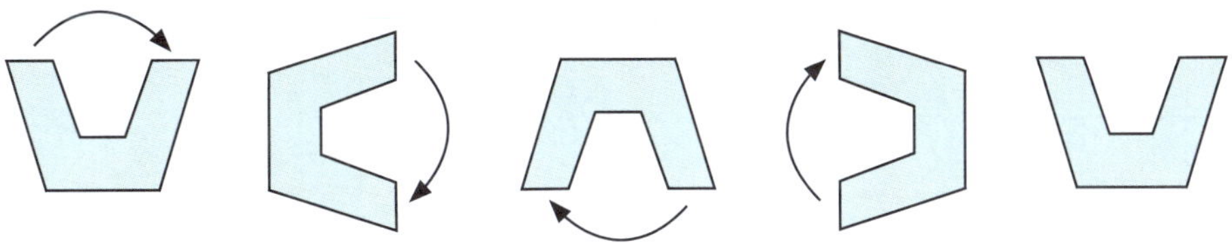 ☐

Chapter 12: Exercise 5, page 209

Practice 1

1. Is each figure a symmetric figure?

   a) 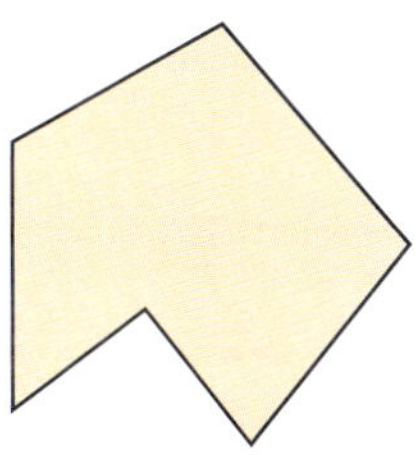

   b) 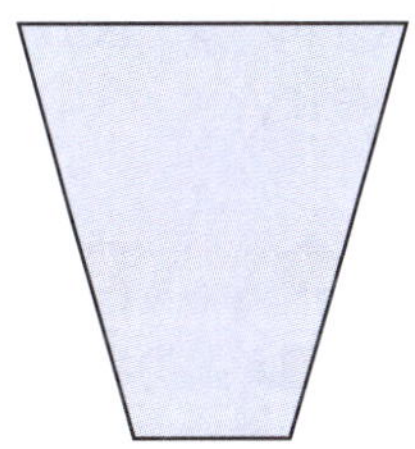

2. Is the dotted line in each figure a line of symmetry?

   a) 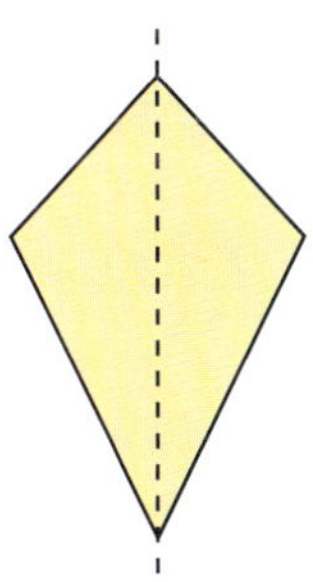

   b) 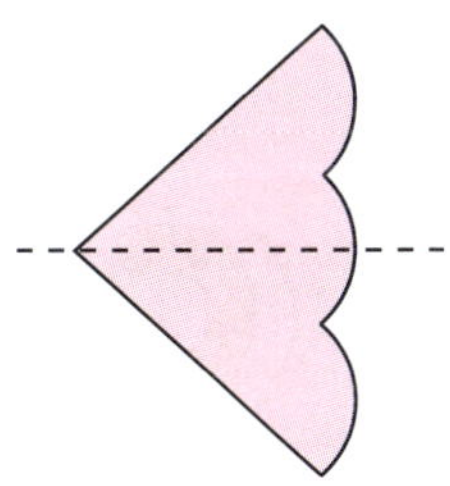

   c) 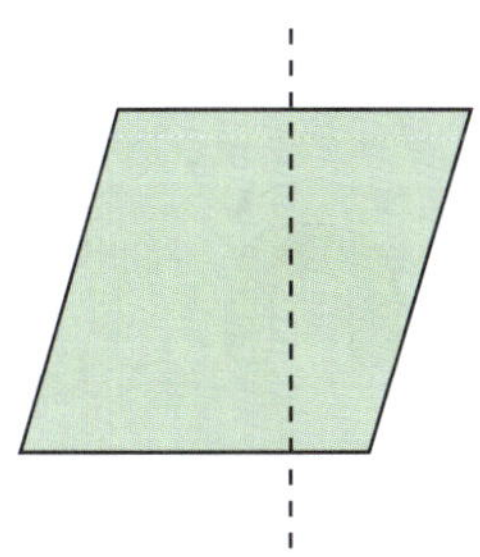

 ISBN 978-93-5103-031-7

3. Each figure below is half of a symmetric figure. Complete each symmetric figure with the dotted line as a line of symmetry.

a)

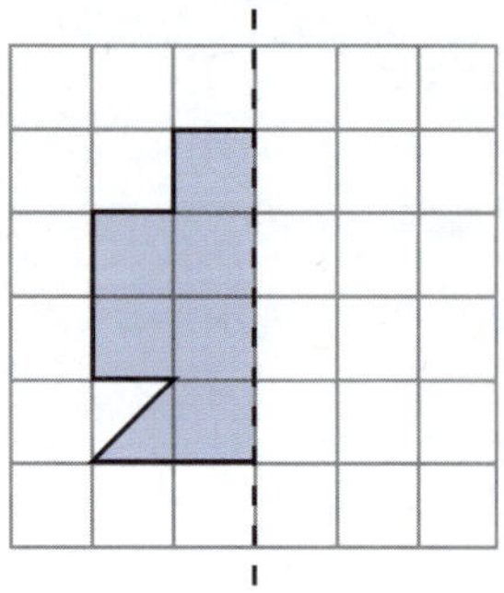

b)

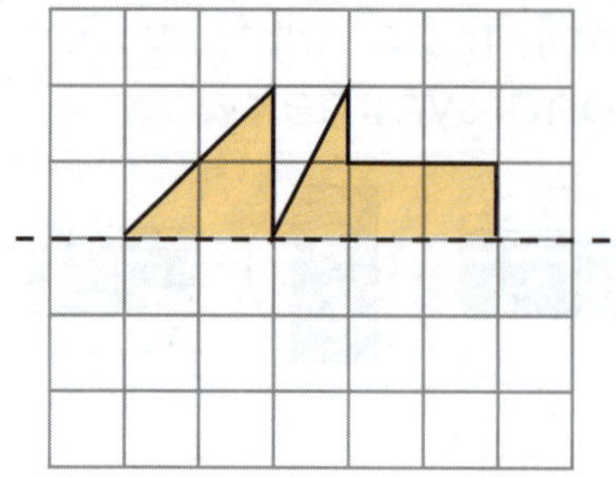

4. Each figure below is half of a symmetric pattern. Complete each symmetric pattern with the dotted line as a line of symmetry.

a)

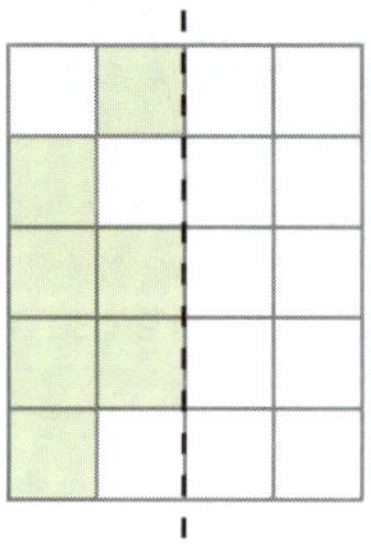

b)

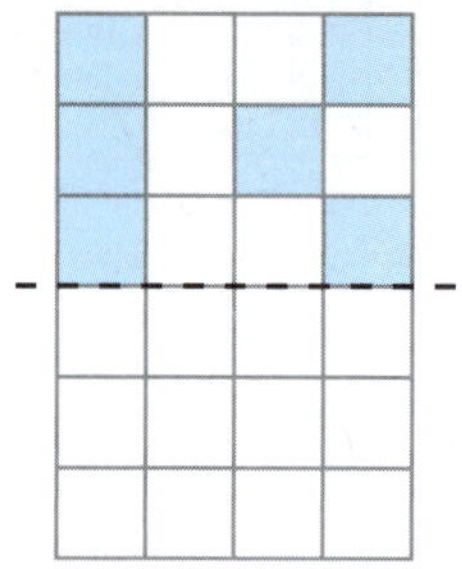

5. The figures below are rotated through four quarter turns until they complete one full turn. Tick the box next to the figure(s) with rotational symmetry.

a)

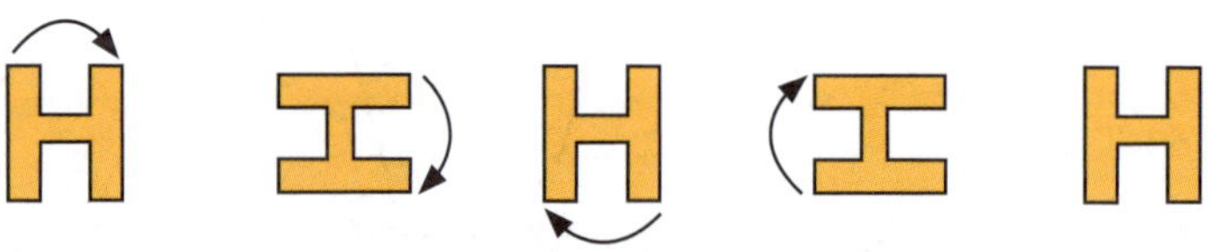

☐

b)

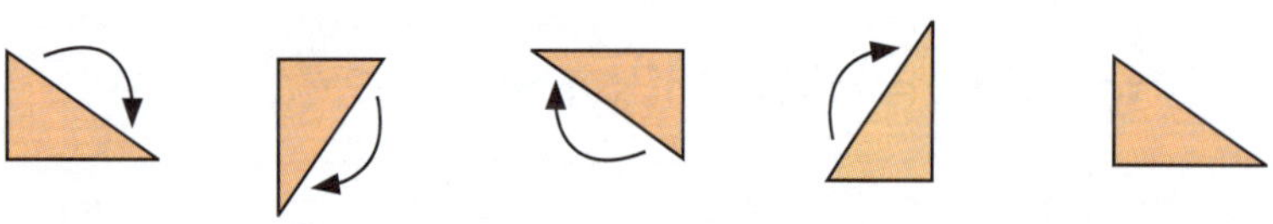

☐

c)

☐

d)

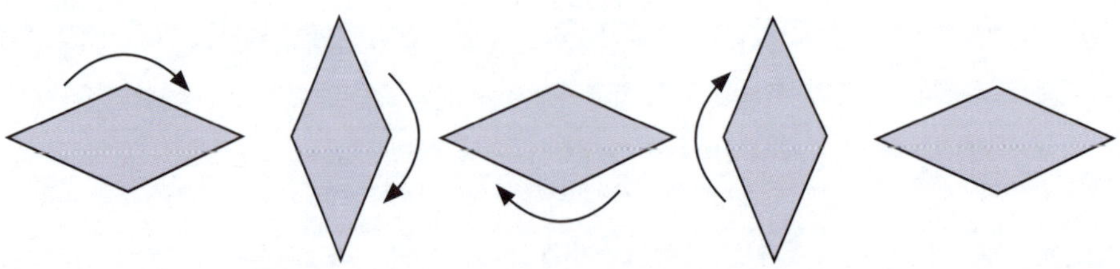

☐

 ISBN 978-93-5103-031-7

Lesson 2 Problem Solving

Mind stretcher

Let's Learn

Colour 4 squares in the figure below to form a symmetric pattern with the dotted line as a line of symmetry.

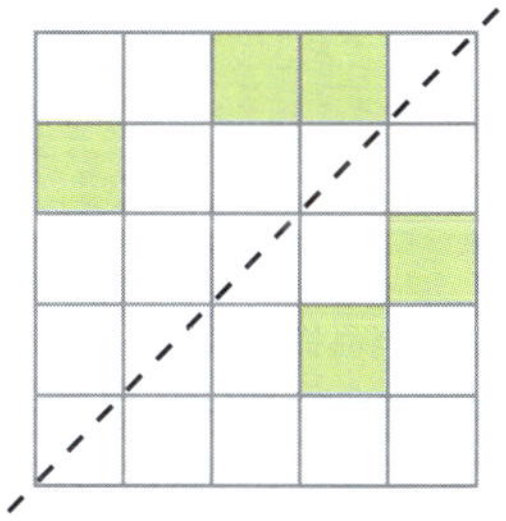

1 Understand the problem.

Where is the line of symmetry?
What is a symmetric pattern?
How many squares do I have to colour?

2 Plan what to do.

I can **act it out**. First, I copy the figure on a piece of square grid paper. Then, I fold the figure along the dotted line to see which squares I have to colour.

3 Work out the **Answer**.

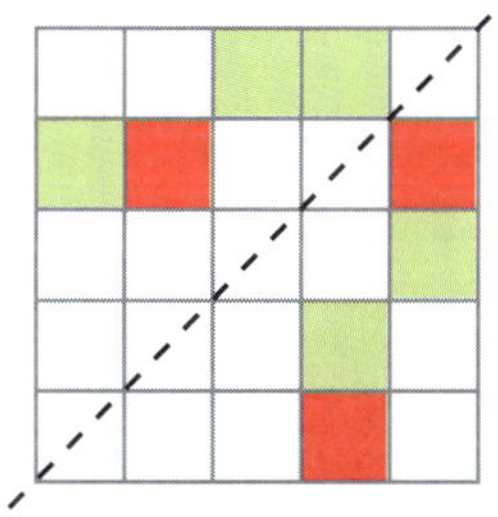

The pattern is symmetric now, but I have coloured only 3 squares. I have to colour another square.

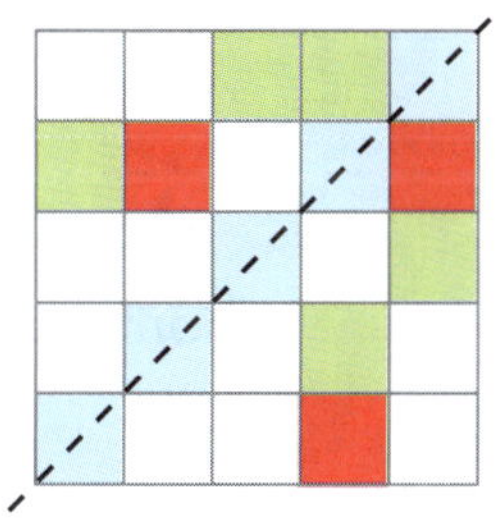

I can colour any one of the squares along the line of symmetry to form a symmetric pattern.

4 Check
Did you answer the question?
Is your answer correct?

I have coloured 4 squares.
The pattern is symmetric along the line of symmetry.

My answer is correct.

- ☑ 1. Understand
- ☑ 2. Plan
- ☑ 3. Answer
- ☑ 4. Check

 ISBN 978-93-5103-031-7

13 Graphs

Lesson 1 Line Graphs

Completing and interpreting broken line graphs

Let's Learn

This table shows the number of visitors at a theme park for five months.

Month	Aug	Sep	Oct	Nov	Dec
Number of visitors	2500	3500	2000	2500	4000

The data can also be presented in a **line graph**.

Picture It

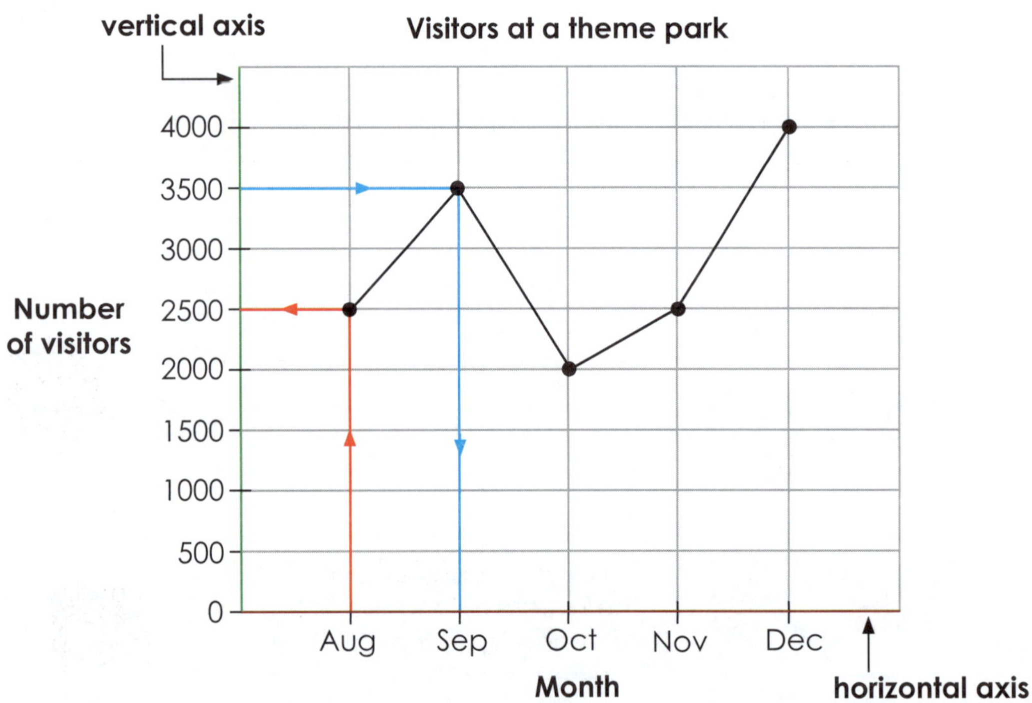

a) How many visitors were there in August?

First, find August along the **horizontal axis**.
Then, move up to a point on the graph.
Lastly, move left to a point on the **vertical axis**.

There were 2500 visitors in August.

 ISBN 978-93-5103-031-7

b) In which month were there 3500 visitors?

There were 3500 visitors in September.

c) What was the increase in the number of visitors from August to September?

3500 – 2500 = 1000

The increase in the number of visitors from August to September was 1000.

d) What was the decrease in the number of visitors from September to October?

There were 2000 visitors in October.

3500 – 2000 = ____

The decrease in the number of visitors from September to October was ____.

e) What was the difference between the number of visitors in September and in December?

There were 4000 visitors in December.

4000 – 3500 = ____

The difference between the number of visitors in September and in December was ____.

 ISBN 978-93-5103-031-7

Let's Do

1. The line graph shows the number of people in a supermarket at every hour from 5 p.m. to 8 p.m.

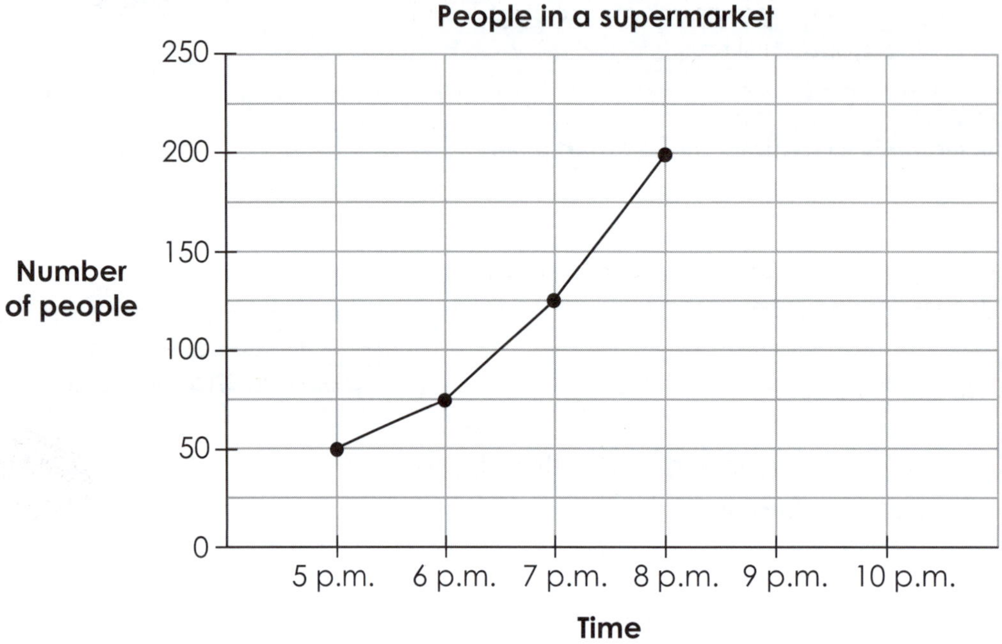

a) The supermarket manager recorded the number of people in the supermarket at 9 p.m. and 10 p.m. Complete the line graph using the data given in the table below.

Time	9 p.m.	10 p.m.
Number of people	100	0

b) What was the increase in the number of people from 7 p.m. to 8 p.m.?

_______ – _______ = _______

The increase in the number of people from 7 p.m. to 8 p.m. was _______.

c) What was the decrease in the number of people from 8 p.m. to 9 p.m.?

_______ – _______ = _______

The decrease in the number of people from 8 p.m. to 9 p.m. was _______.

  ISBN 978-93-5103-031-7

2. Fix a metre ruler upright in the ground of an open field. Measure the length of the shadow of the ruler every hour from 10 a.m. to 3 p.m.

a) Record the length of the shadow. Then, round the length to the nearest 10 centimetres.

Time	Length of shadow (cm)	Length of shadow rounded to nearest 10 cm
10 a.m.		
11 a.m.		
noon		
1 p.m.		
2 p.m.		
3 p.m.		

b) Present your data in the line graph below.

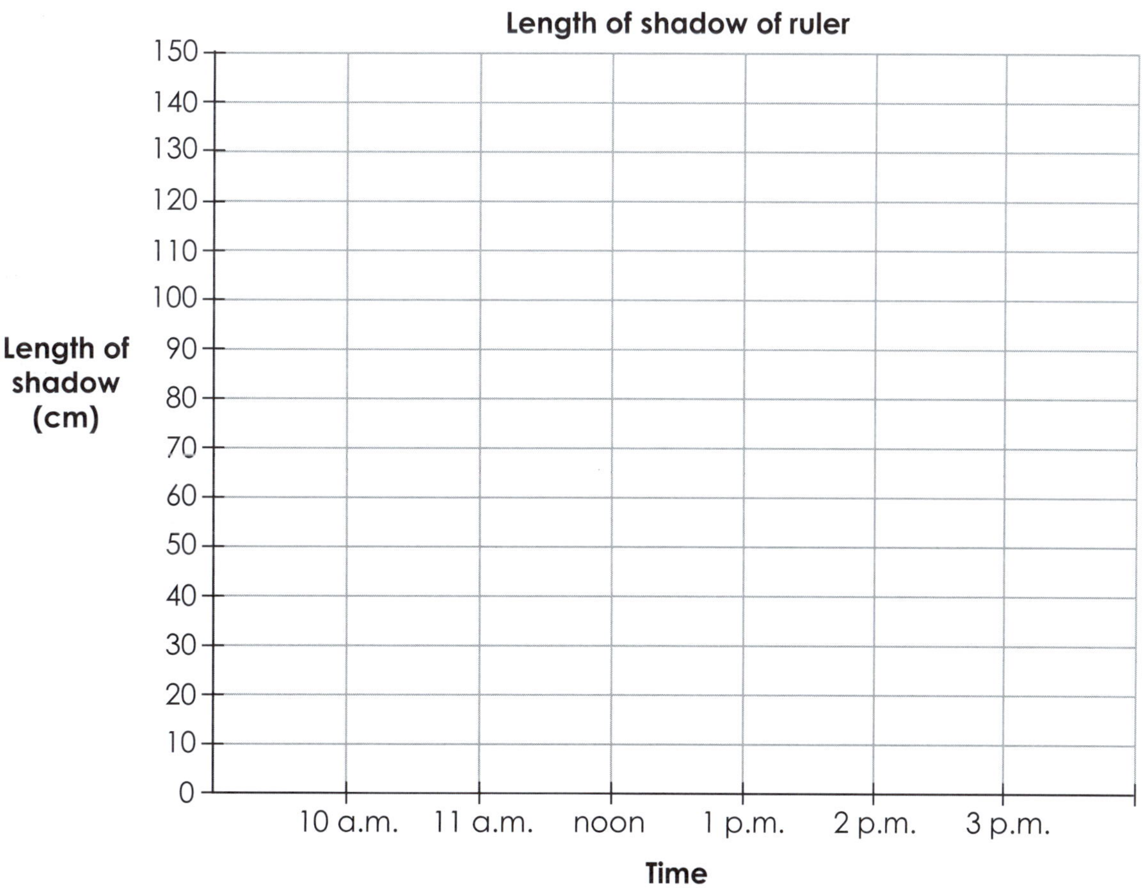

PB Chapter 13: Exercise 1, pages 210–215

 ISBN 978-93-5103-031-7

Reading and interpreting straight line graphs

Let's Learn

The line graph shows the cost of a type of plastic tape sold in a store.

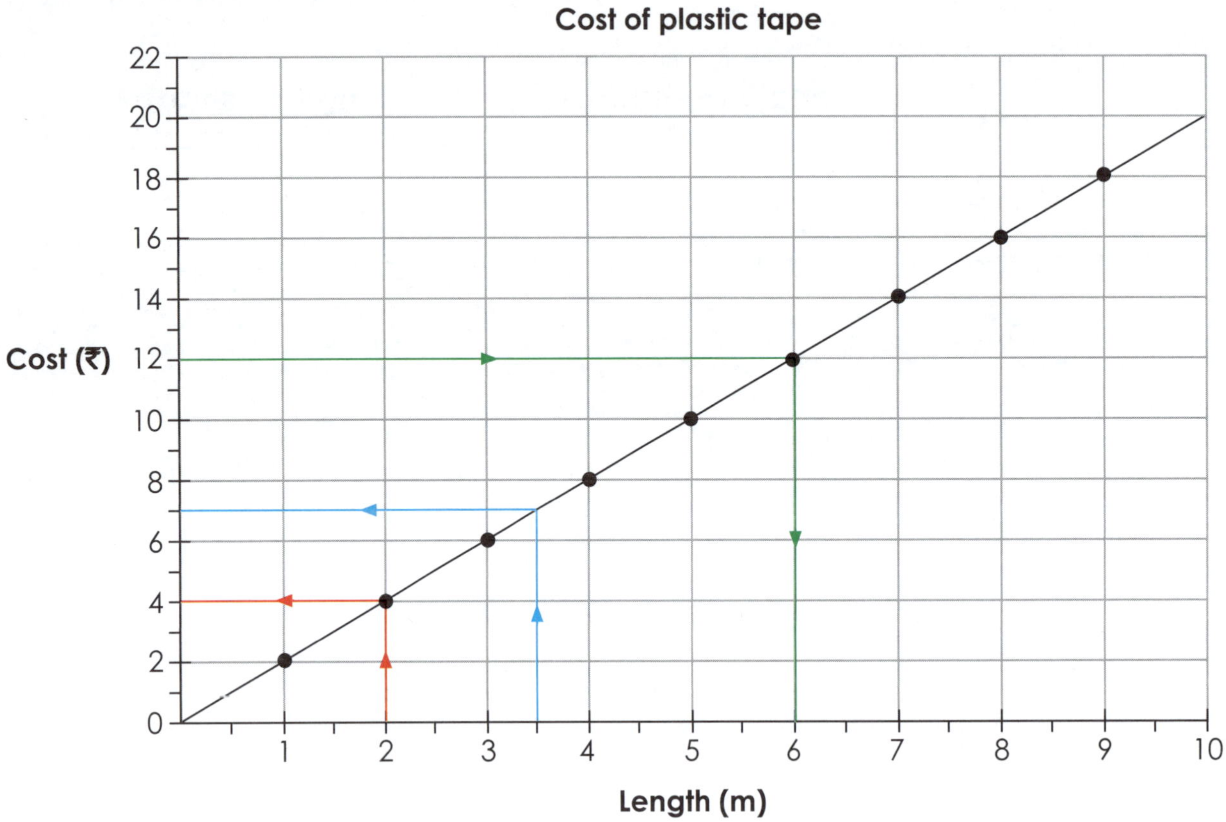

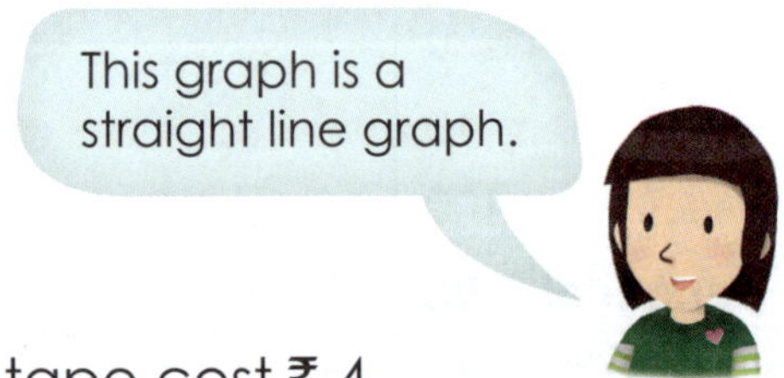

a) The graph shows that 2 metres of plastic tape cost ₹ 4.
7 metres of plastic tape cost ₹ ____.

b) When the cost is ₹ 12, the length of the plastic tape is 6 metres.
When the cost is ₹ 16, the length of the plastic tape is ____ metres.

c) $3\frac{1}{2}$ metres of plastic tape cost ₹ 7.
When the cost is ₹ 17, the length of the plastic tape is ____ metres.

 ISBN 978-93-5103-031-7

Let's Do

1. The line graph shows the temperature of an object heated over five hours.

Temperature of a heated object

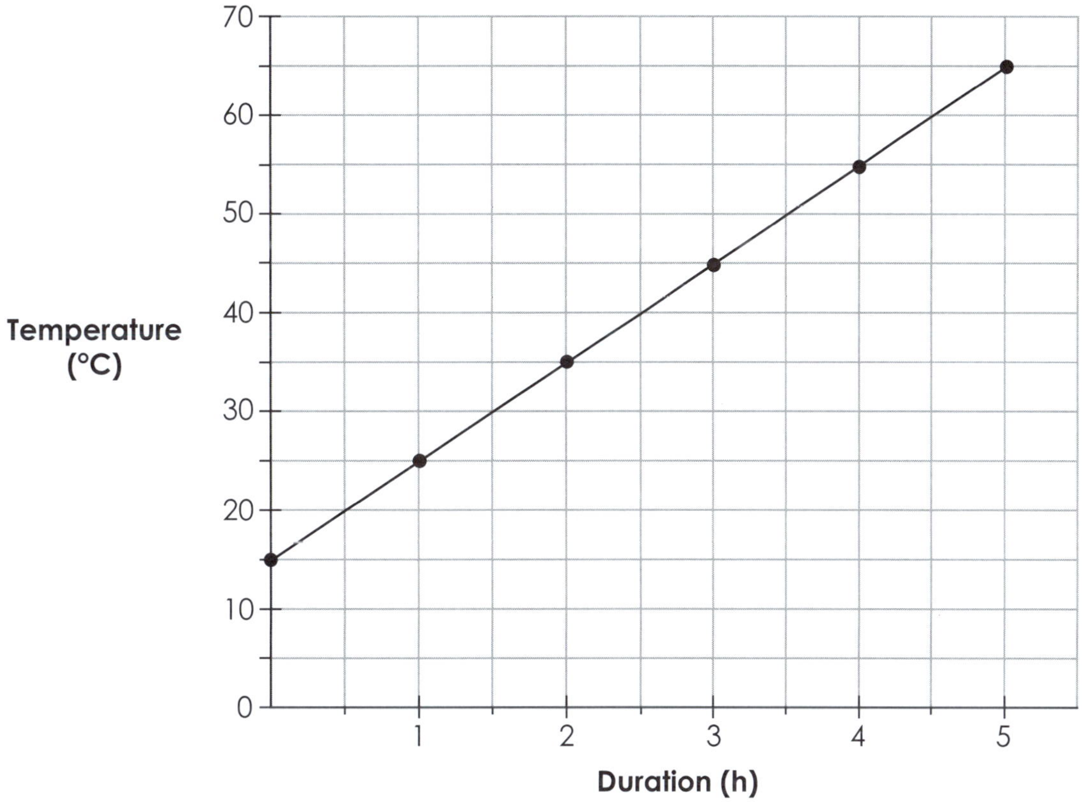

Fill in the blanks.

a) The temperature of the object before it was heated was ______°C.

b) Complete the table.

Duration (h)	1		3		5
Temperature (°C)		35		55	

c) The temperature of the object after 1.5 hours was ______°C.

d) The temperature of the object after ______ hours was 60°C.

e) The increase in temperature between the second hour and the fifth hour was ______°C.

f) The temperature increased by ______°C every hour.

P/B Chapter 13: Exercise 2, pages 216–217

 ISBN 978-93-5103-031-7

Comparing bar graphs and line graphs

Let's Learn

We use different types of graphs to show data in different ways. When we want to compare the number of glasses of different types of fruit juices sold by a stall in a week, we use a bar graph to show the data.

Picture It

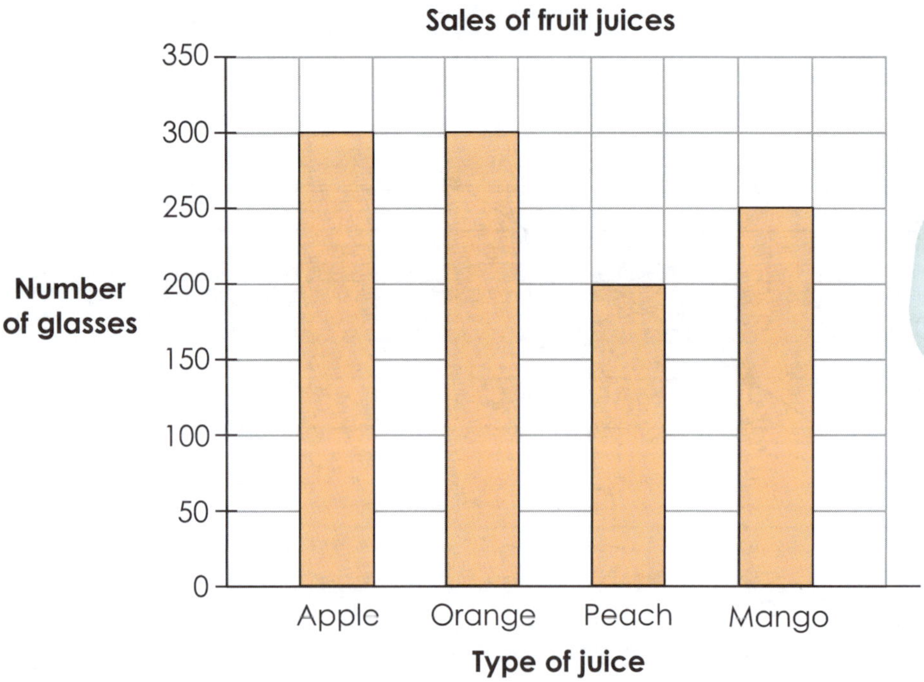

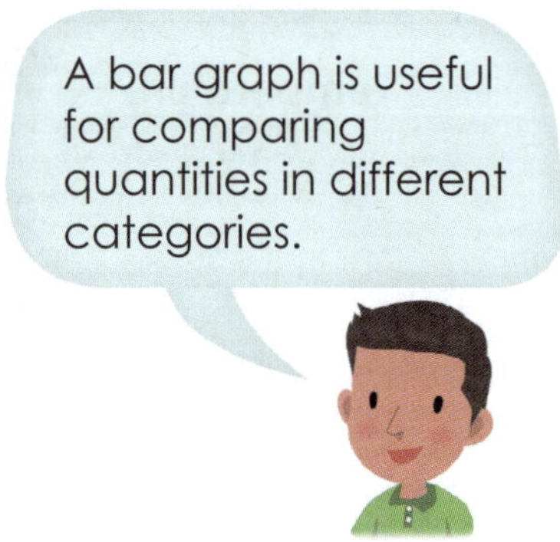

a) The number of glasses of apple juice and orange juice sold was equal.

b) The least number of glasses of peach juice was sold.

c) The stall sold 50 more glasses of mango juice than peach juice.

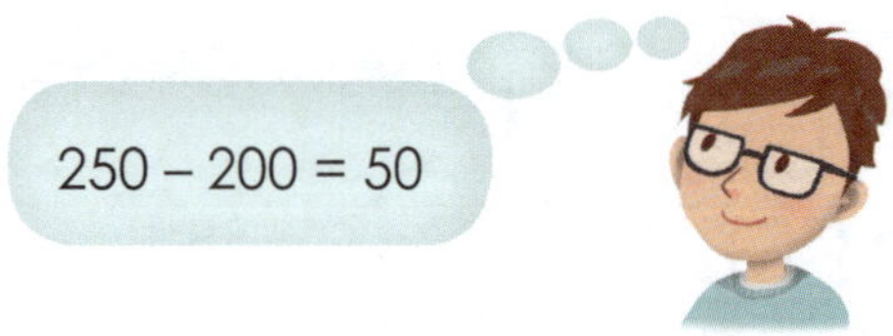

d) The stall sold 100 fewer glasses of peach juice than apple juice.

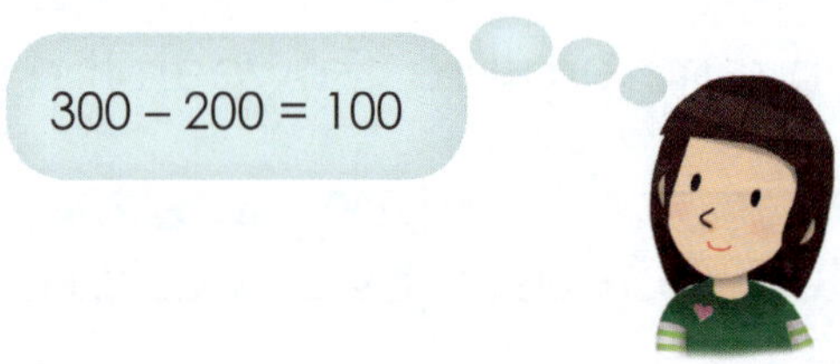

  ISBN 978-93-5103-031-7

We use a line graph to show the number of glasses of fruit juices sold by the stall every day from Monday to Friday.

Picture It

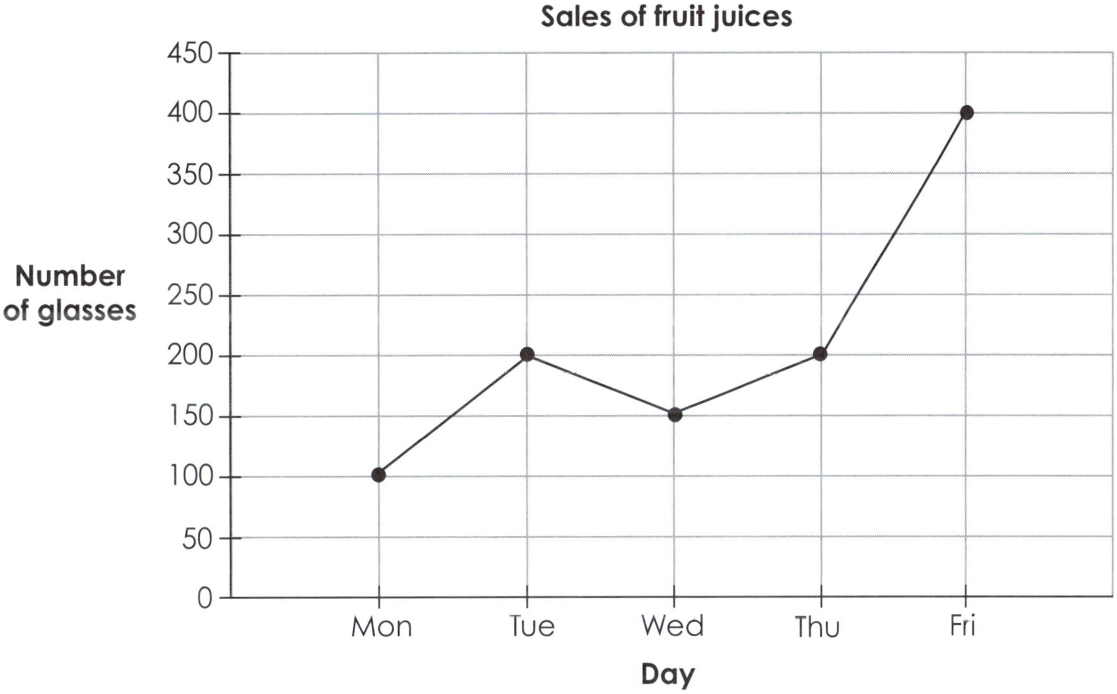

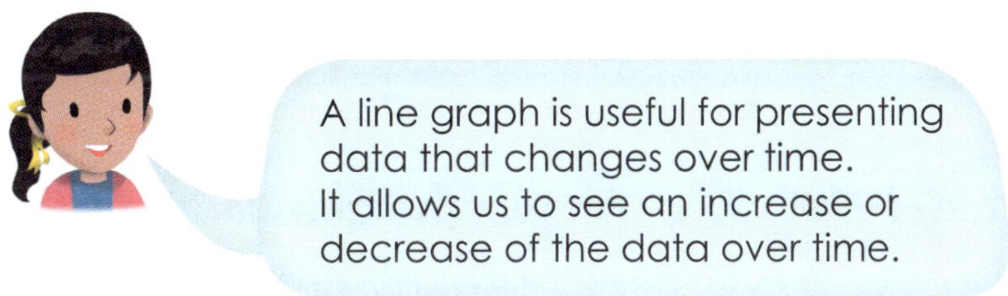

a) The greatest number of glasses of fruit juices was sold on Friday.

b) The sales of fruit juices increased between Monday and Tuesday.

c) The sales of fruit juices decreased between Tuesday and Wednesday.

d) The sales of fruit juices increased the most in one day between Thursday and Friday.

e) On the whole, the sales of fruit juices from Monday to Friday was increasing.

 ISBN 978-93-5103-031-7

Let's Do

1. Choose either a bar graph or a line graph to present the data. Explain your choice.

   a) A group of 30 students was asked to name their favourite type of storybook.

   A ______ graph can be used to present the data

   because ____.

   b) Derek turned on a tap to fill a tank. He measured the height of the water level in the tank over five minutes.

   A ______ graph can be used to present the data

   because ____.

P/B Chapter 13: Exercise 3, page 218

Practice 1

1. The graph shows the amount of petrol Mr. Jordan bought in the last five months.

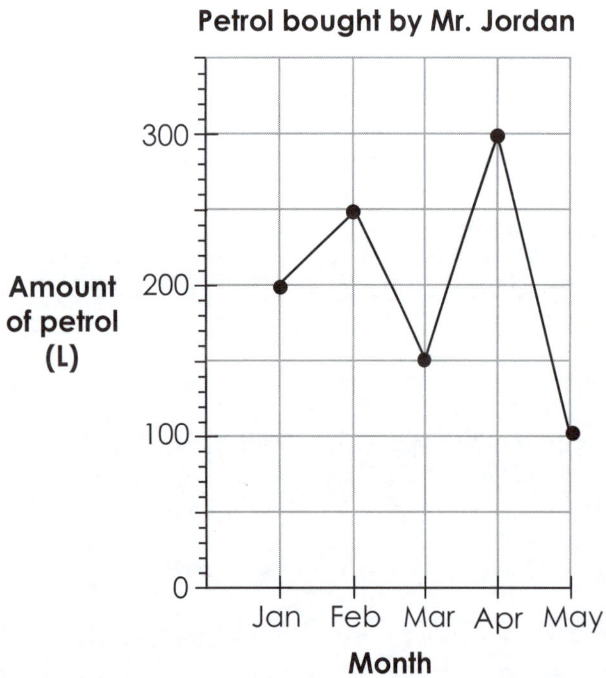

Answer the questions.

a) How many litres of petrol did he buy in February?

b) In which month did he buy 300 litres of petrol?

c) What was the increase in the amount of petrol he bought between March and April?

d) What was the decrease in the amount of petrol he bought between April and May?

 ISBN 978-93-5103-031-7

2. The line graph shows the length of a spring when various weights are hung on it.

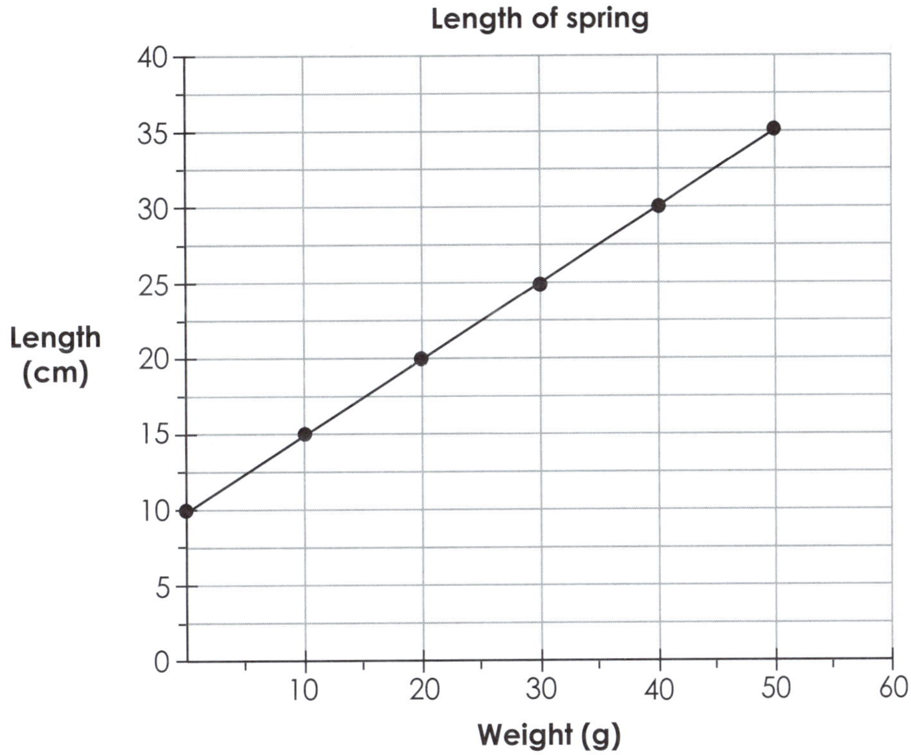

a) Complete the table.

Weight (g)	0	20	45		
Length (cm)				15	27.5

b) By how many centimetres is the spring stretched when a weight of 40 grams is hung on it?

3. Choose either a bar graph or a line graph to present the data. Explain your choice.

a) Abdul recorded the height of a plant for a week after planting the seed.

b) Sara asked 50 students to name their favourite colour.

 ISBN 978-93-5103-031-7

14 Time

Lesson 1 Seconds

Telling time

Let's Learn

The **second** is another unit of time. We write second as **s**.

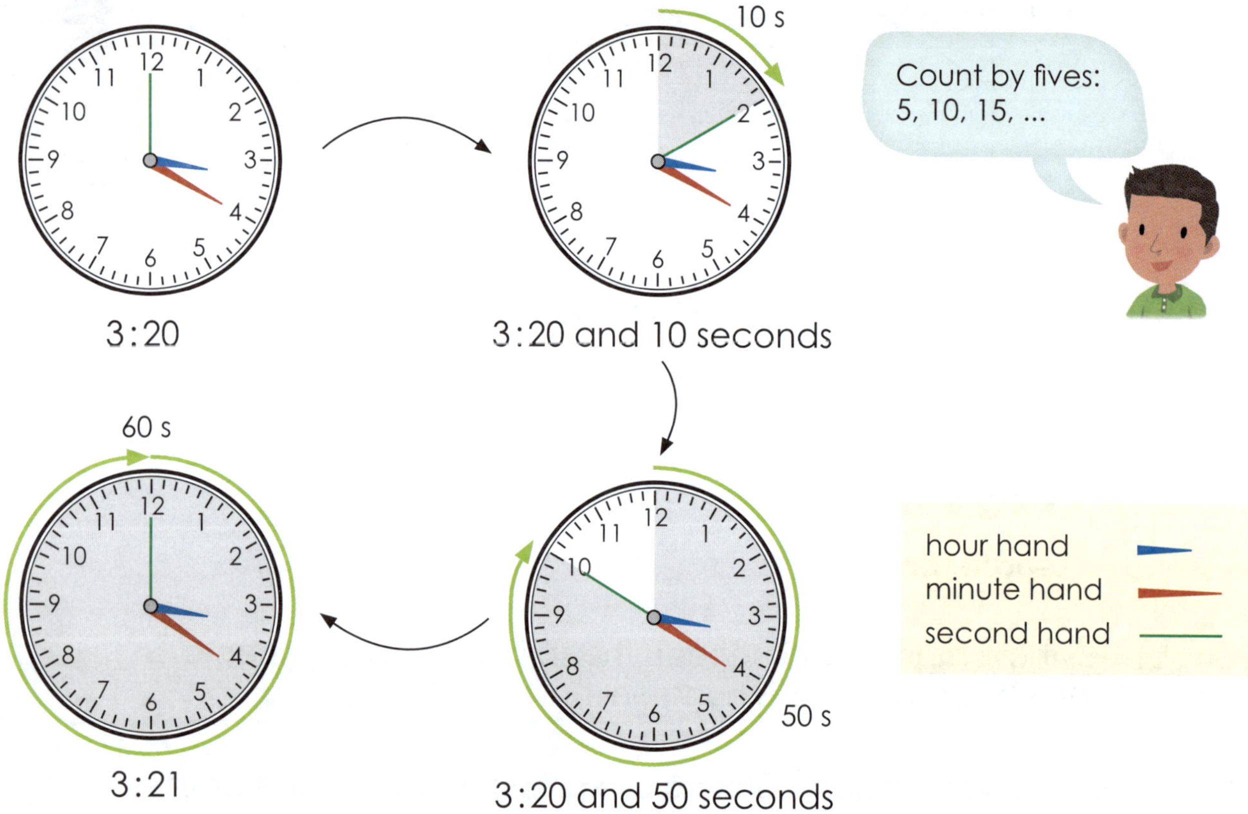

The **second hand** takes 60 seconds to make one complete turn round the clock. Second is a smaller unit of time than the minute.

1 minute = 60 seconds

  ISBN 978-93-5103-031-7

Let's Do

1. Write the time.

a)

12 : 30 and ____ seconds

b)

____ : ____ and ____ seconds

Chapter 14: Exercise 1, page 219

Finding duration in seconds

Let's Learn

Maths Lab

a) Harry started folding a paper aeroplane at 6:45 and 20 seconds.

He finished folding the aeroplane at 6:45 and 50 seconds.

Picture It

6:45 and 20 seconds

6:45 and 50 seconds

6:45 and 50 seconds is 30 seconds after 6:45 and 20 seconds.

Harry took 30 seconds to fold the paper aeroplane.

 ISBN 978-93-5103-031-7

b)

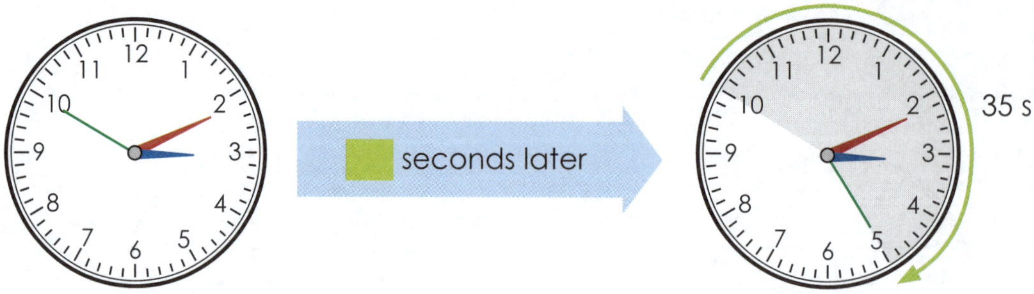

3:10 and 50 seconds

3:11 and 25 seconds

3:11 and 25 seconds is ▇ seconds after 3:10 and 50 seconds.

Let's Do

1. Write the times and find the duration.

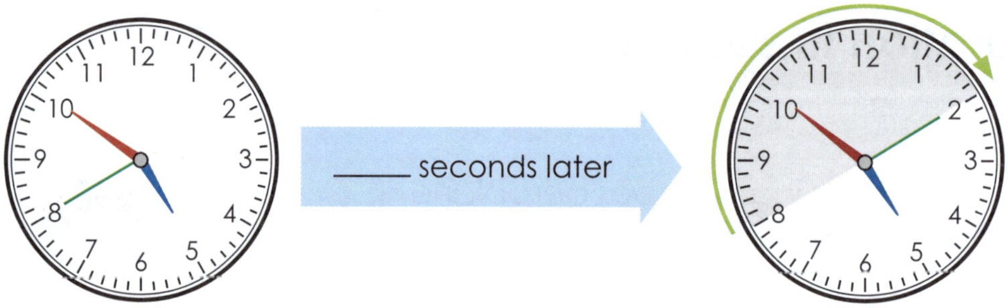

4:50 and _____ seconds

4:_____ and _____ seconds

2. a) Find out how many times you can skip in 10 seconds.

   b) Find out how many seconds you take to write the numbers 1 to 10.

Chapter 14: Exercise 2, pages 220–222

Expressing minutes and seconds in seconds

Let's Learn

Write 3 minutes 40 seconds in seconds.

3 min 40 s → 3 min = 180 s, 40 s

1 min = 60 s
3 min = 3 × 60
= 180 s

3 min 40 s = 180 s + 40 s
= 220 s

 ISBN 978-93-5103-031-7

Let's Do

1. Write in seconds.

a) 2 min 30 s → _______ min = _______ s; _______ s

2 min 30 s = _______ s + _______ s

= _______ s

b) 4 min 15 s = _______ s + _______ s

= _______ s

Chapter 14: Exercise 3, page 223

Expressing seconds in minutes and seconds

Let's Learn

Write 150 seconds in minutes and seconds.

150 s → 120 s = 2 min; 30 s

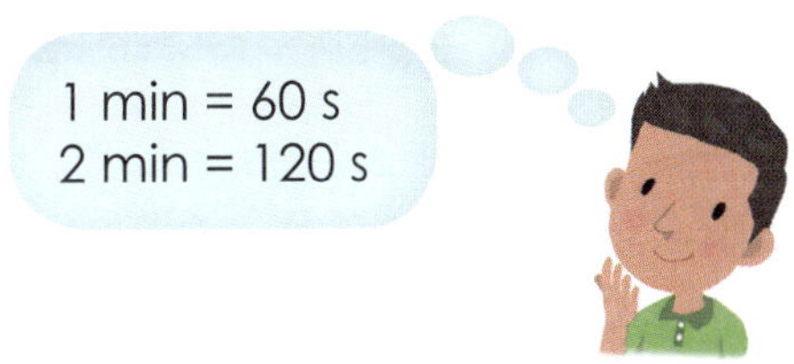

150 s = 120 s + 30 s
= 2 min 30 s

Let's Do

1. Write in minutes and seconds.

a) 130 s → _______ s = _______ min; _______ s

130 s = _______ s + _______ s

= _______ min _______ s

b) 285 s = _______ s + _______ s

= _______ min _______ s

Chapter 14: Exercise 4, pages 224–225

Practice 1

1. What time is shown on each clock?

a)

b)

2. Find the duration.

a)

10:30 and 15 seconds

10:30 and 55 seconds

b)

4:05 and 55 seconds

4:06 and 30 seconds

3. Write in seconds.

a) 1 min 10 s

b) 2 min 12 s

c) 3 min 35 s

d) 4 min 46 s

4. Write in minutes and seconds.

a) 120 s

b) 200 s

c) 220 s

d) 368 s

ISBN 978-93-5103-031-7

Lesson 2 24-hour Clock

Telling time

Let's Learn

a)

Train	Destination	Departure time	Arrival time
Puri Express	Puri	06 32	12 25
Chennai Express	Chennai	09 35	17 50
Puducherry Express	Puducherry	20 05	10 00

The train timings are shown in the **24-hour clock notation**.

Using the 24-hour clock notation, we can tell if the time is before or after noon without writing a.m. or p.m.

b) A day begins at 00 00 and ends at 24 00.

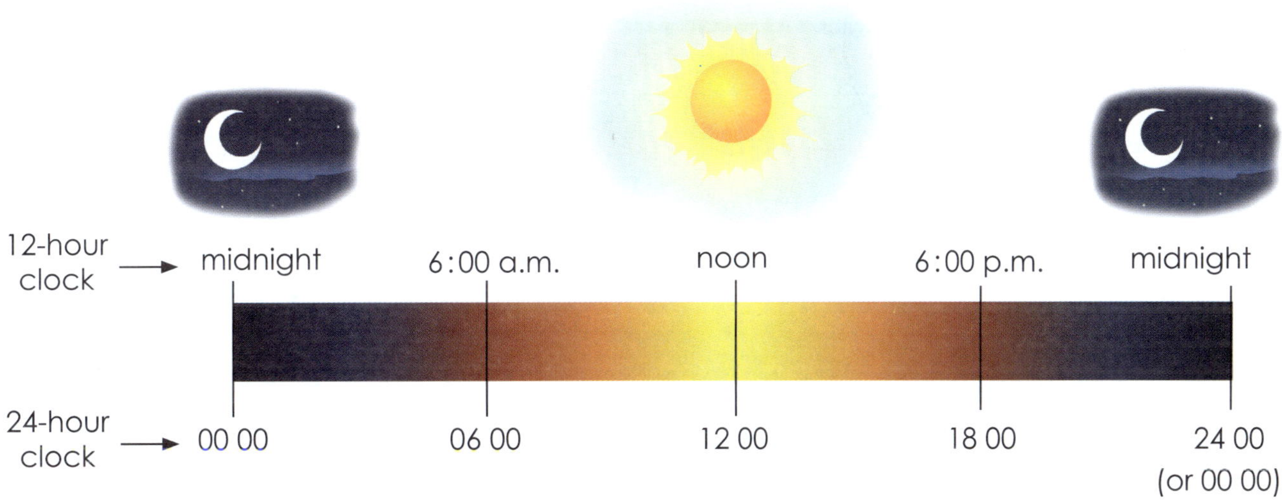

There are 24 hours in a day.

c) 9 o'clock in the morning or 9:00 a.m. is 09 00.

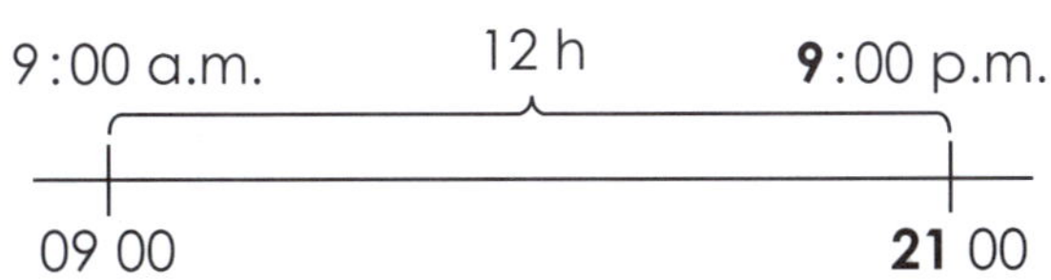

9 o'clock at night or 9:00 p.m. is 21 00.

 ISBN 978-93-5103-031-7

d) 02 15 is 15 minutes past 2 in the morning or 2:15 a.m.

Picture It

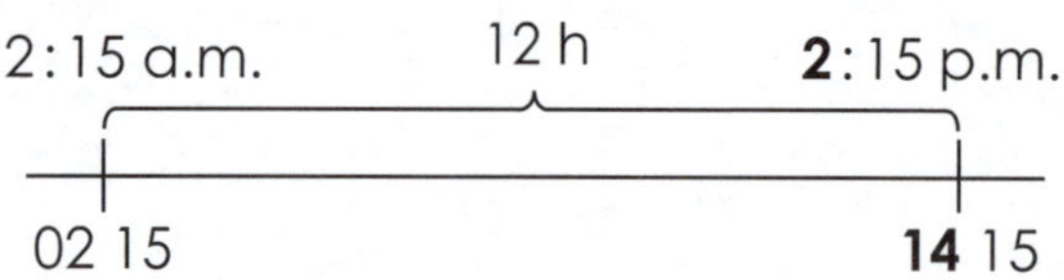

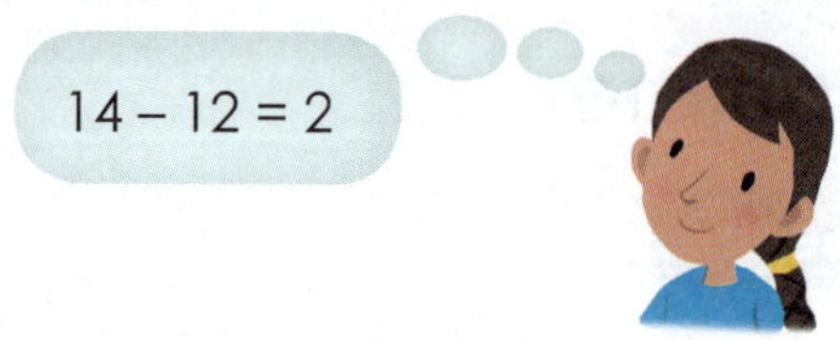

14 15 is 15 minutes past 2 in the afternoon or 2:15 p.m.

Let's Do

1. Write the time using the 24-hour clock notation.

   a) 

   Morning: ______

   Afternoon: ______

   b) 

   Morning: ______

   Night: ______

2. Write the time using the 12-hour clock notation.

   a) 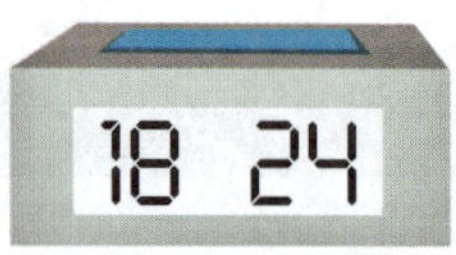

   ______

   b) 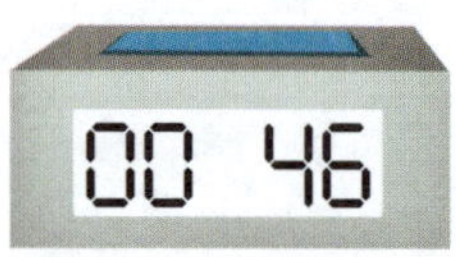

   ______

PB Chapter 14: Exercise 5, pages 226–227

  ISBN 978-93-5103-031-7

Finding duration of time

Let's Learn

James watched a film from 11 30 to 13 45. How long was the film?

Method 1

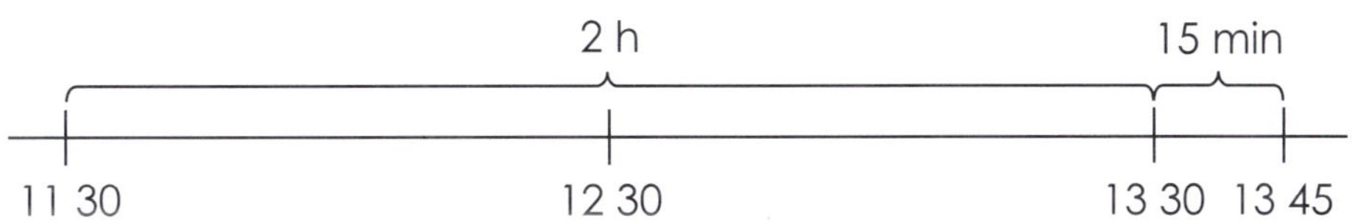

2 h + 15 min = 2 h 15 min

The film was ___ hours ___ minutes long.

Method 2

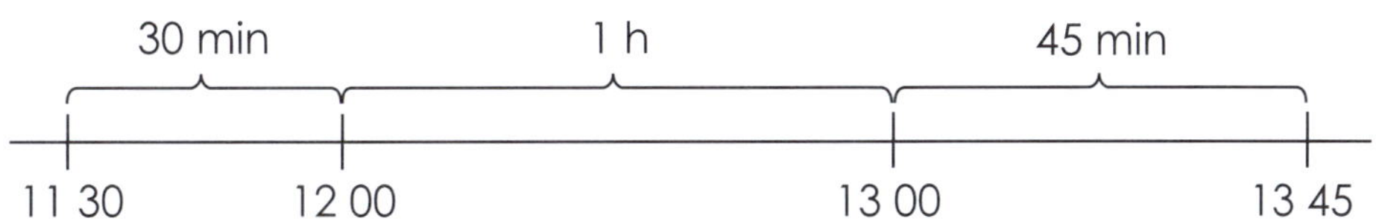

30 min + 1 h + 45 min = 1 h 75 min
= 2 h 15 min

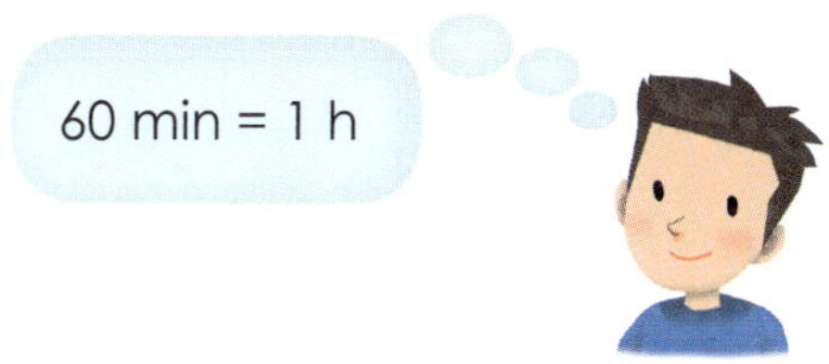

The film was ___ hours ___ minutes long.

Let's Do

1. Kelly read a book from 13 45 to 16 20. How long did she spend reading the book?

Method 1

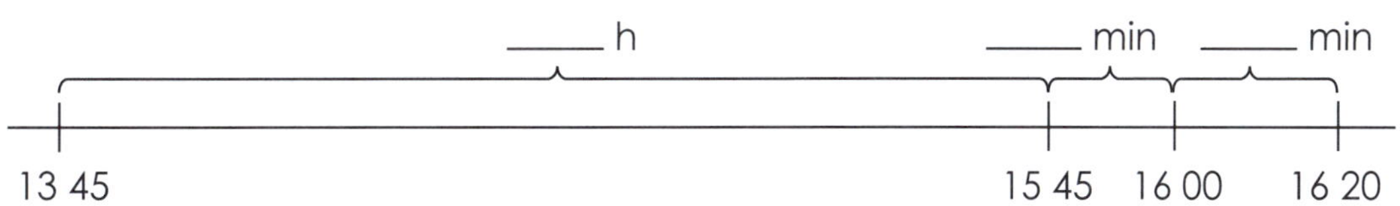

_____ h + _____ min + _____ min = _____ h _____ min

She spent _____ hours _____ minutes reading the book.

 ISBN 978-93-5103-031-7

Method 2

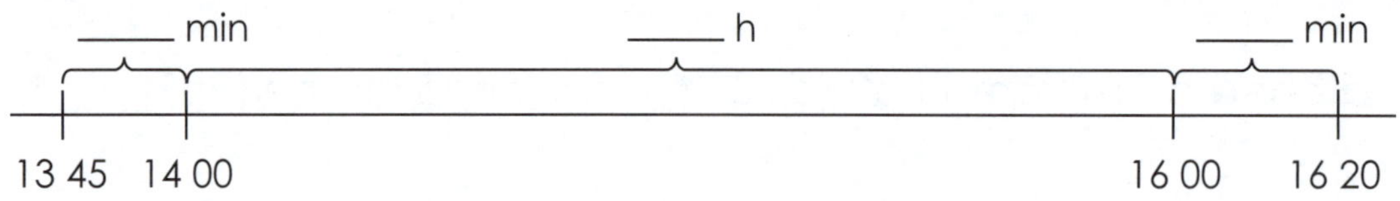

_____ min + _____ h + _____ min = _____ h _____ min

She spent _____ hours _____ minutes reading the book.

Chapter 14: Exercise 6, page 228

Finding end time

Let's Learn

Jamal started playing basketball at 10 15. He played for 3 hours 20 minutes. What time did he stop playing?

Method 1

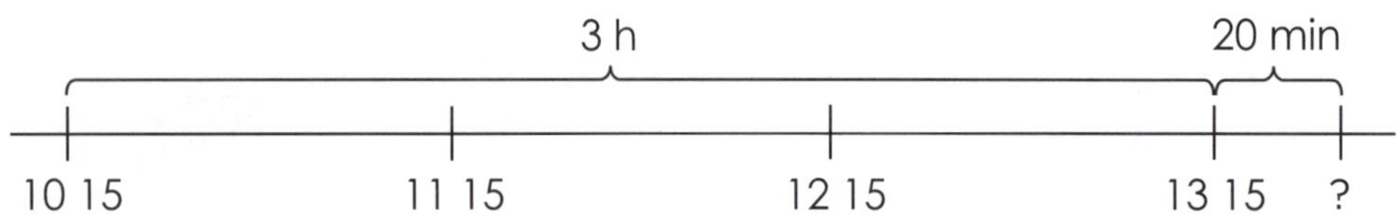

3 hours after 10 15 is 13 15.

20 minutes after 13 15 is 13 35.

He stopped playing at ▇.

10 + 3 = 13

15 + 20 = 35

Method 2

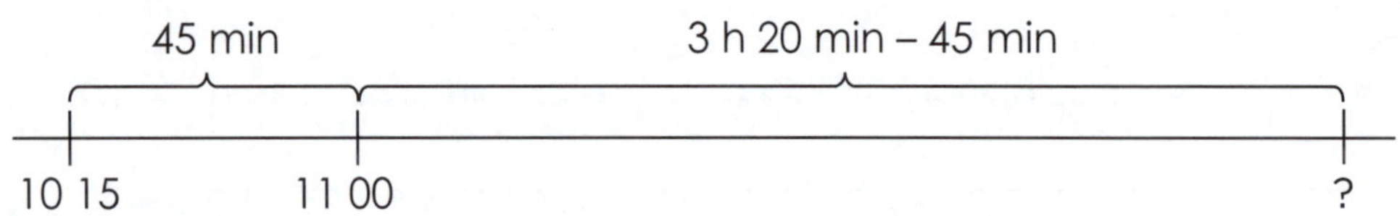

3 h 20 min – 45 min = 2 h 80 min – 45 min
= 2 h 35 min

2 hours after 11 00 is 13 00.
35 minutes after 13 00 is 13 35.

He stopped playing at ▇.

3 h 20 min → 2 h 20 min, 1 h = 60 min

 ISBN 978-93-5103-031-7

Let's Do

1. Naseem took 4 hours 50 minutes to complete a marathon. He started running at 06 40. What time did he complete the marathon?

Method 1

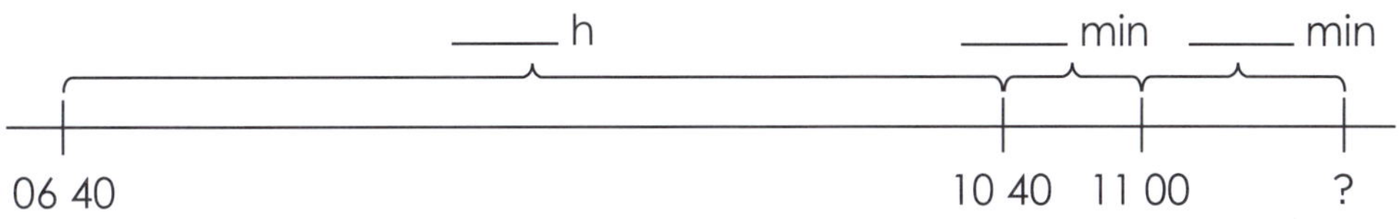

______ hours after 06 40 is ______.

______ minutes after ______ is ______.

______ minutes after ______ is ______.

He completed the marathon at ______.

50 min = ____ min + ____ min

Method 2

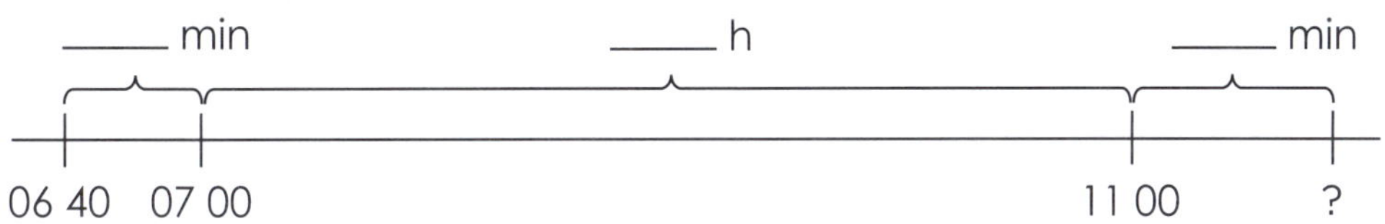

______ hours after 07 00 is ______.

______ minutes after ______ is ______.

He completed the marathon at ______.

P/B Chapter 14: Exercise 7, page 229

 ISBN 978-93-5103-031-7

Finding start time

Let's Learn

Rachel spent 3 hours 50 minutes cleaning up her room. She finished cleaning up at 14 20. What time did she start cleaning up?

Method 1

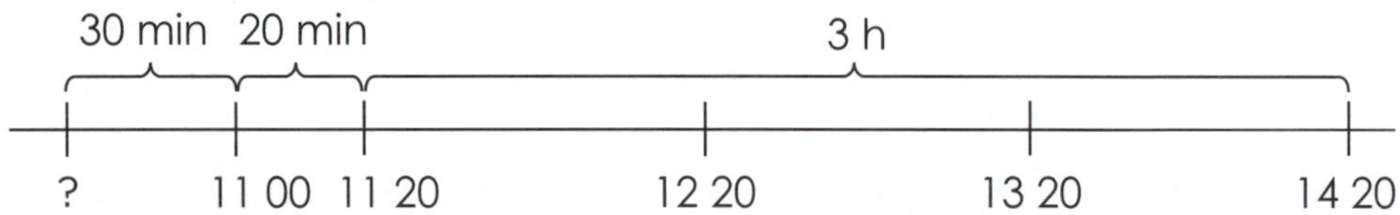

3 hours before 14 20 is 11 20.
20 minutes before 11 20 is 11 00.
30 minutes before 11 00 is 10 30.

She started cleaning up at ▢.

Method 2

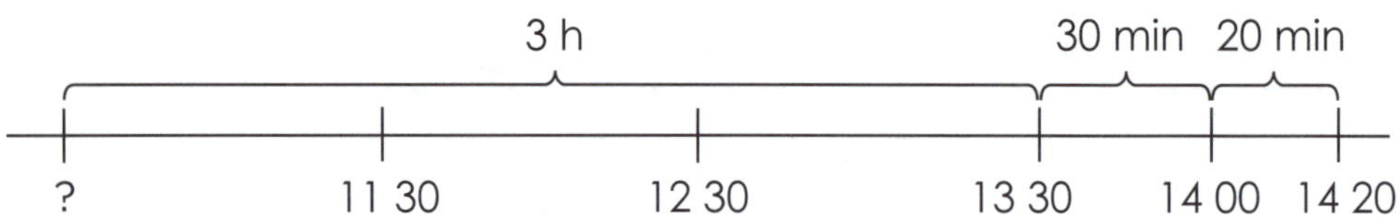

20 minutes before 14 20 is 14 00.
30 minutes before 14 00 is 13 30.
3 hours before 13 30 is 10 30.

She started cleaning up at ▢.

 ISBN 978-93-5103-031-7

1. Rita took 4 hours 35 minutes to knit a sweater. She finished knitting the sweater at 16 20. What time did she start knitting?

Method 1

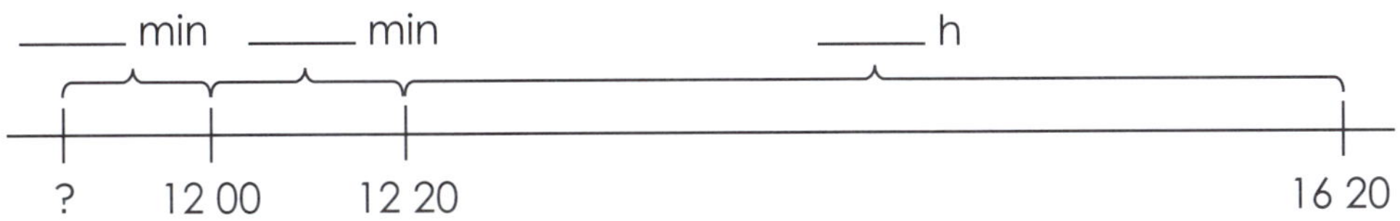

_______ hours before 16 20 is _______.

_______ minutes before _______ is _______.

_______ minutes before _______ is _______.

She started knitting at _______.

Method 2

_______ minutes before 16 20 is _______.

_______ minutes before _______ is _______.

_______ hours before _______ is _______.

She started knitting at _______.

P/B Chapter 14: Exercise 8, page 230

 ISBN 978-93-5103-031-7

Finding duration of time involving two days

Let's Learn

A bus left Bangalore at 22 15. It arrived in Chennai at 04 40 on the next day. How long was the bus journey?

Picture It

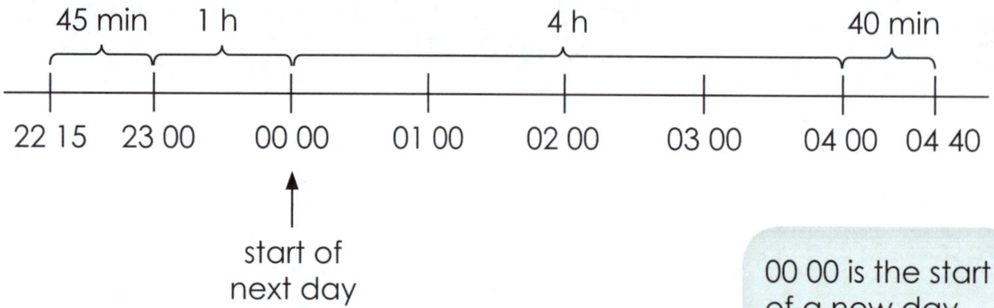

1 h 45 min + 4 h 40 min = 5 h 85 min
= 6 h 25 min

The bus journey was 6 hours 25 minutes long.

Let's Do

1. A plane left City A at 23 15. It arrived in City B at 08 40 on the next day. How long did the flight take?

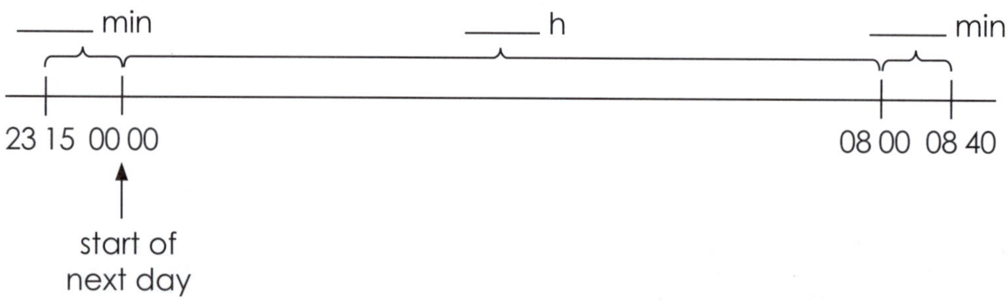

______ min + ______ h + ______ min = ______ h ______ min

= ______ h ______ min

The flight took ______ hours ______ minutes.

PB Chapter 14: Exercise 9, page 231

 ISBN 978-93-5103-031-7

Finding end time involving two days

Let's Learn

A sleeper train departed from New Delhi for Lucknow at 21 10 on Monday. The train journey was 11 hours 40 minutes long.

a) On which day did the train arrive in Lucknow?
b) What time did the train arrive in Lucknow?

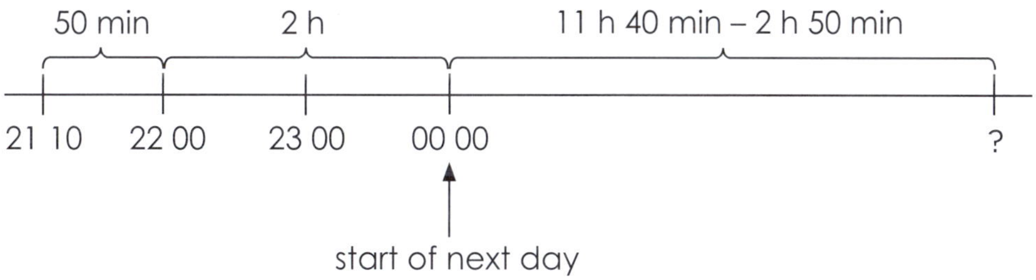

a) The train arrived in Lucknow after 00 00 on the next day.
It arrived in Lucknow on Tuesday.

b) 11 h 40 min – 2 h 50 min = 10 h 100 min – 2 h 50 min
= 8 h 50 min

The train arrived in Lucknow 8 hours 50 minutes after 00 00.
It arrived in Lucknow at 08 50.

Let's Do

1. Kabir attended a new year party for 4 hours 25 minutes. He arrived at the party at 22 30. What time did he leave the party?

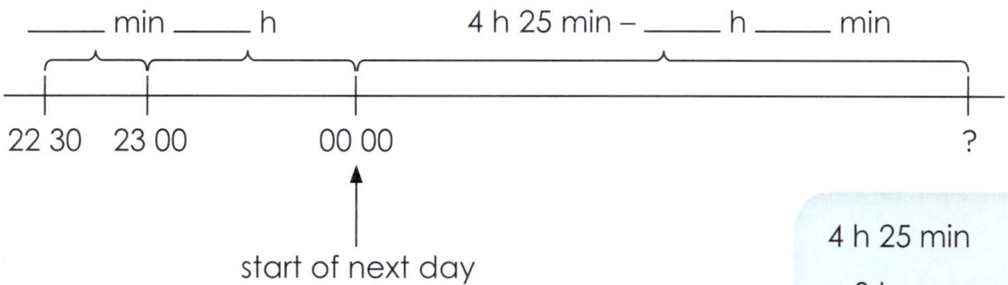

4 h 25 min – _______ h _______ min = _______ h _______ min

He left the party _______ hours _______ minutes after 00 00.

He left at _______.

P/B Chapter 14: Exercise 10, page 232

 ISBN 978-93-5103-031-7

Finding start time involving two days

Let's Learn

Michelle took an overnight bus from Mumbai to Goa. The bus journey took 9 hours 20 minutes. If she arrived in Goa at 05 45, what time did the journey start?

Picture It

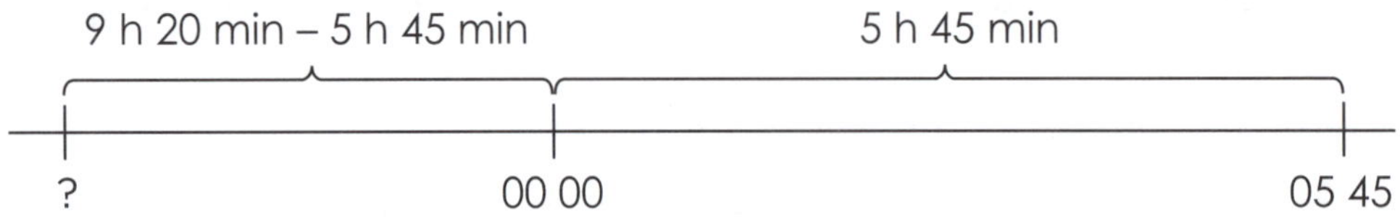

5 hours 45 minutes before 05 45 is 00 00.

9 h 20 min – 5 h 45 min = 8 h 80 min – 5 h 45 min

= 3 h 35 min

3 hours before 00 00 is 21 00.

35 minutes before 21 00 is 20 25.

3 hours 35 minutes before 00 00 is ____.

The bus journey started at ____.

00 00 is the start of a new day.
24 00 is the end of the day.
24 – 3 = 21

Let's Do

1. Tina climbed Mount Kinabalu in 7 hours 15 minutes. She reached the peak of the mountain at 05 20. What time did she start climbing the mountain?

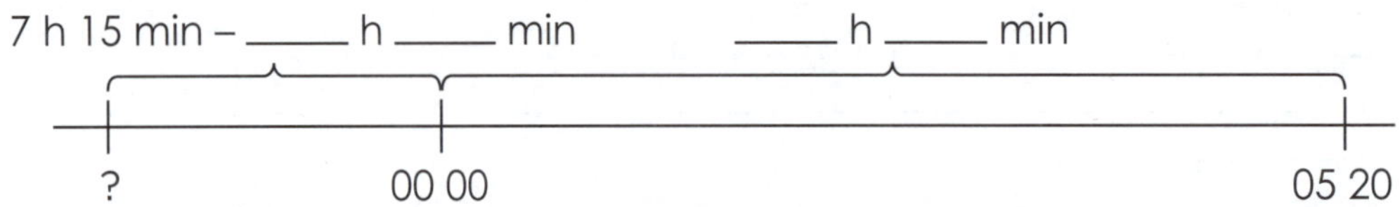

7 h 15 min
= 6 h ____ min

7 h 15 min – ____ h ____ min = ____ h ____ min

____ hour ____ minutes before 00 00 is ____.

She started climbing the mountain at ____.

Chapter 14: Exercise 11, page 233

  ISBN 978-93-5103-031-7

Practice 2

1. Write the time using the 24-hour clock notation.

   a) What time is it in the morning?
   b) What time is it in the evening?

2. Write the time using the 24-hour clock notation.

   a) 6:40 a.m.   b) 9:25 p.m.   c) noon

3. Write the time using the 12-hour clock notation.

   a) 08 05   b) 14 20   c) 00 55

Solve the word problems. Show your work clearly.

4. Sofia attended her piano lesson from 08 45 to 10 30. How long was the piano lesson?

5. Gopal took 3 hours 25 minutes to make a card for his friend. He started making the card at 12 40. What time did he finish making the card?

6. Adil took 5 hours 55 minutes to cook a meal for his family. He finished cooking at 19 20. What time did he start?

7. Cathy watched a film from 23 20 to 01 10 the next day. How long was the film?

8. Mr. Reddy took a plane from City A to City B. He arrived at City B at 02 35 on Tuesday. If the journey took 5 hours 20 minutes, what time did the plane leave City A?

Lesson 3 Problem Solving

Word problems

Let's Learn

Mr. Pandit painted his house from 09 40 to 14 15. He took a break before taking another $3\frac{1}{4}$ hours to complete painting his house. How long did Mr. Pandit take to paint his house altogether?

 ISBN 978-93-5103-031-7

1 **Understand** the problem.

What time did Mr. Pandit start painting his house?
What time did he stop painting his house?
What do I have to find?

2 **Plan** what to do.

First, I find the duration from 09 40 to 14 15.

Then, I add $3\frac{1}{4}$ hours to the duration to find the total time taken.

3 Work out the **Answer**.

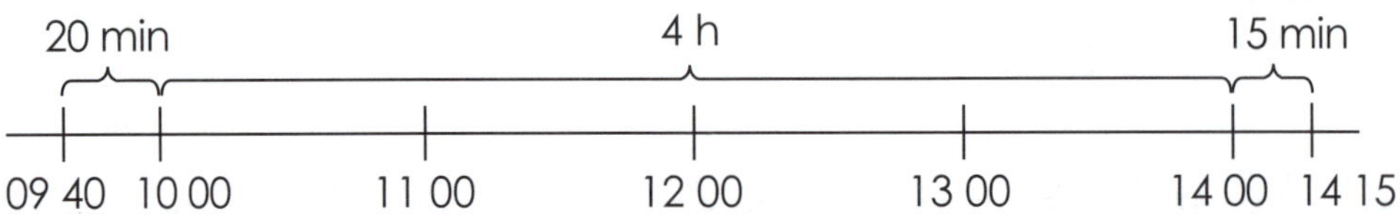

20 min + 4 h + 15 min = 4 h 35 min

The duration from 09 40 to 14 15 is 4 hours 35 minutes.

$\frac{1}{4}$ h = $\frac{1}{4} \times 60$

= 15 min

1 h = 60 min

$3\frac{1}{4}$ h = 3 h 15 min

4 h 35 min + 3 h 15 min = 7 h 50 min

Mr. Pandit took 7 hours 50 minutes to paint his house altogether.

4 **Check**

Did you answer the question? Is your answer reasonable?

There are about 5 hours from 09 40 to 14 15.

$3\frac{1}{4}$ hours is about 3 hours.

5 + 3 = 8

The total time taken is about 8 hours.

My answer is reasonable.

☑ 1. Understand
☑ 2. Plan
☑ 3. Answer
☑ 4. Check

Let's Do

1. Alice shopped at a mall for 2 hours 25 minutes. She then drove $\frac{1}{3}$ hour from the mall back to her house. If she reached her house at 13 35, what time did she begin shopping at the mall?

Draw a timeline to solve the problem.

☐ 1. Understand
☐ 2. Plan
☐ 3. Answer
☐ 4. Check

Chapter 14: Exercise 12, pages 234–235

 ISBN 978-93-5103-031-7

Practice 3

Solve the word problems. Show your work clearly.

1. Gary spent 1 hour 40 minutes revising for a Mathematics test and 45 minutes revising for an English quiz. He started his revision at 17 20.
   a) How long did Gary spend on revision altogether?
   b) What time did Gary end his revision?

2. Sana took $2\frac{1}{2}$ hours to bake a cake. She then took another 1 hour 10 minutes to bake some muffins. If she finished baking the muffins at 12 55, what time did she start baking the cake?

3. A train takes 5 hours and 35 minutes to travel from City A to City B. The train takes another 1 hour 25 minutes before it reaches City C. If the train leaves City A at 22 38, what time will it reach City C?

4. Mr. Singh left Town X for Town Y at 10 24. The usual travelling time from Town X to Town Y is 6 hours 50 minutes. However, there was a traffic jam on the way and he only arrived in Town Y at 19 02. How long was Mr. Singh delayed by the traffic jam?

Mind stretcher

Let's Learn

A snail is climbing up a tree. It can climb 4 centimetres in 5 seconds. It takes 1 second of rest for every 10 seconds of climbing. When the snail rests, it slips down the tree by 2 centimetres. How long will it take the snail to climb 1 metre?

1 Understand the problem.

How far can the snail climb in 5 seconds?
How often does it rest?
What happens when it is resting?
What do I have to find?

2 Plan what to do.

First, I **draw a diagram** to help me solve the problem.
Then, I find how far the snail can climb in 11 seconds.

 ISBN 978-93-5103-031-7

3 Work out the **Answer**.

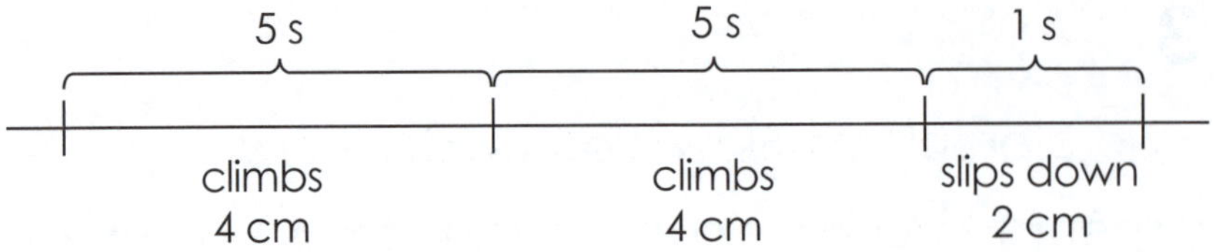

5 + 5 + 1 = 11
4 + 4 − 2 = 6

The snail climbs 6 centimetres in every 11 seconds.

1 m = 100 cm

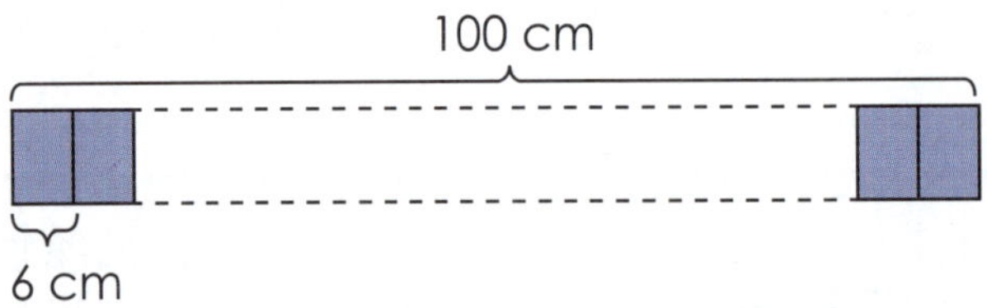

100 ÷ 6 = 16 R4

16 units of 6 cm

×16 (6 cm → 11 s) ×16
96 cm → 176 s

The snail will take 176 seconds to climb 96 centimetres.

It will take another 5 seconds to climb the remaining 4 centimetres.

176 + 5 = 181

The snail will take 181 seconds to climb 1 metre.

4 **Check**

Did you answer the question? Is your answer reasonable?

4 cm → 5 s

1 cm → $\frac{5}{4}$ s

100 cm → 100 × $\frac{5}{4}$ = 125 s

If the snail did not rest, it would have climbed 100 centimetres in 125 seconds.

My answer is greater than 125 seconds. So, it is reasonable.

☑ 1. Understand
☑ 2. Plan
☑ 3. Answer
☑ 4. Check

  ISBN 978-93-5103-031-7

Glossary

A

- **anticlockwise**

  The **anticlockwise** direction is the direction opposite to which clock hands turn.

- **approximately**

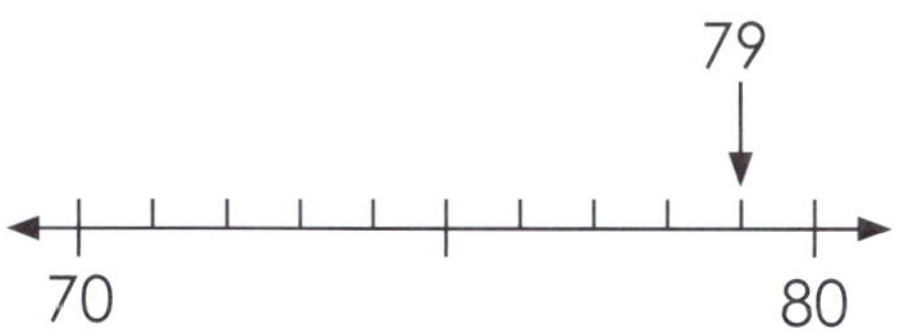

  79 is about 80.
  79 is **approximately** 80.
  We write it as $70 \approx 80$.

C

- **clockwise**

  The **clockwise** direction is the direction in which clock hands turn.

- **composite number**

  A **composite number** is a number that has more than two factors.

  $8 = 1 \times 8$ $8 = 2 \times 4$
  8 is a composite number.
  $3 = 1 \times 3$
  3 is not a composite number.

D

- **decimal**

  A **decimal** is a number with a whole number part and a fraction part separated by a decimal point.
  0.2, 3.02 and 4.538 are decimals.

- **decimal place**

  A **decimal place** is the position of a digit to the right of a decimal point.
  The decimal 15.49 has two decimal places, the tenths place and the hundredths place.

- **decimal point**

  A **decimal point** is used to separate the whole number part from the fraction part of a number.

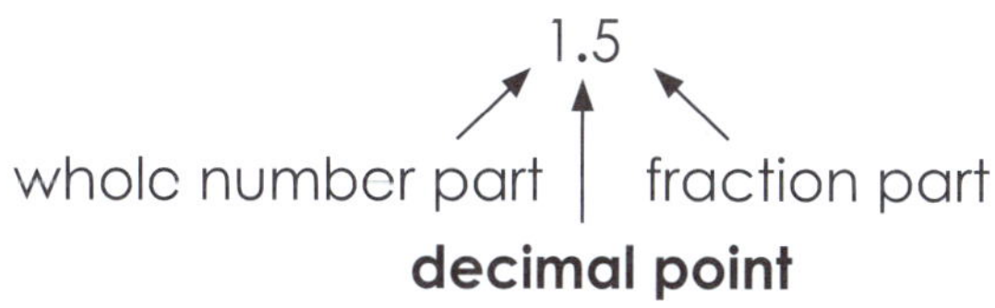

- **degree**

  A **degree** is a unit of angle measure.

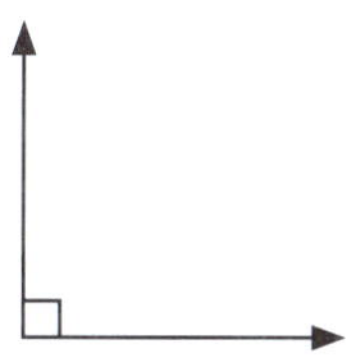

  A right angle measures 90 degrees.
  Write 90 degrees as 90°.

- **divisible**

  A number is **divisible** by another number when the quotient is a whole number and the remainder is 0.
  $8 \div 2 = 4$
  $8 \div 4 = 2$
  8 is divisible by 2 and 4.

E

- **estimate**

  An **estimate** is close to the actual value.
  $312 + 476 = 788$
  The estimated value of $312 + 476$ is $300 + 500 = 800$.

 ISBN 978-93-5103-031-7

F

- **factor**

  Factors are whole numbers that are multiplied to get another number.
  $3 \times 6 = 18$
  3 and 6 are factors of 18.

  A factor is a whole number that divides another whole number exactly, without any remainder.
  $18 \div 6 = 3$ $\quad$ $18 \div 3 = 6$
  6 is a factor of 18. 3 is also a factor of 18.

H

- **horizontal axis**

  The **horizontal axis** of a line graph is the line that runs from the left to the right through 0.

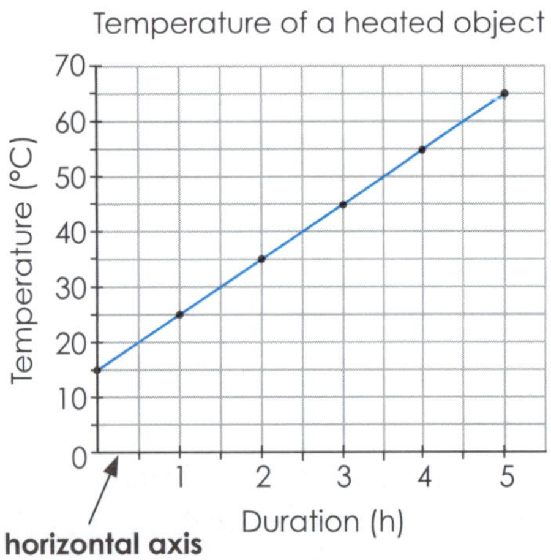

- **24-hour clock notation**

  The **24-hour clock notation** is a way of writing time without using a.m. or p.m.
  10 : 30 a.m. can be written as 10 30.
  1 :25 p.m. can be written as 13 25.

- **hundredth**

  1 **hundredth** is 1 out of 100 equal parts.
  $\frac{1}{100} = 0.01$

I

- **improper fraction**

  An **improper fraction** is a fraction that is equal to or greater than 1. Its numerator is equal to or greater than its denominator.
  $\frac{13}{6}$ and $\frac{11}{11}$ are improper fractions.

- **increasing order**

  To arrange numbers in **increasing order**, arrange the numbers in order beginning with the smallest number.

  These numbers are arranged in increasing order.
  30, 37, 39, 45
  ↑
  smallest

L

- **line graph**

  A **line graph** is a graph used to present data that changes over time.

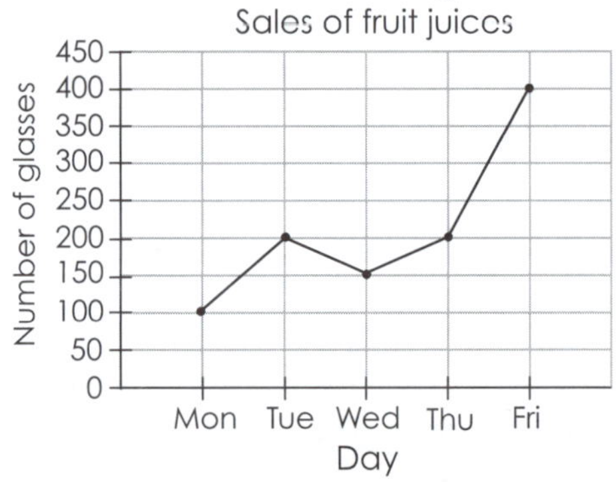

- **line of symmetry**

  A **line of symmetry** is a line that divides a figure into two halves that match exactly when folded along this line. A figure can have more than 1 line of symmetry.

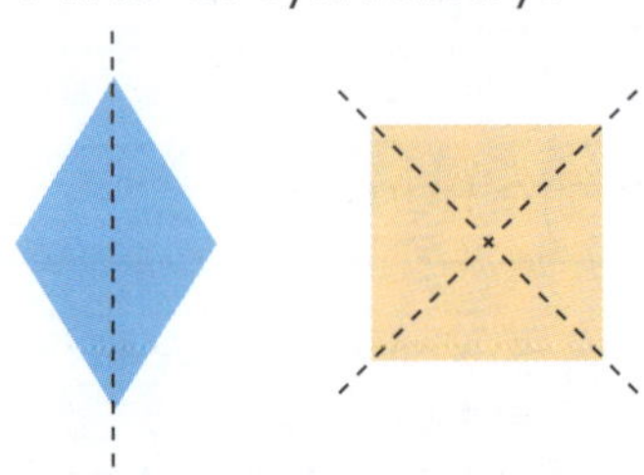

In the figures, the dotted lines are lines of symmetry.

ISBN 978-93-5103-031-7

M

- **mixed number**

  A **mixed number** is made up of a whole number and a fraction.

  $$7 + \frac{1}{2} = 7\frac{1}{2}$$

  7 → whole number; $\frac{1}{2}$ → fraction; $7\frac{1}{2}$ → **mixed number**

- **multiple**

  The **multiple** of a number is the product of the number and any other whole number except zero.

  $1 \times 8 = 8$

  $2 \times 8 = 16$

  $3 \times 8 = 24$

  8, 16 and 24 are multiples of 8.

P

- **perimeter**

  The **perimeter** of a figure is the distance around the figure.

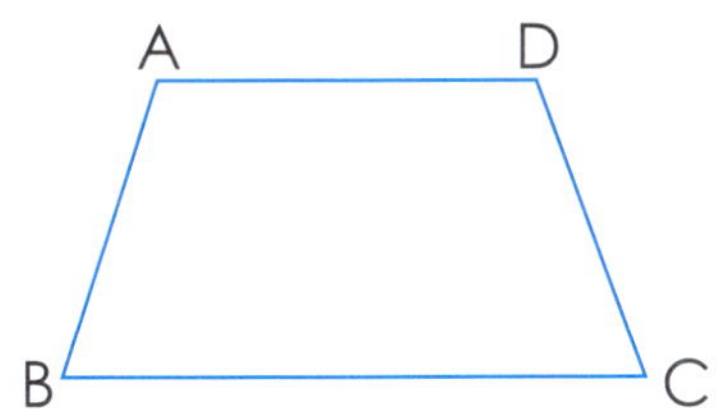

  Perimeter of ABCD = AB + BC + CD + DA

- **prime number**

  A **prime number** is a number that has only two factors, 1 and the number itself.

  3, 5 and 7 are prime numbers.

- **product**

  When we multiply one number by another number, the result is the **product** of the two numbers.

  $$2 \times 3 = 6$$

  2 → factor; 3 → factor; 6 → **product**

R

- **reasonable**

  An answer is **reasonable** if it makes sense.

  $784 - 416 = 368$

  We can use estimation to check if the answer 368 is reasonable.

  $784 - 416 \approx 800 - 400$

  $= 400$

  Since 368 is about 400, the answer is reasonable.

- **rotational symmetry**

  When a shape looks exactly the same more than once during a full turn, it has **rotational symmetry**.

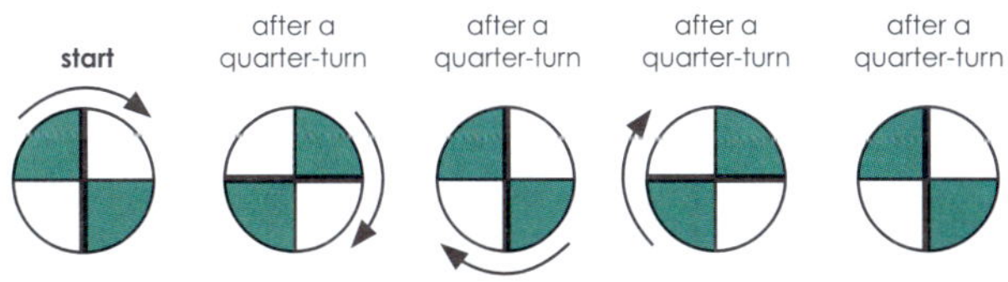

- **round**

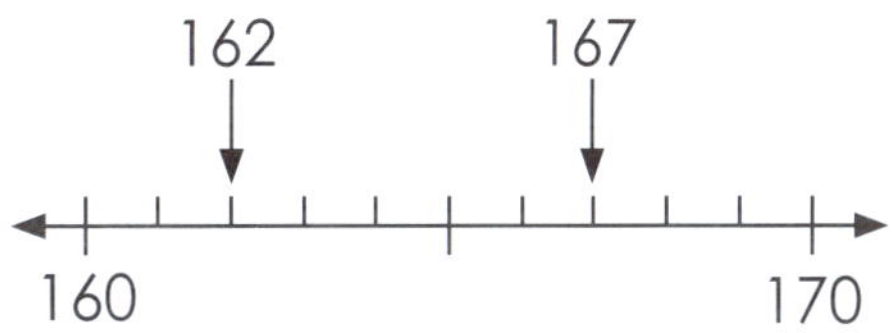

  When we **round** 162 to the nearest 10, we round it down to 160.

  When we round 167 to the nearest 10, we round it up to 170.

S

- **second (s)**

  The **second** is a smaller unit of time than the minute.

  1 minute = 60 seconds

 ISBN 978-93-5103-031-7

• **second hand**

The **second hand** is the clock hand that shows the number of seconds that had passed in a minute.

• **symmetric figure**

A **symmetric figure** is a figure with two halves that match exactly when folded along the line of symmetry.

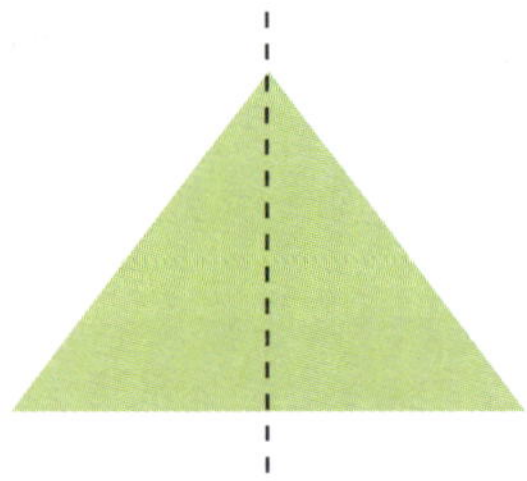

This triangle is a symmetric figure.

• **symmetry**

A figure has **symmetry** if it can be folded into halves that match exactly along the fold line.

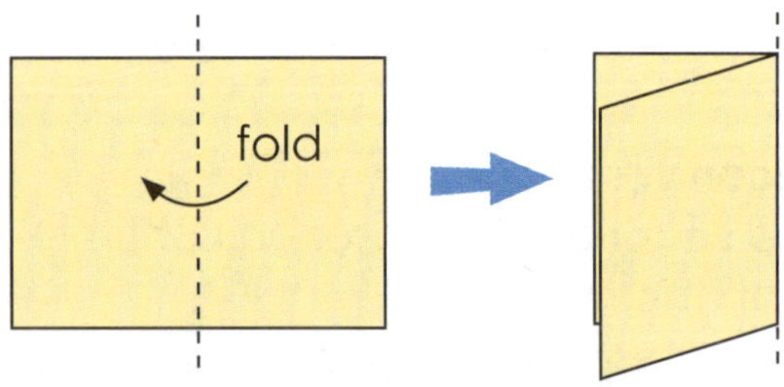

T

• **tenth**

1 **tenth** is 1 out of 10 equal parts.

$\frac{1}{10} = 0.1$

• **thousandth**

1 **thousandth** is 1 out of 1000 equal parts.

$\frac{1}{1000} = 0.001$

V

• **vertex (of an angle)**

The **vertex** of an angle is the point at which the end points of the two rays meet.

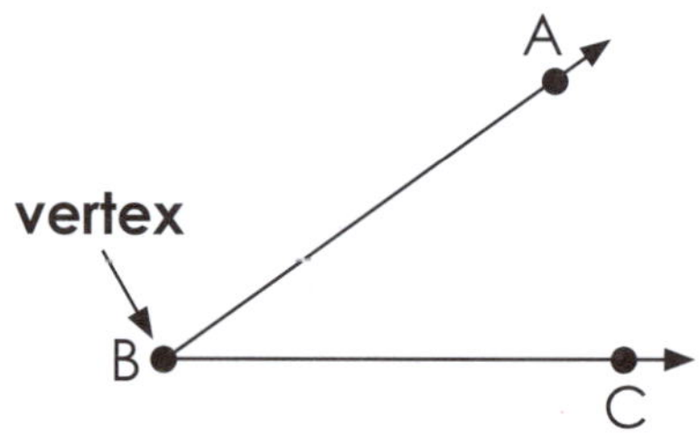

Point B is the vertex of $\angle ABC$.

• **vertical axis**

The **vertical axis** of a line graph is the line that runs from the bottom to the top through 0.

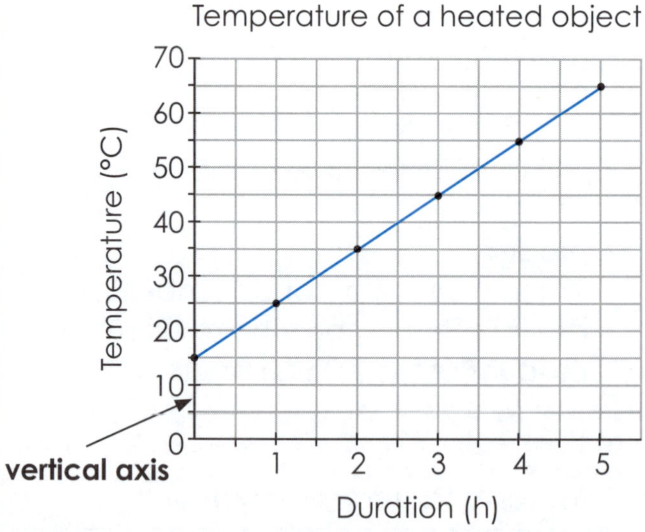

 ISBN 978-93-5103-031-7

Answers

Chapter 1

Page 9, Let's Do

1. **a)** 8012; **b)** 49,501; **c)** 90,090
2. **a)** four thousand nine hundred eight;
b) twenty-seven thousand one hundred sixty-five;
c) eighty-one thousand nine hundred

Pages 9–10, Let's Do

1. **a)** 5000; **b)** 2000; **c)** 100 2. **a)** 800; **b)** 80,000; **c)** 8000

Page 10, Let's Do

1. **a)** ten thousands, 70,000; **b)** 6

Page 12, Let's Do

1. **a)** 50,650; **b)** 81,306; **c)** 11,020; **d)** 9020; **e)** 1,00,000
2.

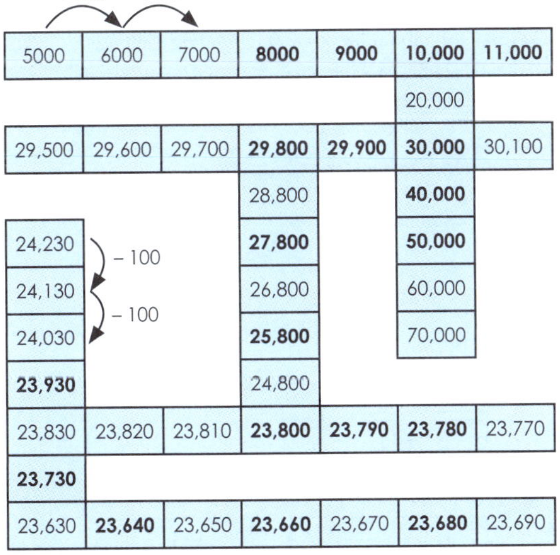

Page 13, Let's Do

1. **a)** 49,000; **b)** 52,000; **c)** 54,000; **d)** 58,000

Pages 14-15, Let's Do

1. **a)** <; **b)** > 2. 79,021, 78,430, 78,409 3. **a)** 9650; **b)** 5069

Pages 15–16, Practice 1

1. **a)** 12,803; **b)** 20,050; **c)** 70,000
2. **a)** one thousand seven hundred fifty-eight; **b)** five thousand three hundred six; **c)** seventy-two thousand nine hundred three; **d)** ninety-one thousand one hundred twenty
3. **a)** 8000; **b)** 20,000; **c)** 54,607; **d)** 40,830 4. **a)** 60; **b)** 600; **c)** 60,000; **d)** 6 5. **a)** 8; **b)** thousands 6. **a)** 5,980, 6,080; **b)** 34,465, 35,465; **c)** 63,700, 53,700 7. A: 47,900, B: 48,200, C: 48,400, D: 48,800, E: 49,100 8. **a)** 35,620; **b)** 4600 9. Circle: 90,530; Cross: 90,305 10. **a)** 30,016, 30,061, 30,160, 30,601; **b)** 20,990, 29,909, 29,999, 90,000 11. **a)** 98,750; **b)** 50,789 12. 97,430

Page 17, Let's Do

1. **a)** 10,911; **b)** 90,717; **c)** 99,153 2. 44,712

Page 18, Let's Do

1. **a)** 81,307; **b)** 51,925; **c)** 19,791 2. 56,019

Page 20, Let's Do

1.

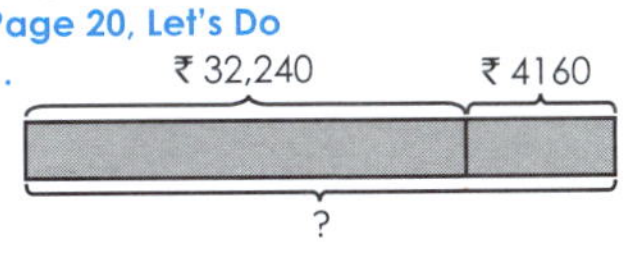

₹ 32,240 + ₹ 4160 = ₹ 36,400
The laptop costs ₹ 36,400 altogether.

2.

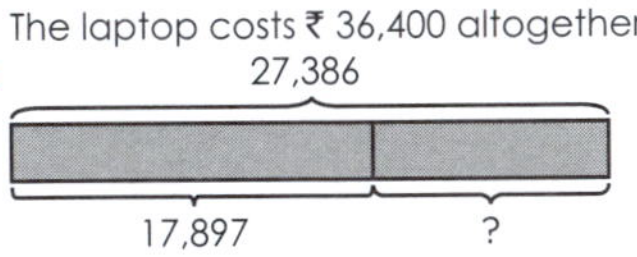

27,386 – 17,897 = 9489
The company must buy 9489 more bricks.

Page 20, Practice 2

1. **a)** 69,991; **b)** 63,956; **c)** 79,008
2. **a)** 80,831; **b)** 8742; **c)** 29,502

3.

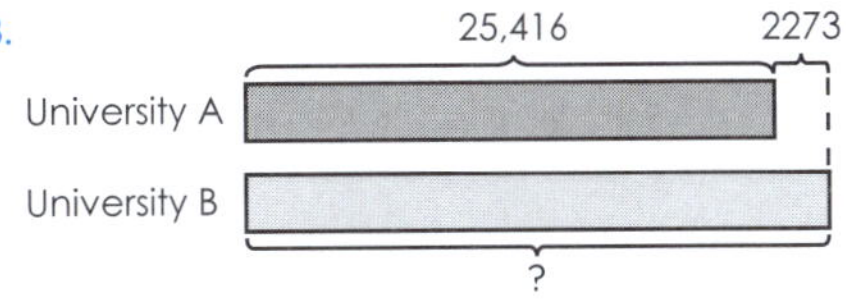

25,416 + 2273 = 27,689
University B has 27,689 students.

4.

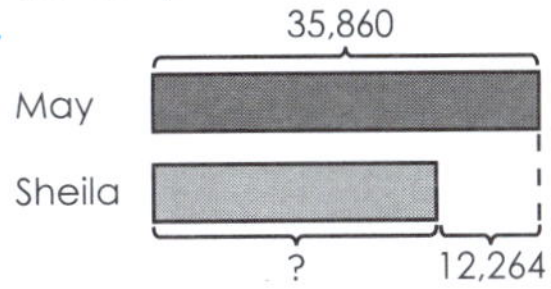

35,860 – 12,264 = 23,596
Sheila distributed 23,596 pamphlets.

5.

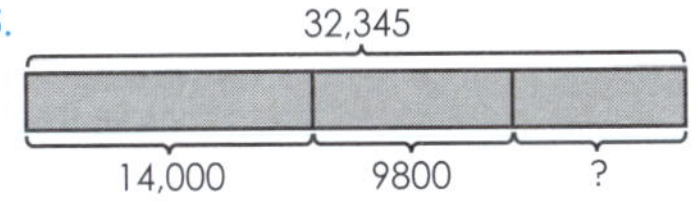

14,000 + 9800 = 23,800
There were 23,800 men and women.
32,345 – 23,800 = 8545
There were 8545 children at the parade.

Page 22, Let's Do

1. **a)** 30; **b)** 80; **c)** 100

Page 24, Let's Do

1. **a)** 130; **b)** 450; **c)** 4810

Pages 25–26, Let's Do

1. **a)** 300; **b)** 3700; **c)** 4900; **d)** 42,600

Pages 26–27, Let's Do

1. **a)** 700; **b)** 1300; **c)** 300; **d)** 85,000

Page 27, Let's Do

1. Estimates vary. 621, 600

Page 28, Practice 3

1. **a)** 90; **b)** 730; **c)** 4620; **d)** 9100 2. **a)** 800; **b)** 15,500; **c)** 40,000; **d)** 46,100 3. Estimates vary. **a)** 905, 900; **b)** 3041, 3100; **c)** 39,688, 39,700; **d)** 475, 500; **e)** 6840, 6900; **f)** 71,026, 71,000

Page 29, Let's Do

1. 1, 2, 4, 8, 16 2. 1, 2, 3, 4, 6, 12 3. 8, 10, 24

Page 30, Let's Do

1. **a)** Yes; **b)** No

Page 31, Let's Do

1. Circle: 23, 17 Cross: 8,12 2. 2, 3, 5, 7, 11, 13

Page 33, Let's Do

1. 2, 3, 5, 7 2. 12, 14, 15, 16, 18, 20
3. 2 4. 9

Page 33, Practice 4

1. 1, 2, 3, 6, 9, 18 2. **a)** 4; **b)** 8; **c)** 9
3. 1, 2, 4, 8, 16, 32
4. **a)** 1, 2, 4, 8; **b)** 1, 3, 5, 15; **c)** 1, 2, 4, 5, 10, 20; **d)** 1, 2, 5, 10, 25, 50; **e)** 1, 3, 5, 15, 25, 75; **f)** 1, 2, 7, 14, 49, 98 5. 15, 20, 25, 80
6. 2, 3, 5, 7, 11, 13, 17, 19, 23, 29, 31, 37, 41, 43, 47, 53, 59, 61, 67, 71, 73, 79, 83, 89, 97 7. 72, 74, 75, 76, 77, 78, 80, 81, 82, 84, 85, 86, 87, 88, 90

Page 34, Let's Do

1. 15, 20, 25, 30 2. 27, 36, 45, 54

Page 35, Let's Do

1. **a)** factor; **b)** multiple; **c)** factor 2. **a)** Yes, Yes; **b)** Yes, Yes; **c)** Yes; **d)** No

Page 37, Let's Do

1. **a)** No; **b)** Yes; **c)** No

Page 37, Practice 5

1. **a)** 12, 15; **b)** 25, 30, 35, 40 2. Circle: 98, 50, 88, 54, 32
3. **a)** 20, 24, 28; **b)** 30, 36, 42 4. **a)** factor; **b)** multiple
5. **a)** Yes; **b)** Yes 6. **a)** No; **b)** Yes; **c)** No
7. Answer varies. Example:
24 is a multiple of 3.
2 + 4 = 6
6 is a multiple of 3.
The sum is a multiple of 3.

 ISBN 978-93-5103-031-7

Chapter 2

Page 38, Let's Do
1. **a)** 90, 90, Method 2

Page 39, Let's Do
1. **a)** 140; **b)** 60

Page 40, Let's Do
1. **a)** 17,700; **b)** 25,960

Page 42, Let's Do
1. **a)** 4400; **b)** 44,400

Page 42, Let's Do
1. Estimates vary. **a)** 25000, 24880; **b)** 18000, 18240

Page 43, Let's Do
1. 9890

Page 44, Practice 1
1. **a)** 60; **b)** 84; **c)** 240 2. **a)** 6033; **b)** 8428; **c)** 17,250; **d)** 25,290; **e)** 27,419; **f)** 56,322 3. Estimates vary. **a)** 20,500, 20,380; **b)** 24,000, 23,922; **c)** 18,900, 18,450; **d)** 49,000, 48,797; **e)** 30,000, 30,160; **f)** 48,000, 47,840

4.
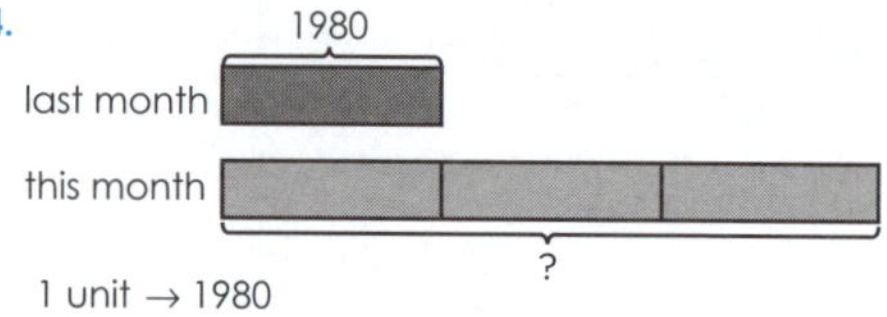

1 unit → 1980
3 units → 3 × 1980 = 5940
He sold 5940 loaves of bread this month.

5.
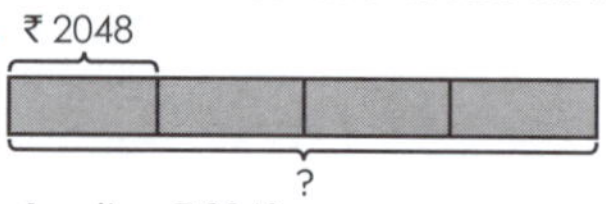

1 unit → ₹ 2048
4 units → 4 × ₹ 2048 = ₹ 8192
Mr. Rao earns ₹ 8192 in 4 weeks.

Page 46, Let's Do
1. **a)** 1439; **b)** 650 R4; **c)** 605

Page 48, Let's Do
1. **a)** 44; **b)** 440

Page 49, Let's Do
1. **a)** 400; **b)** 400

Page 50, Let's Do
1. 526

Page 50, Practice 2
1. **a)** 703; **b)** 1009; **c)** 502; **d)** 1202; **e)** 496; **f)** 909; **g)** 918 R5; **h)** 475
2. **a)** 200, 235; **b)** 500, 511 R3; **c)** 400, 388; **d)** 810, 812 R8; **e)** 2500, 2509 R1; **f)** 1200, 1196 R4

3.
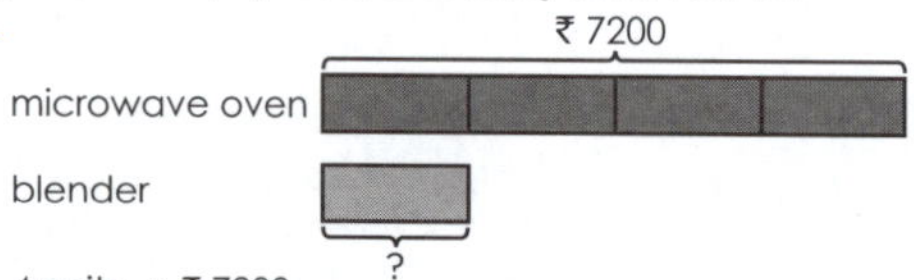

4 units → ₹ 7200
1 unit → ₹ 7200 ÷ 4 = ₹ 1800
The blender costs ₹ 1800.

4.
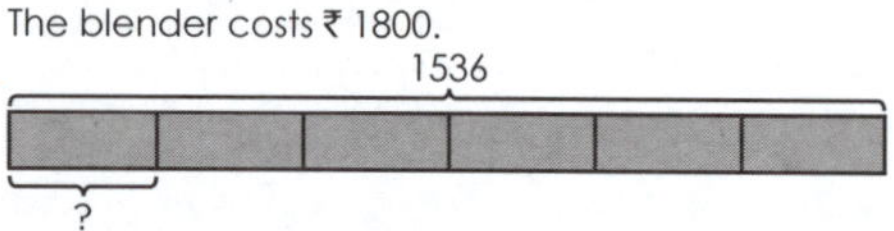

6 units → 1536
1 unit → 1536 ÷ 6 = 256
There are 256 rubber bands in each box.

5.
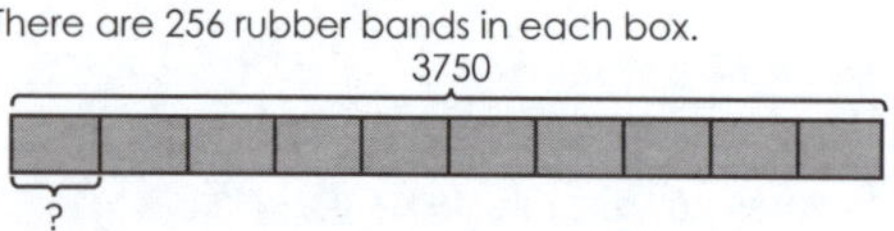

10 units → 3750
1 unit → 3750 ÷ 10 = 375
Mr. Sharma had 375 bags of rice.

6.
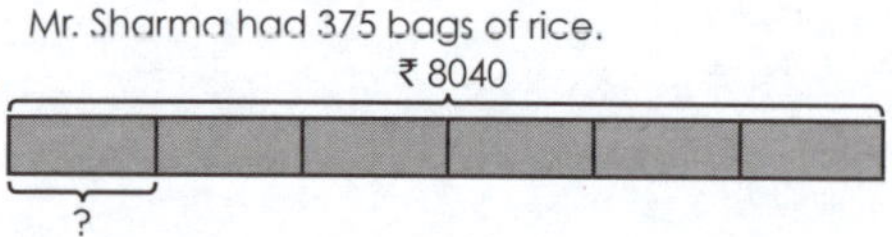

₹ 8040 ÷ 6 = ₹ 1340
She paid ₹ 1340 for each pair of earrings.

Page 52, Let's Do
1. 420, 420

Page 53, Let's Do
1. **a)** 31,360; **b)** 12,360

Page 54, Let's Do
1. **a)** 1728; **b)** 1674; **c)** 2232; **d)** 1653

Page 55 Let's Do
1. **a)** 24990; **b)** 15300; **c)** 22214; **d)** 54234

Pages 56–57, Let's Do
1. Estimates vary. **a)** 1000, 882; **b)** 8000, 9476; **c)** 21,000, 21,920

Page 57, Let's Do
1. 14,645

Page 58, Practice 3
1. **a)** 690; **b)** 4760; **c)** 1800; **d)** 4050; **e)** 14,050; **f)** 33,600 2. Estimates vary. **a)** 500, 528; **b)** 1800, 1769; **c)** 6300, 5896; **d)** 1000, 1313; **e)** 15,000, 15,317; **f)** 64,000, 61,308 3. 4950 copies 4. 375 stamps 5. ₹ 3375 altogether 6. 105 chicken sandwiches 7. 13,248 red balls

Page 59, Let's Do
1. 124 – 78 = 46 people visited the zoo in the evening
124 + 46 = 170 visited the zoo that day
170 × ₹ 21 = ₹ 3570 was collected

Page 60, Practice 4
1. 20 × 11 = 220 cakes each month
12 × 220 = 2640 cakes in a year
2. 3140 – 11 = 3129 children remaining
3129 ÷ 7 = 447 groups
447 + 1 = 448 groups

3.
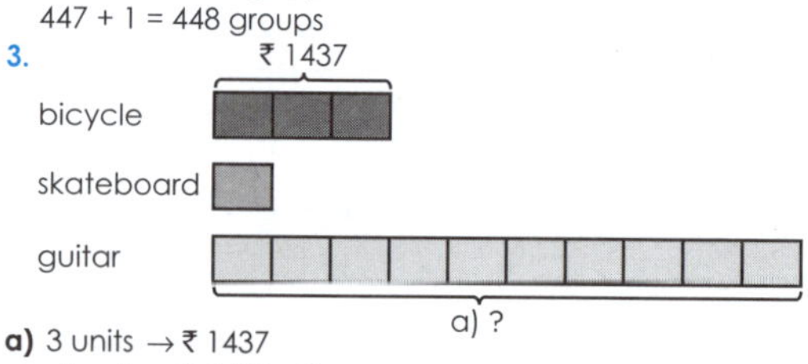

a) 3 units → ₹ 1437
1 unit → ₹ 1437 ÷ 3
= ₹ 479
10 units → 10 × ₹ 479
= ₹ 4790
The guitar costs ₹ 4790.
b) 3 + 10 = 13
13 units → 13 × ₹ 479
= ₹ 6227
Total cost of the bicycle and the guitar is ₹ 6227.
4. 15 × 130 = 1950 grams of clay was given to 15 boys
3390 – 1950 = 1440 grams of clay remained
1440 ÷ 9 = 160 grams of clay was received by each girl

Chapter 3

Page 63, Let's Do
1. **a)** $3\frac{4}{5}$; **b)** $2\frac{1}{6}$

Page 64, Let's Do
1. **a)** $1\frac{2}{3}$, $2\frac{1}{3}$; **b)** $1\frac{5}{6}$, $2\frac{1}{3}$, $3\frac{2}{3}$ 2. **a)** $1\frac{1}{2}$; **b)** $2\frac{1}{3}$; **c)** $4\frac{2}{3}$

Pages 64–65, Practice 1
1. **a)** $2\frac{1}{2}$; **b)** $3\frac{3}{4}$ 2. **a)** $3\frac{2}{3}$; **b)** $2\frac{4}{5}$; **c)** $4\frac{7}{10}$ 3. A: $1\frac{1}{2}$, B: $2\frac{1}{4}$, C: $2\frac{3}{4}$
4. **a)** $1\frac{1}{2}$; **b)** $2\frac{1}{2}$; **c)** $3\frac{5}{6}$; **d)** $7\frac{2}{3}$

Pages 66–67, Let's Do
1. **a)** $\frac{5}{5}$; **b)** $\frac{7}{4}$ 2. 9

Page 67, Let's Do
1. **a)** 3; **b)** $2\frac{1}{6}$

Page 68, Let's Do
1. **a)** $\frac{19}{6}$; **b)** $\frac{13}{5}$

Page 69, Let's Do
1. **a)** 7; **b)** 5

Page 70, Let's Do
1. **a)** $3\frac{3}{5}$; **b)** $4\frac{3}{4}$

 ISBN 978-93-5103-031-7

Pages 70–71, Practice 2

1. a) $\frac{8}{3}$; **b)** $\frac{12}{6}$ **2.** 9 halves **3.** 17 fifths **4. a)** $4\frac{1}{4}$; **b)** $3\frac{1}{3}$; **c)** 4; **d)** $2\frac{2}{5}$; **e)** $2\frac{1}{2}$; **f)** $1\frac{1}{2}$ **5. a)** $\frac{9}{5}$; **b)** $\frac{8}{3}$; **c)** $\frac{9}{4}$; **d)** $\frac{23}{6}$ **6. a)** 9; **b)** 3; **c)** 7; **d)** 7

7. a) $2\frac{1}{4}$; **b)** 4; **c)** $4\frac{3}{8}$; **d)** $5\frac{8}{9}$

Page 73, Let's Do

1. a) $1\frac{2}{3}$; **b)** $1\frac{1}{5}$

Page 74, Let's Do

1. a) $1\frac{1}{3}$; **b)** $1\frac{3}{4}$

Page 75, Let's Do

1. $1\frac{1}{8}$

Page 76, Practice 3

1. a) $1\frac{2}{5}$; **b)** $1\frac{4}{7}$; **c)** $1\frac{5}{8}$; **d)** $1\frac{4}{9}$ **2. a)** $1\frac{1}{8}$; **b)** $1\frac{2}{3}$; **c)** 2; **d)** $1\frac{1}{2}$

3. $\frac{5}{6}+\frac{2}{3}=\frac{5}{6}+\frac{4}{6}$

$=\frac{9}{6}$

$=1\frac{3}{6}$

$=1\frac{1}{2}$ metres

4. $\frac{7}{12}+\frac{3}{4}+\frac{1}{4}=\frac{7}{12}+\frac{9}{12}+\frac{3}{12}$

$=\frac{19}{12}$

$=1\frac{7}{12}$ kilograms

Page 77, Let's Do

1. a) $1\frac{1}{5}$; **b)** $4\frac{1}{3}$

Pages 77–78, Let's Do

1. a) $2\frac{1}{3}$; **b)** $3\frac{1}{3}$

Page 78, Let's Do

1. $2\frac{1}{6}$

Page 79, Practice 4

1. a) $3\frac{1}{4}$; **b)** $1\frac{5}{6}$; **c)** $3\frac{1}{2}$; **d)** $1\frac{7}{10}$; **e)** $2\frac{2}{5}$; **f)** $2\frac{2}{7}$ **2. a)** $1\frac{1}{2}$; **b)** $2\frac{2}{5}$; **c)** $\frac{5}{12}$; **d)** $5\frac{1}{2}$

3. $2-\frac{2}{3}=1\frac{3}{3}-\frac{2}{3}$

$=1\frac{1}{3}$ pizza

4. $10-\frac{1}{4}-\frac{3}{8}=9\frac{8}{8}-\frac{2}{8}-\frac{3}{8}$

$=9\frac{3}{8}$ kilograms

5. $2-\frac{1}{5}-\frac{3}{10}=1\frac{10}{10}-\frac{2}{10}-\frac{3}{10}$

$=1\frac{5}{10}$

$=1\frac{1}{2}$ litres

Page 80, Let's Do

1. a) $\frac{1}{2}$; **b)** $\frac{3}{4}$

Page 81, Let's Do

1. 3, 12

Page 82, Let's Do

1. 15 **2.** $6\frac{2}{3}$ **3.** $11\frac{2}{3}$

Page 84, Let's Do

1. 36 **2.** $2\frac{1}{4}$

Page 85, Let's Do

1. $\frac{1}{7}$

Pages 85–86, Practice 5

1. a) $\frac{2}{3}$; **b)** $\frac{5}{6}$ **2. a)** 4; **b)** 24; **c)** $\frac{2}{3}$; **d)** $5\frac{5}{8}$; **e)** 49; **f)** 45

3. $\frac{3}{4}\times 5=3\frac{3}{4}$ metres **4.** $6\times\frac{2}{3}=4$ litres **5.** $\frac{8}{40}=\frac{1}{5}$ of the children

6. $\frac{2}{9}\times 81=18$ cards

Page 87, Let's Do

1. a) 300; **b)** 9

Page 88, Let's Do

1. a) 4, 40; **b)** 14, 900

Page 88, Let's Do

1. 54

Page 89, Let's Do

1. $\frac{2}{5}$

Pages 89–90, Practice 6

1. a) 250; **b)** 4; **c)** 10; **d)** 18 **2. a)** 2, 20; **b)** 7, 500; **c)** 5, 300; **d)** 6, 3
3. a) 250; **b)** 1900; **c)** 84; **d)** 33; **e)** 1300; **f)** 2100

4. $\frac{3}{4}$ **5.** $\frac{3}{5}$ **6.** $\frac{3}{10}$ **7.** $\frac{5}{12}$

Page 91, Let's Do

1. 30

Page 92, Let's Do

1. $84-49=35$ adults

$\frac{35}{84}=\frac{5}{12}$

The number of adults is $\frac{5}{12}$ of the total number of people at the carnival.

Page 93, Let's Do

1.

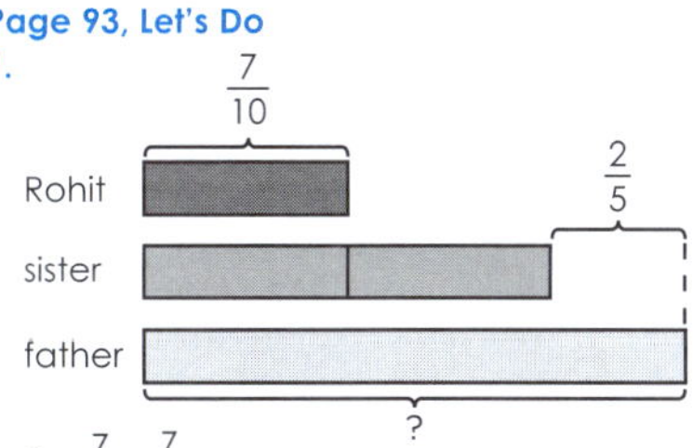

$2\times\frac{7}{10}=\frac{7}{5}$

$=1\frac{2}{5}$

His sister is $1\frac{2}{5}$ metres tall.

$1\frac{2}{5}+\frac{2}{5}=1\frac{4}{5}$

His father is $1\frac{4}{5}$ metres tall.

Page 94, Practice 7

1.

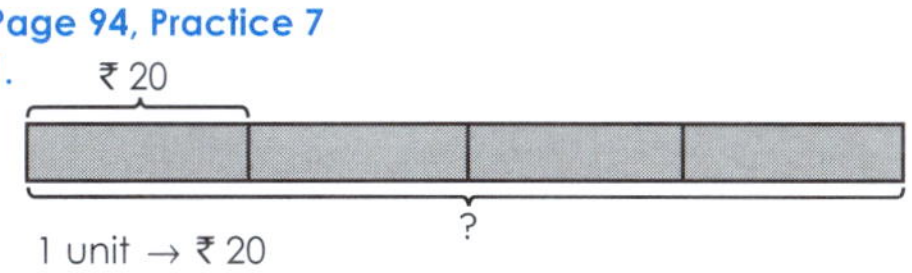

1 unit → ₹ 20
4 units → 4 × ₹ 20 = ₹ 80
He had ₹ 80 at first.

2. $35-21=14$ students wear glasses

$\frac{14}{35}=\frac{2}{5}$ of the students wear glasses

3. $7-\frac{5}{6}=6\frac{6}{6}-\frac{5}{6}$

$=6\frac{1}{6}$ metres long

$7+6\frac{1}{6}=13\frac{1}{6}$ metres

4.

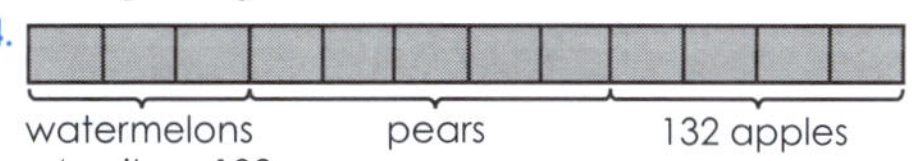

4 units → 132
1 unit → 132 ÷ 4
= 33
12 units → 12 × 33 = 396
There are 396 fruits at the stall.

Chapter 4

Pages 97–99, Let's Do

1. a) chicken; **b)** 6 **2. a)** 15; **b)** February, June; **c)** January; **d)** 6; **e)** February; **f)** 18, 8, 15, 10, 16, 5

Page 101, Let's Do

1. a) 106; **b)** 3; **c)** 37

Page 103, Let's Do

1. a) 4; **b)** 3; **c)** 12

 ISBN 978-93-5103-031-7

Pages 104–105, Practice 1
1. **a)** 12, 20, 8, 10; **b)** 12; **c)** 12; **d)** pears; **e)** 50
2. **a)** 20; **b)** 27; **c)** 20; **d)** 42; **e)** 8

Chapter 5
Pages 108–109, Let's Do
1. **a)** LKJ or JKL; **b)** HGF or FGH
2. **a)** c or YXW; **b)** e or WZY; **c)** ZWX or XWZ; **d)** XYZ or ZYX

Pages 110–111, Let's Do
1. **a)** 20°; **b)** 140°; **c)** 45°; **d)** 115°
2. Estimate: Answers vary. Example: 60°; Measure: 62°, 107°, 92°

Page 114, Practice 1
1. **a)** ∠JLK or ∠KLJ; **b)** ∠XYZ or ∠ZYX 2. **a)** 77°; **b)** 120°

Page 115, Let's Do
1. **a)** $\frac{3}{4}$; **b)** $\frac{1}{2}$; **c)** 4

Pages 116–117, Let's Do
1. **a)** east; **b)** west; **c)** school; **d)** park; **e)** market; **f)** southeast

Pages 118–119, Let's Do
1. **a)** police station; **b)** community centre; **c)** 225°; **d)** south

Pages 119–120, Practice 2
1. **a)** 4, 360°; **b)** 2, 180°; **c)** 1, 90°; **d)** 3, 270°
2. **a)** Clockwise: northeast, east, southeast, south, northwest; **b)** east, southwest, 180°, 45°, southwest, southeast, southwest

Chapter 7
Page 132, Let's Do
1. **b)** X, Y 2. **a)** 20, 9 ; **b)** 10, 10

Page 133, Let's Do
1. **a)** 45°; **b)** 41°

Page 135, Let's Do
1. 14

Page 135, Practice 1
1. **a)** 45°; **b)** 27°; **c)** 6 cm 2. **a)** 57°; **b)** 21°; **c)** 10 cm
3. NO = 5 cm, KL = 7 cm

Chapter 8
Page 140, Let's Do
1. **a)** 10; **b)** 14; **c)** 14; **d)** B, C 2. **a)** 99 cm; **b)** Answer varies.

Page 141, Let's Do
1. **a)** 7, 14, 8, 18, 9, 16, 8, 16, 7, 14; **b)** Q, S; **c)** R, S; **d)** P, T

Page 142, Let's Do
1. **a)** 30; **b)** 39

Pages 143–144, Let's Do
1. 32 2. 26

Page 144, Practice 1
1. **a)** B, C; **b)** A, B 2. **a)** 12 cm; **b)** 24 m 3. **a)** 14 cm; **b)** 18 cm; **c)** 20 cm; **d)** 24 m

Page 146, Let's Do
1. **a)** 21; **b)** 20

Page 147, Let's Do
1. 16

Pages 147–148, Practice 2
1. 20 cm², 10 cm², 16 cm²
2. 48 cm², 27 cm², 49 m², 60 m², 64 cm²

Page 149, Let's Do
1. **a)** 13; **b)** 78

Page 149, Let's Do
1. **a)** 9; **b)** 81

Page 150, Let's Do
1. **a)** 9; **b)** 36

Page 151, Let's Do
1. **a)** 12; **b)** 38

Page 152, Practice 3
1. 10 cm, 100 cm²; 15 cm, 120 cm²; 11 m, 165 m² 2. 6 m, 18 m; 12 cm, 42 cm; 11 cm, 44 cm 3. **a)** 15 cm; **b)** The square has a bigger area.

Page 153, Let's Do
1. **a)** 10, 14; **b)** 14, 16

Page 155, Let's Do
1. 140

Page 157, Let's Do
1. 90 m²

Page 158, Let's Do
1. 78 m²

Page 159, Practice 4
1. **a)** 40 cm², 28 cm; **b)** 59 m², 40 m; **c)** 168 m², 68 m; **d)** 483 m², 112 m
2. **a)** 440 m²; **b)** 225 m²

Page 161, Let's Do
1. **a)** 180 cm²; **b)** 72 cm

Page 162, Let's Do
1. 80 m²

Page 163, Practice 5
1. Area of rectangular piece of paper = 60 cm × 46 cm = 2760 cm²
Length of table = 4 + 60 + 4 = 68 cm
Breadth of table = 4 + 46 + 4 = 54 cm
Area of table = 68 cm × 54 cm = 3672 cm²
Area of tabletop not covered by paper = 3672 – 2760 = 912 cm²
2. Area of the room = 8 m × 7 m = 56 m²
Length of carpet = 8 – 1 – 1 = 6 m
Breadth of carpet = 7 – 1 – 1 = 5 m
Area of carpet = 6 m × 5 m = 30 m²
3. 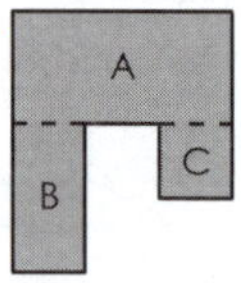

Area of A = 20 m × 15 m = 300 m²
Length of B = 28 – 15 = 13 m
Area of B = 13 m × 10 m = 130 m²
Area of C = 8 m × 5 m = 40 m²
Area of Mr. Lee's house = 300 + 130 + 40 = 470 m²
470 × ₹ 50 = ₹ 23,500
It will cost ₹ 23,500 to tile the entire floor area.

Chapter 9
Page 166, Let's Do
1. **a)** 0.4; **b)** 0.6; **c)** 0.7; **d)** 0.9

Page 167, Let's Do
1. **a)** 0.5; **b)** 0.7

Page 168, Let's Do
1. 4

Pages 168–169, Let's Do
1. **a)** 2.4; **b)** 2.8

Page 169, Let's Do
1. **a)** 1.1; **b)** 3.3

Page 170, Let's Do
1. **a)** 3.2, 3.6, 3.9; **b)** 6.1, 6.4, 6.8

Page 170, Let's Do
1. **a)** $\frac{4}{5}$; **b)** $2\frac{4}{5}$

Page 171, Let's Do
1. **a)** 35.7; **b)** 50.4

Page 172, Let's Do
1. **a)** 70; **b)** 4; **c)** 0.2

Page 173, Let's Do
1. **a)** 3.4; **b)** 5.2

Page 174, Let's Do
1. **a)** 8.5 2. **a)** 3.1, 3, 1.3, 0.3; **b)** 9, 7.8, 7.2, 2.7

Pages 174–175, Practice 1
1. **a)** 0.8; **b)** 0.6; **c)** 0.5 2. 3.3 L 3. **a)** 0.3; **b)** 0.9; **c)** 1.7; **d)** 3.2
4. **a)** $\frac{3}{10}$; **b)** $\frac{1}{2}$; **c)** $1\frac{2}{5}$; **d)** $3\frac{3}{5}$ 5. 10.4, 11.4, 12.7 6. **a)** 1.2; **b)** 25.4; **c)** 30.8 7. **a)** 4; **b)** 0.8; **c)** 6 8. **a)** 4.7; **b)** 6.5; **c)** 8.4 9. 5, 5.3, 6.2, 6.8

Page 176, Let's Do
1. **a)** 0.03; **b)** 0.05

Page 177, Let's Do
1. **a)** 0.23; **b)** 0.45

Page 178, Let's Do
1. **a)** 2.84; **b)** 80.57

Page 178, Let's Do
1. **a)** tenths, 0.9; **b)** 2, 0.02

Page 179, Let's Do
1. **a)** 0.6; **b)** 2.48; **c)** 3.07

Page 180, Let's Do
1. **a)** 0.20; **b)** 0.45; **c)** 6.50; **d)** 8.05

ISBN 978-93-5103-031-7

Page 181, Let's Do
1. 4.62, 4.69, 4.78
Page 182, Let's Do
1. **a)** 31.35; **b)** 42.47; **c)** 125.84; **d)** 248.90
Page 182, Let's Do
1. **a)** $\frac{3}{50}$; **b)** $\frac{7}{25}$; **c)** $2\frac{1}{20}$; **d)** $3\frac{13}{20}$
Page 183, Let's Do
1. **a)** 0.75; **b)** 0.35; **c)** 0.32; **d)** 1.5; **e)** 2.4; **f)** 3.54
Page 185, Let's Do
1. 1.68 2. 243.5 3. **a)** 2.2, 2.02, 0.2, 0.02; **b)** 80.7, 74.5, 7.8, 7.45
Pages 185–186, Practice 2
1. **a)** 0.04; **b)** 0.43 2. **a)** 0.68; **b)** 0.72; **c)** 0.09 3. **a)** 0.07; **b)** 0.2; **c)** 2; **d)** 0.08; **e)** 4; **f)** 100 4. **a)** 6; **b)** 3; **c)** 3; **d)** 2 5. **a)** 0.3; **b)** 0.03; **c)** 2.18; **d)** 3.42 6. **a)** ₹ 0.30; **b)** ₹ 0.50; **c)** ₹ 0.75; **d)** ₹ 0.95; **e)** ₹ 3.50; **f)** ₹ 5.05
7. 2.14, 2.26, 2.38 8. **a)** 20.18; **b)** 20.07; **c)** 35.1 9. **a)** $\frac{2}{25}$; **b)** $1\frac{1}{4}$; **c)** $4\frac{9}{20}$; **d)** $6\frac{3}{50}$ 10. **a)** 0.25; **b)** 0.6; **c)** 5.75; **d)** 10.85 11. **a)** 42.6; **b)** 2.5 m; **b)** 32.6 kg 12. **a)** 3.3, 3.03, 0.3, 0.03; **b)** 63.5, 6.4, 6.35, 5.63
Page 187, Let's Do
1. **a)** 0.024; **b)** 0.315; **c)** 4.002
Page 188, Let's Do
1. **a)** 0.02; **b)** 3, 100, 1000, 345
Page 189, Let's Do
1. **a)** 0.008; **b)** hundredths, 0; **c)** 5, 0.5
Page 190, Let's Do
1. **a)** 0.485; **b)** 0.064; **c)** 0.003; **d)** 5.476; **e)** 2.018; **f)** 3.04
Page 190, Let's Do
1. 3.251, 3.257, 3.263, 3.269
Page 191, Let's Do
1. **a)** 27.048; **b)** 27.158; **c)** 27.147
Page 192, Let's Do
1. **a)** $\frac{3}{125}$; **b)** $\frac{69}{200}$; **c)** $3\frac{1}{500}$; **d)** $2\frac{51}{125}$
Page 193, Let's Do
1. 52.071 2. 74.65 3. **a)** 3.02, 0.32, 0.302, 0.032; **b)** 2.628, 2.189, 2.139, 2.045
Page 195, Let's Do
1. 7.231, $1\frac{3}{4}$, 0.35, $\frac{7}{25}$
Pages 195–196, Practice 3
1. **a)** 1.143; **b)** 2.036 2. **a)** 0.2; **b)** 0.005; **c)** 2; **d)** 1000 3. **a)** 0.6; **b)** 6; **c)** 0.06; **d)** 0.006 4. **a)** 4; **b)** 7; **c)** 0.08; **d)** 0.004 5. **a)** 0.567; **b)** 0.049; **c)** 3.007; **d)** 2.009 6. **a)** 1.703; **b)** 0.085; **c)** 5.069; **d)** 10.052
7. 4.359, 4.365, 4.371, 4.378, 4.383 8. **a)** 5.509; **b)** 2.819; **c)** 13.52
9. **a)** $\frac{29}{200}$; **b)** $\frac{51}{125}$; **c)** $4\frac{253}{500}$; **d)** $2\frac{3}{500}$ 10. **a)** equal to; **b)** greater than; **c)** smaller than; **d)** equal to; **e)** greater than; **f)** greater than
11. **a)** 0.09, 0.08, 0.009, 0.008; **b)** 3.502, 3.25, 3.205, 3.025; **c)** 4.9, 4.683, 4.638, 4.386; **d)** 10, 9.932, 9.923, 9.392
Page 198, Let's Do
1. **a)** 4; **b)** 14; **c)** 30; **d)** 5; **e)** 16; **f)** 19
Page 199, Let's Do
1. **a)** 4.3; **b)** 4.3; **c)** 4.4 2. **a)** 0.9; **b)** 2.5; **c)** 7.1; **d)** 24.6; **e)** 18; **f)** 11
Page 199, Practice 4
1. **a)** 3; **b)** 1; **c)** 13; **d)** 10; **e)** 4; **f)** 5; **g)** 10; **h)** 20
2. **a)** 0.8; **b)** 0.1; **c)** 2.7; **d)** 8.1; **e)** 10.9; **f)** 19.1, **g)** 20.6, **h)** 10

Chapter 10
Page 200, Let's Do
1. **a)** 0.8; **b)** 0.06
Page 201, Let's Do
1. **a)** 1.3; **b)** 1.2; **c)** 0.10; **d)** 0.17
Page 202, Let's Do
1. **a)** 3.5; **b)** 4
Page 203, Let's Do
1. **a)** 6.0; **b)** 10.1; **c)** 6.7
Page 203, Let's Do
1. **a)** 0.96; **b)** 1.14; **c)** 0.4; **d)** 1.03
Page 204, Let's Do
1. **a)** 2.52; **b)** 0.90; **c)** 0.85
Page 205, Let's Do
1. **a)** 33.12; **b)** 7.17
Page 206, Let's Do
1. Estimates vary. Example: **a)** 10, 9.76; **b)** 6, 5.92
Page 207, Let's Do
1. 2.5
Page 207, Practice 1
1. **a)** 0.9; **b)** 1.7; **c)** 4.1; **d)** 0.10; **e)** 0.11; **f)** 1.26; **g)** 8.3; **h)** 0.82; **i)** 2.02; **j)** 48.74; **k)** 19.43; **l)** 40.02 2. Estimates vary. Example: **a)** 8, 7.55; **b)** 7, 6.34; **c)** 7, 7.18; **d)** 3, 3.70; **e)** 13, 13.08; **f)** 9, 8.85; **g)** 8, 7.58; **h)** 20, 20.04
3.
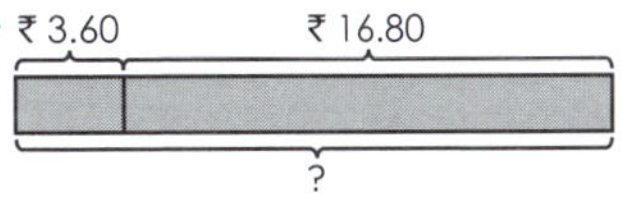

₹ 3.60 + ₹ 16.80 = ₹ 20.40
He had ₹ 20.40 at first.
4.
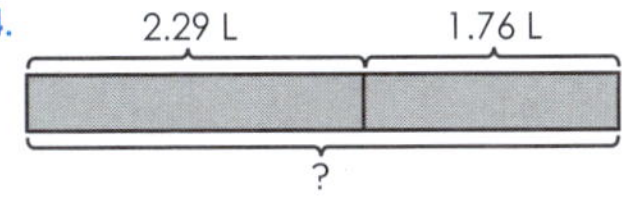

2.29 + 1.76 = 4.05 litres
The volume of the mixture was 4.05 litres.
5.
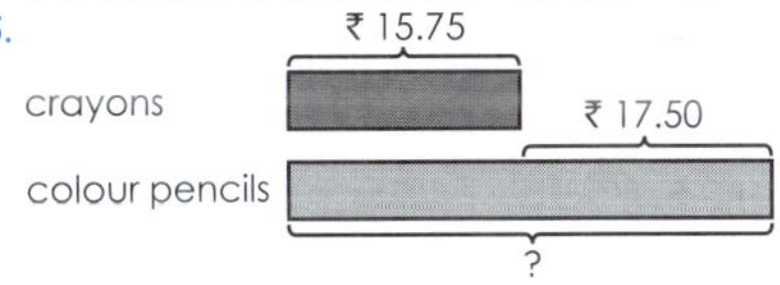

₹ 15.75 + ₹ 17.50 = ₹ 33.25
She spent ₹ 33.25 on colour pencils.
Page 209, Let's Do
1. **a)** 0.2; **b)** 0.7; **c)** 0.6; **d)** 3.1
Page 209, Let's Do
1. **a)** 4.1; **b)** 0.6; **c)** 3.55
Page 210, Let's Do
1. **a)** 0.07; **b)** 0.47; **c)** 0.06; **d)** 0.26; **e)** 0.93; **f)** 1.93
Page 211, Let's Do
1. **a)** 0.55; **b)** 3.14; **c)** 4.33; **d)** 6.28
Page 212, Let's Do
1. **a)** 3.23; **b)** 4.16; **c)** 6.13
Page 213, Let's Do
1. **a)** 3.6; **b)** 3.5; **c)** 4.8
Page 214, Let's Do
1. **a)** 3.74; **b)** 3.73; **c)** 2.66
Pages 214–215, Let's Do
1. **a)** 5.86; **b)** 9.98; **c)** 2.04
Page 215, Let's Do
1. Estimates vary. Example: **a)** 2, 2.63; **b)** 21, 21.89
Page 216, Let's Do
1. 1.88
Pages 216–217, Practice 2
1. **a)** 0.1; **b)** 1.6; **c)** 2.6; **d)** 0.95; **e)** 3.35; **f)** 2.5; **g)** 0.84; **h)** 0.87; **i)** 13.33; **j)** 22.23; **k)** 4.89; **l)** 36.65 2. **a)** 17.31; **b)** 19.98; **c)** 11.05; **d)** 10.61
3. Estimates vary. Example: **a)** 3, 2.80; **b)** 4, 4.51; **c)** 4, 3.64; **d)** 23, 22.22; **e)** 15, 14.89; **f)** 45, 45.55
4.
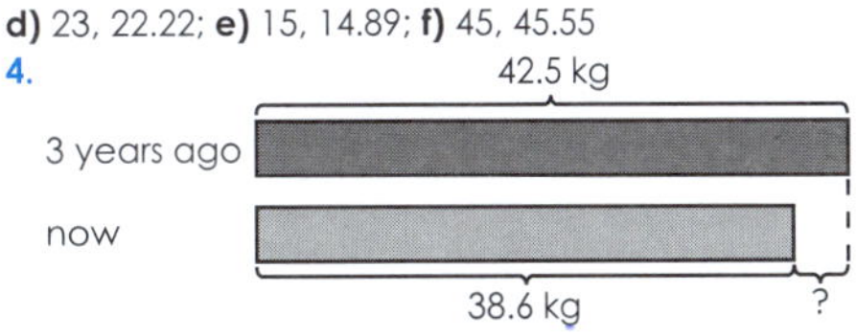

42.5 – 38.6 = 3.9 kg
Hassan has lost 3.9 kilograms.
5.
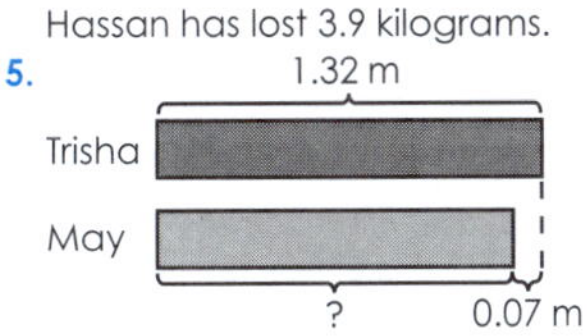

1.32 – 0.07 = 1.25 m
May is 1.25 metres tall.
6.
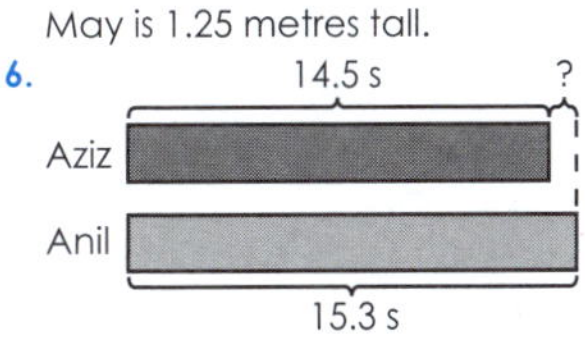

15.3 – 14.5 = 0.8 s
Aziz ran faster by 0.8 seconds.

 ISBN 978-93-5103-031-7

Page 218, Let's Do
1. **a)** 0.6; **b)** 0.06
Page 219, Let's Do
1. **a)** 2.8; **b)** 4; **c)** 3.20
Page 219, Let's Do
1. **a)** 0.28; **b)** 0.40; **c)** 0.24
Page 220, Let's Do
1. **a)** 6.9; **b)** 124.2; **c)** 260.8
Page 223, Let's Do
1. **a)** 1.04; **b)** 102.06; **c)** 289.56
Page 224, Let's Do
1. Estimates vary. Example: **a)** 20, 19.5; **b)** 180, 178.38
Page 225, Let's Do
1. 80.20
Page 225, Practice 3
1. **a)** 3.6; **b)** 0.56; **c)** 1.86; **d)** 1.35; **e)** 32.8; **f)** 6; **g)** 15.87; **h)** 19.30; **i)** 26.32; **j)** ₹ 0.90; **k)** ₹ 16.20; **l)** ₹ 30.60 2. Estimates vary. Example: **a)** 18, 19.2; **b)** 6, 7.44; **c)** 20, 20.45; **d)** 36, 39.24; **e)** 30, 31.50; **f)** 14, 13.58

3.
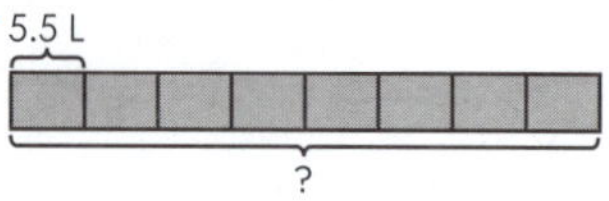

8 × 5.5 L = 44 litres
He used 44 litres of paint altogether.

4.
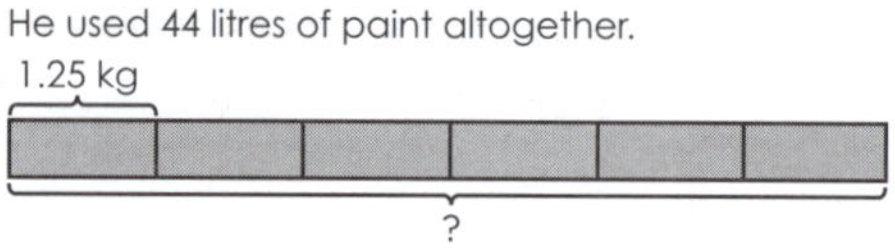

6 × 1.25 kg = 7.5 kilograms
The total weight of 6 bottles of orange juice is 75 kilograms.

5.
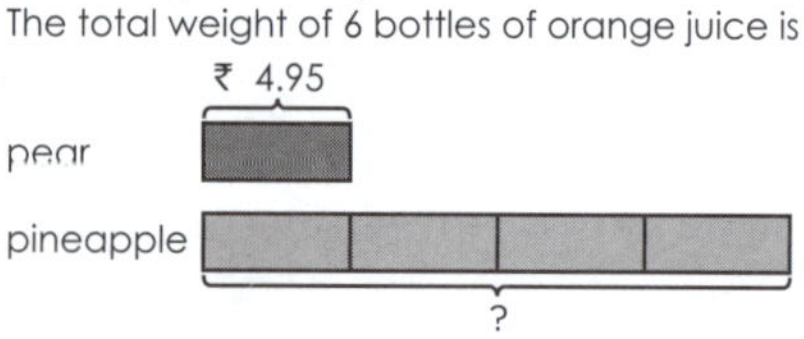

4 × ₹ 4.95 = ₹ 19.80
The pineapple costs ₹ 19.80.

6.
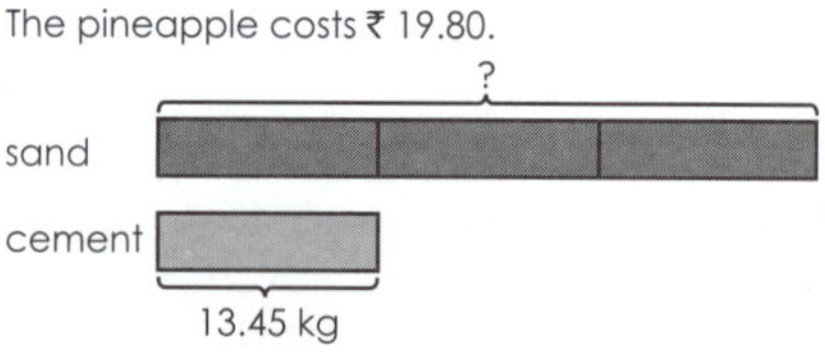

3 × 13.45 kg = 40.35 kilograms of sand used

Page 226, Let's Do
1. **a)** 0.2; **b)** 0.02
Page 227, Let's Do
1. **a)** 0.5; **b)** 0.6; **c)** 0.70; **d)** 0.60
Page 228, Let's Do
1. **a)** 0.05; **b)** 0.06; **c)** 0.05; **d)** 0.05
Page 230, Let's Do
1. **a)** 0.15; **b)** 0.56; **c)** 2.30; **d)** 2.43
Pages 232–233, Let's Do
1. **a)** 6.08; **b)** 1.5; **c)** 4.25; **d)** 2.75
Page 234, Let's Do
1. Estimates vary. Example: **a)** 0.3, 0.27; **b)** 0.9, 0.89; **c)** 5.2, 5.15
Page 235, Let's Do
1. 1 2. 5.4
Page 236, Let's Do
1. 1.80
Pages 236–237, Practice 4
1. **a)** 0.6; **b)** 0.8; **c)** 0.21; **d)** 0.11 **e)** 0.15; **f)** 0.71 **g)** 3.2; **h)** 0.42; **i)** 1.36; **j)** 1.6; **k)** 2.5; **l)** 3.05 2. **a)** ₹ 0.15; **b)** ₹ 0.60; **c)** ₹ 0.85 3. Estimates vary. Example: **a)** 3, 2.95; **b)** 4, 3.99; **c)** 9, 8.76 4. **a)** 7; **b)** 5; **c)** 14 5. **a)** 0.6; **b)** 0.6; **c)** 2.0

6.
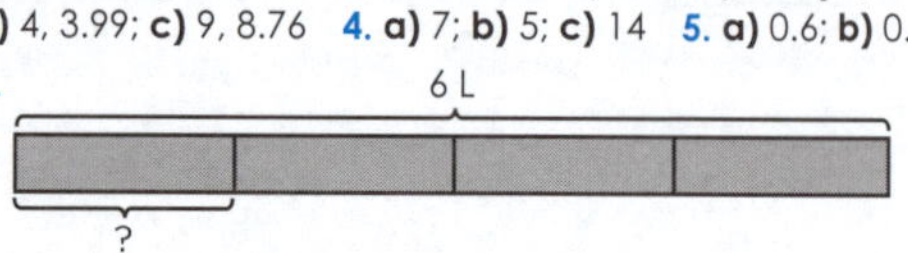

6 L ÷ 4 = 1.5 litres of syrup in each bottle

7.
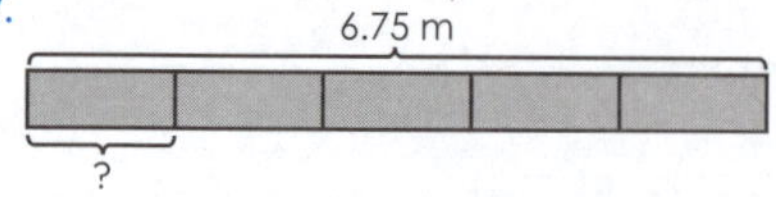

6.75 m ÷ 5 = 1.35 metres long

8.
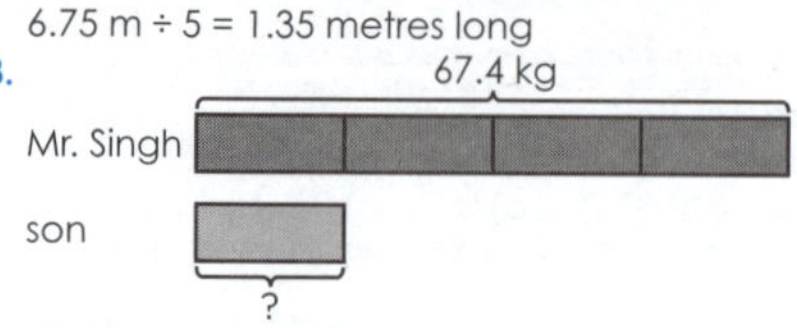

67.4 kg ÷ 4 = 16.85 kg
His son's weight is 16.85 kilograms.

9.
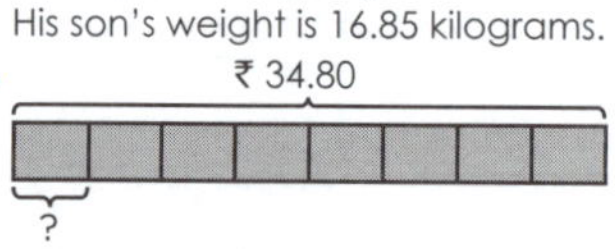

₹ 34.80 ÷ 8 = ₹ 4.35

Page 238, Let's Do
1. 5 – 0.25 = 4.75
5 bottles contain 4.75 litres of orange juice.
4.75 ÷ 5 = 0.95
There is 0.95 litre of orange juice in each bottle.

Page 238, Practice 5
1. 1 unit → ₹ 3.40 ≈ ₹ 3
7 units → 7 × ₹ 3.40 ≈ 7 × ₹ 3 = ₹ 21
Neeta needs to pay about ₹ 21 for 7 pencils.
1 unit → ₹ 25.75 ≈ ₹ 26
2 units → 2 × ₹ 25.75 ≈ 2 × ₹ 26 = ₹ 52
Neeta needs to pay about ₹ 52 for 2 notebooks.
₹ 21 + ₹ 52 = ₹ 73
Neeta needs to pay about ₹ 73 altogether.
₹ 73 is less than ₹ 100.
Neeta has enough money.

2.
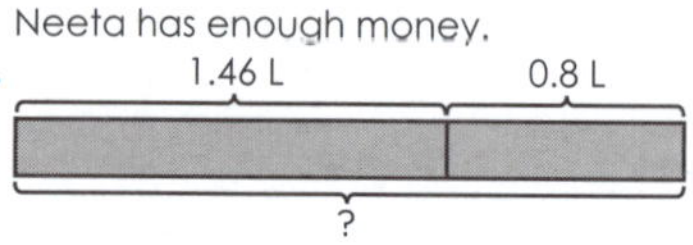

1.46 + 0.8 = 2.26
He had 2.26 litres of grey paint.

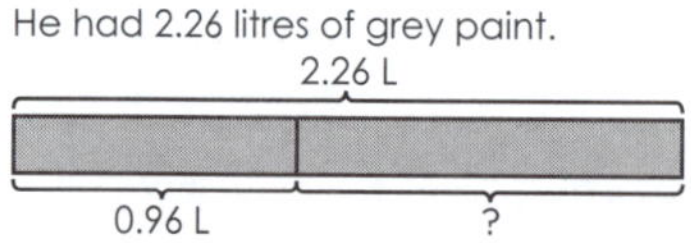

2.26 – 0.96 = 1.3
He was left with 1.3 litres of grey paint.

3.
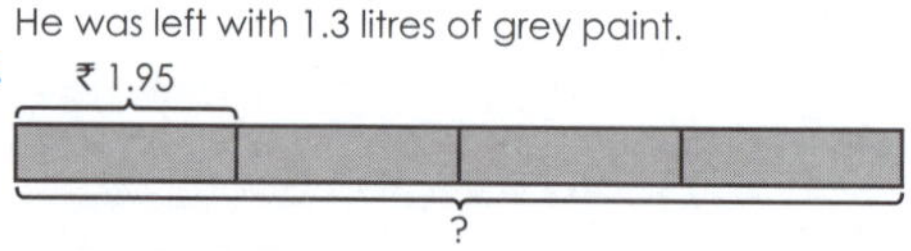

4 × ₹ 1.95 = ₹ 7.80
4 stamps cost ₹ 7.80

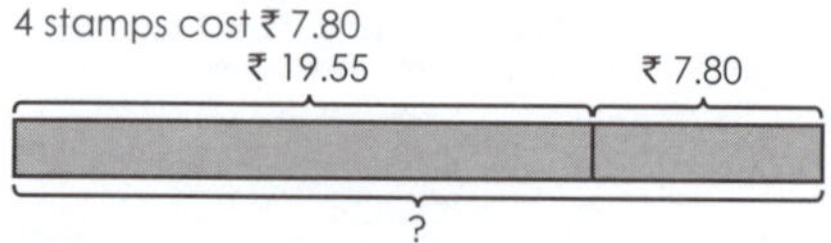

₹ 19.55 + ₹ 7.8 = ₹ 27.35
He spent ₹ 27.35 altogether.

4.
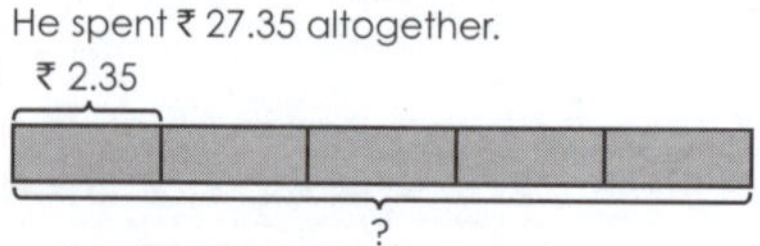

5 × ₹ 2.35 = ₹ 11.75

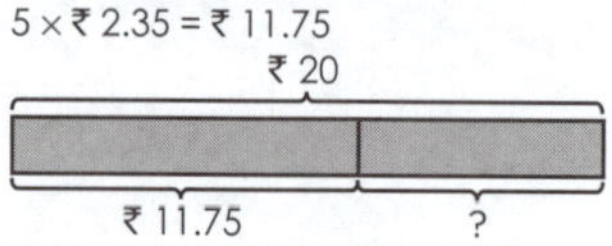

₹ 20 – ₹ 11.75 = ₹ 8.25
She received ₹ 8.25 in change.

 ISBN 978-93-5103-031-7

5.

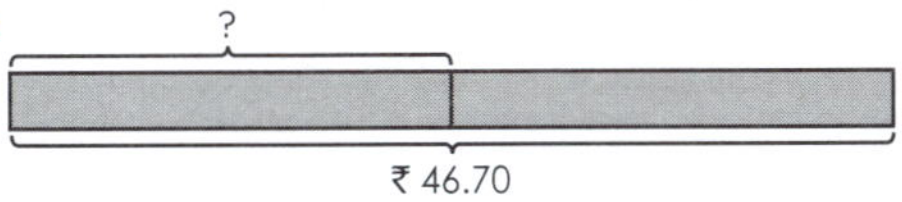

₹ 46.70 ÷ 2 = ₹ 23.35
Each girl paid ₹ 23.35 for lunch.

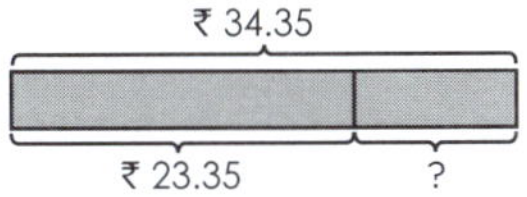

₹ 34.35 – ₹ 23.35 = ₹ 11
Alice had ₹ 11 left.

6.

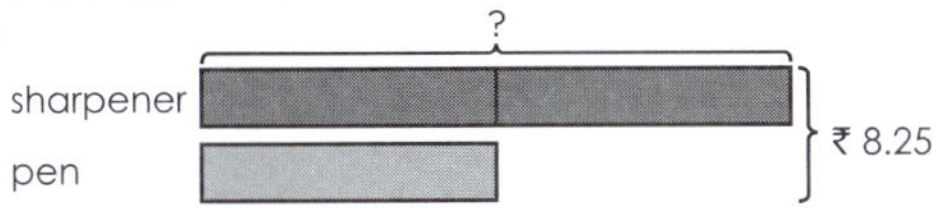

3 units → ₹ 8.25
1 unit → ₹ 8.25 ÷ 3
= ₹ 2.75
2 units → 2 × ₹ 2.75
= ₹ 5.50
The sharpener cost ₹ 5.50.

7. 1 unit → ₹ 4.50
4 units → 4 × ₹ 4.50 = ₹ 18
4 comic books cost ₹ 18.
1 unit → ₹ 25
3 units → 3 × ₹ 25
= ₹ 75
3 exercise books cost ₹ 75.
1 unit → ₹ 38.75
2 units → 2 × ₹ 38.75
= ₹ 77.50
2 art and craft books cost ₹ 77.50.
Total cost = ₹ 18 + ₹ 75 + ₹ 77.50
= ₹ 170.50
Total amount to be paid is ₹ 170.50

Chapter 11

Page 240, Let's Do

1. 5, 400

Page 241, Let's Do

1. 6

Page 242, Practice 1

1. **a)** 3 cm 6 mm; **b)** 4 kg 600 g; **c)** 12 L 200 ml; **d)** 20 km 25 m; **e)** 10 m 40 cm; **f)** 10 km 200 m; **g)** 14 L 400 ml; **h)** 28 kg 750 g

2. 2 kg 250 g

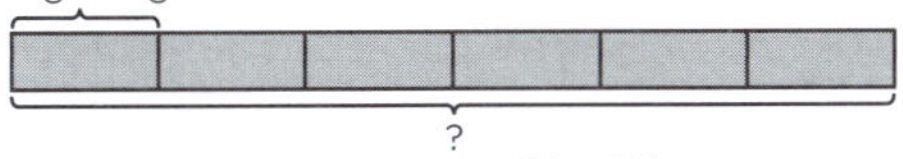

6 × 2 kg 250 g = 12 kg 1500 g = 13 kg 500 g
The total weight of flour that Alice has is 13 kilogram 500 grams.

3. 2 L 300 ml

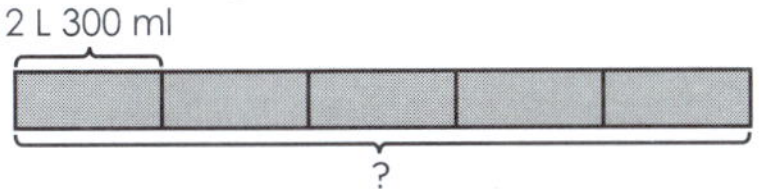

5 × 2 L 300 ml = 10 L 1500 ml = 11 L 500 ml
Ram drinks 11 litres 500 millilitres of water in 5 days.

4. 3 km 650 m

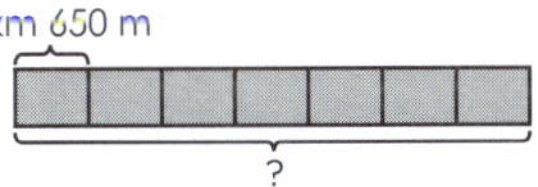

7 × 3 km 650 m = 21 km 4550 m = 25 km 550 m
Roger cycles a total distance of 25 kilometres 550 metres in a week.

Page 242, Let's Do

1. 1, 90

Pages 243–244, Let's Do

1. 1, 750 **2.** 1, 550

Pages 244, Let's Do

1. 800

Pages 244–245, Practice 2

1. **a)** 2 L 120 ml; **b)** 2 kg 120 g; **c)** 2 km 650 m; **d)** 2 m 50 cm; **e)** 2 L 855 ml; **f)** 6 mm; **g)** 655 m; **h)** 560 ml

2.

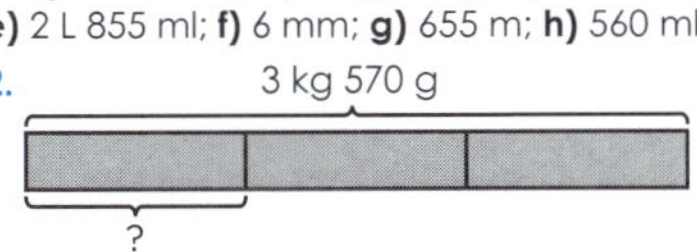

3 kg 570 g ÷ 3 = 1 kg 190 g
The weight of the kidney beans in each bag was 1 kilogram 190 grams.

3.

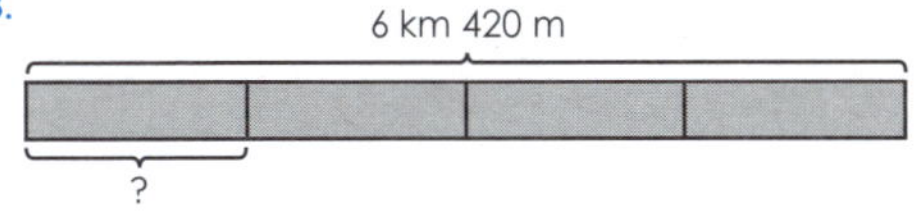

6 km 420 m ÷ 4 = 1 km 605 m
Each of them walked 1 kilometre 605 metres.

4.

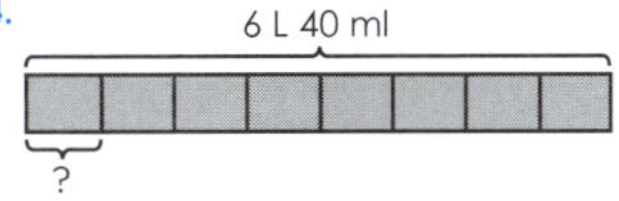

6 L 40 ml = 6040 ml
6040 ml ÷ 8 = 755 ml
The volume of water in each glass was 755 millilitres.

Page 246, Let's Do

1.

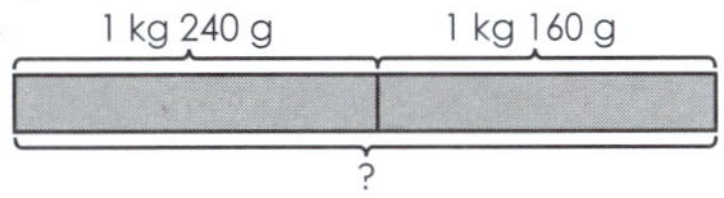

1 kg 240 g + 1 kg 160 g = 2 kg 400 g
The total weight of flour Mrs. Lee used is 2 kilograms 400 grams.
2 kg 400 g ÷ 8 = 300 g
She used 300 grams of flour for each pie.

Page 246, Practice 3

1.

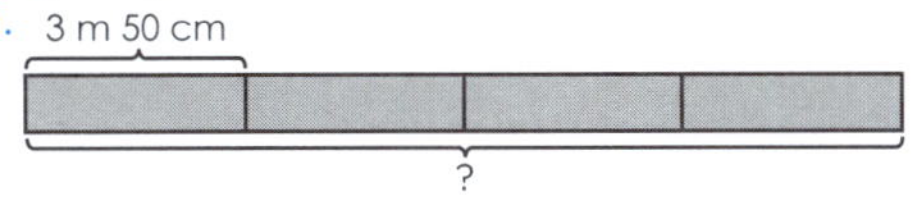

4 × 3 m 50 cm = 12 m 200 cm
= 14 m
The total length of ribbon was 14 metres.
14 m ÷ 2 − 7 m
She used 7 metres of ribbon for each present.

2.

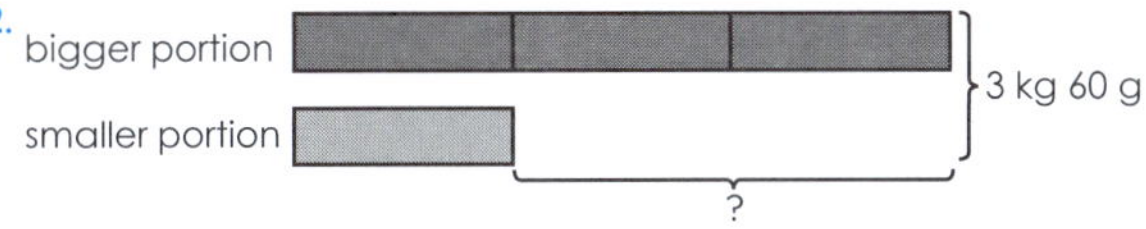

3 kg 60 g = 3060 g
4 units → 3060 g
1 unit → 3060 g ÷ 4
= 765 g
2 units → 2 × 765 g
= 1 kg 530 g
The bigger portion was 1 kilogram 530 grams heavier than the smaller portion.

Chapter 12

Page 250, Let's Do

2. Circle: a, c, d

Page 252, Let's Do

1. **a)** Yes; **b)** Yes; **c)** No; **d)** Yes

Page 255, Let's Do

1. Tick: **a)**; **b)**

Pages 255–256, Practice 1

1. **a)** No; **b)** Yes
2. **a)** Yes; **b)** Yes; **c)** No
5. Tick: **a)**; **d)**

Chapter 13

Pages 260–261, Let's Do

1. **b)** 75; **c)** 100 **2.** Answers vary.

Page 263, Let's Do

1. **a)** 15; **b)** 2, 4, 25, 45, 65; **c)** 30; **d)** 4.5; **e)** 30; **f)** 10

Page 266, Let's Do

1. **a)** bar, it can show the comparison between the number of students who chose each type of storybook; **b)** line; it can show how the height of the water level increases over five minutes.

Pages 266–267, Practice 1

1. **a)** 250 L; **b)** April; **c)** 150 L; **d)** 200 L **2. a)** 10, 35, 10, 20, 32.5; **b)** 30 cm **3. a)** A line graph can be used to present the data because it can show how the height of the plant increases over the week after the seed is planted; **b)** A bar graph can be used to present the data because it can show the comparison between the number of students who chose each type of colour.

 ISBN 978-93-5103-031-7

Chapter 14

Page 269, Let's Do

1. **a)** 15; **b)** 9:00, 30

Page 270, Let's Do

1. **a)** 40, 30, 4:51, 10 2. **a)** Answer varies. Example: 8; **b)** Answer varies. Example: 8 s

Page 271, Let's Do

1. **a)** 150; **b)** 255

Page 271, Let's Do

1. **a)** 2, 10; **b)** 4, 45

Page 272, Practice 1

1. **a)** 5:40 and 5 seconds; **b)** 7:55 and 25 seconds 2. **a)** 40; **b)** 35
3. **a)** 70 s; **b)** 132 s; **c)** 215 s; **d)** 286 s 4. **a)** 2 min; **b)** 3 min 20 s; **c)** 3 min 40 s; **d)** 6 min 8 s

Page 274, Let's Do

1. **a)** 04 45, 16 45; **b)** 10 30, 22 30 2. **a)** 6:24 p.m.; **b)** 12:46 a.m.

Pages 275–276, Let's Do

1. 2, 35

Page 277, Let's Do

1. 11 30

Page 279, Let's Do

1. 11 45

Page 280, Let's Do

1. 9, 25

Page 281, Let's Do

1. 02 55

Page 282, Let's Do

1. 22 05

Page 283, Practice 2

1. **a)** 07 00; **b)** 19 00 2. **a)** 06 40; **b)** 21 25; **c)** 12 00 3. **a)** 8:05 a.m.; **b)** 2:20 p.m.; **c)** 12:55 a.m.
4. 15 min + 1 h + 30 min = 1 h 45 min
   The piano lesson was 1 hour 45 minutes long.
5. 20 minutes after 12 40 is 13 00.
   3 hours after 13 00 is 16 00.
   5 minutes after 16 00 is 16 05.
   He finished making the card at 16 05.
6. 20 minutes before 19 20 is 19 00.
   5 hours before 19 00 is 14 00.
   35 minutes before 14 00 is 13 25.
   He started at 13 25.
7. 40 min + 1 h + 10 min = 1 h 50 min
   The film was 1 hour 50 minutes long.
8. 2 hours 35 minutes before 02 35 is 00 00.
   5 h 20 min – 2 h 35 min = 4 h 80 min – 2 h 35 min
   = 2 h 45 min
   2 hours before 00 00 is 22 00.
   45 minutes before 22 00 is 21 15.
   2 hours 45 minutes before 00 00 is 21 15.
   The plane left City A at 21 15.

Page 284, Let's Do

1. $\frac{1}{3}$ h = $\frac{1}{3} \times 60$
   = 20 min
   2 h 25 min + 20 min = 2 h 45 min
   35 minutes before 13 35 is 13 00.
   2 hours before 13 00 is 11 00.
   10 minutes before 11 00 is 10 50.
   She began shopping at the mall at 10 50.

Page 285, Practice 3

1. **a)** 1 h 40 min + 45 min = 1 h 85 min
   = 2 h 25 min
   Gary spent 2 hours 25 minutes on revision altogether;
   b) 25 minutes after 17 20 is 17 45.
   2 hours after 17 45 is 19 45.
   Gary ended his revision at 19 45.
2. $\frac{1}{2}$ h = $\frac{1}{2} \times 60$
   = 30 min
   $2\frac{1}{2}$ h = 2 h 30 min
   2 h 30 min + 1 h 10 min = 3 h 40 min
   She baked for 3 hours 40 minutes.
   40 minutes before 12 55 is 12 15.
   3 hours before 12 15 is 09 15.
   3 hours 40 minutes before 12 55 is 09 15.
   She started baking at 09 15.
3. 5 h 35 min + 1 h 25 min = 6 h 60 min
   = 7 h
   The train journey from City A to City C took 7 hours.
   7 hours after 22 38 is 05 38.
   It will reach City C at 05 38.
4. 36 min + 8 h + 2 min = 8 h 38 min
   The journey took 8 hours 38 minutes.
   8 h 38 min – 6 h 50 min = 7 h 98 min – 6 h 50 min
   = 1 h 48 min
   Mr. Singh was delayed by 1 hour 48 minutes by the traffic jam.

 ISBN 978-93-5103-031-7

Problem Solving Process

Solve problems using these 4 steps:

1 **Understand** the problem.
Can you describe the problem in your own words?
What information is given?
What do you need to find?
Is there information that is missing or not needed?

2 **Plan** what to do.
What can you do to help you solve the problem?
Here are some things you can do:

- Draw a picture
- Make a list
- Make a supposition
- Guess and check
- Look for a pattern
- Act it out
- Work backwards

3 Work out the **Answer**.
Solve the problem using your plan in Step 2.
If you cannot solve the problem, make another plan.
Show your work clearly.
Write the answer statement.

4 **Check**
Read the question again. Did you answer the question?
Does your answer make sense?
Is your answer correct?
You may use the following to help you check your answer:

- fact families
- replace the unknown in the problem with your answer

If your answer is not correct, go back to Step 1.

 ISBN 978-93-5103-031-7

The content of this Scholastic ALPHA™ Mathematics Coursebook 4 Edition is adapted from Primary Mathematics Project 3B, 4A, 4B, 5A, 5B (3rd Edition) originally developed by the Ministry of Education, Singapore. This edition contains new content developed by Scholastic Education International (Singapore) Private Limited which is not attributable to the Ministry of Education, Singapore. We would like to acknowledge the Project Team from the Ministry of Education, Singapore, who developed the original Singapore Edition:

Project Director: Dr Kho Tek Hong
Team Members: Hector Chee Kum Hoong, Liang Hin Hoon, Lim Eng Tann, Rosalind Lim Hui Cheng, Ng Hwee Wan, Ng Siew Lee, Chip Wai Lung

Original edition published under the title of Primary Mathematics Project 3B, 4A, 4B, 5A, 5B (3rd Edition)

Published by Marshall Cavendish Education Pte Ltd

This edition

Published by Scholastic Education International (Singapore) Private Limited